Between Citizens and the State

POLITICS AND SOCIETY IN TWENTIETH-CENTURY AMERICA

SERIES EDITORS

William Chafe, Gary Gerstle, Linda Gordon, and Julian Zelizer

A list of titles in this series appears at the back of the book

Between Citizens and the State

THE POLITICS OF AMERICAN HIGHER
EDUCATION IN THE 20TH CENTURY

Christopher P. Loss

PRINCETON UNIVERSITY PRESS   PRINCETON AND OXFORD

Copyright © 2012 by Princeton University Press
Published by Princeton University Press, 41 William Street,
Princeton, New Jersey 08540
In the United Kingdom: Princeton University Press, 6 Oxford Street,
Woodstock, Oxfordshire OX20 1TW
press.princeton.edu

Jacket art: *Three Graduates Looking to New Horizons*. © Paul Barton/CORBIS

Library of Congress Cataloging-in-Publication Data

Loss, Christopher P.
Between citizens and the state : the politics of
American higher education in the 20th century / Christopher P. Loss.
p. cm.   (Politics and society in twentieth century America)
Includes bibliographical references and index.
ISBN 978-0-691-14827-4 (hardback)
1. Higher education and state—United States. 2. Federal aid to
higher education—United States. 3. Education, Higher—Aims and
objectives—United States. 4. Education, Higher—Political aspects—
United States. 5. Education, Higher—Social aspects—United States.
6. Education, Higher—Economic aspects—United States. 7. Education,
Higher—United States—History. I. Title.
LC173.L67 2011
379.1'2140973—dc23   2011017423

British Library Cataloging-in-Publication Data is available

This book has been composed in Minion Pro

Printed on acid-free paper. ∞

Printed in the United States of America

10   9   8   7   6   5   4   3   2   1

For Catherine, Susannah, and Jack,
and in memory of my dad, Archie K. Loss (1939–2010)

Contents

Illustrations and Appendix Charts

❖❖❖

Illustrations

Acknowledgments

———————— ❖❖❖ ————————

It all started innocently enough. It was 1993. I was in my junior year of college and needed to talk to someone. So, after gathering my courage, I picked up the phone and dialed Penn State University president Joab Thomas.[1] He didn't answer. His secretary did. I told her I loved Penn State but was distraught over the direction of the institution, particularly its approach to undergraduate education. I explained that many of the general education classes were too big, too impersonal, and that I needed a one-on-one meeting with the president to let him know what I thought. She took my name and student number and said she'd call me back. Moments later the phone rang. I picked up. The president would be delighted to meet me, she said. We agreed to a time. I promised to be there.

President Thomas greeted me warmly. He offered me a Pepsi. I accepted. He asked me to sit down, to share my concerns. I did. He listened intently, nodded often, occasionally uttering a sympathetic "hmmm" followed closely by an affirming "yes." When I finished, he thanked me for my time. Without missing a beat he then asked me if I'd serve as an undergraduate representative to the Penn State Faculty Senate. Thrilled, I jumped at the chance. A few weeks later I became a member of the undergraduate life committee.

I did not realize it at the time, but that moment marked my introduction to the politics that lay near the center of this book. And one way or another, I've spent most of my time ever since thinking, reading, and writing about the politics of American higher education: What is the purpose of higher learning? How does it benefit society? And what sorts of citizens and politics does it produce? In short, what happens to students when they go to college—when they spend four years, as the historian Richard Hofstadter memorably put it, in 1968, "suspended between . . . the external world, with all its corruption and evils and cruelties, and the splendid world of our imagination?"[2]

I have been fortunate to have lived most of my adult life hovering somewhere between the real world and the world of my imagination. I like both places. And I've been lucky to have had comfortable homes wherever I've landed. It is my pleasure to acknowledge the institutions and individuals that have helped me along the way.

This book started as a dissertation at the University of Virginia. I split my time between the Curry School of Education and the Corcoran Department of History, ultimately doing doctorates in both. At the Curry School, I'd like to thank Annette Gibbs, Brian Pusser, and Jennings Wagoner, who taught me a lot about the history of education. In the Corcoran Department of History, I'm indebted to Ed Ayers, Joe Kett, and Brian Balogh. Brian was my dissertation advisor. I met him in my first year of graduate school. He took me under his wing, and I'm grateful he did. Brian is a really smart guy. But I know a lot of smart people. What makes Brian different is that he's also an unfailingly generous person who cares deeply about his students. Long after he put the pro in "pro-ministrator," Brian was a consummate professional. He read and commented on all the different drafts of this manuscript—from précis to dissertation to book. I've joked with him a million times that he's thanked in more book acknowledgments than just about anyone in the business. I have no idea if this is true, of course, but it doesn't make thanking him here any less satisfying.

While at the University of Virginia, I had the good fortune of being on the receiving end of a number of wonderful research fellowships and unique work opportunities. Each of them in different ways contributed to this project. For research support, thanks to the School of Education and the Department of History; and, for year-long fellowships, to the Graduate School of Arts and Sciences, the Miller Center of Public Affairs, and the Governance Studies Program at The Brookings Institution. The FDR Library, the Truman Library, and the LBJ Library each awarded me research grants. I also worked part time in the Office of the Vice President and Provost for four years. That's where I learned how universities *really* work. Anda Webb, the vice provost and chief of staff, and Gene Block, then provost and now the chancellor at UCLA, taught me a ton. What better way to learn about the intricacies of the promotion and tenure process, or employee compensation, or maternity leave, or student health insurance, or the budget process, or how to fill budget gaps, then to do so "on the job?" Anda was an excellent teacher. I tried my hardest to take good notes.

The dissertation was turned into a book at Vanderbilt University—a fantastic place to teach, write, and work. In Peabody College, thanks to everyone in the Department of Leadership, Policy, and Organizations, and especially to my colleagues in the higher education program; they're an amazing group. I've been rescued a number of times by our crack team of administrative officers, led by the indomitable trio: Rosie Moody, Renee Morgan, and Susie Smith. Thanks also to the Dean's Office for the Small Research Grant and for generously covering the copyright and reproduction costs for the illustrations in this book. Serena Hinz helped design the charts.

It's been a pleasure working with Princeton University Press. Julian Zelizer first approached me about my book after he heard me present my work at a Miller Center Fellows' Conference. He encouraged me to send the manuscript his way when I was done. It took a few years. When I did finally submit it, however, my editors, Clara Platter and Chuck Myers, received it with enthusiasm. They have taken good care of it ever since. Not only did they solicit two supremely generous reader reports, they made sure I was well treated by Princeton's stalwart production team: Natalie Baan, Jack Rummel, and Sarah Wolf.

Colleagues have knowingly and unknowingly read and commented on portions or entire versions of this manuscript at various stages of its development.

Sometimes this occurred because I was presenting at a conference and they had no choice; other times because I asked and they willing agreed; in both cases I benefited immensely from their questions, comments, and insights. Thanks to Michael Bernstein, Sarah Binder, Burton Bledstein, Katherine Chaddock, Elizabeth Clemens, Alon Confino, Bob Crowson, Linda Eisenmann, William Galston, Roger Geiger, Scott Gelber, Ellen Herman, Sarah Igo, Paul Kramer, Melvyn Leffler, Lorraine McDonnell, Pat McGuinn, Pietro Nivola, Margaret O'Mara, Wade Pickren, G. Kurt Piehler, Doug Rossinow, Lynn Sanders, Michael Sherry, John Skrentny, John Thelin, Harold Wechsler, Allan Winkler, and last but not least (though he is almost always last in any alphabetical list), Jonathan Zimmerman—a real flesh-and-blood public intellectual. Hugh Hawkins and Gareth Davies, both of whose work I have long admired and even taught in my classes, read the whole manuscript and provided more than a few good suggestions on how to make it better. So did Derek Hoff. Derek's book went into production at the same time as mine, and it was his idea that we should exchange chapters as we worked our way through the revision process. I'm glad we did. Finally, thanks to Jack Spielvogel, who made me want to study history.

My deepest gratitude is for my family, which has grown in size the last few years and suffered some devastating losses. Thanks to my in-laws, Marie and the late Tom Gavin, for being so utterly wonderful. Chicago is their home, and when we visit we always feel like we're home, too. My parents, Suzanne and Archie Loss, were thrilled when I decided to go to graduate school. That never changed. Professors themselves, they well understood the gnawing ache of the academic calling, and what it really meant when I said I was "almost finished" with my book. It takes time to write one of these things—and time does march on. Sadly, my dad did not live to see this book's completion. An unfair fight against cancer took his joyful soul long before he was ready to let it go. My mom, sisters and I cradled him as he drew his last, quiet breath. It was a hell of a thing—a poignant reminder that no one escapes the ravages of time. I miss him.

Time occasionally feels as if it stands still, of course, which brings me to my most important thank you of all. I met Catherine Gavin in a history seminar during our first year of graduate school. We've been together ever since. She's all grace, beauty, and intelligence, and along with our children, Susannah and Jack, the love of my life. This book is for her.

Between Citizens and the State

Chapter 1

Introduction
The Politics of American Higher Education in the Twentieth Century

❖

During the twentieth century, political leaders and university officials turned to one another with increasing frequency in order to build an expansive national state and educational system. They abandoned their shared tradition of laissez-faire relations and forged a powerful partnership that transformed the country's plural system of colleges and universities into a repository of expertise, a locus for administrative coordination in the federal government, and a mediator of democratic citizenship. Slowly during the interwar period, then rapidly after World War II, the state and higher education joined forces to fight economic depressions and poverty, to wage world wars hot and cold, and to secure the rights of previously marginalized Americans. Ironically, at the very moment the partnership reached its peak in the 1960s, it turned sour, only to reconstitute itself, if in a different form, following the conservative political ascendance of the 1980s. *Between Citizens and the State* tells this story.

To date, scholars have only captured a sliver of the relationship between higher education and the American state. This book advances the literature on the emergence of the American university beyond the rise of the professions and the growth of the federal-academic research matrix. Without question the ascendance of large-scale scientific research during World War II radically altered the nature of federal-academic relations, and it is exhibit A in the birth of what some scholars call the "proministrative state." But the emphasis on "big science," and the handful of elite institutions and experts that produced it, has concealed other developments in state-academic relations that occurred outside federally funded labs before and after World War II. Throughout the last century, state policymakers and academic administrators turned the nation's colleges and universities into multipurpose institutions that not only produced cutting-edge defense and medical research but also mediated access to democratic citizenship for millions of Americans.[1]

Why has higher education's role in twentieth-century American life been so narrowly drawn? There are two reasons. One is the scholarly fixation on the birth of the World War II–era federal-academic research matrix. The other is the difficulty of fitting higher education into the larger story of American political and social history.[2] To craft a new narrative of the politics of American higher education thus requires thinking differently about its placement within the nation's mix of social and political institutions. So, where does higher education fit? The answer explored in the pages that follow: higher education fits between citizens and the state.

By relocating American higher education at the crossroads of state-society relations—between citizens and the state—this book seeks a deeper understanding of higher education's role in twentieth-century American political development (APD).[3] Over the past twenty-five years, scholars from political science, sociology, and history have resituated the study of American politics within a polity-centered frame that conceives the state as an evolving, time-bound amalgamation of institutions and ideas. On a theoretical level, APD posits that a combination of public, private, and voluntary institutions—from executive branch agencies to the military to big business and charitable foundations—gives the American state its physical form across space and time. Historically contingent ideas about the appropriate scale and scope of the American state—whether described as strong or weak, big or small—determine the particular institutional arrangement deployed at a given moment in time. In this project, higher education serves as the key institutional embodiment of the American state and the central intellectual construct that helped policymakers and the American people define the very meanings of government, knowledge, and democratic citizenship in the twentieth century.[4]

Between Citizens and the State builds on a burgeoning literature about the American state that has revealed the importance of intermediary institutions—sometimes called "parastates"—in national governance.[5] According to this literature, since the nation's founding the polity's strong preference for a noninvasive central state directed state development toward interventions that relied on institutions at least once removed from the federal government's immediate family of bureaucratic agencies. In the nineteenth century, when that family was small, state builders turned to political parties, the law, subsidies, and all manner of third-party providers, especially state- and local-level government, to facilitate westward expansion and economic growth throughout the country. In a polity afraid of big government, state builders used intermediaries to mete out federal authority at the local level. What they discovered along the way was that the federal government worked best when it operated by proxy, or as one astute scholar has recently described this phenomenon, "out of sight."[6]

This pattern of mediated governance endured—and thrived—in the twentieth century even as the family of federal bureaucracies grew. During the New Deal and after World War II, a rich mix of intermediary organizations, still anchored by state- and local-level government but joined by interest groups, professional-voluntary associations, and the private sector, worked with the federal government's growing network of bureaucratic agencies to regulate the economy, defend the homeland, and deliver goods and services to the American people.[7] Ultimately, the picture of the American state gleaned from this literature is of a state of parastates, and of an ironic state at that: in order to aggregate governing authority in Washington in the twentieth century, state builders first had to disaggregate that authority among a diffuse arrangement of parastates.

I contend that American higher education emerged as a predominant parastate in the twentieth century. Situated between citizens and the state, completely beholden to neither party but expected and committed to serve both, higher education proved perfectly suited for the task. For one thing, the higher education sector grew dramatically during the twentieth century (see appendices A.1 and A.2): despite economic crises and global wars the number of schools increased four times (from roughly 1,000 to 4,000 institutions) and enrollments more than fifty times (from 250,000 to 14 million students).[8] For another, higher education's geographically diffuse complex of institutions provided a ready-made administrative network to reach students as well as the millions of other local people who resided nearby. The potential for higher education's ideas and individuals to migrate into the heart of society proved particularly seductive to state builders. That higher education could be used to shape citizens' political commitments resonated with national leaders, such as Franklin Roosevelt and Lyndon Johnson, who wanted to build a new and more powerful state but had to do so using homegrown materials, all the more effective if they were locally produced. From such stuff was the American state made.

In the name of state building, national leaders had tapped higher education since the early days of the republic. Following the Revolutionary War, college building expanded rapidly beyond the original 9 colonial colleges to include nearly 250 by 1860. The central government's sale of "land grants" stimulated some of this growth. The Northwest Ordinance of 1787 disbursed land grants in order to pay down the nation's revolutionary war debt and promote the creation of schools and colleges in newly conquered lands. Congress built on this earlier precedent with the Morrill Land-Grant Act of 1862. Passed in the throes of the Civil War, the legislation secured the government's role as a key supporter of public higher education. And during Reconstruction the federal government relied on the Freedmen's Bureau and northern missionaries to coordinate the organization of the thousands of new schools that ex-slaves built to protect their hard-fought freedoms. Subsequent federal legislation, for agricultural research stations and the general development of the land-grant system itself, upped the government's financial stake in the operation of the nation's emerging constellation of educational institutions. Add to this the construction of privately financed German-style research universities, such as Johns Hopkins University, opened in 1876, and by the close of the nineteenth century the country's decentralized, public-private higher education system was complete. The only thing missing was students.[9]

Between Citizens and the State picks up where this earlier story ends, offering a new synthetic history of the politics of American higher education in the twentieth century. It examines the role of higher education in twentieth-century state building—when higher education finally got "big." I argue that World War I precipitated a long period of bureaucratic reinvention—both within the university and between the university and the state—that eventually converted higher education into a key adjunct of the New Deal administrative state. The effects of this new institutional arrangement on the meaning of democratic citizenship surfaced during World War II, when opinion leaders and expert psychologists discovered that educated citizens were better citizens—a point seemingly substantiated by veterans' surprising success under the G.I. Bill of 1944. Convinced that higher education created prosperous, civic minded, psychologically adjusted democratic citizens worthy of special rights and privileges, cold war policymakers embarked on a global education strategy that culminated in the National Defense Education Act of 1958.

Yet the state's reciprocal understanding of democratic citizenship, in which educational opportunity was granted to individuals in return for national service, proved impossible to contain. By the 1960s, the state's rigid conception of the educated citizen, which had been constructed around the memory of the hero citizen-soldiers of World War II, exploded under pressure from campus protesters, especially black and female students and their sympathizers in university administration, on Capitol Hill, and in the White House. Alienated by the modern bureaucratic university and provoked by what they perceived as an imperialist, racist, and sexist bureaucratic state, groups of black and female students forced a national debate about the uses of the university in a democratic society. Their ensuing political struggle—framed by the civil rights movement, the War on Poverty, the Higher Education Act of 1965, and the broader "rights revolutions" of the 1960s—altered the reciprocal relationship between citizens and the state. Swept away by the existential quest for individual and group liberation, and the unconditional demand for respect and self-determination, minority students around the country advanced a rights-based definition of democratic citizenship closely related to a variant of interest group politics known as diversity. Diversity became the watchword to ensure an educated citizenry prepared to meet future challenges. The rapid formation of black and women's studies programs, combined with the passage of the Education Amendments of 1972, served as harbingers of the ascendant diversity regime. Together they signaled the arrival of a new rights-based, identity-group political order on campuses that mirrored in miniature the political organization of the American state itself.

Specifically, *Between Citizens and the State* explores higher education's role in state building from three overlapping institutional and ideational perspectives. First, I examine the "big three" federal higher education policies of the past century: the 1944 G.I. Bill, the 1958 National Defense Education Act, and the 1965 Higher Education Act. While truly monumental pieces of public policy, these laws do not alone define the extent of the federal government's role in higher education policymaking. Taking my lead from political scientists, my project also examines the incremental, in some cases forgotten, policy developments that bracketed those landmark legislative moments. My use of "policy feedback"—the idea that "new policies create a new politics," as political scientist E. E. Schattschneider famously put it—provides a more complete examination of the origins and outcomes of federal higher education policy.[10] I place the G.I. Bill, the NDEA, and the Higher Education Act in historical context rather than using them as mere markers in what is typically depicted as the triumphant march of American higher education in the twentieth century. These policies remain turning points in the story that I tell, but without the air of inevitability of previous studies that have failed to explore how wars, economic crises, and campus upheavals, at different times in the past century, pushed American higher education to its breaking point. By focusing on policy developments that have figured marginally if at all in the extant literature, this book seeks to restore a dimension of contingency to the existing account of the history of American higher education that has been distorted by an infatuation with purely quantitative measures of institutional vitality, such as the growth in student enrollments, federal research support, and endowment size.[11]

Second, I explore the lives of students, faculty, and administrators in and outside bounded campus settings, studying at home and around the world, as civilians and soldiers, as farmers and television viewers, as political actors and citizens. To capture the complexity of the relationship between the state and higher education in the twentieth century accurately requires looking at educational experiences that occurred away from brick-and-mortar collegiate settings: in the American countryside and on battlefronts, in foreign countries and in suburban households, and in a whole host of other spaces and bandwidths located beyond campus borders. During the New Deal, for example, the Roosevelt administration and the Department of Agriculture tapped the land-grant university extension system, and its force of three thousand county agricultural agents, to implement the Agricultural Adjustment Act and other New Deal programs. During World War II, the U.S. Army partnered with higher education to deliver educational programs before, during, and after combat to millions of G.I.s. During the height of the cold war, higher education experimented with educational television, poured millions of dollars into so called "adult education," promoted study abroad, and infused the undergraduate curriculum with courses and activities intended to furnish global understanding. And during the 1960s, freedom schools, teach-ins, consciousness raising groups, and experimental colleges offered students a parallel but alternative educational universe to explore ideas about race, feminism, sexuality, war, and politics not included in official undergraduate course directories or convened in buildings named in honor of wealthy donors.

My exploration of the outer reaches of organized higher education provides a significant corrective to scholarship that has drawn rigid boundaries between different types of higher education institutions and the services those institutions provide.[12] In contrast, I place the institution in a capacious framework that reveals the extent to which higher education really was used to penetrate deep into the polity and to mediate relations between millions of citizens and their government. Although public and private universities and colleges rest at the heart of this analysis, I also track the role of administrators, faculty, and students teaching and learning in other institutional settings. By delving into all the ways that higher education insinuated itself into other institutions not concerned primarily with education delivery, this project demonstrates higher education's important, if underappreciated, role as a vehicle of political change in the twentieth century. It spotlights what is arguably higher education's core social and political function: educating citizens for life in a democracy.[13]

Unearthing the social and political functions of higher learning presents a host of challenges. Getting at the private, day-to-day experiences of students and professors is not easy; revealing source material is meager. It is perhaps for this reason that most of the studies that purport to probe higher education's social and political uses are usually thinly veiled polemics against, and occasionally defenses of, the institution. The basic contours of the genre work well on nightly news shows and in other debate-style venues in which "conservative" and "liberal" commentators take turns blaming one another for ruining the modern university since the 1960s. On closer inspection, however, most of these works rely on caricatures of the academy. Conservatives rail against what they perceive to be higher education's liberal professoriate and curriculum, wishing instead for a return to the good old days of the American college they think existed before the 1960s.[14] Old left, New Left, and identity left liberals, meanwhile, vociferously counter such criticisms with their own exaggerated rejoinders against post-1960s conservatism. Liberals correctly defend their right to teach and research under the doctrine of academic freedom, yet they err in parodying conservatism as inherently anti-intellectual. They lambast conservatism as inimical to the modern research enterprise, blaming conservative administrators and trustees for turning the academic grove into a bazaar where students are customers, knowledge is a product, and everything is for sale.[15]

Both sides have played fast and loose with the past and either ignored or forgotten how politically moderate and market-driven American higher education has been and continues to be.[16] Rather than rehash this hoary debate, I hope to move the discussion beyond the fateful 1960s, even as the story I tell passes through it. The politics examined in this book move between and among the international and national, the state-level and local, the institutional and disciplinary, and from movement to organizational to personal politics. In order to make sense of the politics of higher education in the twentieth century—to understand why the federal government turned college going into a national priority—we must seek to capture the dynamics of each of these relationships. A good way to do this is to look at the iterative relationship between policymakers in Washington, DC, and administrators, professors, and students living, working, and learning in a variety of different institutional settings elsewhere. In addition to using a wide array of secondary sources, I have also mined federal education data and reports, presidential papers, government documents, military records, and congressional testimonies combined with surveys, opinion polls, and newspapers to reconstruct higher education at the national level; campus newspapers, student letters, institutional studies and surveys, and administrative records and course syllabi have been used to illustrate the role of higher education in state building and in defining citizenship at the campus level. Because the objective of this study is to reveal hidden aspects of American political development, the evidence that I use draws on a broad range of social—and not simply political—relationships. It is this combination of "bottom-up" and "top-down" approaches that distinguishes this work from most work on higher education.[17]

Finally, I trace the influence of psychological knowledge on the organizational, political, and social transformations that drive my story. Over the course of the last century, professional psychologists, and their allies in other branches of the social and behavioral sciences, shaped Americans' perception of their government, their interaction with their government, and their understanding of themselves as citizens. Some scholars who have studied this widening jurisdiction of psychological thought refer to it as the "therapeutic ethos" and have located its epicenter in the rise of consumer capitalism during the decades around the turn of the twentieth century. The broad consensus among these scholars is that a therapeutic mode of self-understanding—denoted by a belief in dynamic personhood and penchant for conspicuous self-referencing and narcissism—offered individuals a way to cope with the psychological challenges of modern life. The standard story carries a powerful critique of the vanishing public sphere as it was eclipsed by self-absorbed efforts to adapt to a heartless world. Rather than focusing on the therapeutic as merely a source of individual transformation, however, this project also traces the different ways in which psychological expertise transformed higher education and the American state, changing the organizational structure of universities and colleges and the meanings of citizenship in the twentieth century.[18]

I follow three professional communities of psychologists as they moved between academe and the state from World War I through the cold war. As historians Ellen Herman and James Capshew have shown, warfare offered psychologists an especially propitious arena in which to demonstrate the utility of their expertise in solving organizational and human problems; and because wartime disrupted colleges and universities as much as any institution, they proved particularly susceptible to psychological understandings of problems and prescriptions for rehabilitation.[19] Following World War I, for example, university leaders turned to personnel specialists—the first community of psychologists that I examine—for guidance in accommodating the intellectual and emotional needs of their students. Having honed their techniques in the U.S. Army during the war, personnel specialists returned from battle with new ways to help harmonize individuals' interactions with large-scale organizations. Personnel specialists thought of institutions and individuals as interconnected and endowed with unique personalities that could be adjusted and readjusted—indeed, perfected—by expert interventions. This discovery profoundly changed the way colleges and universities operated, how they packaged and delivered knowledge, and the ways professors and administrators interacted with their students. A heightened emphasis was placed on personalizing and individualizing the academic experience, using what I refer to as the "personnel perspective," in order to ensure that all students made a smooth adjustment into and out of college.

"Adjustment" and its opposite, "maladjustment," served as a social scientific catchall for much of the twentieth century. Variously understood from one discipline to another, leading definitions of adjustment typically mirrored the white, middle-class behavioral and psychological norms of the male investigators who created and used it.[20] Within higher education, administrators plotted students along the adjustment spectrum to chart their academic, social, and psychological progress, or lack thereof. Administrators and faculties believed they could guide students' adjustment by readjusting higher education's academic, administrative, and social structures. As a practical issue this belief obligated administrators and faculties to make college fun as well as personally fulfilling, to do whatever was necessary to improve students' chances of success in order to keep more students in school. It also forced college officials to revise the nineteenth-century student management doctrine of in loco parentis, which defined students as "children" and administrators and faculties as "parents." College leaders maintained their parental privileges but updated the definition of childhood to accommodate new theories of psychological development. No doubt, the emergence of the American research university occurred in the last quarter of the nineteenth century, but the psychologically informed theory of in loco parentis that dominated the undergraduate experience in the twentieth century dated to the 1920s, when educators adopted the personnel perspective to help students adjust to hierarchical organizations.

The fascination with adjustment extended to the 1930s as New Deal planners marshaled the power of the federal government to readjust the nation's social and political institutions. Building on political scientist Stephen Skowronek's foundational premise that "state building is most basically an exercise in reconstructing an already established organization of state power," I show how the Roosevelt administration used higher education to achieve some of its state-building goals.[21] Geographically diffuse with strong regional allegiances, higher education assisted New Dealers in naturalizing relations with an American people who trusted their colleges and universities more than they did their government. Led by publicly supported land-grant institutions, which enjoyed close ties to the federal government and the public, programs in agricultural adjustment, student work-study, and civic education helped national opinion leaders forge a mutually beneficial partnership with the entire higher education sector, public and private. Hamstrung by ideological antistatism and a lack of administrative capacity, federal government leaders saw higher education as a great way to reach out and touch the lives of farmers, students, and average Americans everywhere. Policymakers learned their lessons well. Even as none of these efforts endured as originally conceived beyond the immediate economic crisis, the idea of using education to adjust citizens and the state was not forgotten.

World War II revealed the full potential of educational adjustment when a new generation of social psychologists migrated to the U.S. Army and to key nodes of the wartime government. Relying on emergent opinion survey technologies to gauge soldiers' attitudes about life in the military, they forged an idealized conception of the adjusted citizen-soldier that inextricably linked psychological health to educational attainment. This finding not only prompted the military to join forces with higher education to bring educational opportunities to soldiers during the war, it also shaped the creation and meaning of the G.I. Bill of 1944 afterward. The G.I. Bill consecrated the relationship between education and psychological adjustment and moved American higher education, and the veterans that swarmed to it, closer to the center of democratic citizenship. After World War II, democratic citizens, by definition, were college educated.

A third community of psychologists—public opinion researchers—deepened and complicated the relationship between education and democratic citizenship during the cold war. As a measurement of psychological adjustment writ large, public opinion was tracked with feverish intensity during that endless crisis. Opinion polling offered intimate knowledge of citizens' private lives and political beliefs and thus presented state policymakers with a new means of democratically governing a distended polity. Significantly, just as social psychologists' study of psychological adjustment in World War II linked better citizenship to educational attainment, opinion researchers also established a causal relationship between informed opinion and education. College-educated citizens, research showed, registered the most sophisticated understanding of cold war politics and global affairs. This finding strengthened policymakers' belief that higher learning could improve national security. It also convinced academic leaders that the study of the global cold war should be incorporated into the college curriculum and extended to adults in cities and in the countryside. By decade's end both developments became synthesized within the National Defense Education Act of 1958, which affirmed the notion that higher education was a bastion of democracy not only at home but around the world.

The psychological link between higher education and adjusted citizenship snapped in the 1960s when students, aghast at the bureaucratic menace that was the "multiversity," revolted against it. The mass New Left led the charge before dissolving into competing student identity groups by the late 1960s. Black and female student groups—in search of liberation rather than adjustment—emerged as the two most influential identity groups, each pressing for an educational and political order that approximated the nation's racial and gender diversity. Because of their efforts, race and gender moved to the center of national politics and black and women's studies programs were incorporated into the academic mainstream. These new interdisciplines represented diversity incarnate, confirming students' belief that they not only had a right to attend college, but also a right to an education all their own.

However, students did not discard the psychological premises that suffused the modern university and politics. Rather, they harnessed psychology for their own purposes in order to topple the despised adjustment regime and, in its place, erect a new institutional and ideational structure that made the cultivation of personal identity the aim of a college education. In other words, groups of black and female students shared much in common with the "expert" communities of psychologists whose ideas about human behavior, racial and gender norms, and organizational development they sought to overturn. This was ironic because the New Left, black power, and the women's liberation movements all considered psychology to be a tool of oppression, not freedom. The psychological evoked an endless litany of negative associations: personnel management with in loco parentis; personal adjustment with corporate automation; personality with plasticity; public opinion with politics as usual; interest groups with narcissistic self-interest; and Freudianism with male oppression, if not misogyny. Yet in attempting to overcome their own alienation, student protesters found it impossible to resist the allure of the psychological. They explored their inner emotions and private knowledge, often in small group settings, to recover personal, often painful experiences for political purposes; in turn, they discovered that politics and education were personal and that the path to self-discovery required self-knowledge and introspection. At the end of the day, black and female students, like the expert psychologists before them, also believed that psychological insights could help make America's higher education system and politics, and the citizens who participated in both, democratic.[22]

Admittedly, the relationship between higher education and democratic citizenship explored here was not entirely new to the twentieth century. Throughout American history higher learning had always been closely linked to better citizenship. One of the major goals of the old-time denominational college, which dominated the nation's education landscape before the Civil War, was to train citizens for a life of public service in the new nation. This belief was likewise embedded within the educational mission of the ascendant university model after the Civil War. Even as the new university moved well beyond the classical curriculum, offering students courses of study in a host of practical and scientific fields, citizenship training remained a core function. "All the colleges boast of the serviceable men they have trained," reflected Harvard president Charles W. Eliot, in 1908, "and regard the serviceable patriot as their ideal product. This is a thoroughly democratic conception of their function."[23]

My study adds three dimensions to this older story. First, and most important, full citizenship, like college going, was sharply divided along racial and gender lines in the nineteenth century, the near-exclusive privilege of well-off, white men of Protestant faith. It was not until the twentieth century that the state began to extend full citizenship and educational opportunity to everyone else. Second, this study brings the state back into the history of American higher education, and in a new way. While citizens have always been trained to serve the state, not until the twentieth century did the state take an active interest in, and provide financial support for, training democratic citizens. Finally, this study brings psychology into the history of democratic citizenship. Over the course of the last century social scientists advanced new ways to think about and measure citizens' political and personal behavior that changed how the state and its citizens thought about one another, and citizens thought about themselves. Infusing politics with therapeutic potential changed the ways in which higher education policy was framed and along with it the very meaning of citizenship. During the twentieth century, higher education policy, and the meanings of citizenship that it helped define, were worked out between citizens and the state.[24]

Part I, "Bureaucracy" (chapters 2 and 3), examines the bureaucratic conquest of higher education and the state during the interwar period. As I explain in chapter 2, during the 1920s American higher education became truly massive in scale and scope. Enrollments climbed to exceed a million students as college building took off around the country. The dramatic growth in institutions and students, which more or less continued for the rest of the century, caught university administrators off guard. High student dropout rates coupled with general administrative disarray seemed poised to bring the university building project to its knees. The realization, as one university president put it, that "many students enter at the bottom but comparatively few go over the top," raised serious doubts about the future of higher learning.[25]

University leaders' search for administrative order led them back to the crucible of wartime. Though the war caused havoc at many campuses, some fields of study, such as psychology, exploited the war in order to extend their professional influence beyond the university laboratory. Two competing camps of psychologists—intelligence testers and personnel specialists—populated the U.S. Army Committee on Classification of Personnel during the war; both camps, while possessed of differing conceptions of human behavior, found the army fertile ground for fine tuning the use of their psychological technologies to adjust and readjust large-scale institutions and the individuals who populated them. For administrative, scientific, and economic reasons, however, the personnel community achieved a critical advantage over the intelligence testers. After the war, a multidisciplinary personnel movement, led by personnel guru Walter Dill Scott, the director of the Army Committee on Classification of Personnel, co-opted the intelligence testing community. Scott and his team of psychologists had harmonized the army's troop induction and placement processes, and now wanted to extend their expertise to all large-scale organizations. They persuaded college administrators, in part because many of them ascended the administrative ranks after the war, that personnel management could help them better understand their students and thus improve students' chances of success. During the 1920s, the focus on adjustment turned higher education into an institution that not only imparted knowledge and credentials to students, but also offered students training to navigate hierarchical organizations. Higher education pioneered work on personal adjustment, which during and after World War II became the very heart of educated citizenship.

Prior to that happening, however, higher education and the state needed to join forces. Chapter 3 shifts the focus from organizational change within higher education in the 1920s to venues that linked the New Deal state and higher education in the 1930s, when federal policymakers used higher education to help adjust the American people to life in a bureaucratic state. The country's land-grant colleges and universities proved absolutely indispensible to this state-building effort. Resting at the literal and metaphoric intersection of the state and society, but completely beholden to neither, the land grants captured the attention of entrepreneurial New Dealers in search of discreet ways to extend federal power at the grassroots. Attention to the land grants eventually spilled over to the entire higher education sector as President Roosevelt and a handful of top New Deal administrators encouraged and rewarded higher education institutions, and many of the students who attended them, for their help in combating the Great Depression. Higher education won, extending the government's reach into citizens' lives.

Roosevelt's interest in higher education was driven primarily by raw political considerations, not his personal affection for colleges and universities. But he was also persuaded by congressmen, university presidents, professors, and students and parents who let him know that higher education was in dire need of a new deal, too. For Roosevelt and his brain trust, then, higher education offered a popular and relatively uncontroversial way to fight unemployment, deliver social amelioration and services, and at its most ambitious, help average Americans to make sense of the growing bureaucratic regime in which they lived. "No institution," declared a New Dealer in 1936, "is more interested in all aspects of national life than is the college or university"—and for good reason.[26] My examination of land-grant colleges and universities' role in dispensing agriculture adjustment, the Office of Education's federal forum project, and the National Youth Administration's college work-study program illuminates the ways in which the New Deal experience sympathetically disposed higher education's leaders to the possibilities of still greater cooperative endeavors during World War II.

Part II, "Democracy" (chapters 4 and 5), explores how higher education and democratic citizenship became deeply intertwined during World War II and the cold war. Chapter 4 moves the story from the New Deal to the U.S. Army. As the state's main wartime hub for psychological research, the Army Research Branch, headed by University of Chicago sociologist Samuel A. Stouffer, presented evidence to military commanders that better-educated soldiers were more efficient, exhibited higher morale, and were less likely to desert or suffer a psychoneurotic breakdown than their educationally deprived peers. Military and educational policymakers were galvanized by this finding and joined forces to create the Army Information and Education Division—the education clearinghouse for the common soldier. With the steady support of General George C. Marshall, the chief of staff of the army, who believed wholeheartedly in the transformative power of education, millions of G.I.s made use of the educational services provided to them. Soldiers learned how to read in an army literacy course, earned degrees-by-mail through the U.S. Armed Forces Institute, and even pursued a college-level education at one of the army's four Army University Centers. Although army officials and psychologists interpreted soldiers' enthusiasm for higher learning as evidence that education could be used to shape soldiers into psychologically balanced and adjusted citizens, most soldiers just felt fortunate for the chance to improve their lot during the war. Many soldiers shared the excitement of one fortunate G.I. safely stationed at Camp Cooke, California: "Yes, there is definitely something I would like to learn in the Army."[27]

If for wholly different reasons, then, policymakers' and soldiers' enthusiasm for higher education carried over to the postwar period. Record numbers of veterans, the vast majority of whom were white males, tapped the education provision of the G.I. Bill. Their widely heralded academic success and seemingly smooth readjustment to civilian life appeared to confirm that education not only produced good soldiers, it also produced democratic citizens. The excitement generated by the passage of the G.I. Bill proved infectious, triggering policy effects that extended well beyond the lives of veterans and shaped policymaking for decades to come. The legislation fueled the polity's interest in higher learning and remade the institution into a training ground for democratic citizenship.

As I explain in chapter 5, replicating the stunning outcomes of the G.I. Bill, however, proved more difficult than expected on the cold war campus—and not only because of Senator Joseph McCarthy's (R-WI) well-documented hunt for political subversives in academia. Though McCarthyism dominates most studies of the cold war university, and figures in the story told here, McCarthyism did not completely dominate higher education. Despite suffering a torrent of anticommunist attacks—and more than a few casualties—higher education also played a leading role in the government's battle for hearts and minds in the 1950s. At home and abroad the American state deployed education in order to produce democratic citizens and then used public opinion polls to evaluate the integrity of the production process. Obsessively tracked during the cold war, "public opinion" offered policymakers and educational elites access to the American people's collective psychological adjustment and mental health, to their intellectual fitness and their knowledge of the bipolar cold war world in which they lived. Although polling was by no means bulletproof, as pollsters' misreading of the 1948 presidential election embarrassingly revealed, the exploration of the relationship between attitudes and opinions, and between the public's opinions and the state's prosecution of the cold war, indicated time and again that educated citizens were better citizens.

But higher education's effort to shape public opinion yielded unpredictable results as students' private experiences commonly differed with official educational aims. "We have a more aggressive state of mind," fumed one professor. "But I'll be damned if students see much connection between higher learning and better citizenship."[28] This was not for lack of trying. Senator J. William Fulbright (D-AR) and Representative Karl E. Mundt (R-SD), along with midlevel government administrators such as Freida B. Hennock of the Federal Communications Commission, turned to higher education to beat back communism and make the world safe for democracy. University leaders and foundation officers, led by C. Scott Fletcher of the Ford Foundation, pursued the same goals by different means. They collaborated to make the study of global politics a central feature of the undergraduate experience and to convince millions of adults everywhere to watch educational television. In both areas higher education's effort to create globally aware citizens, be it in the cold war classroom or in front of the family television, continued to disappoint. Students and their parents shunned politics and their "citizen duty" to an alarming degree during the cold war. Undergraduates wanted to have fun, study business, and graduate to a well-paying corporate job, while most adults preferred to watch anything but educational television. This discovery raised the possibility that Americans might be motivated by private self-interest and not some overriding concern for the public weal. The public's political apathy proved particularly discouraging to state policymakers who had come to believe that educated citizens were model citizens. Not even the 1958 National Defense Education Act seemed to register very deeply with students. Though students surely appreciated increased access to NDEA-sponsored fellowships, loans, and loan-forgiveness options, whether they were becoming better citizens as a result of attending college was anyone's guess by the end of 1950s.

The book's final part, "Diversity" (chapter 6), answers this question. It explores how students' private concerns came to occupy the center of campus and national politics in the 1960s and in so doing thrust higher education into the thick of the nascent rights revolution. Students' rights-based reconstruction of the educated citizen marked a departure from the older reciprocal-based formulation that had been decisive in the creation of past higher education policy. From the 1930s through the 1950s, the state provided citizens with educational opportunities in order to repay them for their sacrifices during the Great Depression and the brutal war years that followed. But the gradual expansion of educational access and of federal involvement in higher education set in motion a sequence of unexpected social and political reactions that prepared the way for the shift from a reciprocal to a rights-based conception of the educated citizen founded on the principle of diversity. Awarding higher education benefits to war veterans under the G.I. Bill of 1944 expanded to include additional categories of student-citizens under the NDEA of 1958 and again under the Higher Education Act of 1965. Where the G.I. Bill provided educational opportunities to a single class of citizens—veterans—and the NDEA to citizens in federally sanctioned national-defense-related fields of study, the 1965 Higher Education Act, and its subsequent amendments, theoretically offered the promise of higher education to everyone else. The Higher Education Act increased the flow of federal funds for the support of "developing institutions" and scholarships for students of "exceptional financial need." Along with other War on Poverty educational programs created to equalize "opportunity," the act increased college access for black and minority students, laying the groundwork for the emergence of diversity as the main organizing principle of the post-1960s university.

The institutionalization of diversity was not simply a by-product of a single piece of federal higher education legislation, of course. It occurred in stages, turning on the actions of students and university administrators as well as federal officials, and contained as many unintended consequences as the immigration reform legislation passed the same year as the Higher Education Act. After illuminating the surprising policy origins of diversity, I then examine how groups of rights-conscious black and women students—roused by the ideology of black power and women's liberation and by psychologically derived understandings of oppression and liberation—organized identity groups to pressure administrators into creating black and women's studies programs. The mobilization of rights-conscious black and female students in the late 1960s and early 1970s diversified the college curriculum and helped introduce a new style of identity group politics to the national scene. Subsequent student groups—Jews, Asians, Latinos, gays and lesbians, and countless others—rallied around identity in order to secure their place within the college curriculum. Students' quest for identity and a true historical self personalized and diversified American higher education and American politics.[29]

College administrators also benefited from this new political model. They quickly learned that converting black power into black studies, and women's liberation into women's studies, proved an effective way to cope with students' personal and political grievances. By using the university's existing organizational and academic infrastructure to their advantage, administrators discovered that decision making in the name of diversity was an effective approach to address stakeholders' demands and to manage the day-to-day affairs of their institutions. By the early 1970s, well before the Supreme Court's 1978 *Bakke* decision underscored "diversity" as a core value in higher education, many students agreed that they had a "right" to attend college. College administrators, for their part, embraced the notion that the right to education meant little if the student body and curriculum did not reflect the broader society's demographic, intellectual, and cultural diversity. In the end, it was this odd and unexpected mix of federal policy, student identity-group activism, and administrative maneuvering that propelled the idea of diversity into the institutional core of the present-day university.

The conclusion, chapter 7, offers an overview of the state of higher education in an age of diversity. Without the Great Depression, World War II, and the cold war to thicken the relationship between the state and higher education, a rightward political shift commenced during the economic downturn of the 1970s that reached its climax with the election of President Ronald Reagan in 1980. Ideological differences dating back to the campus turmoil of the 1960s, combined with real financial concerns, helped to drive a wedge between the government and higher education. Funding cuts and the introduction of market-driven student-aid policies altered the nature of college going for the rest of the century and beyond. Ultimately, the drift toward "privatization" in the final two decades of the twentieth century readjusted higher education's role as a mediator between citizens and the state once again—changing how students paid for college and moving students closer to a privatized conception of democratic citizenship inextricably tied to the "personal politics" of identity.

PART I

Bureaucracy

———— ❖ ————

Chapter 2

Reorganizing Higher Education
in the Shadow of the Great War

———————— ❖❖❖ ————————

The story begins in World War I. After Congress answered President Woodrow Wilson's call for war on Germany in April 1917, the U.S. government extended its reach into the lives of average Americans in ways not seen since the Civil War. The Selective Service System conscripted 2.8 million young men for military duty; the War Industries Board, headed by the indomitable Bernard Baruch, exerted strong-armed federal oversight of American business; and the Committee on Public Information, the government's official propaganda wing, directed by newspaperman George Creel, whipped up home-front patriotism to lethal levels. In rapid order, the Great War made clear what had been obvious for a long time: when need be the federal government could become a powerful bureaucratic machine.[1]

No institution was haunted more by the specter of wartime bureaucracy than the modern university. The loss of half of all male students to military duty, combined with the resultant loss of tuition income, compelled many university heads to wonder whether the complete discontinuance of normal educational activities could be too far off.[2] To make up for war's human and financial tolls, American higher education sought aid and comfort from the federal government. What it got instead was a full frontal assault from the U.S. Army, in the fall term of 1918, when some five hundred colleges and universities were converted into de facto army boot camps. College presidents, desperate to boost enrollments and contribute to the war effort, cut a deal with the army that granted student deferments in exchange for participation in one of the army's reserve officer or special training corps' programs. The largest program was the Student Army Training Corps, which inflamed passions by reminding students "It's patriotic to go to college." As college leaders had hoped, the program lifted enrollments and revenues as well as many students' nationalist fervor.[3]

Initial excitement quickly faded. Martial imperatives—morning drill, mandatory "war issue" courses, and the presence of army commanders—overwhelmed normal, day-to-day campus operations. No doubt academic freedom was the first casualty. Defined in 1915 in the American context by the American Association of University Professors, "absolute freedom of thought" surrendered as several dozen professors were summarily fired for admitted or alleged opposition to U.S. involvement in the war.[4] Many professors thought the whole wartime experience an utter disaster, regretting that their leaders had ever permitted the university to become, in the words of Edward S. Corwin, a noted scholar of constitutional law at Princeton University, "a cog of the military machine."[5] Not until the Great Depression would academic leaders again entertain the possibility of direct state engagement—and only then because they had no other choice.

This raises an important question: If the 1920s was notable for the state's absence in higher education affairs, why do I start my study there? Because it was in this decade that higher education first approximated its current size and shape—when the sector started to look and behave something like it does today. It was also during this decade that higher education administrators embraced a psychologically informed conception of individuals and institutions that helped higher education expand its scope and authority, particularly its administrative capacity, which would prove indispensible later, when the state once again came calling. Believing that they needed to know their students more intimately in order to manage them more effectively, educational elites across the country pursued a sweeping bureaucratic reorganization that would decisively shape the politics of American higher education on and off campus for the rest of the century. Academic administrators combined educational with therapeutic practices and created an organizational structure that would prove remarkably adaptable to the personal and political demands of successive generations of students, especially in the 1960s and 1970s when students' quest for ethno-racial and gender diversity engulfed many campuses. In sum, to understand how higher education became the institution it is today requires looking closely at the administrative innovations created during the crucial decade of the1920s.[6]

At the time, of course, the decision to innovate higher education was driven by the present not the future, and by students—lots of students. The postwar decade was a remarkably fecund one for higher education: nationally, enrollments doubled to exceed 1.1 million and a new college or university—or at least an institution that called itself by that name—opened every ten days.[7] The combination of more discretionary income, record high-school graduation rates, and the belief that a college degree improved upward social mobility intensified middle- and upper-class Americans' demand for higher learning.[8] "The insatiable appetite of American youth for higher education," opined the editors of the *Washington Post*, in 1927, "is the most significant and healthy sign that could be exhibited in connection with the future development of the country."[9]

Yet big demand begot even bigger problems. Colleges struggled to oblige all their students. Ballooning faculty-student ratios and a lack of space seemingly confirmed students' growing sense that "impersonalism" was the defining feature of the modern university. And, perhaps worst of all, half or more of all students never earned a degree. Between 50 and 60 percent of college students dropped out of college in the 1920s, 35 percent of these during the first year. Numerous reasons were cited for this sad state of affairs—financial hardship, academic unpreparedness, and low enthusiasm were leading causes of high attrition, what administrators dourly referred to at the time as "student mortality."[10]

High dropout rates were hardly news in the 1920s. Since the late nineteenth century, when the demand for college was starting to pick up steam, and academic standards were notoriously lax, most colleges admitted any student who had the time, inclination, and money to attend. These students were often poorly prepared and many left college as a result—even though minimal pass-work well below a "gentleman's C" was often good enough to earn a degree.[11]

But as enrollments climbed in the twentieth century, the trickle of student departures came to feel more like a flood tide. Some old-time professors predictably pinned the travails of the university on the surplus of marginally prepared students who "don't think—can't think, and never can be taught to think."[12] College going was a privilege, they insisted, and students who did not graduate had only themselves to blame. A growing number of professors and administrators, however, took a more sympathetic view. They shouldered some of the blame and increasingly agreed with the opinion leveled by one distraught undergraduate: "The students of this generation are clamoring for attention . . . demanding consideration of our special problems . . . asking strange, new things of the university."[13]

College administrators turned to the new psychological sciences for solutions to their students' problems. They began to accept psychological diagnoses of and prescriptions for the adjustment and readjustment of individuals living and working in large-scale institutions. The fixation on adjustment and its opposite, maladjustment, dominated the social scientific imagination beginning in the 1920s. Even as psychology fragmented into increasingly specialized applied subfields, a focus on personal adjustments, or some variation of it, endured.[14]

What was the profile of this perfectly adjusted individual? Then and later, he was a white male of respectable means—a reflection of the values and tastes of the very middle- and upper-class white males who comprised professional psychology and who filled the seats in most college classrooms. Beyond this point, the consensus around adjustment ended. While investigators agreed on the goal of adjustment, they disagreed over the best way to achieve it. As I explain in the first part of this chapter, this debate boiled over in the Committee on Classification of Personnel in the Army during the war. Intelligence testers believed adjustment was fixed and that by testing soldiers' intelligence they could be sorted properly to rationalize bureaucracies. Personnel specialists sympathized with intelligence testers, and some even dabbled in intelligence testing, but they questioned the ability of such instruments to gauge adjustment unilaterally. Rather, they believed that a more accurate appraisal of adjustment could be obtained by considering each individual as a "total personality" in which intelligence was one of many factors considered.[15] They asserted that adjustment was both inherited and learned, intellectual and experiential. Creating harmonious organizations, they argued, depended on more than a single measure; it required the continuous adjustment and readjustment of individuals and institutions.

After the war, both camps sought to reshape large-scale organizational life in their respective images. For reasons that I explore in the middle half of this chapter, personnel theory—what I refer to throughout this book as the "personnel perspective"—proved especially conducive to the institutional design and the political preferences of the white, middle- and upper-class playground that was the modern university. The personnel perspective emphasized flexible personhood and environments, which fit perfectly with higher education's postwar institution-building agenda and with existing understandings of the dominant student management doctrine of the day, in loco parentis. Inherited from the British Common Law, the doctrine crystallized as an American legal concept in the nineteenth century. Literally translated, in loco parentis sanctioned the college to serve in "the role of the parent" and granted administrators and faculty plenary authority over students' intellectual, physical, and moral development.[16]

The explosion in psychological knowledge after World War I opened up higher education's parental powers beyond the academic and bodily to include students' emotional health and well-being. The extension of the college's parental power into the mysteries of the psychological, as I document in the closing section of this chapter, had enduring administrative and intellectual consequences. At all but the most elite institutions, administrators gave up on weeding out would-be failures and on deliberately limiting access to certain groups of students. Instead they tried to make the total environment more flexible as well as fun.[17] They attempted to forge adaptable bureaucratic settings in order to accommodate and adjust a range of personalities because personality, unlike intelligence, was regarded as malleable. And once institutionalized, this revised meaning of in loco parentis demanded that educational elites do whatever they could to keep more students in school. As we shall see, building institutions that were both socially appealing and financially solvent seemed to depend on it.

"No Intention of Wasting a Drafted Man": Psychology Goes to War

Sigmund Freud's celebrated 1909 Clark University lectures and young Walter Lippmann's exploration of Freudian ideas in *Preface to Politics* four years later introduced members of New York and Boston high society to the role of the unconscious in shaping human behavior.[18] For the American public, however,

World War I represented psychology's true coming out. Placing psychology in the thick of average soldiers' introduction to military life, according to one historian, "put psychology on the map of the United States."[19]

Personnel specialists were the first group of expert psychologists to march off to war. Organized by Walter Dill Scott and Walter Bingham of the Carnegie Institute of Technology (CIT), the personnel community matriculated from a wide array of professional contexts, including industrial and individual psychology, psychiatric social work, mental hygiene, and corporate marketing and advertising. Despite the odd assortment of professional affiliations, these experts shared a belief that "human relations" problems lay at the root of modern life's most vexing challenges. Unlike Frederick Winslow Taylor's theory of scientific management, which rigidly defined a worker solely in terms of the quantity of his productive output, personnel managers insisted that increased productivity required an appreciation for the "maximum well-being of the human element in industry."[20]

On the eve of U.S. entry into the war, personnel theory's utopian sentiments won over few adherents inside the federal government. What did interest policymakers, however, was personnel management's apparent skill at coordinating and rationalizing the organizational life of large-scale organizations and the men who populated them. Desperate and pressed for time, Bernard Baruch, director of the War Industries Board, and William Redfield, the secretary of commerce, sought to increase the available supply of qualified personnel specialists in the federal government. In less than a year the government—in concert with the University of Rochester, the New School, the CIT, and the University of California, Berkeley—trained six hundred personnel managers to streamline governmental-business relations and to bring a semblance of administrative order to the rapidly expanding federal universe.[21]

The War Department took note. Scott, with Bingham at his side, convinced the department to let them manage the army's nascent personnel operation. Having previously established personnel departments at companies such as AT&T, Carnegie Steel, and Westinghouse, and having worked on developing selection processes for commissions in the Reserve Officers' Training Corps, Scott and Bingham appealed to military leaders who were overwhelmed by the prospects of mobilizing a military force that had grown seventeenfold in less than six months. Scott requested and received nearly total control. By August 1917, the Committee on Classification of Personnel in the Army was up and running.[22]

Scott's background and training had prepared him well for his new assignment. He earned his doctorate in psychology under Wilhelm Wundt at Leipzig University in 1900. After a brief stint at Cornell University working under Edward B. Tichener, Scott decided to pursue a career in the emerging, if lightly regarded, field of applied psychology. His journey from a pure scientist to an applied psychologist interested in the nitty-gritty application of psychological techniques to everyday life was retraced innumerable times by others in the early twentieth century, including Bingham. Following a short stay at Dartmouth, the Chicago-trained Bingham headed to CIT to head its new department of applied psychology. He was immediately struck by the school's brazen vocational outlook and convinced Scott to join him there. CIT specialized in training industrial managers and engineers, and Bingham became interested in using psychology to help graduates—and the firms for which they worked— cultivate "their ability to understand and influence people."[23] Like others who counted themselves members of the small but growing ranks of the field of applied psychology, Scott and Bingham were energized by finding practical solutions to quotidian bureaucratic challenges. Psychology may have flourished in Europe as a pure science of mind, but in the United States practitioners earned their stripes by rolling up their sleeves to help construct the nations' administrative order.[24]

In Scott and Bingham's case this meant using psychology to resolve business problems. From their headquarters at the Bureau of Salesmanship Research at CIT, they and their junior associates designed a host of novel psychological technologies to help business firms systematize the selection and placement of new salesmen. The instruments they developed and popularized—the personal history blank, the application blank, the reference letter, and the interviewer's scale and rating sheet—provided business firms with an ostensibly objective way to select the right person for the job.[25]

In fact, the bureau's suite of tools was anything but objective, even for a fringe-branch of applied psychology not known for rigorous experimental design. The construction of the interviewer's scale and rating sheet illustrates this point. First, Scott and Bingham tapped business leaders to develop a list of traits found in the "ideal salesman." Next, the top five traits—appearance, convincingness, industry, character, and value to the firm—were provided to raters who rank-ordered the strength of those traits in twenty-five known salesmen. Finally, a rater used this list to gauge the extent to which those five traits were observable in a particular job candidate. Using the ideal salesman as their normative referent point, the "man-to-man" selection method that Scott advocated was really little more than an elaborate exercise in finding men that looked and behaved like the tester.[26] These and other tools were packaged and sold to companies as *Aids in Selecting Salesmen*.[27]

Ironically, it was precisely the subjective, makeshift quality of Scott's psychological tools that appealed to the army command. The subjective design and administration of the tools made them serviceable for any personnel situation, offering a user as many possible options as his opinions or tastes. The personal history blank and rating scale were merged to form the soldier qualification card—the centerpiece technology of the army's entire personnel operation designed to help select army officers and place soldiers into appropriate military occupations. The Scott Rating Card—created with the help of trade-test

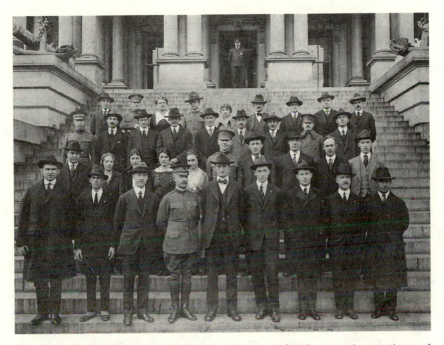

Figure 2.1. The Committee on Classification of Personnel in the Army (ca. 1919) served as a hub of activity for personnel specialists during World War I. Walter Dill Scott (bottom row, center, in the bowtie), Walter Van Dyke Bingham (first row, third from left), and Louis Hopkins (first row, last man on the right) were among the committee's most notable members. Courtesy Northwestern University Archives.

specialist Louis B. Hopkins from General Electric and psychologist James R. Angell from the University of Chicago—contained a record of all the personal information "deemed necessary in order to utilize [recruit] services to the greatest advantage in the Army."[28]

The card expediently organized each recruit's occupational, educational, and personal qualifications—the mix of factors necessary to determine a soldier's fit. Boards of trained personnel specialists interviewed recruits at each army cantonment to learn what, if any, "special talents" they possessed. Although labor intensive, interviewers processed 3 million recruits and were credited with identifying individuals of exceptional talent whose skills the army needed. Walter Bingham likened it to "a great employment bureau" and explained its utility in an equally practical way: "We have no intention of wasting a drafted man who happens to be a repairer of surgical instruments by placing him in the ammunition train." The army command was impressed with the results obtained through the recruit placement process and established Scott's committee on a permanent basis after the war.[29]

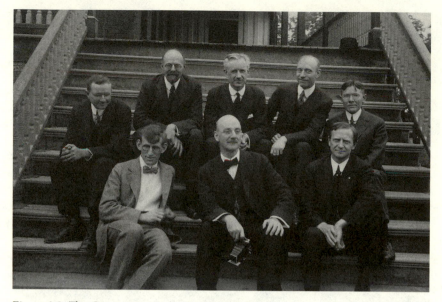

Figure 2.2. The Committee on the Psychological Examination of Recruits during the early development of its group intelligence tests for the U.S. Army (ca. 1917). Robert Yerkes is in the middle of the top row. To his left are Walter Van Dyke Bingham and Lewis Terman. H. H. Goddard is seated directly in front of Yerkes. Courtesy Robert M. Yerkes Papers, Manuscripts and Archives, Yale University Library.

The personnel community's long-term organizational achievements were unexpectedly eclipsed by intelligence testers, the second group of expert psychologists to descend on the army. Led by Robert M. Yerkes of Harvard University, at the time the president of the American Psychological Association, they organized as the Committee on the Psychological Examination of Recruits. Joined by Lewis H. Terman of Stanford, Carl C. Brigham of Princeton, Henry H. Goddard of the Training School for the Feebleminded in Vineland, New Jersey, and for a brief period in 1917, Walter Bingham, Yerkes and his intelligence testers submitted that a more efficient mass system of testing was possible through the measurement of native intelligence.[30]

The relative novelty of mass intelligence testing, the need for more—not fewer—soldiers, and Scott's personal dislike of Yerkes, despite Bingham's professional connection to him, cooled the military to intelligence testers' initial petition for a wartime role. It was only after behind-the-scenes negotiations that Yerkes secured a beachhead for intelligence testing in the Surgeon General's Sanitary Corps. From there trial runs of the intelligence tests, which had been designed in less than two weeks at Goddard's Vineland asylum using sample tests developed by Carl Brigham, revealed some utility in pinpointing mentally deficient recruits. Scott and the army command, persuaded that intelligence testing could be useful in conjunction with other types of examinations, appointed Yerkes to the Committee on Classification of Personnel.[31] In the months that followed, Yerkes and his team administered their Alpha (for literate recruits) and Beta (for illiterate recruits) examinations to half of the recruits interviewed by the committee. While the exams did help identify the mentally "feeble" draftee, the majority of results derived from the Army Alpha and Beta tests were downright absurd, laden with racist assumptions that members of the committee shared as a matter of course. Yerkes' testing corps determined that the average "mental-age" of the army's white recruits was 13.08 years, or slightly higher than that of a "moron," following their official lexicon. Army commanders were not impressed. They generally ignored Yerkes' wartime recommendations, discharged few soldiers for "low" intelligence, and disbanded his testing unit after the war.[32]

"Every Industry Is Struggling to Get upon a Firm Basis for the Future": The Triumph of the Personnel Perspective

Despite the army's summary rebuff, the public's and policymakers' interest in intelligence testing grew apace after the war thanks to a well-orchestrated promotional blitz by former testers. A traveling exhibit showcasing the committee's work crisscrossed the country in the months following the armistice, drawing big crowds of curious onlookers wherever it stopped.[33] A number of published accounts offered readers a glimpse of the wartime findings of the testing community and prescriptions for how best to apply those findings in the resolution of pressing social problems. In 1921, Robert Yerkes released his massive monograph, *Psychological Examining in the United States Army*.[34] Too long and tedious to be of access to lay readers, the book generated buzz only among junior researchers who lavished increasing time and resources on studying the nuances of intelligence in the postwar period.[35]

Carl Brigham published a much more influential book two years later. *A Study of American Intelligence* exposed the "plain, if somewhat ugly, facts" about the declining prospects of the American nation. Awash in the main currents of early-twentieth-century eugenic thought, Brigham's conclusions were as predictable as they were racist: the relentless influx of inferior immigrant racial stock—from Africa and, more recently, from eastern and southern Europe—had depleted the nation's intellectual capacities, driving it perilously close to extinction. He recommended that the American people and national policymakers join together to work "toward the prevention of the continued propagation of defective [racial] strains in the present population."[36]

Fears of racial and national degeneration had been smoldering since well before the war years. But the pursuit of "100 percent Americanism" during the war ignited nativist fires that the work of Brigham's and others' stoked. The widespread eugenic belief that "Mediterranean" and "Negro" races were putting the nation at risk galvanized public officials to try and prevent further degeneration. First of all, the alleged inferiority of African Americans offered a new justification for segregation in the South. Writing in the *Atlantic Monthly* in 1922, Cornelia James Cannon declared the separation of the races as not only a function of "race prejudice," but a necessity since blacks "never reach a mental age of 10."[37] Second, eugenic ideas and data derived from the army intelligence testers decisively shaped the nature of America's increasingly restrictive immigration policy. Legislation was passed in 1917, 1921, and 1924—the last of which, the Immigration Restriction Act of 1924, terminated Asian immigration altogether and bottlenecked immigration flows from southern and eastern Europe. On signing the legislation, President Calvin Coolidge declared that "America must be kept American."[38] This racist policy would not be substantively altered for more than four decades, until the passage of the 1965 Immigration Act ended the quota system designed to limit immigrant flows from all but western and northern Europe.[39]

At the institutional level, meanwhile, education and business supported the ascendant intelligence testing regime for bureaucratic reasons. The discharge of more than 3 million veterans eager to find work, go to college, or both, made the selection and placement of workers and students a major issue after the war. The measurement of intelligence appeared to hold the key to overcoming worker unruliness. Strikes had halted production of key military materiel during the war and promised to slow postwar reconversion unless addressed. Intelligence testing seemed like a way to do just that. Although harsh working conditions, low pay, and brutal managerial oversight were the most direct causes of the labor-management divide, Yerkes highlighted another, less obvious reason: "It has come to be recognized . . . [that] however well the physical requirements of a job are met by the individual, his intelligence may be inadequate or he may be unsuited temperamentally to his occupation."[40] Eager to control workers and thwart unionization, corporate leaders agreed.

Education leaders also looked to the measurement of native intelligence as a solution to the related problems of student selection and placement. Interest in intelligence testing proved keenest among high-school officials, and as early as 1920, Yerkes reported being swamped by "many hundreds of requests" for customized versions of his Army Alpha intelligence test.[41] With a twenty-five-thousand-dollar grant from the General Education Board, a branch of the Rockefeller Foundation, the country's leading nonprofit supporter of the social sciences, Yerkes and Terman designed the widely used National Intelligence Test for students in grades three through eight.[42] The rise of compulsory education laws, which increased enrollments a staggering 711 percent (from 202,963 to 1,645,171) between 1890 and 1919, persuaded school leaders of the value of mass intelligence testing for the measurement and placement of students. For all these reasons, the compulsory high-school arena provided the perfect mar-ket for intelligence testers to peddle their wares.[43]

The noncompulsory collegiate market proved a more difficult case in spite of runaway enrollment growth. Intelligence testers pressed college administra-tors to adopt their exams to "make room for the fit by keeping out the obvi-ously unfit," according to R. L. Duffus of the *New York Times*.[44] Yet no more than a few dozen elite private colleges in the Northeast could afford to limit enrollments, and these institutions relied on the College Board subject exami-nations (first unveiled in 1901 to gauge aspiring college students' mastery of high-school content) rather than intelligence tests.[45] This is not to suggest that intelligence tests failed to make any inroads on college campuses but to point out that they penetrated the higher education universe slowly after the war. To be sure, the future of student selection would belong to the Army Alphas-derived Scholastic Aptitude Test (SAT), designed by Carl Brigham after the war. At its first administration, in 1926, however, it was not the "big test" that it was to become: only eight thousand students were tested, a number that actually declined during the 1930s before climbing steadily upward after World War II. Led by Harvard president James Conant, who believed the SAT could be used to identify the nation's true intellectual elite—its "natural aristocracy"— Ivy League institutions enthusiastically adopted the SAT in the 1950s. Schools located down the prestige chain followed deferentially behind. But in the 1920s, the overwhelming majority of institutions used intelligence tests—if they used them at all—for the assessment of students after they had passed their subject exams, not before.[46]

At the end of the day, intelligence testers' desire to use their exams to check enrollment growth only occurred at a handful of private, elite institutions. Ad-ministrators elsewhere puzzled over how to use mental exams while at the same time fulfilling higher education's democratic mission. The use of intelligence exams for the express purpose of limiting student enrollments seemed contrary to many college presidents' sense of duty. "No American institution, unless pri-vate and restricted, has the right to adopt a method of selecting candidates that in any way violates the principles laid down in the Declaration of Indepen-dence," said Josiah M. Penniman, provost of the University of Pennsylvania, a private institution.[47] David Kinley, president of the University of Illinois, a public institution, agreed: "No man has any right under a government like ours to undertake to determine that only a few shall be permitted to get an education of higher grade." For many university leaders, then, the use of intelligence tests to limit enrollments flew in the face of America's democratic creed.[48]

In addition, postwar intelligence tests were no more predictive of students' academic performance than they had been of a soldiers' military service. When combined with other subjective factors of student performance—such as grades, class rank, letters of recommendation, and subject examinations— mental exams achieved acceptable correlations. Absent these additional factors the exams failed to forecast much of anything. By 1926, Arthur Klein, chief of the division of higher education at the Federal Bureau of Education, spoke for many members of the higher education community when he reported that "mental testing has made enormous strides since the Army tests . . . but the results have not been so satisfactory as the friends of psychological testing would desire." Mental tests, Klein concluded, "are not to be trusted."[49]

Finally, the economic realities confronted by American higher education made limiting admissions a practical impossibility at the vast majority of schools. Many university leaders certainly shared intelligence testers' desire to limit the influx of thousands of new students, many of whom, chided one dean, "showed neither great interest nor ability in college work." Their desire to exclude inferior students was mitigated by a 79 percent rise in postwar inflation.[50] "Every producer of raw material, every industry is struggling to get upon a firm basis for the future," surmised Eliot Wadsworth, president of the Harvard Alumni Association, in 1920. "The American industry of education is going through the same process." In the near term the postwar decline in higher education's purchasing power meant that most schools needed more—not less— tuition revenue to get by.[51]

Private and public institutions responded differently to the increased-demand/decreased-revenue postwar economic climate. Elite private schools in the Northeast—led by Harvard, Yale, and Princeton—raised tuition and established selective and exclusionary admission policies to slow the rate of institutional growth. The unique institutional characteristics of Ivy League schools permitted them to follow this path—namely large endowments, established benefactor networks, and close relationships with private college preparatory schools such as Groton, Hotchkiss, and Choate. At the same time, the Ivy's push toward selective admissions was the result of boldfaced anti-Semitism. At Harvard, Yale, and Princeton officials sought to limit the admission of Jewish students in order to preserve a majority of seats for the sons of Protestant upper-middle-class families. Alumni and top administrators at the "Big Three" identified the "Jewish problem" as one that needed to be dealt with straight away.[52] Columbia University offered a cautionary example: Jewish students had comprised nearly 40 percent of the student body during the 'teens before administrators instituted quotas that halved that number in the 1920s. At Harvard, Yale, and Princeton administrators conspired to keep Jewish enrollments around 10 percent. "The presence of Jews in large numbers," wrote Harvard's president Lawrence A. Lowell, one of the chief proponents of the Jewish embargo, "tends to drive Gentiles elsewhere."[53]

A far different approach was undertaken by schools outside the Northeast. Public institutions in the Midwest and West adapted to the gloomy postwar economic climate by raising their modestly priced tuitions and admitting more students. Although not all publics charged tuition, most did, and among those enrollment caps resulted in a "reduction in tuition income" that produced "a unit which is not economical," according to an official at the Federal Bureau of Education.[54] The mere suggestion of disqualifying an applicant who possessed a high-school certificate in the 1920s, as the intelligence testers recommended, was thus to misunderstand the demand-driven, tuition-dependent nature of American higher education. With a new university or college popping up practically every week, and with more students than ever wanting access to advanced study, to deny admission to a student bearing a high-school certificate made little sense when a competitor located literally down the road would in all likelihood admit the same applicant the very next day.

Then again, whether an institution opted for a selective or open admission policy—and the overwhelming majority of schools chose the latter—neither private nor public institutions needed the help of intelligence tests to limit student enrollments. Students were quite skilled at leaving school on their own. Student mortality, what university officials sometimes called the "freshman problem," posed a major threat in the 1920s. No region or institutional type was spared. Data secured from thirty-six two-year junior colleges in the Midwest, the South, and the Far West revealed a dropout rate of 66 percent. Officials at Virginia's Sweet Briar Women's College, in 1922, reported that a mere 25 percent of entering students matriculated to graduation, and most who dropped out did so in the first year. Larger institutions performed better, but still poorly. At the University of Pittsburgh the average first-year mortality rate was 35 percent. Institutions in the South reported similarly high mortality rates. Hugh H. Caldwell, registrar at the University of Georgia, found that schools in the South had a 32 percent freshman mortality rate. Any temptation to blame the South's poor performance on its history of low education funding was belied by the fact that elite universities with "good holding power" experienced similar rates of student withdrawal. In the Northeast, Harvard and Yale lost an average of 25 percent of freshmen in the early and middle 1920s; in the Midwest, 13 percent of freshmen left the University of Wisconsin during the freshman year; 30 percent left the University of Minnesota; and 37 percent left the University of Chicago. Based on the findings of a multiregion study, fully one-third of all college freshmen did not return as sophomores in the 1920s.[55]

The failure of the intelligence testing community to control access left the schoolhouse door open for the multidisciplinary personnel community. Not surprisingly, given their own preoccupation with studying institutions, personnel specialists made the creation of professional organizations their first order of business. Scott, along with other former members of the Committee on Classification of Personnel, established the Scott Company to help spread the personnel gospel of "the worker as an individual" throughout American business. The Scott Company oversaw the establishment of personnel offices at forty leading industrial firms after the war and played a key role in ending industrial strife in the Chicago garment trade battles of 1920. Two years later, James McKeen Cattell and John B. Watson connected with Scott, Bingham, Yerkes, Terman, and 160 other applied psychologists to form the Psychological Corporation. As evidenced by its core membership, the corporation attracted a diverse collection of experts—including intelligence testers—from across the spectrum of applied psychology. By attracting members from numerous fields and with varying methodological outlooks, the corporation offered an explicit acknowledgment that the most effective approach to professionalization lay in working with rather than against one another, even if that required doing so in a loosely organized way. In the years that followed, the corporation served as a publicity agent, referral service, and supply company for all applied psychologists.[56]

The personnel community also created research organs to disseminate emergent knowledge into the field. The Personnel Research Federation served as the intellectual nerve center of the nascent personnel community, publishing the *Journal of Personnel Research*, edited by Walter Bingham. The journal provided a forum for personnel experts, labor leaders, and corporate heads, and served as a vehicle for the extension and promotion of new practices and theoretical innovations. In 1922, James R. Angell, the new president of Yale University, said that the founding of the federation marked "a definite forward step in the solution of those crucial problems which center about personnel in industry."[57]

It was Scott, however, who left the most indelible mark on the theoretical underpinnings of the personnel movement and the evolving personnel perspective. Scott's experiences working in the army as well as for major industrial firms served as the basis of his book *Personnel Management: Principles, Practices, and Point of View*, (1923). More than any other work on the subject, *Personnel Management* crystallized existing thought on personnel theory and pointed the way for its subsequent development. During the war, the guiding belief of the personnel community had been "the right man in the right place." But Scott's mammoth exegesis offered a more nuanced rendering of the personnel perspective. Drawing from Freudian psychoanalysis, philosophical pragmatism, social and industrial psychology, and Frederick Winslow Taylor's efficiency school of worker productivity, Scott's somewhat trite wartime mantra had evolved into an elaborate seven-part schema founded on the "principle of individual difference." According to Scott, "individual difference"—what he elsewhere called the "human conception of labor"—was the recognition by managers that each "individual differs from another" and that "different kinds of work are done best by persons who, temperamentally, are particularly interested in them." Scott challenged business managers to disavow their old belief in the commodification of labor—of "putting square pegs into round holes." Personality, as Scott's wartime experience had revealed, was dynamic, and the key to efficient production lay in creating a cooperative working relationship between management and labor. A difficult task under the best of circumstances, Scott's prescription for the cessation of labor unrest would only occur if managers recognized that "work" was social and psychological as well as physical. Scott believed managers should take workers' desire for "self-expression" and "self-realization" seriously because contented workers were better workers.[58] The importance of job satisfaction was seemingly elemental, long assumed by personnel theorists but not scientifically confirmed until psychologist Elton Mayo and his Harvard Business School associates published the results of their Hawthorne Studies a few years later. They discovered that worker productivity increased when managers expressed appreciation for, and interest in, a job well done.[59]

Even before the so-called "Hawthorne Effect" was widely known, Scott's understanding of personnel theory provided an important ideological justification for the spread of "corporate welfarism." Although it was not institutionalized by many firms, corporate welfarism provided employees with representation on corporate boards, generous health plans, stock options, and subsidized recreational opportunities. It is true, as numerous critics of corporate welfarism have suggested, the managers who agreed to such concessions did so only because they offered a relatively painless way to avoid worker unionization. It is also true, however, as one historian has advised, that "busting unions" was not the only motive behind corporate leaders' interest in personnel theory. It also appealed to business leaders because they believed it would help change the corrupt business firm of old into a model democratic institution. In attempting to treat each worker as an individual, personnel specialists like Scott honestly believed that the business firm could be the cornerstone of a more democratic society.[60] For a brief time, business leaders endorsed this view. The proportion of business firms with at least two hundred fifty employees that established a personnel department increased between 1915 and 1920 from 5 to 25 percent.[61]

Though the future of white collar employment would indeed turn on personnel theory and its promise of pleasing personalities, its infiltration of blue-collar work stalled after the war. Authoritative federal oversight combined with a worker deficit during the heat of battle had forced many industries to build personnel offices and to adopt what surely was a more conciliatory posture toward organized labor. Both factors dissipated in the conservative, laissez-faire, antiunion 1920s. A widespread Red Scare, dramatized by the federal government's thuggish crackdown on alleged anarchists and Communists, many of whom were believed to be housed in or affiliated with organized labor, prefigured the corporate sector's rapid retreat from personnel theory and practice. Widespread anxiety over the spread of anarchist forces in the American homeland—fueled by the Russian Revolution and, more proximately, by the simultaneous detonation of bombs in eight U.S. cities on June 2, 1919—lent some credence to the theory that a Bolsheviklike coup d'état was near at hand. One of the intended victims of the bombing spree, A. Mitchell Palmer, the attorney general of the United States, acted aggressively to preempt further chaos. Federal as well as voluntary organizations contributed crucial tactical support. The Justice Department's Bureau of Investigation added a new antiterror wing, the

General Intelligence Division, headed by J. Edgar Hoover, to root out domestic anarchists. Together with a reinvigorated Ku Klux Klan, a newly formed American Legion, and scores of local vigilante organizations, the Justice Department plotted a series of surgical strikes against a number of leading Communist labor unions and political organizations in dozens of cities. The ensuing spate of "Palmer Raids"—authorized under the dubious legal auspices of the Alien Act of 1918—resulted in the deportation of at least ten thousand alleged subversives. Not only did the government's attack on organized labor in 1919–20 crush union activities until the Great Depression, it convinced corporate leaders to shelve personnel management. Believing that most workers were in fact radicals, firms thus reverted to get-tough labor policies that stressed worker discipline rather than morale.[62]

The corporate sector's anti-Communist-inspired rejection of personnel theory forced personnel specialists to find new organizational venues in which to advance the personnel perspective. They did not have to look for very long. Despite their countless attempts to leave the university and reinvent the outside world, personnel specialists ended up back where they started. The university—rife with student turnover and administrative chaos—emerged as a main laboratory for the application of the personnel perspective.[63]

"Being on the Threshold of a College Career Involves an Emotional Crisis of Exceptional Intensity": The Personnel Perspective Remakes In Loco Parentis

Professional psychologists did not alone control their own destiny during the interwar period. Their numbers grew tenfold between 1919 and 1939, from three hundred to three thousand practitioners, but more often than not midlevel administrators and faculty, some but not all of whom had formal disciplinary training, were tasked with spreading the personnel perspective.[64] The main professional body behind this effort was the American College Personnel Association (ACPA). Organized in 1924 from the remnants of the National Association of Appointment Secretaries, the group changed its name to reflect its new interest in the advancement of personnel theory to the college setting, and by 1930 the ACPA boasted a distinguished membership that included many of America's leading colleges.[65] According to Louis B. Hopkins, one of the organization's major boosters, the formation of a professional community dedicated to "bringing the college into closer organizational touch with its students" commenced higher education's effort to do whatever it could to "serve the individual."[66]

Hopkins dedicated the better part of his postwar professional life promoting the personnel perspective. He spent the first five years after the war working alongside his mentor, Walter D. Scott—first at the Scott Company, then as the director of personnel at Northwestern University, where Scott became president. In 1924, Hopkins followed suit as president of Wabash College. He took his interest in personnel theory with him to central Indiana, where he achieved renown as the country's leading college personnel expert. His groundbreaking 1926 report, *Personnel Procedures in Education: Observations and Conclusions Resulting from Visits to Fourteen Institutions of Higher Learning*, became a master plan for the college personnel movement.[67] In 1937, Hopkins's study formed the basis for the American Council on Education's landmark publication *The Student Personnel Point of View*, the standard guide on the subject for years afterward.[68]

Hopkins supported comprehensive personnel services that extended from admission through graduation. Vocational, academic, and personal counselors, armed with the latest tests of aptitude and attitude, were needed to assist students in overcoming the difficult challenges presented by the transition into and out of college life. Whatever the problem, Hopkins believed it could be solved if administrators relied on "the point of view which concerns itself primarily with the individual." According to Hopkins, this required overhauling undergraduate life to meet the individual needs of students, to "show the relationship of one piece of work to another and that there [was] a unity in the movement to individualize education."[69] Harmonizing individuals and institutions mattered because going to college presented all sorts of challenges. A college president made this point quite clear, warning a new class of freshman that "when you come to college, you make a violent break with your past." Hopkins believed that the personnel perspective could prevent violent breaks and help students adjust to college.[70]

A belief that college was a time of intense emotional upheaval was captured by psychologist G. Stanley Hall's work on adolescence. A pioneer in the psychological sciences and a leading expert of evolutionary childhood development and pedagogics, Hall depicted adolescence as a period of psychological and physiological change. Though others before him had pointed to adolescence as a unique social category between childhood and adulthood, Hall's work was novel in its characterization of the teen years as filled with psychic distress. In Hall's magnum opus *Adolescence* (1904), he described adolescence as a time of *strum und drang*—storm and stress—marked by combative interpersonal relations, especially with parents, psychological instability, and risky, libido-driven behaviors. According to Hall's leading biographer, his theory was really a "product of the frustrations of his own maturity," the working through of his own incredibly dysfunctional life that included a tumultuous tenure as the president of Clark University from 1899 to 1920.[71] Whether Hall's theory derived from personal rather than empirical evidence is beside the point. What mattered was that Hall's conception of adolescence resonated among college officials whose institution served as the pivot point from childhood to adulthood. Hopkins recognized this. "For a very large percentage of freshmen," he wrote, "the very fact of being on the threshold of a college career involves an emotional crisis of exceptional intensity."[72]

That the personnel perspective easily adapted to accepted understandings of in loco parentis mattered immensely. This doctrine granted administrators and faculty parental power over students' social conduct and academic training.[73] The doctrine developed a sturdy legal meaning in the nineteenth century in cases that pitted angry parents against allegedly abusive teachers.[74] Just as the parent could discipline his children at his pleasure, the courts declared, so too could the schoolmaster or the tutor in their role as a surrogate parent. Within higher education the Kentucky Supreme Court articulated a leading definition of the term in *Gott v. Berea College* (1913). The court agreed that the college's parental power permitted it to prohibit students from patronizing a local restaurant: "College authorities stand in loco parentis concerning the physical and moral welfare, and mental training of pupils, and . . . they may . . . make any rules or regulations for the government or betterment of their pupils that a parent could for the same purpose. Whether the rules or regulations are wise . . . is a matter left solely to the discretion of the authorities, or parents as the case may be."[75]

Two years later, the American Association of University Professors (AAUP) published the General Report of the Committee on Academic Freedom and Academic Tenure in which the doctrine of in loco parentis gained strength by negation. In codifying the American academic profession's first definition of "academic freedom," the fifteen-member committee, chaired by Columbia economist E.R.A. Seligman, bypassed *Lernfreiheit* (freedom of the student) and focused instead on *Lehrfreiheit* (freedom of the teacher)—"freedom of inquiry . . . of teaching . . . of extramural utterance." The committee's silence about student freedom departed from the Germanic tradition that regarded the freedom of the teacher and the student as theoretically constitutive. No such equivalency existed in the American context, where the doctrine of in loco parentis was the law of the land.[76]

Faculty and administrators embraced their parental powers with as much, if not more, vigor as students did in resisting it.[77] Boilerplate language outlining the college's parental power was buried deep within most college handbooks. Few students and their families were even aware of the language, and fewer still grasped its full meaning and legal implications until it was too late. Bryn Mawr's policy, pulled from its 1923 handbook, captured the sentiment if not wording of similar clauses elsewhere: "The college reserves the right to exclude at any time students whose conduct or academic standing it regards as undesirable."[78]

Countless students unsuccessfully sought legal redress for summary expulsions and suspensions throughout the 1920s. Time and again the doctrine of in loco parentis withstood legal challenge. In 1924, a Michigan court sided with college administrators who kicked a student out of school for smoking. That same year a Maryland judge ruled against a group of coeds in search of a court injunction to halt their dismissal after filing a complaint against a predatory administrator. Given this precedent, it was not at all surprising that in 1928 the New York Supreme Court declined to reinstate an expelled female student at Syracuse University who administrators claimed exhibited conduct "unbecoming a typical Syracuse girl."[79]

These cases were not atypical. While most students remained blithely unaware, those who did stray too far from the simple fun and games of college life faced dire consequences indeed. In different times and places students were expelled for reasons that would be considered unconscionable in today's academic world: for not attending chapel, for conscientiously objecting to military drill, for writing private letters critical of the administration, and marrying in a civil rather than religious ceremony.[80] Students' infantilizing relationship to their schools dated back to antiquity: the Greek word for education was derived from the word for *child* and akin to the word for *play*.[81] In the twentieth century, the American judicial system's reliance on the so-called "right-privilege distinction" helped implant the traditions of in loco parentis deep within higher education.[82] Certain professional occupations, like a police officer or a physician, and institutions, like higher education, were regarded as privileges in which participation could be and often was conditioned on the willing suspension of elemental constitutional rights. In the case of college going, students relinquished their rights to equal protection, to due process, as well as to First Amendment rights, in exchange for the privilege and fun of going to school. This would begin to change in World War II, when veterans flooded college campuses, before finally crumbling in the 1960s and 1970s under pressure from rights-conscious student groups in search of full citizenship on and off campus. Until then, students were legal minors, possessed few rights, and could be summarily suspended or expelled at any time and for almost any reason, however slight or unsubstantiated that reason might be.

Yet the doctrine of in loco parentis was not intended to be exclusively punitive.[83] It had a gentler side that compelled faculties and administrators to show tenderness and warmth toward their students, to care for them as if they were their own flesh and blood. This was never a legal dictate. The Common Law expressly limited the scope of "natural affection" to relations between biological parents and children.[84] Just as it was impossible to prevent malice under in loco parentis, it was also impossible to prevent strong bonds of affection. Not for nothing was the college also known as an alma mater—a nourishing mother—that guided children into adults and into expansive, fictive kinships with hundreds and thousands of past and future alumni siblings and relatives. The belief that college officials were supposed to care for their students as if they were their own children presented a truly awesome burden. It was the college's responsibility to ensure that their children's needs were met at all times and in all possible ways.[85]

When students' needs grew to include their psychological health and personal adjustment, the jurisdiction of in loco parentis grew with it. Prior to the war, the college confined its parental role to students' academic and moral upbringing; afterward their parental obligations extended to include students' psychological health. The recognition that a student's life outside the classroom might well impinge on her performance in it forced administrators to take greater responsibility for their students' total development—intellectual and moral, social and emotional. "This change of attitude," according to Dean Herbert E. Hawkes of Columbia University, a leading proponent of the personnel perspective, "involved the explicit assumption of responsibility for, attention to, and, if possible, education of the entire individual."[86] In 1924, the president of the University of Chicago, Ernest D. Burton, described the same change in a different way: "The main thing I want to say and to emphasize is that the business of the college is to develop personalities, personalities that are capable of large participation in life and of large contribution to life."[87]

"The All-Round Development of Personality": Higher Education Adopts the Personnel Perspective

College officials deployed new managerial techniques and intellectual innovations as part of incorporating the personnel perspective into higher education's existing framework. Many of these advances were put in place by registrars, deans of students, and even faculty from across the disciplines, particularly education, who in time would occupy the core of the student-service professions. By exploring the ways in which these middle managers latched onto the personnel perspective, it is possible to chart the path by which personality became institutionalized within higher education in the 1920s.[88]

Personality and the belief in pliable selfhood eclipsed character as the "chief purpose of a college education." It did not happen overnight. Character was the hallmark of the nineteenth-century educated gentleman, and vestiges of it endured deep into the twentieth century even as personality became ascendant. Indeed, the two terms where often juxtaposed and then confused, or used interchangeably. This state of disorientation was evoked by Oscar Werner, author of a popular college self-help manual, *Every College Student's Problems*, published in 1929. "Unfortunately much confusion exists at the present time in our thinking about the relationship of personality to character . . . ," he wrote. "Some say that our character is what we really are, our personality is the expression we give to our character, and our reputation is the opinion that people get of our character through . . . our personality."[89] Werner's synopsis, inelegant as it may have been, was about right.

Within the academic enterprise, a combination of factors gradually weakened character's purchase during the 1920s. First, the slow but steady secularization of the academy devalued character's cultural capital. Character implied moral rectitude, integrity, self-restraint, and religious conviction—values threatened by a campus environment in which mandatory chapel and capstone courses in moral philosophy were becoming increasingly passé.[90] Second, the religious heterogeneity and sheer size of many campus populations made the cultivation of character difficult. Though the student body was and would remain virtually all white until after World War II, coeducation was dominant and the student body more and more religiously diverse, at least in comparison to the nineteenth century. If not always welcomed, Jews, Catholics, and Protestants of all persuasions were nevertheless represented at most colleges, especially those located in or near urban centers. American higher education was also big. By 1920, Columbia's enrollment topped twenty thousand making it "the largest university in the world." Many of the nation's most prestigious schools were also among the very biggest: at Michigan, the University of California, Berkeley, and Pennsylvania enrollments exceeded ten thousand; at Harvard, Chicago, and Wisconsin, five thousand. The great rush to go to college after the war, and for the rest of the century, made educating in the name of character increasingly difficult to do.[91]

Finally, professional psychologists considered the study of character unscientific. According to one leading historian on the subject, American social scientists made a professional commitment to objectivity and value neutrality in order to achieve the status of the physical sciences.[92] Among psychologists this shift portended the abandonment of character and the embrace of personality. The time-bound code words of character—duty, honor, restraint, and self-sacrifice—mattered little to professional psychologists interested in a plastic conception of selfhood characterized by adaptability and development—that is, adjustment. In all these ways, personality served as an ideal object of inquiry for psychology's energetic professionalizing agenda in a bureaucratic age.[93] Dean John B. Johnston of the University of Minnesota thought so, declaring at a meeting of the National Association of Deans of Women that the goal of higher education was "the all round development of personality."[94]

So, how was protean personality institutionalized? College administrators' increasing interest in the collection and analysis of ever greater amounts of students' personal information was one way. According to the Committee on Personality Measurement of the American Council on Education, higher education's eagerness to measure student personality grew directly out of the Great War. Colleges required students to submit detailed case-history information on their academic and personal lives using a variation of the army's admission blank. This information, according to Frank O. Holt, the registrar of the University of Wisconsin, helped administrators develop an individualized program of counseling to increase the likelihood of a new student's "success and happiness."[95]

After the war, colleges demanded increasing amounts of personal information from their applicants. Admission officers asked for all types of personal information "concerning such matters as the date and place of the student's birth;

his special interests with regard to study, athletics, and self-support; his intentions with regard to college and vocation; his school offices, honors, and other activities." Most admission blanks posed many more additional questions. A study charting the rise in the amount and detail of personal data required for collegiate admission reported that an average admission application required students to respond to more than sixty personal questions on a whole range of subjects.[96]

The proliferation of personal data reflected admission counselors' growing interest in applicants' backgrounds and trainings, upbringings and personalities. According to Hopkins, administrators at the schools he studied concurred that the highly subjective measure of personality and disposition was the most reliable means of determining an applicant's suitability for college. Harvard officials, for instance, reminded applicants that while scholarly attainments were necessary for admittance, high "regard [was also] given to character, personality, and promise."[97] Administrators at Columbia likewise stressed that the "satisfaction of the minimum academic requirements does not insure admission." Evidence of nonacademic intangibles such as "character and personality" aided the decision-making process.[98]

College officials also turned to former teachers, principals, employers, ministers, and friends to ensure an accurate sketch of each applicant's personality. The most common tool, again descended from the U.S. Army, was the comparative rating blank. Like its wartime progenitor, the college blank required referees to rate the presence and strength of specific personality traits—including "industriousness," "straightforwardness," "public spirit," and "leadership"— and to compare those traits with "boys graduating from secondary schools the country over." Because comparisons of this sort were impossible, administrators also required letters of recommendations. Northwestern University, for example, "in order to develop . . . students in intellect, personality, and character," requested that referees provide meticulous written expositions on applicants' "popularity," "seriousness," and likelihood of "being benefited by college life."[99] Elsewhere institutions made targeted appeals to the people they presumed knew their students best of all—parents. Beginning in 1924, the dean of students at Harvard, for example, mailed letters requesting parental help. The dean admitted that Harvard was too big, and that it took too long to gather all the personal information needed to work effectively with students as "individuals." "Will you, as a service both to your boy and to the college," he begged, "write us about him, with reference to his individual qualities and needs, as fully as you are willing to do, so that even from the beginning we may feel that we know him!"[100]

Then and later, the personnel perspective was a moving target. Its chief benefit was that it could be used to accommodate the changing admission criteria of different administrators and institutions, at different times. At Harvard, Yale, and Princeton, and at other elite colleges that instituted selective admissions, the interest in personality was partially predicated on a desire to cull Jewish and other supposed racial and ethnic undesirables from the admission cycle. Indeed, the subjective nature of personality provided admission committees with more than enough leeway to build a case for or against practically any applicant. Its pliability was what made it so popular among admissions officials and administrators—and, ultimately, so volatile. Beginning in the 1960s, and then for the rest of the century, admissions officials recalibrated the personnel perspective in order to create an ethno-racially diverse student body. As the definition of educated citizenship changed over the course of the twentieth century, so did the personnel perspective, and with it the composition of the undergraduate student body and curriculum.[101]

In the 1920s and later, higher education's commitment to shape-shifting personality was instrumental as well as genuine. Administrators maintained a focus on personality development after the admission process was completed. At Northwestern University, for example, the personnel department gathered and analyzed students' personal information throughout their tenure. They actively solicited and catalogued faculty and peer ratings to determine whether a student's personality was "inspiring," "indifferent," or "repellant."[102] At the University of California, Berkeley, personnel officials in the engineering department declared faculty- and peer-generated "personality records" to be "equally or more valuable than scholastic achievements." Potential employers, explained Professor Blake E. Vanleer, "put a high value on the personal recommendation."[103] With clear measures for prognosticating student achievement lacking, personnel officials submitted that the collection and evaluation of personal information provided access to the personality traits of successful and unsuccessful college students. "This process may seem at first a rather long and tedious one," admitted the registrar of Clemson Agricultural College, James L. Littlejohn, "but it makes for greater uniformity and produces satisfactory results."[104]

Administrators and faculty also developed programs and services that, in time, became the foundation of the modern profession of student affairs. The goal was to minimize the psychological disruption of college by maximizing the personal attention lavished on students the moment they stepped on campus. Freshman week programs emerged as one of the preferred techniques of doing so. "If a college is interested in the success and welfare of its newcomers," said an administrator at the University of Chicago, "it is worthwhile to concentrate for a few days on the task of adjusting freshman rightly to their new situation."[105] The registrar at Mount Holyoke detected "a desirable psychological effect in having the freshman class meet . . . during these first days of the year."[106] Many administrators apparently felt the same way. In 1924, Mary Frazer Smith, the registrar at Wellesley College, reported to the membership of the American Association of Collegiate Registrars that forty-one colleges had organized freshman week programs—a number that climbed to almost 150 by the close of the decade.[107]

Freshman week was dedicated to student adjustment and socialization, guidance and academic placement. The University of Maine, a freshman week pioneer, unveiled its program in 1923—among the first schools to do so. "Freshman week has among its objects the providing of an opportunity . . . ," explained University of Maine's president Clarence Cook Little, "to study carefully the individual problems of freshmen and to assist in estimating their ability to meet the responsibilities and difficulties of college life."[108] Maine's program required all freshmen to arrive on campus one week before upperclassmen. Students were assigned to cohorts of between ten and twenty pupils and given an itinerary consisting of forty-five different lectures, tests, and social events. Required sessions included Taking Notes and Examinations, Use of Books, Social Conduct, and College Students' Day's Work and College Customs, among others. Placement tests in mathematics, English, foreign languages, and chemistry were also administered. Evenings were spent socializing. Scheduled events included a "mixer," "stunt night," athletic rally, and a trip to the Orono Theater to watch a movie.[109]

A survey conducted at the University of Maine found broad support for freshman week along with a few suggestions for improvement. Nearly half of all students thought it should be made "less intensive" while others requested "more time to themselves for rest, for getting settled and for making acquaintances outside . . . [their] . . . particular group."[110] Faculty at Ohio State University voiced similar concerns. In 1927, at a meeting following the inaugural run of Ohio State's freshman week program, a group of faculty members, possibly chagrined by the fact that the bulletin they prepared for the freshman week was filled with "grammatical errors," agreed that too many activities had been compressed into too short a time period. "Students [became] so tired," reported the Ohio State student newspaper, "they were unable to do their best work in the examinations and placement tests and [did] not enjoy the tours of the campus."[111] Nevertheless, administrators and national policymakers praised the freshman week experiment. Researches at Teachers College concluded that freshman week programs enhanced students' adjustment, morale, and retention. The Federal Bureau of Education leveled its own optimistic assessment of freshman week activities: "The plan is so simple, results obtained so excellent . . . that general adoption of the device . . . may be looked for among institutions which are seriously trying to meet their educational and social problems."[112]

College administrators buttressed freshman week with orientation classes to help freshmen "find themselves."[113] Researchers Charles Fitts and Fletcher Swift identified three main types of orientation courses in their 1928 study *The Construction of Orientation Courses for College Freshmen*. All three course types focused on some sort of intellectual, social, or behavioral adjustment. The first was the "Adjustment to the social and intellectual world of today" course—also known as the "world problem" course, instituted most famously at Columbia

Figures 2.3 and 2.4. Freshman Week gained widespread popularity in the 1920s as a commonsense approach to helping new students adjust to the academic and emotional challenges of college life. Above, a group of male freshmen, readily identifiable by the dink, or beanie, on their heads, take a tour of Ohio State University during Freshman Week, fall 1927. Below, Ohio State University president George W. Rightmire (on the balcony with the bullhorn) greets a new class of students during Freshman Week, fall 1929. Courtesy The Ohio State University Archives.

University during the war. Replicated elsewhere, this type of course focused on "social and moral problems, duties, responsibilities, and relationships of the world today."[114] The second was the "Introduction to methodology of thinking and of study."[115] Courses in this category covered a broad array of study skills, including how to study, reading improvement, and effective library utilization—all skills that, if absent, caused maladjustment. The final, and most popular, orientation course according to Fitts and Swift, stressed the "Adjustment to college life." The point of this course was "to help the entering student to make adequate adjustments to his new mental and social environment."[116] Offered at fewer than ten schools before the war, orientation courses exploded after it, penetrating the undergraduate curriculum at more than eighty institutions by 1926.[117]

While administrators turned to orientation courses to level the educational playing field, they also organized specialized educational tracks to accommodate students of varying abilities. The rapid expansion of the two-year junior college sector, which grew from 52 to 277 institutions (public and private) during the 1920s, served as a key index of this trend.[118] Although the junior college came of age after World War I, its distant origins dated back to the founding of the American research university. William Rainey Harper, the first president of the University of Chicago, along with David Starr Jordan, the first president of Stanford University, voiced support for the junior college as early as the 1880s. Their inspiration for the idea came from a number of sources. One was the German university model, which included a similar organizational unit; another was the desire for a larger pool from which to select qualified students. Not surprisingly, many of the biggest boosters were administrators from flagship colleges and universities interested in greater control over the flow of students in and out of their campuses. Ray L. Wilbur, the president of Stanford University, saw the junior college as a "clearing-house" for the university, "culling out those unable to go further and stimulating . . . those for whom a university course is necessary and desirable."[119] In these ways junior colleges theoretically increased students' educational options while offering university leaders with a means to deal with the very real problems of organizational confusion and overcrowding at their own institutions.

The fastest growth in the junior college market occurred in the Midwest and Far West, especially California, home to an extensive system of publicly supported two-year schools. It took time for the California model to spread to other regions of the country, however, and in the immediate postwar period university leaders instead experimented with variations on the junior college model to lighten the weight of their schools' bureaucratic load. Many institutions followed the lead of the University of Chicago and divided the traditional four-year track into two discrete halves: the junior college, consisting of the freshman and sophomore years, and the senior college, consisting of the junior and senior years, where admission to the latter depended on the successful completion of the former. Administrators defended this approach as the so-cially and intellectually responsible way to manage students of limited educa-tional abilities or ambition. University of Chicago's dean Chauncey S. Boucher thought the arrangement made sense given the varied backgrounds of his students: "All of our students, who either end their requirements or who continue . . . have in common this much: an introduction to each of the four large fields of thought, an essential minimum of proficiency in English usage, and a respectable minimum training in a foreign language and in mathematics."[120]

North of Chicago, at the University of Minnesota, administrators and politi-cians organized an entirely separate General College to meet the educational needs of students of "lesser ability." The course sequence was utilitarian and practical, not traditionally scholastic. Students took survey courses only, and were excused from language, laboratory, and all advanced technical study. Stu-dents were drawn from across the socioeconomic spectrum and 20 percent of them emanated directly from working-class, immigrant households. Though the General College remained a source of ill will among professors forced to teach in it, President Lotus D. Coffman recognized the college as a good way to build support for the entire state system of higher learning. Universities that are truly "faithful to their constituencies," he declared, "will be dynamic institu-tions to which society will look with increasing frequency and pride." Coffman was surely right, and within a decade a thousand Minnesotans were enrolled in the General College.[121]

At the other end of the education ladder, the formation of honors programs and classes gained momentum for superior students. Used effectively at Ivy League colleges such as Princeton and Harvard, the intensification and refine-ment of third- and fourth-year study extended to other colleges around the country. President Frank Aydelotte of Swarthmore College organized an hon-ors program that became a model for other institutions. The standard course of instruction, Aydelotte explained, was geared toward a "hypothetical indi-vidual—the average student." The honors program catered instead to the edu-cational needs of those "who are capable of going faster than the average, who do not need the routine exercises which are necessary for those of mediocre ability." Many students appreciated the added attention and rigor of the new honors courses. A student at Smith College described her experiences in glow-ing terms. "The greatest thing we 1924 special honors students can hope for," she said, "is that we may start a tradition of the love and fellowship of study, for that is what special honors has brought us." Between 1923 and 1927, the number of colleges offering this type of specialized undergraduate instruction increased from forty-four to one-hundred-fifty institutions.[122]

The new emphasis on personalized education ironically raised questions about the purported impersonalism of the average undergraduate educa-tional experience. Complaints abounded. Some were precipitated by balloon-ing class sizes and overall institutional growth. At the University of Michigan, for example, one student fretted about the absence of "personal contact with instructors in many large classes"; another likened the school to a "huge, heartless place."[123] Others sprung from the style of instruction itself. Here, according to critics, the professoriate's growing obsession with original research appeared to be taking a toll on the quality of undergraduate education. Sociologist Robert C. Angell of the University of Michigan, himself a very productive researcher, arrived at this conclusion in his 1928 study *The Campus*: "No one can deny that professors are interested in their fields of study; but many believe that frequently they have little ability in, or enthusiasm for, imparting their knowledge and interest to immature undergraduates."[124] Having dedicated themselves "to research in some narrow field," he said, their teaching "is apt to be dry, pedantic, boring."[125] A graduate of the University of Chicago echoed these sentiments when he recalled the impoverished pedagogy of the young political scientist, Harold Lasswell. "I thought him a bit of a freak," he said, "[Lasswell] lectured us desperately, with a glazed stare into space, conspicuously unaware of whether we understood him and visibly unconcerned with what we might be thinking."[126]

Educational elites believed something had to be done to moderate the potentially deflating influence of "bone-dry scholastics . . . lacking in personality."[127] In 1922, the Land Grant College Association passed a resolution "in favor of professional training of college teachers," and at many institutions administrators did make the improvement of classroom instruction a real priority.[128] Some schools set their sights on creating smaller, more intimate lectures and increasing the amount of time dedicated to professor-student interaction. Others organized teacher training and administrative courses for aspiring college professors that explored the problems of the college and its students, typically from a psychological vantage point. Purdue University offered a course entitled Psychology of Learning and Teaching Applied to College Work; Ohio State University offered many more, including courses on college teaching, administration, and the Psychological Problems of Higher Education.[129] And still others created teaching awards and introduced student evaluations to goad poor performing professors to improve their pedagogical style.[130] Predictably, some professors questioned the point: "[Students] will pass on us favorably by seeking our product," said one, "unfavorably, by avoiding us."[131]

Other factors beyond personality also contributed to the surge of interest in better teachers and more fluid instruction. The expansion of graduate education during the 1920s, when earned doctorates increased 250 percent, raised fresh questions about how best to prepare would-be professors for a life of teaching, research, and service. Different disciplines, now demarcated by evermore rigid departmental bounds, advanced particular research techniques and modes of inquiry: in psychology, the laboratory was the venue of choice; in history, the seminar; and in sociology and anthropology, the field study. In other words, new ways of producing knowledge required new ways of teaching it.[132]

The heightened attention to students' needs was in many ways more evident outside the classroom. An important precedent for the coordination of this arena occurred before the Great War when university presidents banded together to bring order to the wild and unruly world of college football. Originally run by and for students, with the help of alumni hangers-on, college football achieved spectacle status in the last decades of the nineteenth-century. Tens of thousands of fans crowded stadiums in the Northeast and Midwest to cheer their gridiron heroes to victory. Absent administrative oversight, however, the sport became plagued by corruption. Nonstudents regularly suited up. Players reaped in-kind and cash payments for good play. And coaches wielded incredible power and collected incredible salaries. With thousands of dollars and more than school pride on the line, football passed from being a game to a war where young men really died. During the bloody 1905 season, eighteen players were killed on the field of battle. Most of the casualties succumbed to the "flying wedge," a play that pitted an entire charging squad—the "wedge" against a lone opposing player. Shocked by the level of carnage, the "Rough Rider" himself, President Theodore Roosevelt, convened an emergency meeting of college presidents at the White House. One year later a number of the attendees formed an athletics governing and regulatory body that led to the founding of the National Collegiate Athletic Association in 1909.[133]

After the Great War, college leaders expanded their focus from the physical to the emotional health of all students, not just athletes. Beyond revising laissez-faire housing policies it also meant coming to grips with the secret, all-white Greek system, which continued to dominate the social organization of college life, as it had since the middle of the nineteenth century. A few college presidents sought to abolish the Greek system, or its "secret society" equivalent, agreeing with the professoriate that fraternities and sororities fractured the student body and encouraged drinking, cheating, and general slothfulness. Just as Woodrow Wilson had failed to abolish Princeton University's exclusive "eating clubs" during his presidential tenure there between 1902 and 1910, those few who dared do the same in the 1920s met strong alumni resistance and a similar fate. Loyalties ran deep between and among the "brothers" and "sisters" of the Greek system—and so did their pockets. At every turn, they let college leaders know that future bequests hinged on the Greek system's continued existence. Given these realities, most college leaders opted to bring the entire infrastructure of the Greek system, which housed and fed between a quarter and third of all students nationally, under tighter bureaucratic control. Instead of keeping the Greek system at a geographic and administrative distance, as had traditionally been the case, administrators thus endeavored to convert it into a de facto residential college.[134]

The remainder of the student body, known as independents, boarded in private residences or in modest dormitory rooms. A Michigan freshman claimed that his room "crushed his spirit . . . [and] typified all the loneliness that a freshman can have." He was so "ashamed" of his room that he would not allow friends to visit. In order to improve adjustment and democratize the collegiate experience, wealthy schools, such as Harvard and Yale, along with elite women's colleges, expanded and enhanced their undergraduate dormitory space during the 1920s in an effort to equalize the living conditions for all students.[135] At poorly funded public institutions, however, students' living arrangements remained precarious. "The housing problem is serious," wrote a house-mother at a large coeducational university. "The present houses are none too sanitary; the rules, which have gradually evolved, need revision; e.g., the one made long ago, that students must be permitted at least two hot baths a week, is now generally interpreted not more than two, and the practice of watching the bathing hours and turning on the heater makes for friction."[136] Administrators at a public college located in the Midwest reported finding a student "living in a shack which he had erected with his own hands from discarded lumber."[137] More than one student, according to a personnel official, had "no place where he can sit down in comfort . . . entertain his chosen friends . . . and develop his taste and personality, his individuality."[138] The provision of better housing and greater administrative oversight was deemed a key part of helping students adjust to and stay in school.

So was the coordination of the extracurriculum. The intricate web of student-run clubs and teams—what one historian has described as the rudiments of a true "peer society"—had long represented the heart and soul of the undergraduate experience.[139] Its network of preprofessional organizations (Civil Club, Mechanical Club, Forestry Club, Future Teachers of America Club, and Home "Ec" Club, for example) and Greek-letter societies offered students ready-made professional identities and social networks that followed them well into their adult lives. Like those professional bodies and the wider society in which they were linked, the extracurriculum reflected the interests and sensibilities of the white middle- and upper-class students who went to college. This would not materially change until the 1960s when previously marginalized groups, led by African Americans and women, created their own clubs and organizations at predominantly white-serving colleges and universities that directly challenged the legitimacy of the white, patriarchal status quo. Following the example of the existing Greek club culture, emergent student groups organized around a variety of ethno-racial, gender, and sexual affiliations to create clubs that would serve as vessels of diversity after the 1960s. Until then, however, Greek-letter "Big Men" of one stripe or another—athletic stars and socialites whose very existence hinged on the status achieved outside the classroom—controlled the extracurriculum.[140]

Perhaps because of the time and attention that most students lavished on their extracurricular pursuits, faculty and administrators naturally assumed it perpetrated maladjustment. This outlook began to change in the 1920s as research linked academic achievement and healthy personality development to more, not less, extracurricular involvement.[141] In 1927,

Northwest Missouri State Teachers College, for instance, reported "the students who make the best grade tend to find an outlet for their extra-curricular activities."[142] Other studies, conducted at the University of Kansas, University of California, and University of Minnesota, for example, also suggested that students who refused extracurricular activity actually registered lower scholarly accomplishments.[143] At Middlebury College, administrators considered the extracurriculum so important that they started assigning grades for participation.[144] Frank Aydelotte, the president of Swarthmore College, once again chimed in. An outspoken advocate of the extracurriculum, he believed administrators had much to learn from the excitement that undergraduates brought to their campus activities and clubs: "If the regular curriculum could offer the same opportunity for the development of independence and initiative that is now offered by clubs and teams . . . some of the energy which undergraduates put into the miscellaneous pursuits would go into their studies with infinitely greater educational results."[145] Across the country, savvy academic administrations took heed and offered official recognition and financial resources to entice the student-run shadow bureaucracy out of the darkness. For psychological and practical reasons, accommodating students made sense, and by the end of the 1920s, most administrators were persuaded that the extracurriculum was a key ingredient in their recipe for student success.[146]

Despite increasingly close administrative oversight, students were still victimized by deadly cases of maladjustment. A rash of student suicides during the spring semester of 1927 raised public fears about the dangers of college to a frenzied level. National newspapers described it as an "epidemic." From a statistical standpoint this was an inaccurate description. Yet the brutality of nearly thirty student suicides in the span of one semester—by shooting, poison, gas, hanging, and by stepping in front of a moving train—seemed to suggest that "the period of adolescence," as one neuropsychiatrist put it, "is the most dangerous age that young men and young women have to pass through."[147] McIntyre Harsha, a freshman at the University of Chicago, provided fodder for what was an especially lurid case. Road workers near Harsha's hometown of Chesterton, Indiana, found his body beside the highway, a .38-calibre pistol clutched in his hand. His parents speculated that he had been driven to suicide by a "love affair" gone awry. Chesterton police were not so sure. In Harsha's coat pocket they found a crumpled newspaper clipping "discussing the failure of boys quitting school early in life."[148]

Critics of the modern university speculated as to the source of the crisis. Religious leaders linked the death craze to students' belief that "this life is hell," according to Reverend C. Everett Wagner of the West Side Methodist Episcopal Church, in New York City. "A machine age without the counterbalancing influence of Christianity makes a man inevitably feel that he is a little cog within a big machine," he said. President James L. McConaughy of Wesleyan University pointed his finger at temporal causes, especially the spread of John B. Watson's "psychological behaviorism." Watson, who had previously connected the suicide outbreak to "present-day religion . . . and unbending Christians," now suffered McConaughy's wrath. The spread of mechanistic behaviorism, McConaughy retorted, had "caused students to think of themselves as playthings of fate without God-given wills."[149]

Other students and administrators considered psychology to be a solution, rather than cause, of maladjustment. At the University of Baltimore, for instance, students formed an antisuicide club with the motto "Live and Let Live." Its thirteen members pledged to take psychology courses and to apply psychological insights across campus to avert the spread of the "germ of self-destruction." Elsewhere the National Committee on Mental Hygiene (NCMH) oversaw the establishment of a small but influential network of thirty mental hygiene facilities around the country, half of which it located on college campuses. The medical director of the NCMH, Dr. Frankwood E. Williams, claimed the university had focused too rigidly on cultivating intellect without properly caring for the whole mind. President William H. P. Faunce of Brown University, home to one of the NCMH clinics, concurred: "The chief troubles of students . . . lie deeper than the mere physical. . . . Students struggle with fears, repressions and other obstacles. . . . They come to college and are faced at once with the necessity of readjusting their lives. . . . They need help in that very delicate process." A perceptive clinician surmised that the advent of the campus mental hospital represented the logical extension of administrators' ongoing fascination with the personal lives of their students. "Attention has been given to the gifted student and the probationer, [but] the maladjusted student, whose emotional development is confused . . . is just beginning to attract notice." By the mid-1930s, 16 percent of colleges had established clinical services—a number that was to grow rapidly in the years ahead.[150]

Because of limited clinical staff, however, professors were sometimes tapped to serve as the frontline psychological forces of the college campus. At the University of Minnesota, Donald Patterson and his protégé E. G. Williamson organized a novel means of coordinating their institution's hygienic regimen. They set up a faculty-run "Contact Desk" to take calls from students and to arrange for referrals to the campus mental health clinic. During the 1929 stock market crash, for example, the desk fielded more than two thousand student requests. In time, students became comfortable seeking help on their own. "The patients, of course, were few at first and the growth of the service has been gradual," explained a psychiatrist at the University of California, Berkeley. "However, as the knowledge of it has spread in the student body, by word of mouth and by lectures on mental problems by the staff psychiatrists in the freshman hygiene course, the material has come to assume fairly sizeable proportions."[151]

That undergraduates independently patronized their mental hygiene clinics is not that surprising. The *Ohio State Lantern* encouraged students to seek help: "Psychology Clinic Will Give Help on Student Problems," announced one headline. Open discussion about the role of the clinic in the daily life of college students possibly helped those students who did seek assistance feel better about doing so. At Ohio State, for example, it was reported that "every class and practically every college is represented among those consulting the clinic."[152] What would have been a rarity a generation before had become commonplace. Using psychology to adjust to modern life had become part of what it now meant to go to school and to get an education.

No doubt, students were well versed in the language of psychology and increasingly adept at crude self-diagnoses. Undergraduates were exposed to psychology during the admission process, at freshman week, in orientation classes, in psychology courses, where they commonly served as experimental subjects, and when they visited the campus personnel office or psychiatric clinic for counsel and guidance.[153] At each of these stops, college students were encouraged to imagine themselves in a process of continuous adjustment and readjustment. At Syracuse University, in 1925, a study of undergraduate attitudes highlighted the extent to which students' college experience and sense of self-understanding had been shaped by America's postwar psychological culture: student-respondents ranked "personality development" as their number-one personal problem.[154]

❖❖❖

The spread of the personnel perspective throughout American higher education marked the end of a search for an answer to the institution's bureaucratic problems. After intelligence exams proved inadequate to the task, college officials turned to personnel experts for help. Administrators' conviction that the cultivation of student personality was a worthy goal of higher learning did not take root simply because they lacked better alternatives. Before and after the war, the deliberate attempt to adjust and readjust individuals and their environments had been a central concern of the leaders of all large-scale organizations. University administrators embraced personnel theory, and promoted personality development, because they believed it worked. It never worked as well as administrators hoped, of course: future generations of college students would continue to drop out of school at rates nearly equal those of the 1920s.[155] Ironically, this fact did not weaken administrators' faith in the personnel perspective; it strengthened it. Once the belief in psychological understandings of human and organizational development expanded administrators' parental responsibilities under the doctrine of in loco parentis, there was no looking back.

Even so, the new psychologically infused parent-child relationship that emerged out of the shadows of the Great War defied easy description. The only way to make sense of it, mused one observer, was by way of an all-too-familiar comparison with the business sector: when it came to improving output, "the manufacturer and the educator have exactly the same opportunities and limitations. He can procure a better grade of raw material and he can refine the processes of manufacture." University administrators tried both in the 1920s, and the formula they concocted turned out to be far more intoxicating than they could have imagined. Originally dispensed to what was a growing but still relatively homogenous student population, higher education's ingestion of psychological prescriptions for human and organizational problems was loaded with side effects. The belief in the adjustment and readjustment of individuals and institutions would prove critical to forging a new pattern of state-academic relations during the New Deal and, later, to a new understanding of citizenship and politics, too.[156]

Chapter 3

Building the New Deal Administrative State

—————————— ❖❖❖ ——————————

The reorganization of American higher education in the 1920s was followed by a second period of institutional adjustment during the Great Depression. After more than a decade of distant relations with the federal government following the debacle of World War I, educational elites were forced by the painful realities of the worst financial crisis in U.S. history to chart a new course away from their laissez-faire past. Even professors thought it was time to try a different tack: "The cuts contemplated this year are so cruel and destructive as to threaten seriously our whole educational system," wrote an anguished professor to a newly inaugurated President Roosevelt, in March 1933. "I appeal to you in the name of downtrodden and oppressed teachers, will you not do something for us, the forgotten men and women of America?"[1]

Although scholars have forgotten it today, higher education helped bridge the gap between citizens and the state during the 1930s. This chapter explores the ways in which higher education served the New Deal, and how that service contributed to the creation of an expansive centralized state in a political culture hostile to big government. The existing scholarship has highlighted the academy's role in crafting New Deal social and economic policy.[2] Yet the role that higher education played in delivering services and programs to citizens, in implementing many of the social and economic policies developed by its own faculty, the coterie of executive-level policymakers known as Roosevelt's brain trust, has remained unexamined. New Dealers were never beholden to psychological conceptions of human behavior and organizational effectiveness to the extent that business leaders and university administrators had been in the 1920s. But they did seek to adjust and readjust institutions and individuals—and on a truly national scale—in order to build a new and more powerful state. One of the institutions they turned to was higher education. It proved crucial to the New Deal's achievement of national administrative capacity and to the preparation of citizens for life in a bureaucratic state.

This argument challenges the prevailing belief that the nation's higher education sector was inconsequential to national policymakers in the 1930s.

According to the received view, after the overreach of World War I the state-academic partnership remained cold during the 1920s, simmered on low in the 1930s, and rocketed to life in World War II.[3] The exigencies of total war, combined with the introduction of cost-plus-a-fixed-fee and master contracts, vanquished the memory of World War I. World War II, then, convinced academic administrators and scientists that the government could be trusted to sponsor research without corrupting either the research process or the tradition of decentralized federal-academic relations.

This version of events is not so much incorrect as incomplete. In concentrating on elite scientists' anticipated partnership with the state in World War II, scholars have utterly missed the real state-academic partnership that took root in the 1930s.[4] It occurred far removed from the scientific laboratory, in regions of the academic estate long overlooked by scholars in search of evidence of state building in the 1930s. In areas such as agricultural extension, student aid, physical plant modernization, and adult education, higher education requested and received support from the government, and the government requested and received support from higher education. That this mutually reinforcing relationship has remained obscured speaks to the scholarly fixation on the birth of big science in World War II, and to the profound difficulty of making sense of the Roosevelt administration's penchant for state building by proxy.[5]

The New Deal's mediated state-building model stemmed from two interrelated sources. The first was the American polity's longstanding preference for a noninvasive central state—the widespread fear of consolidated authority that shaped (and by most accounts, constrained) state expansion since the American Revolution. The second, more proximate cause was the strength of the southern Democratic wing of the New Deal coalition. "Dixiecrats," who occupied an inordinate number of prime congressional chairmanships, wielded their outsized authority with impunity during the New Deal. No aggrandizement in federal power went unchecked, particularly if it threatened the South's segregated, antiunion social and economic system.[6]

The force of ideological and congressional antistatism channeled the American state toward partnerships with all types of intermediary institutions, or parastates. During the 1930s, the most common intermediary was state and local government itself, whose functionaries administered the vast majority of federal programs. Unemployment insurance and welfare programs were managed in this fashion, and so too the New Deal's bevy of "workfare" and cultural uplift programs. Where Roosevelt's hand seemed too heavy or government too big—for instance, when he clumsily tried to "pack" the Supreme Court, and later, to consolidate the country's economic and social welfare programming under the National Resources Planning Board—the antistatist political tides turned against him.[7] The New Deal achieved more durable results when it buried regulation in arcane mechanisms such as the tax code or when it provided funding and coordination but turned program administration over to third-party providers like colleges and universities. Led by the public land-grant university system, whose longstanding if poorly understood partnership with the state helped bring awareness to the struggles of the entire academic sector in the 1930s, higher education proved to be an adept mediator at the grassroots.[8]

This chapter charts the escalating relationship between the state and higher education during the New Deal by observing the experiences of public and private higher education. Three programs that relied on higher education to mediate relations between citizens and the state are explored: agricultural adjustment policy, public works and student work-study, and the civic training experiment known as the federal forum project. While these programs may appear unrelated, when examined together they reveal higher education's incredible organizational dexterity, and help explain why state builders turned to the institution to rehabilitate the countryside, to put the unemployed back to work, to keep students off the dole, and to help Americans everywhere come to terms with living in a New Deal state. No doubt, had these programs been lumped together and administered by a federal agency explicitly devoted to harnessing the planning capacity of universities, they would have been derailed before getting started. But that is the point: disaggregated and diffused through existing outlets, these programs drew minimal attention just long enough to cultivate partnerships and popular support that permitted them to survive the immediate economic crisis and, if in altered form, beyond. Before World War II, New Dealers used colleges and universities as intermediary institutions to connect with the American people and to connect the American people with their government.

"One of the Major Educational Agencies in the United States": Agricultural Adjustment and University Extension

In the late winter months of 1933 the Roosevelt administration inherited a farm economy that had been in steady decline for well over a decade. Unlike the industrial sector downturn that dated back to the market crash of 1929, the agricultural depression had been ongoing since the end of World War I. By 1932 farmers' gross income was $5.3 billion, $12 billion less than it had been in 1919, and their total debt burden exceeded $9 billion.[9] "Unless something is done for the American farmer," the president of the American Farm Bureau Federation warned Congress in January 1933, "we will have revolution in the countryside within less than twelve months."[10] The spontaneous formation of desperate "farmers' holiday" organizations across the Midwest, which threatened to withhold crops from markets until farmers could be guaranteed the cost of production, seemingly corroborated such claims. In Lemars, Iowa, for example, a farmer mob, aggrieved over rampant foreclosures and rock-bottom prices, "marched in and carried off a judge" with the intention of killing him.

The judge's life was spared, but not before a standoff with a battalion of Iowa National Guardsmen resulted in seventy-nine arrests.[11]

The farm collapse, the presence of powerful agricultural interest groups, and a large agricultural workforce comprising 30 percent of the nation's total ensured that farm policy would be central to the administration's economic recovery program. Yet the administration's commitment to agricultural adjustment was guided by more than interest-group capture.[12] There were legitimate, widely held economic rationales that privileged a sweeping federal overhaul of rural America. Leading New Dealers, including Henry A. Wallace, the secretary of agriculture, and his undersecretary, Rexford Tugwell, believed that the Great Depression had been caused by poor farming practices and the dramatic loss of farmers' purchasing power since the war.[13]

The duress in the farm sector resulted from systemic agricultural overproduction on the one hand, and the decline of consumers' incomes on the other. Farmers' inability to purchase everyday consumables, to say nothing of the expensive equipment required for modern mechanized farming, had dragged down the industrial sector and destabilized the nation's entire economic order. Readjusting farmers' purchasing power toward "parity"—the ratio between farm prices and costs during the period from 1909 to 1914, the supposed golden age of American agriculture—surfaced as the immediate objective of the Agricultural Adjustment Act, which passed in May 1933, one month prior to the National Industrial Recovery Act. It was no coincidence that agricultural legislation preceded industrial legislation: New Dealers believed that a full and complete macroeconomic recovery of necessity depended first on the full and complete recovery of the agricultural economy.[14] "Millions of the unemployed in the cities lost their jobs because farm people lost their power to buy," declared a U. S. Department of Agriculture (USDA) official. "Restoring farm purchasing power will set men to work in the cities, making the things that farmers need and will buy if they can."[15]

The Agricultural Adjustment Administration (AAA) was established to implement the act. But as a practical matter the AAA and its chief administrator, George N. Peek, an Illinois farm equipment manufacturer, were subordinate to the USDA and its new secretary, Henry A. Wallace.[16] No one person wielded more influence over New Deal agricultural policy than did Wallace. An agricultural economist by training, a hybrid corn innovator, and publisher of *Wallace's Farmer*, a popular farming newspaper, his grasp of agricultural issues was unmatched. Wallace, whose father had served a frustrating term as secretary of agriculture in the Harding and Coolidge administrations, was determined to do what his father could not: organize farmers across the country by increasing federal support for agriculture through a controversial policy known as voluntary domestic allotment. Conceived by William J. Spillman of the Bureau of Agricultural Economics and popularized by Milburn L. Wilson, an agricultural economist at Montana State College and a Roosevelt adviser, voluntary domestic allotment emerged as the remedy to the overproduction problem. The program disbursed cash payments to farmers, funded by processor taxes, in return for farmers agreeing to reduce, or to use the official terminology, adjust, their agricultural output.[17]

This effort was complicated by the fact that the countryside's fear of federal power cut deep. Though farm groups had sought help from the government throughout the 1920s, the idea of the government paying farmers not to farm—and slaughtering thousands of animals—particularly when so many Americans were going hungry, was disturbing.[18] "To have to destroy a growing crop is a shocking commentary on our civilization," admitted Henry Wallace, in his book *New Frontiers* (1934). "I could tolerate it only as a cleaning up of the wreckage of the old days of unbalanced production."[19] His undersecretary, Rexford Tugwell, agreed, but thought it was the only option available to the USDA "under the competitive and money economy."[20] Strong reservations were voiced in and outside Washington in part because nobody was sure whether the plan would actually work. Past efforts at agricultural coordination had invariably fractured along commodity, regional, racial, and class lines. Would domestic allotment be different? Even though no one knew the answer to this question, major farm organizations, led by the Farm Bureau, whose leadership recognized the AAA as a way to extend its policymaking influence and organizational jurisdiction beyond its Midwest stronghold and into the South, threw their support behind the allotment plan. There was no other choice. All farmers, save for a handful of agribusiness firms, were desperate for help and agreed to march alongside the AAA down what Roosevelt himself called a "new and untrod path . . . to rescue agriculture."[21]

Time was of the essence. With the spring planting season already well underway, and the prospects of another year of uncontrolled agricultural output looming, the AAA's organizational challenges were nothing if not monumental. Rather than constructing a whole new bureau and hiring thousands of new bureaucrats, the savvy Wallace turned to the USDA Cooperative Extension Service and its force of county agricultural demonstration agents, more commonly known as county agents, to implement the AAA—the lone New Deal program assigned to an existing government agency.[22] The web of institutions that made up the USDA Extension Service reached far and wide, and included federal, state, and local government; the American Farm Bureau Federation; and the nation's sixty-six land-grant colleges and universities.[23]

To be sure, Wallace's choice to partner with the publicly supported "cow colleges"—which comprised 5 percent of the nation's total number of colleges but enrolled nearly a quarter of all students—was that of a seasoned agricultural man keenly aware of the mutually constitutive partnership between and among the USDA, the Farm Bureau, and the agricultural colleges.[24] The creation of the USDA and the Morrill Land-Grant Act occurred nearly simultaneously, in 1862, during the Civil War. Over the next several decades the USDA and the land-grant colleges competed with one another to fulfill their overlapping statutory mandate to produce and disseminate up-to-date information and education on farming techniques, home economics and household management, and agricultural marketing to farmers and their families. Subsequent federal legislation made the de facto relationship legally binding. The 1887 Hatch Experiment-Station Act, passed one year after the USDA achieved cabinet-level status, provided each of the state land grants with an annual appropriation of $15,000 to support its college research station; later the second Morrill Land-Grant Act of 1890, and the Adams Act of 1906, increased the federal government's largess. The secretary of agriculture supervised the experiment station program, and occasionally recommended research topics, but permitted station directors significant autonomy in conducting research and managing their own operations.[25]

Station directors quickly discovered that the production of new agricultural research was pointless if that research failed to find an audience. The USDA and the land-grant colleges responded to the need for greater contact with farmers by forming extension divisions to communicate new research findings and agricultural practices to farmers and to collect firsthand knowledge of emergent issues from the field. The land-grant colleges and the USDA differed over how best to do this—the former preferring to have farmers come to the faculty, the latter preferring to have faculty go to the farmers. Variations on both approaches were tried in the late nineteenth century. Faculty from the land-grant colleges and research stations convened mass-meeting farmer institutes and small-group short courses; they tried mailing bulletins and organizing correspondence classes to pass on to farmers their latest scientific discoveries. None of these traditional instructional techniques worked. Farmers had neither the time nor inclination to parse densely written academic jargon or to go to school; schools would have to go to the farmers. The USDA's direct-to-customer model, delivered by county agents using a pedagogical style known as the "demonstration method," eventually won out.[26]

The demonstration method avoided bookish instruction and instead emphasized applied learning—"showing" rather than "telling" farmers what worked. This seemed especially appropriate as many farmers in the South and Midwest, where extension proliferated, lacked formal education. Agents met with farmers to demonstrate preferred plowing, fertilizing, planting, and crop rotation techniques and practices. The method first achieved national acclaim in Terrell, Texas, in 1904. The USDA and the Rockefeller-endowed General Education Board had provided funds for the organization of community demonstration farms and to train county agents to help cotton farmers combat the invasion of the Mexican boll weevil. Dr. Seaman A. Knapp headed the Terrell, Texas, demonstration farm. Knapp was born in New York in 1833 and graduated from Union College in 1856. After spending the next decade as a teacher, minister, physician, and farmer, he and his family moved to Ames, Iowa in 1866, where he again busily pursued all of these vocations, and more. In addition to running a school for the blind with his wife, he ministered, raised hogs, and served as the editor of a local farm paper. This final assignment introduced him to members of Ames's farming elite that, in turn, led to a faculty position and, later, to a brief stint as president of the Iowa State College of Agriculture from 1883 to 1884. It was a frustrating experience for the no-nonsense Knapp, who discovered that he disliked academic agriculture and the men who engaged in it. Not surprisingly, his biggest accomplishment in these years was a practical one: he drafted an early version of the bill that eventually became the Hatch Experiment-Station Act of 1887.[27]

Having grown tired of deskwork, Knapp jumped at the opportunity to again get his hands dirty. In 1885 Knapp headed south to Lake Charles, Louisiana. He spent a decade there in land reclamation and speculation, and in developing new techniques for large-scale rice cultivation. After helping to turn Louisiana into the "rice milling center of the nation,"[28] Knapp joined the USDA as a special agent for the promotion of agriculture in the South in 1902. It was in this capacity that he began experimenting with demonstration farming in Texas and in placing responsibility for the method in the hands of roaming agricultural educators. The agent was not an entirely new social invention. The Farmers Alliance, which sprouted in Texas in the 1880s and 1890s, relied on "traveling lecturers" to spread its cooperative vision among producers in the South and Midwest. The "education" it disseminated alerted farmers throughout those regions to the possibilities of fluid currency finance, subtreasury credit systems, and organized political insurgency under the banner of the "People's Party." Using farmers to organize and educate other farmers was a trusted method and had been since the "Populist Moment."[29]

Knapp recruited his first team of agents from around Terrell. He paired each agent with a professor from the Texas Agricultural College, assigning them eight hundred miles of railroad to stump on behalf of demonstration, to persuade farmers to try new seeds, fertilizers, and plowing techniques so that others nearby might be compelled to do the same. He also asked them to identify a leading farmer in their territory to serve as a USDA county agent. Who was chosen for this role? Not the land-grant faculty; Knapp considered them too theoretical. He insisted on real farmers who understood what it really meant to live off the land.[30] Knapp explained his agent selection process to Congress, a few years later: "We take men who are the progressive farmers. We aim to get the best farmers in their own section, men whom their neighbors believe in, and they will listen to. . . . We find that these men are more influential than if they knew ten times as much about science, as they know what the farmer considers the best science in the world—and that is the science of winning out, of making a good crop and making money on the farm."[31]

Agents found the work difficult. The pay was meager and the days were long. An early agent recalled traveling "on horseback, usually leaving home on Monday morning and returning about the end of the week."[32] But the biggest challenge was that most farmers were suspicious of the county agents and had to be sold on the idea of demonstration. Knapp was aware of this, admitting that "sometimes farmers have peculiar views about agriculture." Let them believe what they want, Knapp instructed, so long as they agree to "faithfully try our methods." He implored his agents to "avoid discussing politics or churches. Never put on airs. Be a plain man, with an abundance of good practical sense."[33]

An agent in the Mississippi Delta closely followed Knapp's advice, and to good effect. The most important thing, recalled the agent, was "to interest [farmers] and gain their confidence." He did this by requesting "from the experiment station specimens of cotton boll weevil and other weevils often mistaken for the cotton pest," which he carried in his pocket, into the field, for demonstration. "I stopped at . . . all the places where I could see farmers meeting or loafing, giving my little show, and enlisting farmers willing to receive information through visits, correspondence, bulletins, etc. I listed them as cooperators and tried to convince them that I had no axe to grind, no ambition in politics and that no cost was attached to this work, undertaken by the federal government."[34] This was homespun education of the sort the agricultural colleges and the research stations could not have delivered on their own. For agents and farmers alike, the demonstration method was nothing less than a revelation. "Under [Knapp's] organization," gushed an awestruck agent, "all formerly dry agricultural principles became alive and potent as did the dry bones in Ezekiel's Valley when the spirit of the Lord brought bone to bone and clothed them with miraculous flesh and sinew."[35]

Knapp's county agent demonstration model resurrected agricultural education for the masses. The passage of the 1914 Smith-Lever Act, which created the USDA Cooperative Extension Service, made it a matter of record. The act harmonized relations between the USDA and the land-grant colleges by merging the land grants' research and extension functions and channeling both into the person of the county agent. The colleges and the USDA both got what they wanted. The colleges received new funding in exchange for adopting the USDA's county agent-led demonstration method; the USDA, in turn, agreed in principle that future agents would be land-grant graduates with professional ties to the land-grant colleges.[36] To augment the funding of this cooperative enterprise, the act authorized "matching grants" in which the local match could derive from a combination of "public" and "private" sources. Cost sharing of this sort built support for the program and helped the land grants quickly ramp up their extension operations. In the four years after the passage of the Smith-Lever Act the force of county agents climbed from 929 to 2,435. The combined impact of the Smith-Hughes Vocational Education Act of 1917 and the U.S. entry into the Great War had a lot to do with that, relying as they did on county agents to help with rural vocational education and to rally farmers on behalf of the war effort. Agent numbers held steady during the 1920s before climbing to 3,300 by 1935—enough to assign at least one agent to every county in the coun-

Figure 3.1. County Agent Fred Stewart, seated at his desk, meeting with the directors of the Limestone County, Alabama, Farm Bureau, 1926. During the New Deal, county agents leaned on the Farm Bureau, one of the most powerful agricultural interest groups of the twentieth century, to help educate farmers at the grassroots about the benefits of agricultural adjustment. Courtesy Auburn University Libraries Special Collections and Archives.

try. This growth was made possible because the USDA Cooperative Extension Service developed its administrative capacity at the local level: out of a total workforce of 8,400 personnel, a mere 61 employees worked in the Extension Service headquarters in Washington, DC.[37]

The Extension Service also discovered tangible political and bureaucratic advantages in sharing power with other stakeholders. The most important of these was the American Farm Bureau Federation, arguably the most powerful farm organization of the twentieth century. The Smith Lever Act's "private" matching-grant provision paved the way for the Farm Bureau's critical administrative role.[38] Private county "farm bureaus" made up of local farmers and businessmen grew in tandem with the Extension Service, eventually becoming a reliable "matching grant" contributor to the program and to county agents' salaries. An informal version of this relationship dated to the founding of the agent system under Dr. Seaman Knapp but did not crystallize until the Great War when local farm bureaus formed a federated national network whose membership and geographic reach exceeded that of all other farm groups combined. This arrangement was encouraged by the Extension Service and the land-grant colleges, who viewed their partnership with the Farm Bureau as an expedient way to legitimize agricultural extension activities at the grassroots.[39]

The Farm Bureau had multiple agendas, and from the start imagined using county agents for political as well as educational purposes. This posed something of a dilemma, and in 1921 the secretary of agriculture attempted to sever the county agent system's ties to the Farm Bureau, ruling that county agents were supposed to be educators, not interest group agitators. No such clear delineation of agent duties and responsibilities was ever achieved, however, and by the dawn of the New Deal, the interdependent relationship among the Extension Service and land-grant colleges, the Farm Bureau, and key legislatures had hardened into an "iron triangle."[40] Wallace knew this better than anyone, and his decision to link the AAA to the Extension Service and its legion of "semi-governmental employees," county agents, was thus shrewd.[41] By activating local interests and minimizing the visible presence of the federal government, Wallace and the AAA achieved administrative capacity and a critical mass of built-in rural support while expending minimal political capital. As Wallace later mused, in 1935, "Fortunately, we had the extension services with their corps of . . . county agricultural agents and a background of 20 years of experience with which to contact farmers."[42]

The AAA's early production control sign-up campaigns by most accounts went smoothly. Agents collaborated with local advisory committees to introduce production controls on seven of the nation's basic agricultural commodities—wheat, cotton, corn, hogs, rice, tobacco, and milk and milk by-products. Some farmers complained of strong-armed sign-up tactics, but most others embraced the county agents with open arms. Indeed, corn-hog and wheat farmers in the Midwest, and cotton and tobacco farmers in the South, the two main regional recipients of AAA largesse in 1933 and 1934, agreed to reduce acreage and curtail production at an astounding rate. The vast majority of growers signed up: 75 percent of cotton growers; 95 percent of flue-cured tobacco producers; and upward of 95 percent of corn and wheat growers in the farm belt in the Midwest and Great Plains. In Madison County, Mississippi, 1,863 cotton reduction contracts were accepted and a scant 25 refused.[43]

As the "front line forces" of the AAA, county agents used every possible resource available to them to contact farmers and to personalize the expanding New Deal state. Agents primarily relied on timeworn retail methods. Agent R. E. Hughes, of Bacon County, Georgia, devoted eighty-one straight days to his cotton reduction sign-up campaign; during that stretch he made ninety-seven farm visits, received seven hundred office calls, wrote fifty-six letters, mailed out seven different circulars, wrote two news articles, and held eight meetings. Agent Hughes, in his annual report, credited himself with making the sign-up campaign a success: "The cotton reduction program was received with out stretched arms and open hands."[44] Hughes's dogged effort was mirrored by countless agents across the country who went about their business determining allotments and securing contracts often "without pay other than perhaps a mileage allowance."[45] In Iowa, for instance, agents held an estimated two thousand corn-hog meetings over a five-week stretch. Nationwide the Extension Service reported that, in 1934, office calls from farmers jumped from 8 to 21 million, and that 3.5 million telephone calls were logged, more than double the number tallied the year before.[46]

Given the amount of responsibility foisted on agents, controversy not surprisingly followed them into the field. Their alleged transformation from nonpartisan educators "into a tool for politicians . . . a rural ward-healer," as one critic put it, invigorated debates about higher education's relationship to the federal government and about the appropriate role of academic experts in American politics.[47] The Association of Land Grant Colleges and Universities approved of the AAA because the promotional work required only a "minimum amount of activity." Some extension leaders in the upper Midwest and Northeast remained unconvinced. In Pennsylvania and New York—the regional stronghold of the National Grange of Patrons of Husbandry, the Farm Bureau's chief rival—extension officials resisted the AAA for a number of reasons. They insisted that the AAA subverted the educational intentions of the Smith-Lever Act and cited anecdotal evidence of agent malfeasance to support this claim. In 1939 the *Washington Daily News* reported that a county agent in Perry County, Alabama, had mailed an extension-franked letter to farmers in his county to let them know their government checks had arrived. The agent also urged his farmers to "express their gratitude and assure themselves of continued payments by joining the county farm bureau." Another agent devised a similar plan in Nebraska when he recommended that farmers allocate a portion of their government checks to cover their Farm Bureau membership dues.[48] Duplicity such as these fueled the conspiracy theory that agents really were pawns of an all-powerful "Farm Bureau-Extension Axis."[49]

The other reason why some farmers disparaged the AAA and its agent emissaries was that some regions and commodity groups benefited more than others. In Pennsylvania and New York, and throughout the dairy farming mid-Atlantic and Northeast, farmers and extension officials correctly surmised that they were being hurt by commodity programs in the Midwest.[50] The AAA's wheat and corn programs had increased the cost of the feed grains needed by dairy farmers to produce their milk. "The farmers of the east," wrote the director of extension in New York State, "believe, and probably justly so, that the program of the Agricultural Adjustment Administration has been more harmful than helpful to them."[51] Then and later, farmers' complaints subsided when government payments were increased.

For its part, the Extension Service defended agents' service as a logical outgrowth of their role as itinerant agricultural educators and as distantly affiliated members of the academic professions. Officials sought to inoculate their agents against charges of corruption and of private cooptation by reminding challengers of agents' multifaceted professional pedigree. They mounted a three-pronged defense that turned on agents' unique social role as a mediator of state-society relations with ties to higher education and government both. They reminded critics that a farming background and graduation from an agricultural college remained prerequisites for the agent position, and that working with the state land grant was an agent's primary professional affiliation. They also argued that the agricultural depression was a national emergency that required the organization and support of every branch of government, even those branches with tertiary relationships to the central government. And finally, they claimed that the definition of "education" in the Smith-Lever Act—which covered the diffusion of "useful and practical information"—was so broadly conceived as to encompass practically any activity undertaken by an agent.[52] A county agent from New York, Earl Flansburgh, defended this view in a 1933 radio interview. Education, as far as Flansburgh was concerned, was about encouraging "the production and prevention of change"—to encourage farmers to do what they were already doing, if that was best, or to do something new, if that was judged better. This definition of education was fluid if not "abstract," Flansburgh admitted, because education itself was "abstract." "In the broadest sense, man is an educator in every act that changes another man"; education "is a continuous and ever alive process."[53]

Most agents felt the same way. They subscribed to a wide-ranging definition of education that allowed them simultaneously to serve the AAA, the Farm Bureau, the land-grant extension offices, and the farm families in their respective counties without hesitation. A county agent from Georgia, who devoted nearly all of his time to the AAA cotton reduction plan, carefully described that work as "an educational program." Even less charitable agents located outside the South thought the AAA possessed some educational merits. A county agent from Wood County, Wisconsin, grumbled that his AAA duties had cut into the time he could spend on other things and complained of the embarrassment caused by "delays in inquiries and in getting materials from Washington." This agent nevertheless concluded that the AAA "has served a very definite purpose in bringing about a greater confidence in farmers" and "will directly influence producers in keeping better records . . . and any agricultural statistics that they are called upon to give." In the end, agents supported the AAA because it represented a continuation of the same local educational and interest group activities and services they had always provided. As one Louisiana agent recalled late in his life, during the Great Depression agents did whatever they could to help "farm and rural families . . . to increase their efficiency and [raise] their standards of living."[54] No doubt the increased cultural and political authority derived from their relationship with the Farm Bureau and the land-grant colleges greatly assisted county agents' efforts in the 1930s. In stark contrast to the failed organizing efforts of the past, agents' multifaceted institutional base and proven commitment to the countryside strengthened their purchase among farmers, a population not easily won over to coordinated intervention, especially if that intervention emanated from the federal government.[55]

Agents' thorough penetration of the countryside begot unexpected policy outcomes for the state and higher education both. This was ironic as President Roosevelt initially did not view the land-grant system as an obvious administrative response to the federal government's lack of administrative capacity. In 1933, during a round of cost-cutting measures, he signed an executive order that slashed federal support to the land grants by 25 percent. Protests from Henry Wallace and the Farm Bureau, to say nothing of countless "educators, state officials and representatives of agricultural interests," as one senator put it, persuaded Roosevelt to rescind his order. And following the Extension Service's virtuoso delivery of the AAA production-control program, the White House's opinion of the land-grant institutions changed completely. By 1934, Roosevelt and his fellow Democrats, at the urging of the Farm Bureau and the land-grant colleges, began lobbying to increase permanently the Extension Service's federal appropriation and to grow its bureaucratic infrastructure.[56]

Southern Democrats held the key to increasing the Extension Service's funding and to mooring the land-grant system's bureaucratic structure to the New Deal state. Democrats had regained the House in 1931, the entire Congress in 1933, and no region benefited more from the Democratic restoration than the noncompetitive, one-party South. Its long-serving congressmen collected key committee chairmanships in both houses: between 1933 and 1952, they controlled nearly one half of chairs and ranking minority posts in Congress, including coveted slots on the House Ways and Means Committee and the Senate Finance Committee. They used these posts to their advantage by killing all legislation that threatened their racially segregated, antiunion political culture while they fast-tracked agricultural policies of every stripe. In sum, virtually all New Deal policymaking—but especially agricultural policymaking—was southern policymaking.[57]

Senator John H. Bankhead II (D-AL) spearheaded efforts to increase the Extension Service's funding. Born into prosperity near Old Moscow, Alabama, in 1872, Bankhead graduated from the University of Alabama and, later, Georgetown University's law school. He practiced corporate law and helped run his family's substantial coal properties before turning his attention to his family's other, equally prosperous business—politics. His father, a former Confederate Army officer, served thirty years in the House and Senate until his death in 1920; his younger brother, William, served twelve terms in the House, three of those as Speaker, until his death in 1940. Bankhead came to politics somewhat later, in 1930, when he was elected to the Senate, where he remained until his death in 1946. All told, at least one member of the Bankhead family served in Congress for fifty-nine straight years.[58] The secret of their success could be summed up in one word: agriculture. According to one of Bankhead's Senate colleagues, "No man ever took to himself the problems of our farm people more than did John Bankhead."[59]

Bankhead acquired his knowledge of farm politics the hard way. He lost a close Senate race against Hugo L. Black, the future Supreme Court justice, in 1926. Bankhead attributed the loss to his lack of support among lower income groups, especially farmers. In preparation for his second Senate run four years later, Bankhead spent most of his time mending political fences with farmers. Bankhead, according to his biographer, "based his political future on a close alliance with farmers . . . and began his senatorial career as a spokesman for cotton farmers." During his fifteen-year Senate career, he talked about little else.[60] He supported the AAA and domestic allotment in 1933, and later drafted and sponsored several of the New Deal's most important agricultural policies, including the Bankhead Cotton Control Act of 1934, which mandated cotton producers' participation in domestic allotment; the Soil Conservation and Domestic Allotment Act of 1936, which continued the programs of the AAA after it was ruled unconstitutional; and the Bankhead-Jones Farm Tenant Act of 1937, the largely unsuccessful program to help tenant farmers and sharecroppers finance the purchase of their own land. As long as the legislation raised farm prices and in some way improved farmers' lot, or at least held out the possibility of doing so, Bankhead supported it.[61]

The same practical politics guided his sponsorship of increased agricultural extension funding. The Bankhead-Jones Act of 1935—cosponsored by Representative Marvin Jones (D-TX), chairman of the Committee on Agriculture—increased the federal government's funding for cooperative extension by $8 million in 1935, nearly doubling its annual appropriation without any requirement for state and local matching funds. Southern states benefited disproportionately from the legislation. By 1941 Texas was the top grantee at more than a million dollars annually, with North Carolina, Georgia, and Bankhead's home state of Alabama following closely behind. Overall, eight of the top ten largest appropriations went to southern states; only Pennsylvania, ranked eighth, and Ohio, ranked tenth, managed to crack the top ten.[62]

Spreading federal largess far and wide paid handsome political dividends. The Farm Bureau, higher education leaders, even the National Grange, found reasons to support the legislation, which benefited more than county agent work, though that was its primary focus. The act also increased the government's annual contribution to experiment station research and to the endowments of the land-grant institutions themselves. By 1940 the federal government's annual contribution for extension activities was $20 million, or nearly 60 percent of the nation's total cooperative extension budget.[63] The increase in extension funds was not lost on agents in the field. "The new Bankhead-Jones funds," reported the New York State extension director, in 1935, "have enabled us to do many things and to perform many services which we have long wanted to do and which have been asked of us and which were impossible without additional funds."[64]

Even with the magnanimity of the Bankhead-Jones Act, however, the total federal commitment to cooperative extension was relatively small compared to the size of the appropriations given to other New Deal ventures. But the significance of the act must be measured using more than a financial yardstick: the Bankhead-Jones Act solidified the relationship among the New Deal, the Farm Bureau, and the land-grant extension units created to organize and manage the AAA at the local level.[65] According to one scholar, the act was passed with the implicit understanding that the land-grant extension divisions would thereafter carry out educational, informational, and administrative work for all federal agencies without any request for additional funds.[66] The Soil Conservation Service, the Farm Credit Administration, the Rural Electrification Administration, the Tennessee Valley Authority, and the Works Progress Administration, among other New Deal action agencies, deployed their own representatives along with those from the extension bureaucracy to deliver services. That work, in turn, "educated" millions of farmers about the value of federally sponsored programs, easing acceptance, and silencing charges of big government. It is difficult to explain how some of the nation's most skeptical citizens ultimately embraced a landmark extension—so to speak—of national authority, especially in the South, without understanding the mechanisms by which that authority was infused into America's supposedly antistatist soil. The Advisory Committee on Education, appointed by Roosevelt, in 1936, did not exaggerate when it concluded: "The Extension Service has developed into one of the major educational agencies in the United States."[67]

Not all parties approved. Two years later the battle over the Extension Service and the county agent's dual role as educator and interest group operative came to a head. In 1938, H. R. Tolley, the head of the AAA, finalized the Mount Weather Agreement with representatives from the Association of Land Grant Colleges and the USDA, effectively breaking up the monopoly on New Deal agricultural outreach and implementation held by the land-grant colleges, the Extension Service, and the Farm Bureau. Anti-Farm Bureau forces certainly contributed to this development, but mostly it resulted from the growth of the New Deal state itself. According to one expert on the subject, "The relative unity of farm program administration during the first AAA, with authority concentrated in the USDA and executed through the Extension Service, broke down under the weight of increasing government complexity."[68] The rise of mission-driven agricultural agencies dedicated to conservation and modernization, land reclamation and relocation, marketing and price supports, among others, previewed the pluralist future of the American state. In a pattern that would be repeated with increasing frequency in other policy areas in the coming decades—from defense research and healthcare to welfare and education— the New Deal "broker state" dispersed the administration of agricultural policy among a host of agricultural agencies and their allied interests following the execution of the Mount Weather Agreement. Though the Extension Service and the land-grant colleges maintained their leadership roles in the state and county agricultural planning committees that were organized, from then on their power was shared with personnel from other agricultural agencies.[69]

The thinning jurisdiction of the land-grant colleges and the Extension Service's command over agricultural policy after 1938 does not diminish the importance of what preceded it. Between 1933 and 1938, county agents scoured the countryside in behalf of agricultural adjustment, changing farmers' relationship to the state. "The hand of the federal unit reaches every family," observed sociologist Paul Landis of the State College of Washington, in 1936. Even though most farmers did not understand the theoretical underpinnings of agricultural adjustment, "when he gets his check for fifty dollars as a result of letting some of his acreage lie fallow, he feels that government is a real part of his life."[70] Having succeeded at aggregating and addressing millions of individual farmer's demands, county agents made the Extension Service, the land-grant colleges, and farmers themselves key players in the New Deal state. "By decentralizing the responsibility . . . and using the full facilities of the Cooperative Agricultural Extension Service," remarked Secretary Wallace before the U.S. Senate Committee on Agriculture and Forestry, in the late 1930s, "it has been found practical to carry through operations involving from hundreds to millions of individual farmers."[71] Hundreds to millions of individual farmers, Wallace might have added, who remained steadfastly opposed to big government.

"The Students Need This Money": The National Youth Administration and Federal Work-Study

The New Deal did not limit its use of universities to the public land grants and to the various causes of struggling farmers. The dilemma of the land grants exposed the challenges faced by the entire higher education sector in ways that forced the state to move boldly to strengthen its relationship to millions of other citizens by shoring up public and private colleges, thus paving the way for the lessons in citizenship that these intermediaries would soon be delivering to America's college students. Federal programs covered massive physical plant expansion and aid to needy college and graduate students. The New Deal made the preservation and improvement of the higher education sector a major policy priority. Like the government's plan for agricultural adjustment, acceptance of the government's increased role was abetted by laundering national authority through the country's mix of twelve hundred (and growing) public and private colleges and universities.

Initially, the market downturn affected higher education more slowly than other economic sectors. Enrollment growth in 1930 and 1931 helped offset the 10 to 20 percent state-level funding cuts for higher education. As the recession slipped into a depression and as enrollments started to wane, financial solvency became nearly impossible at many institutions.[72] College leaders thus turned to the Hoover administration for help. President Hoover obliged them when he convened the Citizens' Conference on the Crisis in Education, in January 1933. The conference recommended bold federal action on behalf of the nation's entire education system, but none was ever taken.[73] Hoover, who had worked his way through Stanford University as a young man, was disinclined to enact direct federal assistance, and after losing badly in his reelection bid, was rendered powerless to do so.[74] Higher education's increasingly dire financial situation left a bad taste in many a college professor's mouth. "It is a matter of getting used to hamburger," explained a professor, "after you've been used to steak."[75]

By the time Roosevelt assumed office, in March 1933, some professors and students claimed to be hardly eating at all. After three years of economic contraction and federal handwringing, the nation's higher education economy was beginning to show visible signs of wear. The Office of Education reported that higher education income was down from 10 to 40 percent, the result of continuing state-level budget cuts and declining tuition revenues driven by a 10 percent enrollment decrease. All of these factors boded poorly for faculty. Though only thirty-one small, private institutions closed for financial reasons, virtually all professors and staff took pay cuts regardless of institutional type.[76] "How can any man or woman," wondered a distraught professor, "harassed and worried by a constant effort to balance a decreasing income against a scale of living that was assumed to be secure, maintain the calm of mind that is essential to both scholarly thought, and effective teaching?"[77]

Students fared even worse. Officials at the Iowa State College of Agriculture found a student living in his car surviving on homegrown vegetables; another student arrived at campus penniless with a "few butchered hogs to sell." Students elsewhere, as they had since the turn of the twentieth century, formed student agencies and cooperative organizations to buy and sell goods to other students.[78] At the University of Michigan the girls' social center, the University of Michigan League, offered three-a-day meal packages at $3.50 per week. At the University of Pittsburgh, meanwhile, students formed a Cooperative Buying Association to lower food costs.[79] Some institutions gave away food. The cafeteria manager at Indiana University formed a "soup line" to help feed hungry students. According to the Associated Press, the soup line proved so popular that cafeteria workers were "hard pressed to find enough soup bones and soup meat to keep the kettles filled."[80] In response to similar crises, students at Boston University contributed ten cents each and raised thirteen thousand dollars for an emergency student loan fund.[81]

Heightened demand for student aid of all types pushed students and university budget offices to their fiscal and emotional limits. Prior to the depression half of all students financed their education through a combination of small private loans (ranging from $25 to $200) and part-time employment.[82] The economic downturn all but blocked student access to both sources of income.

First, students needed more financial aid than ever. Columbia University filled 660 more loan requests in 1932 than the year before on its way toward disbursing a record $487,000 in student aid. It was not enough. "In spite of all our efforts," admitted Columbia's director of aid, "some students . . . had to drop out."[83] Second, and of greater concern, students no longer had access to outside employment. According to an analysis conducted by the Office of Education and the National Student Federation, the depression devastated the $26 million part-time student employment sector—the main funding stream for student self-support.[84] At Hunter College the head of the Bureau of Occupations, Harriet L. Lowenstein, informed students that the part-time "Saturday salesgirl" positions at New York City department stores were no longer available. In the past those positions had helped one thousand women subsidize their college education. All that was available now were "private positions, as companions and governesses," said Lowenstein.[85]

Pervasive economic anxiety raised fresh questions about the causes and remedies of student maladjustment. Numerous studies suggested financial worries impeded students' academic progress. A four-year study of students at the State College of North Carolina, in Raleigh, revealed the importance of outside employment to steady matriculation. Four-fifths of all students paid for part or all of their college expenses—half of whom were responsible for covering at least 50 percent of the cost of attendance. "Students largely preoccupied with their financial situation," concluded the study, "cannot be expected to do classwork of a high quality."[86] An analysis of freshmen at the University of Chicago substantiated these findings, suggesting the ways in which economic insecurity, a factor previously minimized in studies of student maladjustment, now appeared to be a prime source of it. "I have not money for extras or for clothes," said one coed. "My parents say I can't have any more. Who would have thought that college would cost a fortune!" Her classmate offered a less specific if more anguished plea. "I am not satisfied in college and am quite disillusioned with everything."[87] She was not alone. Reported incidences of student mental health problems grew rapidly over the course of the 1930s. A 1938 study in the journal *Mental Hygiene* showed that 90 percent of 479 four-year colleges surveyed now regarded students' mental health as a fundamental issue of concern.[88]

In Washington these reports exacerbated New Deal policymakers' fears of a widening "youth problem." A few members of Roosevelt's inner circle viewed the youth problem in the darkest of lights. They drew comparisons to youth movements in Soviet Russia, Nazi Germany, and Fascist Italy and posited that the rootlessness and anger caused by the depression would propel hopeless college-age youth toward radical politics. John W. Studebaker, who became the commissioner of the Office of Education, in 1934, was a leading proponent of this position. In a radio address on NBC, in April 1935, Studebaker said the "nation was unable to absorb its youth" and warned that the "lack of constructive activity" would lead to "deep resentment, a vague and bitter antagonism

as they stand at the gateway of life futilely knocking." Citing psychological research, Studebaker predicted a general "breakdown in morale" and an increase
in "antisocial thinking and . . . acting."[89]

While nobody in the Roosevelt administration doubted the connection between economic depression and emotional maladjustment, the chance of a pervasive youth uprising—at least among the college set—seemed remote. Most
college students were politically and socially conservative. In a 1932 presidential straw poll of forty thousand college students, Hoover easily outdistanced
Roosevelt by a margin of almost two to one.[90] So even though increasing numbers of students flirted with radical politics during the 1930s, membership levels in Socialist and Communist campus groups remained miniscule, especially
compared to that of the Greek-letter societies, whose conservative membership
still defined the political and social mood at a majority of schools—and would
more or less continue to do so until the 1960s.[91] Even at the City College of New
York, one of the country's supposedly more radical campuses, left-wing politics
attracted few students. Irving Howe, a City College undergraduate from 1936
to 1940, counted himself among the small Socialist student community that
he estimated at less than five hundred out of a total population of more than
twenty thousand. Howe, whose leftist literary and political views later found a
home at *Dissent*, which he founded in 1954, bitingly recalled that most of his
peers were either "utterly indifferent to racial or any other politics" or "hopeless
careerists . . . determined at any cost to 'make it.'"[92] A study conducted by the
political science department at Brown University, in 1936, corroborated Howe's
assessment, concluding that students' political mood had shifted softly leftward
since 1932, not radically so: "Students have gone from Hooverism to the liberalism typified by the New Deal."[93] A *Fortune* magazine survey arrived at a similar conclusion. College students, *Fortune* wrote, are "intellectually curious" and
"interested in political and social questions" but concerned, first and foremost,
with "security" and a "job that is guaranteed to be safe and permanent."[94]

The elusive goal of security drove the New Deal's nascent youth policy. Evidence suggested that the nation's 20 million youth (aged sixteen to twenty-four)
bore more than a disproportionate share of the insecurity caused by the Great
Depression. Analyses conducted by the federal government and independent
organizations determined that 6 million youth were unemployed and 2 to 3
million more youth were only employed on a part-time basis.[95] According to
the Federal Census of Unemployment, "unemployment is higher in this age-
range than in any other." The U.S. Employment Service explained why: "Where
qualified experienced workers over 25 years of age are available, few employers
can be expected to hire and train young persons whose capacities and efficien-
cies are yet to be demonstrated."[96] A down-on-his-luck Maryland youth arrived
at a similar conclusion: "There is nothing to do after you leave school."[97] American youth did not have an out: too inexperienced to compete for the scarce jobs
that were available, yet too poor to do anything else, including going to college.

The Roosevelt administration responded in a number of ways to help youth adjust to these new realities. The creation of the Civilian Conservation Corps (CCC) in the spring of 1933 was the most conspicuous example of direct federal intervention in the life of young America. Organized by the War Department, the CCC combined strenuous labor and uplift to become one of the most popular New Deal programs. The CCC employed nearly 3 million displaced young people over the course of its decade-long existence, providing jobs in forestry and flood control, and in rural beautification and urban gentrification.[98] The CCC also organized a camper education program with the assistance of the Office of Education. Given the mix of campers' educational backgrounds, the program not surprisingly spanned a wide range of interests and ability levels; it included literacy training, which was required for all illiterate campers starting in 1938, as well as high school and even college-grade work. But the real focus of the CCC education program was on no-frills vocational training and the preparation of campers for future employment. Camp education materials linked working to learning in order to demonstrate to campers the relationship between both activities. Learning for the pure joy of learning was of little concern to CCC officials. Rather, according to Howard W. Oxley, the director of CCC Camp Education, the pedagogical aim was to correct "common school deficiencies" to make "each enrollee more employable and a better citizen."[99]

In other words, the CCC did little to improve the lot of either higher education or its students. College leaders and desperate students thus pressed the federal government for additional aid. President Glenn Frank of the University of Wisconsin, responding to the Wisconsin state legislature's most recent funding cut, bitingly remarked that higher education was paying the price for "the sins of the economic leadership" who wanted to "balance budgets by cutting the very heart out of the only things that make government a creative social agency."[100] A parent sent a letter to President Roosevelt on behalf of his daughter, a student at the financially pinched Eastern Nazarene College, requesting a "small donation towards the saving of this wonderful college."[101] Additional appeals and the prospect of creating more space in the saturated job market convinced Roosevelt and his confidant, Harry L. Hopkins, that aiding college students promoted overall economic recovery.[102]

They weighed several different aid options. Wary of the dole and the degradation associated with federal handouts, Roosevelt and his advisers limited their plans to ones that involved paid labor. The first form of federal support to public higher education included aid for the construction of administration and classroom buildings, dormitories, medical schools, libraries, and even football stadiums. Although the land-grant colleges had received modest annual federal appropriations since the passage of the second Morrill Land-Grant Act of 1890, this funding paled in comparison to the funding that accompanied the New Deal.[103] Two agencies headed up the federal government's effort. The Works

Progress Administration (WPA), headed by Hopkins, was the first. It supplied workers while individual institutions covered the remaining costs. In most cases those costs were subsidized by a second agency, the Public Works Administration (PWA). An offshoot of the National Industrial Recovery Act and headed by Harold Ickes, the PWA distributed $200 million in federal matching grants to assist universities in expanding and modernizing their physical plant. While higher education's allocation represented a small portion of the PWA's total purse, which topped $3 billion in its first year, a majority of which was funneled to the Army Corps of Engineers and the Bureau of Reclamation, the government's education-bound largess nevertheless represented an unprecedented windfall. Nearly every county in the country received PWA funds (3,068 out of 3,071), and so did practically every state university and land-grant college.[104] More than six hundred different public university building projects—including thirteen alone at the University of Alabama—broke ground with the help of the PWA. And with each foundation poured and brick laid entire campuses and their surrounding communities were given a glimpse of state building not previously seen—even at public universities with longstanding federal relationships. The projects were bigger, the funding greater, and the visibility wider—thanks in large part to the presence of huge worksite placards festooned with Roosevelt's name—than anything that had come before.[105]

Manual labor also played a central role in the Roosevelt administration's college aid plan. After briefly toying with the idea of a loan and fellowship program, the president came down in favor of a comprehensive work-study program. He and his advisers agreed to provide select needy students with an opportunity to earn their way to a college diploma. The program was placed under the control of the Federal Emergency Relief Administration (FERA), with Harry L. Hopkins as director. All institutions—public, private, and sectarian—were permitted to participate in the program. After a two-month trial run at the University of Minnesota in the fall of 1933, in February 1934 Hopkins announced that the program would be expanded nationwide and earmarked $5 million to help finance 100,000 students' educations.[106]

The following year, Roosevelt transferred the college aid program to the newly created National Youth Administration (NYA), under the nominal jurisdiction of Hopkins's WPA. The NYA extended the aid program to an additional twenty thousand students (raising the maximum eligible population to 120,000) and permitted graduate students to participate. Undergraduates could earn up to twenty dollars per month, and graduate students up to twice that, working at approved on-campus and off-campus jobs. Over a ten-year period, at a cost of nearly $100 million, the work-study program helped 620,000 students (13 percent of all depression-era matriculates) partially finance their college education.[107] It also benefited their institutions. Following national enrollment declines in 1932 and 1933, higher education registered modest enrollment increases every year thereafter until America entered World War II.[108]

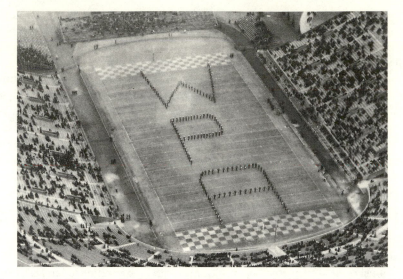

Figures 3.2 and 3.3. New Deal funds triggered a campus building boom in the 1930s. Above, an aerial shot of the Louisiana State University marching band in W-P-A formation captured a festive mood at the rededication of a newly expanded and updated Tiger Stadium, November 1936. Harry Hopkins, head of the WPA, was the guest of honor. Below, gigantic construction site placards like this one at the Physics and Mathematics Building (ca. 1937) at Louisiana State University provided the university community with a glimpse of New Deal state building in progress. Courtesy Franklin D. Roosevelt Presidential Library.

The decentralized bureaucratic structure of the work-study program mirrored the organizational configuration of other New Deal recovery and relief efforts. State-level emergency relief administrators, educational bureaucrats, and university leaders handled the day-to-day managerial duties of the work-study program. A divided administrative framework met southern Democratic leaders and university officials' demand for local control—that is, for freedom from centralized governmental power. Each institution arrived at this demand from slightly different points: southern congressional leaders feared a strong federal government for political reasons; university leaders for academic ones. But safeguarding against the slow creep of statism proved challenging in an era of acute economic and social need. Southern Democrats and university leaders, as the case of federally funded student aid revealed, found it increasingly difficult to juggle requests for federal help with requirements for unfettered autonomy.

Consider the case of Virginia and its flagship public university, the University of Virginia. Virginia's Democratic senators, Carter Glass and Harry F. Byrd, were among the most aggressive opponents of the New Deal regime. Both senators opposed virtually every New Deal program, save for AAA money, and Glass even raised issue with that. According to one scholar, their opposition to the New Deal was beyond compare. Even though Roosevelt was immensely popular in Virginia and throughout the South, the Glass and Byrd political machine was so well oiled that they could openly criticize the New Deal without any fear of either Democratic Party or popular reprisal.[109] The combination of poll taxes, literacy tests, and other discriminatory devices prevented all but 6 percent of eligible voters from casting ballots in Virginia elections—the lowest voter participation rate of any state in the nation. Political scientist V. O. Key denounced Virginia as "a political museum piece." "By contrast," he jibed, "Mississippi," with its 12–16 percent participation rate, was "a hotbed of democracy."[110]

The University of Virginia, founded by Thomas Jefferson in 1819 and opened six years later, was the institutional embodiment of the political and academic antistatism that guided the New Deal's higher education policy.[111] Yet neither its Jeffersonian heritage nor Byrd's and Glass's political posturing prevented the university (along with thirty-seven other schools in the commonwealth) from enthusiastically participating in the federal work-study program. The localized administration of the student-aid program combined with unquestionable student need assuaged Virginia higher education leaders' fear of suffocating federal power. Roughly 130 private schools refused aid, including Harvard and Yale, which used the depression as a convenient excuse to cut enrollments. Most university leaders felt differently, however, and instead shared the view of John Lloyd Newcomb, president of the University of Virginia: "The desirability and even necessity [of the aid program] is, I believe, not open to question."[112]

Newcomb energetically pursued federal money as a way to make up for the 20 percent cut in state support endured by the university in his first two years on the job. In 1934, the inaugural year of the FERA phase of the work-study program, Newcomb cultivated support at every turn. He saw the program as a boon to students, to their colleges, as well as to the larger national recovery effort. In April 1934, Newcomb asked Senator Byrd, who for a time had been the top choice for the post that Newcomb now held, to "do whatever you can to aid in the continuance of this part-time student employment." He reminded Byrd that without the aid "many students . . . would have left college to join the army of unemployed." The next month he solicited Harry Hopkins and requested that the program be extended another term: "The amount of money involved is comparatively small in comparison with the service which is rendered by its expenditures." At the same time, Newcomb kept tabs on the State Emergency Relief Administration (SERA)—FERA's state-level office—located in Richmond. He even upbraided SERA officials, in his characteristically pedantic way, for bureaucratic glitches: "The students need this money in order to buy food, and I am wondering if you will not be good enough to help us out and see if we might not have a little less delay."[113]

While Newcomb handled external relations, Charles H. Kauffmann, director of the Student Self-Help Bureau, managed the internal operations of the federal work-study program. Kauffmann was the gatekeeper, vetting applications, working with the deans to identify occupational needs, and distributing aid to participating students, a small number of whom had grown increasingly agitated by the uncertainty of the economic depression. Although the all-male student body was dominated by wealthy fraternity boys in their "Greek palaces," a tiny faction of less-well-to-do independents pressed the administration for help. Stirred by financial hardship at home and by the spread of militarism abroad, they "chalked" the sidewalks about Grounds—"Down With Imperialistic War. Scholarships Not Battleships."[114] With scholarship money in short supply, however, Kauffmann turned instead to federal work-study funds to placate some of his needy charges. By 1936, he was managing a workforce of more than four hundred students and a monthly payroll of five thousand dollars.[115]

Kauffmann kept busy. He spent a good portion of his time responding to written requests from students and their proxies. An honor student with an "average of 90% or better" asked for a job to supplement his scholarship because "for the past three years my father has been unemployed." The mother of a needy student pleaded: "His father only has a little clerical work. . . . I teach at an adult night-school and am trying to meet an amount of $20 due the University April 1st. If you can help him see anyway to solve his problems he will be glad to come by your office." A father, desperate for additional support, offered a pithier, if highly idiosyncratic, request: "My boy knows how to play the violin and I think he can do something."[116] Frustratingly for Kauffmann, student need outstripped the supply of jobs. Only 12 percent of the student body could participate in the program. With a premium placed on helping academically choice students of proven "need, ability, and promise," Kauffmann more often than not responded with bad news: "I am sorry to report that it will be impossible to give your son additional employment with funds provided by the FERA, as all jobs allotted to our project have already been filled." Students lucky enough to be placed in work-study assignments appreciated the opportunity. A student working at a summer camp in northern Georgia wrote Kauffmann, in August 1935, to thank him for a work-study opportunity for the coming fall term: "Such a job," he said, "is very necessary in aiding me to attend the University."[117]

Congenial correspondences between students and college officials, and between college officials and the federal government, personalized the New Deal's bureaucratic machine. Operating within the largely familiar administrative channels of the university, it would have been understandable had students and faculty, and even a few administrators, lost sight of the federal government's role in sustaining and expanding higher education in the 1930s. But university officials understood that the money flowed outward from Washington, and this realization helped to alter their relationship to the federal government. Rather than inhibiting academic freedom and institutional autonomy, New Deal campus construction projects and the work-study program proved that the federal government could meaningfully contribute to higher education without violating the antistatist tradition of decentralized federal-academic relations.

Although work-study students were paid with federal funds, and thus in some sense federal workers, administrators discovered that the federal government's involvement was benign. The executive director of the NYA, Aubrey Williams, received countless letters lauding the program. The president of Stanford University, Ray L. Wilbur, who initially rejected the aid, now praised the program "for the effective ways in which it has been carried out." His peer at the University of Southern California likewise described the aid program as "wisely conceived and of real value." The president at the State College for Colored Students in Delaware said the program had been "distinctly beneficial to the young men and women assisted here at State College." An assistant dean at the University of Illinois struck a slightly more melodramatic tone in his letter to Williams. He described how the hopes of entire families "centered on the one individual who is attempting to get a higher education." Having helped more than one thousand students secure work-study appointments, the dean confessed to having "learned to know the courage with which [students] persist." A student enrolled at Alabama College held the NYA in the highest possible regard: "When thinking of the values of NYA work and what it has meant to me, first of all I think college, for it is through the NYA program that I have been given the opportunity of a college education."[118]

Despite its success and broad support among higher education leaders and students, the federal work-study program was disbanded in 1943—a casualty of the conservative congressional assault on the New Deal that eliminated the

Figure 3.4. The National Youth Administration's Federal Work-Study Program helped 620,000 college students, like this budding scientist, at work in the lab in 1937, stay in school during the Great Depression. The program was terminated in 1943, only to be revived in 1964 by President Lyndon B. Johnson, the former Texas state director of the NYA. Courtesy Franklin D. Roosevelt Presidential Library.

NYA, the WPA, and the CCC, along with a host of other work and relief programs considered redundant in a booming wartime economy. The work-study program was gone but not forgotten. A young and ambitious congressman from Texas's Tenth Congressional District named Lyndon B. Johnson would remember it well. A 1930 graduate of tiny Southwest Texas State Teacher's College and a former school teacher, Johnson served as the state director of the NYA from 1935 to 1937 before heading to Washington as a freshman member of the House of Representatives. Some three decades later, President Lyndon B. Johnson launched his own New Deal-inspired War on Poverty. One of its signature pieces of legislation, the Economic Opportunity Act of 1964, revived the long-defunct federal work-study program to help capable but needy students work their way to a college degree.[119]

"Some Type of Education, an Education for Citizenship": The Federal Forum Project

While the percentage of young people enrolled in higher education increased during the 1930s, the overwhelming majority of Americans still never set foot on a college campus. College was for "children"; "adults" were not welcome. This fact represented a challenge for New Dealers, who were committed to building a more powerful state and thought that educating the wider public about their plans for doing so was a necessary first step. After all, the New Deal was more than a hodgepodge of loosely related social programs and buildings projects—it was a new form of government that demanded further explanation. According to one leading scholar on the subject, the New Deal was an intellectual and psychological project that endeavored to create a permanent "attitudinal change" among the American people.[120] As Roosevelt himself put it, "The United States still stakes its faith in the democratic way of life. We believe in the representative form of government. We dare not close our eyes, however, to the fact that the only way in which that representative form of government can persist is through an educated and informed electorate."[121]

John W. Studebaker, the commissioner of education, made the education of average Americans his personal mission during the Great Depression. Studebaker was appointed head of the U.S. Office of Education in 1934, after George F. Zook, discouraged by the office's marginal policymaking influence, resigned to become the president of the American Council on Education. Studebaker, a native of Des Moines, Iowa, did his undergraduate work at Leander Clark College and his graduate work at Teachers College. During the war he directed the American Junior Red Cross; afterward he returned to Des Moines to become superintendent of the city's public school system. Studebaker quickly made a name for himself as an educational innovator when he centralized the Des Moines school system and instituted night and extension courses for the residents of central Iowa.[122]

Studebaker attained national acclaim in the early 1930s when he organized the Des Moines Forum Project. He had become convinced that "American schools were not successfully educating boys and girls for American life." The schools covered the "academic fundamentals" well enough, he said; where they came up short was in providing students with "knowledge about the new . . . state and national government which the students as voters would eventually rule." The depression and the social upheaval that accompanied it, combined with the rise of fascist and Communist dictatorships abroad, convinced Studebaker that "some type of education, an education for citizenship, surely, must follow students beyond the school doors into life if popular government [is] to work." Roiling amid a sea of unprecedented societal change, Studebaker was convinced the best way to protect democracy was through locally organized public discussion—what he affectionately described as "a people's university."[123]

The vision for Studebaker's people's university emanated from a number of sources. Distant sources included the mythical New England town meeting, the Lyceum movement of the 1830s and 1840s, and the Chautauqua movement of the late nineteenth century. The most important one, however, was the land-grant university extension model. Studebaker was born and raised in a region where the land-grant extension system was highly revered. Indeed, just north of Iowa, in Wisconsin, the so-called "Wisconsin Idea" inspired a whole generation of Midwestern politicians to look to their land-grant universities for solutions to their most pressing social problems. Studebaker counted himself among those educational leaders enlightened by the "Wisconsin Idea" and the extension model more specifically; and like his friend Henry Wallace, the secretary of agriculture, with whom he shared membership in a Des Moines-area discussion group known as the Pow Wow Club, Studebaker considered the land-grant university the height of democracy in action. Studebaker regularly compared his forum program to the Extension Service. He imagined each discussion group as its own little "experiment station" where citizens could engage leading experts and one another on social, economic, and political questions of the day.[124] Through robust discussion and deliberation headed by a professionally trained expert, Studebaker averred, "We can keep the American way we know and prize."[125]

The Des Moines Forum Project commenced operation in January 1933. With the help of a $125,000 grant from the Carnegie Foundation, Studebaker organized three types of free, public discussions: neighborhood, central, and citywide. The three-tiered discussion format was intended to help participants conceptualize the interconnections between and among local, state, national, and international problems. He forged partnerships with the local school system, radio station, and public library. The *Des Moines Register* and *Des Moines Tribune* provided free publicity; the public library organized reading lists to dovetail with each week's discussion topic; and the local radio station, KSO, established a Friday evening series, "*Critical Conversations on Current News*," that summarized the main discussion points of the past week. Topics covered all manner of social, economic, and political issues: from racial strife to labor unionization; from the New Deal's agricultural policy to the spread of European dictatorships—any subject matter worthy of a newspaper headline. In its first year of operation, thirteen thousand Des Moines residents (17 percent of the total adult population) attended at least one of the five hundred scheduled forums. While twice as many adults did not attend a forum because they were "not interested," the associate editor of the *Register*, W. W. Waymack, who closely tracked the progress of the discussion project, found some reason for optimism. "Results," Waymack told Studebaker, "are at least encouraging to those who believe the masses are not too stupid to make self-government continuously workable."[126]

One of the most impressive aspects of the forum program was the quality and credentials of the discussion leaders themselves. Although the Des Moines School Board presided over the discussion leader selection process, the list of candidates was far from parochial. Leaders were selected from the ranks of the nation's top universities, policy institutes, and opinion-making organizations. "Generally speaking," said Studebaker, "a leader should be a professional educator who devotes his full time to a critical study of contemporary issues." It was the discussion leader's obligation to prevent the forum from devolving into a free-for-all or an extended monologue, neither of which was conducive to a truly democratic style of deliberation. The best leader was not "a lecturer or speaker," explained Studebaker, but a person of "broad training and experience in the field of public affairs as well as a special competency in the guidance of fruitful group discussion."[127]

On paper, anyway, Studebaker and the school board achieved this goal. Notable discussion leaders and guest lecturers included economist Thomas Nixon Carver of Harvard; Chi Meng of the China Institute of America; Karl Polanyi from the *Austrian Economist*; Jerome Frank from the USDA; W.E.B. Du Bois, a founding member of the NAACP and editor of the *Crisis*; and before becoming secretary of agriculture, Henry A. Wallace. By having discussion leaders like these interact with average citizens and help them work through various points of view, Studebaker thought new community leaders would naturally emerge.[128] Studebaker did not think expertly managed group discussion was a contradiction in terms. Although his fundamental goal was the achievement of freedom for all, according to a leading expert on the forum movement, Studebaker thought that democratic discussion-making skills could be learned, that "public conversation would have to be carefully managed so as not to intimidate or offend, and individuals would have to be taught techniques of self-expression and discussion." Fanciful as his vision may have been, Studebaker truly believed that group discussion was the wellspring of democracy.[129]

Studebaker arrived in Washington, in September 1934, committed to extending the Des Moines Forum model to the rest of the nation. This goal proved far more difficult to achieve than he anticipated for a number of reasons. First of all, the Office of Education, as his predecessor George F. Zook had discovered, exercised no formal regulatory power. Since its establishment in 1867 the office had fought for its bureaucratic survival and defended itself against routine calls for its outright abolishment. Originally created as a department without cabinet rank, after two years it was demoted to an office before being demoted again, in 1870, to a bureau within the Department of the Interior. At the time Studebaker assumed the commissionership the bureau had reverted to an office (which happened in 1929) with makeshift headquarters in the Post Office Building.[130] In other words, aside from collecting copious amounts of obscure, dust-gathering statistical data on the American education system, the Office of Education remained far removed from the state and local politics that dominated primary, secondary, and college education policymaking. Having spent two decades running the Des Moines city schools, Studebaker grasped this political maxim as well as anyone. His Des Moines Forum Project was a testament to the importance of local politics in shaping education policy and in the widespread belief that the deliberative assembly was an essential organ of democracy. "When [public forums] are controlled by local education authorities in exactly the same way as is the case with all other local public-education functions," explained Studebaker, "[they] will be genuinely educative in purpose and procedure."[131]

Second, Studebaker's political training in Iowa did not adequately prepare him for the national stage. He badly misjudged the political strength of the Office of Education. He lobbied vigorously for a piece—any piece—of the New Deal's emerging education agenda, and then watched helplessly as the president and Harry Hopkins farmed all of it out to the respective education directors of the CCC, FERA, and NYA. The placement of education policy under the purview of the New Deal's emergency bureaucratic units, and not the Office of Education, diminished the intensity of the political opposition to the Roosevelt administration's embryonic national education agenda. And by keeping education programming out of the permanent executive branch bureaucracy, Roosevelt perpetuated the notion that the expansion of the New Deal state was reversible and that government would return to its previous size after the crisis passed.[132] Studebaker also overestimated his own political skills, making an already difficult job that much harder. He boasted of a federal forum project before having received the go-ahead to do so, and thus raised concerns about governmentally controlled education. In the winter of 1934–35, Studebaker publicly uttered different descriptions of, and costs for, his discussion program. At first he wanted to institute the discussion program in "all communities of the nation," and have the federal government cover 75 percent of the cost since, he awkwardly reasoned, "national problems take up about that proportion of the time."[133] A few months later, in April 1935, Studebaker said his goal was to create ten thousand open forum centers, over a three-year period, with a congressional appropriation of $7 million.[134] A different set of figures followed only days later when Studebaker told the Rotary Club of Salisbury, Maryland, that the forum program would be developed over a ten-year period at a total cost of $70 million.[135] "I am not oblivious to the implications of obnoxious and pestiferous government control," said Studebaker to a group of New York City teachers, "and I don't want to see everything we do locally directed by the Federal government."[136] Genuine though this sentiment was, in publicizing conflicting descriptions of the size and cost of the federal forum project, Studebaker unwittingly stirred fears that his office wanted more—not less—control of the nation's education system.[137]

Studebaker's verbal blunders and political clumsiness nearly crushed all of his aspirations. On August 24, 1935, not quite a year into his commissionership, he wrote the president and complained of feeling "discouraged and embarrassed" at "the lack of opportunity . . . to work effectively from [this] strategic, but at present relatively impotent position." Less than a week later he again wrote the president, apparently feeling a bit more upbeat: "I am eager to *do* something worth while that will really help in the great cause for which we work."[138] Studebaker finally got his wish. After months of negotiating with the administration, Studebaker persuaded his boss that the forum program could "yield not only permanent social values but also immediate and important political advantages" for the New Deal. Roosevelt agreed to a slim-downed version of Studebaker's original plan for a federally financed nationwide discussion program. On November 8, 1935, FERA chief Harry L. Hopkins allocated $330,000 for the establishment of ten federal forum demonstration sites—in cities and counties from Portland, Oregon, to Monongalia County, West Virginia—beginning in 1936. The Des Moines forum project served as the blueprint. Discussion leaders were again recruited from regional colleges, universities, and lower schools and administrative control was handed over to local authorities. School superintendants together with representatives from nearby state universities organized forums and selected discussion topics to address perceived informational needs at the local level. For its part the Office of Education selected and funded test sites, provided training materials and advice on discussion formats, but that was all. In announcing the program to the nation, Studebaker was unequivocal in his description of the federal government's limited role: "There is not going to be any set program dictated by my office to the local communities." As with all New Deal programs, local control again held sway.[139]

The forum movement never achieved the stature of a training ground for national citizenship. From its modest beginnings as a demonstration program, however, a genuine nationwide discussion movement materialized. Despite a reduced operating budget after 1936 the Office of Education received authorization to extend its federal forum project to smaller towns and rural communities believed to be the most geographically and intellectually removed from the New Deal. The Office of Education accomplished this in a number of different

Figure 3.5. In an era when agricultural extension education was the principle means by which colleges and universities connected with adults—when they connected at all—the Federal Forum Project offered a taste of higher learning to average Americans from Portland, Oregon, to Manchester, New Hampshire. An estimated 2.5 million Americans made their way to a federal forum in the 1930s to learn about the important social and political topics of the day. From U.S. Office of Education, *Choosing Our Way: A Study of America's Forums* (Washington, DC, 1938).

ways. The office hit the radio airwaves with a four-part program called *The American Way*—an exploration of the so-called American way of democracy-by-discussion narrated by a fictive small town newspaper editor, Phineas Todd. "The way I look at it," concluded Todd in the fourth installment, "the better understanding of each other's viewpoints, the better adjustment people can make to change. Understanding is the beginning of wisdom, you know!"[140]

The office also organized fifteen Cooperative Forum Centers and sixteen Forum Counseling Programs in partnership with state universities and state departments of education around the country. The cooperative arrangement that emerged closely resembled the Department of Agriculture's university-based extension network. Rather than county agents, however, the Office of Education deputized the graduates of its university-based Forum Counseling Programs to bring the federal forum project to "cities, hamlets, and on the farms throughout the length and breadth of the land," as President Roosevelt envisioned it. As many as thirty communities, in thirteen different states, hired full-time forum counselors. These roving expert discussants organized forums on topics ranging from the Social Security Act to the challenges of consumers, from race relations to birth control. They prepared radio programs, developed and exchanged discussion content and visual-aids with other counselors, and participated in leadership training courses at colleges and universities.[141]

North Dakota Agricultural College (NDAC) served as the headquarters for a federal forum project in the Fargo area during the winter of 1938–39. The new president of NDAC, Frank L. Eversull, sent invitations to a number of nearby communities calling all "forward-looking citizens" to join the college "in intelligent and directed discussions." Five communities agreed to participate (Kindred, population of five hundred, was the smallest; Wahpeton, population of three thousand, the largest), chipping in a thousand dollars to cover speaker costs and related expenses. Eversull convened a local executive committee to work out the logistics and to select discussion topics. They agreed to convene one concurrent forum per week, for twenty weeks, in each town, dividing the sessions among four different topics: "economic problems," "social problems," "art and leisure," and "international relations." Promotional information ran in the newspapers and on the radio and was distributed to local schools and voluntary organizations like the Kiwanis Club and American Legion. In his own study of the forum project, Eversull reported "outstanding results." He praised the forums for being noticeably "free from . . . propaganda" and lively enough to engage "cranks . . . and those with pet hobbies." The Yale-educated Eversull noted the scrupulousness with which the speakers "documented their speeches," crediting it with increasing participants' excitement about and trust in the program. There was also an uptick in the circulation of forum-related library books in the days around each meeting and growing interest in group discussion elsewhere in North Dakota. "Requests came from all over the state for information about the organization and administration of the forum," he said. "This led to the organization of a state-wide movement to provide forums for the less favored sections of the state." During its year of operation, Eversull's NDAC forum held 93 meetings attended by more than 12,000 North Dakotans—a smidgeon of the estimated 2.5 million Americans who attended one of the federal forum project's 23,000 discussion sessions held between 1936 and 1941.[142]

The federal forum project was eventually eclipsed by wartime exigencies and the availability of new mass communications. The coming television age offered a powerful alternative to the face-to-face give and take of the forum model, irrevocably changing the manner in which most Americans received news and participated in democratic deliberation. Still, in its heyday the dramatic growth and popularity of the federal forum program served notice that the central government had a definite stake in the educational progress of the nation, and that its stake extended beyond the learning that occurred inside publicly financed schools and colleges. That Roosevelt and his functionaries permitted the Office of Education to partner with local communities and their school boards in recruiting university professors and leading public intellectuals to direct forum discussions marked a subtle but profound reorientation in the nature of federal-academic relations. The crisis of the Great Depression offered the federal government greater access to the nation's educational development, which traditionally had been considered off limits for federal officials. The scale and scope of the American state was changing and becoming a more immediate presence in the lives of workaday Americans. Studebaker, for one, understood this. A little over a week after he received approval to proceed with the federal forum demonstration project, on November 16, 1935, Studebaker again wrote to Roosevelt, and explained why, after much deliberation, he had revised his assessment of the placement and role of the Office of Education in the federal government. Studebaker told the president he no longer wanted to "confine the purposes, policies and procedures of education to any one department," including his own. Whether Studebaker's change of heart was a consequence of his difficult first year in Washington, he did not say. What was apparent to him now, however, was that education was "essentially different from other governmental functions" because education "runs across all . . . organizations of government." Living and working in the New Deal state, Studebaker implied, had itself become the basis of a true people's university.[143]

❖❖❖

Higher education helped the New Deal achieve administrative capacity in a political culture uncomfortable with a sprawling national bureaucracy. The university's placement between citizens and the state made it an ideal parastate for the federal government to connect with its citizens and, in turn, for citizens to connect with their government. New Dealers relied on colleges and universities to deliver federal programs and services because they naturalized the New Deal's expanded national reach and made it politically palatable to average Americans and to conservative, especially southern, politicians. As the years passed and the New Deal matured, it became increasingly apparent that the polity supported an activist state most when that state operated through providers at least once removed from the federal government's immediate family of bureaucratic agencies. Higher education was one of those kissing cousins.

By uncovering higher education's role in New Deal state building, this chapter alters the existing periodization of the development of the state-academic partnership. While a handful of elite scientists debated endlessly among themselves as to whether they should accept government patronage in the 1930s, literally hundreds of institutions, thousands of faculty and administrators, and hundreds of thousands of students reached an affirmative answer to that question in plain view of the entire polity. A range of key stakeholders at public and private institutions around the country unequivocally expressed their support for government aid. University extension divisions at the nation's land-grant colleges and universities mobilized in the name of agricultural adjustment and were rewarded for their efforts. So too were the hundreds of thousands of college students who worked their way to a diploma with the help of federal work-study. And the federal government tapped leading educators around the country to organize and direct forum discussions where the rapidly changing social, economic, and political world of the New Deal was the primary topic of conversation. Contrary to conventional wisdom that portrays higher education as a closed system cordoned off from the ebb and flow of the real world, this chapter suggests otherwise. Higher education linked millions of citizens to the state, long before World War II.

This chapter also illuminates higher education's development into a key mediator of state-society relations in the 1930s. Situated between citizens and the state, protected from serious criticism by dint of that placement, higher education was able to drill into the social and political spheres. Off campus, county agents traversed the land in the name of agricultural adjustment and professors organized and participated in federal forums in small towns well off the beaten path. Administrators and students had a similarly visceral experience on campus. The campus building boom and the spread of student work-study brought entire campuses and workers from the surrounding community face to face with the New Deal state. Ostensibly inconsequential activities—like county-agent-directed demonstrations, or the construction of new dormitories, or the shelving of a book by a student worker, or the convening of a town forum—foreshadowed the federal government's coming supremacy. That none of the New Deal programs examined here survived as originally conceived much beyond the 1930s should not diminish their long-range importance. For it was through the innumerable if forgotten actions of county agents and farmers, administrators, professors and students, that the New Deal state was made and on which the post–World War II contract state was built, along with its multicultural successor.

As we shall see, the New Deal's experiment in using higher education to connect with and shape the polity's political beliefs revealed tantalizing possibilities for a future in which the state and its citizens would use higher education to adjust and readjust to one another. The state used higher education to connect with citizens and to educate them about the changing political universe in which they lived. The 1930s thus offered a preview of things to come: the federal government had become a major sponsor of higher education, and higher education a major institution of the federal government's burgeoning bureaucratic state.[144]

PART II

Democracy

Chapter 4

Educating Citizen-Soldiers in World War II

———————— ❖ ————————

The New Deal brought the state and higher education into close contact during the 1930s, but it took World War II to make the partnership stick. The education soldiers received during and after the war altered their lives and the life of the nation. Fear of the psychological maladjustment of G.I.s in the field led top military leaders to approve the use of psychological screening mechanisms that seemed to indicate educated soldiers were superior soldiers. That conclusion brought education to the forefront of state policymaking and set the stage for the creation of a vast state-academic partnership that culminated in the 1944 G.I. Bill of Rights.

No development was more vital in forging a lasting partnership between citizens and the state than the passage of the G.I. Bill of Rights. Despite a recent surge of interest in the legislation, scholars have not adequately explained why education became the centerpiece of the G.I. Bill.[1] This chapter does that. First, I situate the legislation in the context of a rapid shift in the state's commitment to educating citizens, providing a rejoinder to those scholars who have branded the G.I. Bill an exceptional piece of federal social policy. While this landmark legislation was exceptional in many ways, it looks less so when placed within the stream of wartime education initiatives that preceded the G.I. Bill. Second, I link fears of psychological maladjustment among soldiers to the state's unprecedented interest in education. Most scholars connect the G.I. Bill's education provision to the state's effort to rebuild the education economy and protect the macroeconomy by using universities as a floodgate to manage the flow of veterans into the postwar labor force. But the role of psychology in the state's attention to higher education has not been explored. This chapter places the quest for adjustment front and center. Third, I connect the state's interest in education to the exigencies of military service: for citizens to fulfill their military obligations, the state had to fulfill its educational obligations. Finally, I provide a perspective beyond that of policymaking elites by examining how the voluntary enrollment of millions of ordinary soldiers in educational programs during the war, and in colleges after it, accelerated higher education's transformation into a powerful parastate—one that would mediate relations between citizens and the state for the rest of the century.

The complete reconstruction of American higher education during World War II was never preordained. With military mobilization and economic recovery commanding national policymakers' attention in the months after the Japanese strike at Pearl Harbor, a total overhaul of the state's approach to educating citizens, despite university leaders' determined push for closer federal relations, seemed remote.[2] This all changed when the Army Research Branch, the state's wartime hub for psychological research, provided America's top military leaders with opinion survey data indicating that recruits craved education and that educated soldiers were better-quality soldiers. According to the Research Branch, regardless of past education, an individual soldier's adjustment to military life improved with continuous educational programming.

Although professional psychologists had moved well beyond the study of adjustment during the interwar period, the wartime Research Branch again fixated on soldier success and failure, if for largely bureaucratic reasons. On the one hand, the branch's investigators, who migrated to the army not only from psychology but from all the social sciences, organized their research around the study of adjustment in order to overcome stark ideological differences in the name of professional unity. On the other hand, the Research Branch discovered that framing its findings in terms of adjustment was the most expedient way to describe soldiers' overall psychological health to results-oriented policymakers, who had neither the time nor patience for professional squabbles. As they had in the Great War, during World War II experts from across the social sciences rallied around the flag of psychology and pledged allegiance to adjustment in order to display the utility of their human technologies in the formulation of public policy.[3]

The Research Branch's technology of choice for tracking soldiers' psychological adjustment was the opinion survey. Contrasting its approach with rigid stimulus-response definitions of adjustment, the Research Branch insisted that a truly democratic measure of adjustment allowed for individual preferences and tastes. Charting soldier adjustment along three dimensions—age, marital status, and education—the Research Branch determined that the best single predictor of adjustment was education level. Their studies presented evidence that better-educated soldiers were more efficient, exhibited higher morale, and were less likely to desert or suffer psychoneurotic breakdown than their educationally deprived peers: individuals who were educated most soldiered best. Military and education policymakers were galvanized by these findings and joined forces to create the Army Information and Education Division (IE Division)—the education clearinghouse for the common soldier. The IE Division, using innovative pedagogical approaches to the mass education of millions of average soldiers, confirmed that higher education created psychologically adjusted citizens.[4]

The alleged positive psychological influence of education on the adjustment of individuals to life in the military meant little to the common soldiers who devoured the IE Division's educational offerings. Rather, education provided soldiers with a sanctuary from the utter boredom and anonymity of military service. As an accepted retreat from the drudgery of army life, education offered soldiers pleasurable as well as potentially rewarding opportunities for intellectual fulfillment and for improved postwar economic prospects.[5]

In other words, the G.I.s who flocked to the army's education programs did so for reasons decidedly different from those hypothesized by the Research Branch. Military leaders looked to education as an instrument to create the soldiers the army most wanted to have, while soldiers gravitated toward education because it offered a pathway to becoming the citizens they most wanted to be. Though they had different ideas about the chief benefits of higher education, by the postwar period the state and its subjects agreed education was central to American citizenship. Even as the battlefield triumphs of the federal-academic research matrix were more visible during World War II, in the long run both the state and the university bet the future on higher education and the student-citizens it produced.

"Today's Soldier Is Not the Same as the '1917–1918' Model": The Army Research Branch and the Measurement of Soldier Opinion

On the eve of America's entry into the war, soldiers and civilians suffered from what the economist John Kenneth Galbraith later dubbed "depression psychosis." High unemployment, public apathy toward American involvement in the war, and low national morale concerned military and political leaders. Despite New Deal programs, roughly 15 percent of American workers remained unemployed as late as 1940. Members of the Roosevelt administration openly complained about the public's "lackadaisical attitude" toward war and wondered whether it would pose a serious "defense problem." Public opinion polls relayed as much. According to a May 1941 Princeton Public Opinion Project poll, only 10 percent of Americans thought the country should declare war on Germany and Italy. Moreover, the *New York Times* reported that military morale was at an all-time low, a result of "spotty leadership . . . lack of imagination . . . and a feeling that time in the Army is wasted." Against this backdrop of general malaise, the embryonic Army Research Branch went to work.[6]

The creation of the Army Research Branch was one of the major administrative outcomes of the War Department's Morale Branch reorganization in March 1941. Established the previous year to manage soldiers' physical welfare—food, clothing, and off-duty activities—the Morale Branch was failing miserably in fulfilling its charge according to reports from the field and the national media. This concerned General George C. Marshall, the army chief of staff, who was particularly sensitive to the personal needs of common soldiers. Marshall's commitment to soldiers' livelihoods stemmed from his own four-decade slog from lowly Virginia Military Institute (VMI) cadet to army chief of staff.[7]

Several other factors help explain Marshall's interest in soldiers' well-being and professional development. Marshall credited his own success to hard work and determination as much as to political connections or battlefield glory, both of which eluded him as a young soldier. Also, in the year Marshall graduated in the middle of his class of thirty-four cadets at VMI (1901), a new professionalized army awaited him courtesy of military reformer Elihu Root, the secretary of war from 1899 to 1904 in both the McKinley and Roosevelt administrations. Beyond centralizing the nation's military forces, Root's reforms sought to replace political patronage and nepotism with military training and education as the officially sanctioned means of career advancement. Professional soldiering meshed perfectly with Marshall's own administrative sensibilities, and he made the most of the specialized training opportunities afforded him in the post-Root era. Like several other rising stars of his generation, including Dwight D. Eisenhower and Omar Bradley, Marshall compensated for the nation's relative isolation and dearth of military engagements during the interwar period by shrewdly navigating the army bureaucracy. Guided by his own experiences, Marshall understood all too well that for most soldiers the benefit of military service often occurred, if it occurred at all, away from the field of battle. As the chief of staff of the army, it was his responsibility to make military service a worthwhile experience. The Morale Branch's alleged ineffectiveness thus forced Marshall to act.[8]

With the blessing of Henry L. Stimson, the secretary of war, Marshall removed the Morale Branch from the Adjutant General's Office and placed it under his own supervision. He then elevated and renamed it, making it the Special Services Division and dividing it into four interdependent branches—Welfare and Recreation, Public Relations, Services, and Planning and Research—the last of which he charged with collecting and analyzing information about current and future morale problems in the army. Finally, Marshall commissioned Frederick H. Osborn to serve as the division's new director. Osborn—an accomplished amateur demographer and longtime advocate of using education as a tool for social progress—proved to be an especially inspired choice. As the previous chairman of the Civilian Committee on Selective Service and of the Joint Army-Navy Committee on Welfare and Recreation, Osborn was well acquainted with the military's ongoing struggle with soldier morale. As a trustee of several leading philanthropic organizations committed to sponsoring social science research, including the Nelson A. Rockefeller Institute of Government and the Carnegie Corporation, Osborn enjoyed ready access to the country's leading social and behavioral scientists. Osborn had little difficulty recruiting the University of Chicago sociologist Samuel A. Stouffer, whom he had met while working on the Social Science Research Council Committee on Social Adjustment in 1940, to lead the Research Branch. Between 1942 and 1945, the Research Branch's staff of 130 administered two hundred different opinion surveys—on topics ranging from alcohol consumption to race relations, from combat performance to demobilization plans—to approximately 500,000 American soldiers worldwide. The complete findings of the Research Branch were later published in a four-volume series entitled *Studies in Social Psychology in World War II*, the first volume of which was *The American Soldier: Adjustment during Army Life.*[9]

At the outbreak of war, however, it seemed unlikely that the Research Branch would be permitted to conduct its opinion surveys. On May 24, 1941, Secretary Stimson banned opinion polling in the military, believing "anonymous opinion or criticism, good or bad, is destructive in its effect on a military organization where accepted responsibility on the part of every individual is fundamental." Memories of World War I and George Creel's Committee on Public Information (CPI), which fanned as much popular opposition to the war as support, had soured Stimson on using cutting-edge but hardly statistically bulletproof opinion-gathering techniques to take the pulse of American soldiers.[10]

Marshall, in contrast, thought advancements in survey design and administration during the interwar years made possible the activities of the Research Branch, even with the secretary's ban. Using opinion surveys designed with the help of the psychologist Rensis Likert of the Program Survey Division of the Department of Agriculture, the Research Branch contended that its surveys differed radically from the dichotomous, "yes-no" polling techniques popularized by George Gallup. Namely, the Research Branch's surveys were self-administered, offered soldiers a range of possible responses, and provided them with space for "free commentary," where they could write about whatever they wished.[11]

Persuaded that the surveys were instruments of democratic decision making, Marshall personally authorized the Research Branch to initiate its first study. On December 8, 1941, a dozen members of the Research Branch descended on the army's Ninth Division at Fort Bragg, North Carolina, to administer Planning Survey I to nineteen hundred new recruits. The results of the Fort Bragg study offered the military, which harbored suspicion of the largely civilian-led Research Branch, compelling evidence that better-educated soldiers adjusted more quickly to military life and possessed significantly higher morale. In the first months of 1942, Osborn delivered the Research Branch's secret Fort Bragg results to Marshall, who received the report with "flattering enthusiasm" and promptly advised Osborn to proceed with Planning Survey II. The report not only confirmed Marshall's own beliefs about the importance of educated soldiers, but also provided him with ammunition to fight for wider educational and research activities throughout the military.[12]

One year after Pearl Harbor, from the Research Branch's new office space in the partially built Pentagon building, Stouffer and his staff prepared the first edition of *What the Soldier Thinks* for limited internal distribution. Using survey data gathered at Fort Bragg and sixty-three additional sites, the report provided the military command with a broad overview of "the new kind of 'raw material' making up [the] Army." Researchers took stock of the marital status, age, and education level of each respondent, but of these three variables they thought education mattered most. Significantly, in World War I only 20 percent of draftees had received instruction beyond grade school; by World War II 67 percent had. High school and college graduation rates had risen as well. For example, among the "old regulars"—enlistees who had joined the army prior to July 1, 1940—only 25 percent were high school (21 percent) or college (4 percent) graduates. By way of comparison, 41 percent of "draftees" had earned a high school (30 percent) or college (11 percent) diploma. "Today's soldier," the report read, "is not the same as the '1917–1918' model." Considering the vast differences in performance between "better educated and less educated" soldiers, the Research Branch warned military leaders against viewing "the problems of World War II . . . through the spectacles of World War I."[13]

The first edition of *What the Soldier Thinks* elaborated on the purported, and seemingly endless, benefits of an educated military. "Better-educated" men (soldiers with at least a high school diploma) were more likely to choose combat duty than were "less-educated" men (soldiers without a high school diploma). The less-educated tended to be "stay at homes" and less "internationally minded" than their better-educated peers. Subsequent research suggested that highly educated soldiers "tended eventually to get better assignments" and that they were "more favorable than others on attitudes reflecting personal commitment to the war." Moreover, better-educated soldiers were more likely to feel that "they should have been drafted, more likely to say that they could be more useful to their country as soldiers than as war workers," and exhibited a "higher personal esprit" and interest in understanding the nature of their service duties and obligations. According to the second edition of *What the Soldier Thinks* (1943), "the educated soldier knows more about the war and has greater facility in acquiring further knowledge." Less-educated soldiers, on the other hand, were four times more likely to go absent without leave (AWOL) or to suffer a psychoneurotic breakdown than better-educated men. Relying on educational attainment as its central frame of reference, the Research Branch established a positive correlation between education and adjustment. In short, educated soldiers were better soldiers. But would they also make better citizens?[14]

Having the "best educated Army in history" posed a unique set of challenges. The survey data pointed to several disturbing developments. Men with some college education were more critical of the army than others surveyed. One new recruit complained, "All my training has been repetitious since I left Training Center and I haven't learned anything new since that thirteen-week period." The monotony of training camp especially exasperated the better educated, who exhibited little difficulty in comprehending and following the army's rules, regulations, and codes of conduct. "I wish the officers would treat us like intelligent adults," opined an exasperated soldier. "Men inducted into the Army are those who were independent in thought and action, in other words worked for a living. I wish there would be less of the monotonous repetition. Treat a man like a nitwit and he'll finally act like one."[15]

Pervasive draftee discontent also caused tension between the old regulars and better-educated newcomers. Even though few of the less-educated soldiers commented at length, those that did made their feelings of dissatisfaction well known. "My own pet gripe is that Selective Service men are treated much better than we soldier. They grunt and gripe too much," explained a discouraged enlistee. Another member of the old guard believed that army discipline had slipped since the arrival of the draftees and noted that they "have been allowed to wise off too much" and that "many of them are too smart for their own good." A wry survey participant described the situation thus: "Sense the number of men [draftees] has to be here the regulars men get put on K.P. [kitchen patrol] over the week-end so the . . . boys can go home. I don't like that cause I . . . got put on K.P. during Easter. I think I am as good as any man. I mean what is good for the goose is good for the gander." That college-educated draftees were ten times as likely to achieve officer candidacy undoubtedly contributed to the enlisted men's growing sense of injustice.[16]

Finally, Research Branch data suggested that regardless of education level, a majority of men felt disenchanted with military service after one year. Soldier malaise, however, was not the product of inattention to soldiers' physical welfare. Studies revealed that a majority of soldiers enjoyed the army's food, felt adequately outfitted in their government-issue olive drabs, and approved of the medical attention they received. The source of discontent lay in the army's perceived inattention to soldiers' emotional welfare—a factor "less tangible," according to Osborn, "but equally important to morale." "The men are usually kept in the dark as to what they are accomplishing, personally or in units," grumbled one soldier, "and questions as to the reasons for orders are barked down immediately." Another soldier concurred: "My first month down here I was allowed to give my opinion on one occasion. I was then told to shut up. . . . I try to keep suggestions to myself now and just take orders."[17]

The Research Branch's self-serving findings, which were used to bolster its organizational prestige and policymaking authority, pointed to possible remedies for the soldiers' disquiet. Research Branch members already believed that highly educated soldiers were better soldiers, but survey data indicated that soldiers desired education and that it could be used to maintain—even enhance—adjustment. A survey administered in the European theater disclosed that 97 percent of soldiers felt that knowledge of current events made them better soldiers. Nearly as high a percentage revealed that they enjoyed listening to talks by their commanding officers on war-related issues even as a survey conducted in another theater of operations revealed that many soldiers were suspicious of military-generated information. The Research Branch's findings demonstrated that American soldiers wanted to learn, desired information on the war effort, and profited emotionally when engaged in educational activities. A fifteen-camp study conducted during the summer of 1942 found that nearly 90 percent of soldiers liked listening to news on the radio about the progress of the war, stories from home, as well as "reports and comments on current happenings." Another study indicated that "letter-writing . . . and magazine reading" were two frequent off-duty activities and that soldiers made regular use of the army's extensive library network. Although lonely, isolated soldiers found the most satisfaction staring at seminude centerfolds in such publications as *Yank: The Army Weekly*, additional research indicated that contemporary fiction, westerns, humors, and historical novels ranked among soldiers' favorite reading materials. Furthermore, the Research Branch discovered that motion pictures aimed at explaining the war effort had a "positive effect" on soldier adjustment at every education level. A study conducted at three Replacement Training Centers in December 1942 of Frank Capra's *Prelude to War*, the first film in the *Why We Fight* series, concluded that "when a particular topic is featured and hammered hard, even the minute facts are remembered. But when a topic—although important—is handled incidentally, little increase in knowledge is evidenced." Marshall—a former army instructor who described his pedagogical philosophy as an exercise in directing "men by trying to make them see the way to go"—praised the films. They helped soldiers understand the events leading up to U.S. entry into the war. "Knowledge of these facts," he concluded, "is an indispensable part of military training."[18]

Simultaneous advances in the use of education therapy by psychiatrists in army hospitals and on the front lines supported the Research Branch's findings linking education and adjustment. Building on therapeutic techniques originally honed during World War I in the treatment of "shell shock," World War II psychiatrists viewed education itself as an effective rehabilitative therapy. Clinical research on educational therapeutics was widespread, but the most far-reaching advances originated in the Topeka, Kansas, home of the Menninger Clinic, operated by the brothers William and Karl Menninger. A groundbreaking 1939 Menninger Clinic study demonstrated the benefits of education therapy in the treatment of mentally ill patients. The study's preliminary findings indicated that education could be used to remold maladjusted personalities. In 1942 a follow-up investigation confirmed the first study's findings and prompted William Menninger to institute educational offerings as a permanent component of his clinic's therapeutic regimen. Classes were offered in foreign languages, dietetics, music appreciation, current affairs, and jewelry making, among other subjects. Nearly 90 percent of patients availed themselves of at least one of the clinic's courses. According to Menninger, educational therapy simultaneously benefited patients and clinicians: success in the classroom in-

Figure 4.1. Soldiers—their identities hidden—participate in reading therapy at a Red Cross reading room at the Eighty-second Field Hospital in Okinawa, Japan, May 1945. From Department of the Army, *Neuropsychiatry in World War II* (Washington, DC, 1973).

creased patients' self-confidence and thus provided clinicians with a new and valuable way of measuring patients' progress toward adjustment.[19]

The Menninger Clinic's interwar experimentation in educational therapeutics had a profound effect on the organization of the military's psychiatric services. As chief of the army Neuropsychiatric Consultants Division, which employed one-quarter of the nation's psychiatrists during the war, William Menninger used his Topeka clinic as a model for the army's neuropsychiatric rehabilitation program. Described by an army psychiatrist late in the war as "simultaneously diagnostic, educational or re-educational, and therapeutic," the army's multifaceted treatment model was replicated throughout the armed services. The combination of rest along with individual, group, occupational, and educational therapy provided psychiatrists with an effective means to return psychologically damaged soldiers to military service quickly. In order to "divert the mind, relieving it of the anxieties and the strains of war," army psychiatrists commenced educational reconditioning "at the moment convalescence begins while the patient is still in bed." The military credited such treatment with the rehabilitation of 85 percent of all psychologically damaged soldiers committed to military hospitals during the war.[20]

Fantastic reports of psychiatry's curative power, later challenged by studies revealing much lower success rates, stoked the army's interest in the use of education as a therapeutic tool.[21] Research Branch data demonstrated that continuing education aided in the personal adjustment of soldiers regardless of circumstance. While psychiatrists pointed to education's rehabilitative functions, psychologists insisted that education possessed important prophylactic uses. Readily available education and information resources and activities could increase soldier morale, improve adjustment, and help avert the onset of psychoneurotic breakdowns. Believing, as Stouffer did, that "one of the uses of education is to help individuals handle their environments realistically," the U.S. Army retooled itself as a school where commanders were "teachers" and soldiers "students."[22]

"The Most of This Opportunity Must Be Made": Educating the Common Soldier

Reports from the civilian sphere—from which the bulk of the wartime army had to be raised—corroborated the army's fear that the nation suffered from an education crisis. While popular support for the war effort jumped significantly after Pearl Harbor, anecdotal evidence suggested that a majority of Americans had little knowledge of why the United States was fighting. Ignorance of U.S. history, which a scant 18 percent of colleges required students to take, was cited as one cause of the problem. Report after report concurred with a massive 1942 *New York Times* study: "American college students are . . . ignorant of even the most elementary aspects of United States History." Fewer than half of all respondents could name four of the freedoms guaranteed to citizens in the Bill of Rights; even fewer could name two of the powers granted to the Congress by the Constitution; and still fewer could identify two of Thomas Jefferson's contributions to the economic and social development of the United States. The Columbia University history professor Allan Nevins captured the sense of dismay within the nation's educational establishment: "What appalls . . . is not merely the blindness that confuses William James with Jesse James and places St. Louis on the Atlantic but the inability of our young people to draw from the nation's past an understanding of the significance of America in the world's history." Among Research Branch personnel, these troubling developments in higher education merely confirmed what they already knew: even America's best and brightest needed further education.[23]

The armed forces soon expanded and consolidated its stockpile of education and information programs for all soldiers. For a select number of soldiers with advanced credentials the army provided specialized training. The program was arranged cooperatively by the National Committee on Education and Defense, higher education's principle wartime lobby group, headed by George F. Zook, president of the American Council on Education, and the Joint Army-Navy Committee on Education and Welfare. The army partnered with higher education institutions to organize and run the specialized training program. More than four hundred different institutions, including five junior colleges, were contracted to take part. But the nation's largest public universities educated a majority of the 380,000 students selected for twelve weeks of specialized instruction in engineering, medicine, dentistry, law, mathematics, physics, and foreign languages.[24]

The army created a separate educational track to accommodate common soldiers without the educational background to qualify for specialized training. In October 1943 Marshall again reorganized the Special Services Division. The purely recreational components of Special Services (that is, athletics and entertainment) were removed from Osborn's control and reconstituted as a separate division. Marshall also divided Osborn's streamlined Special Services Division, officially recognized as the IE Division in February 1944, into four subordinate branches: Orientation, Information, Education, and Research. Those branches directed the army's worldwide radio network, published its collection of soldier newspapers and magazines, and coordinated its growing number of educational programs—everything from recruit orientation and college-level correspondence study during the war to the organization of army university centers after it.[25]

The housing of these diverse services under the roof of the IE Division was an important step in the army's evolving understanding of soldier welfare. To the chief of staff, however, it meant much more. The IE Division would provide soldiers with genuine opportunities for self-improvement and uplift while simultaneously helping prevent soldier maladjustment. In an internal War Department memorandum issued in the wake of the formation of the division, Marshall disclosed that "the most important factor contributing to the spread of psychoneurotics in our Army has been the nation's educational program and environmental background since 1920." Marshall's own bouts with exhaustion and depression (for which he was hospitalized twice) may have contributed to his fear of soldiers' psychoneuroses. However, by the closing months of 1943 it was clear that the army's education program had achieved the organizational integrity that Marshall and Osborn believed it deserved.[26]

The army's growing faith in education as a weapon of adjustment must be weighed against its simultaneous interest in democratic propaganda. Like their totalitarian enemies, American war planners worried endlessly about their soldiers' psychological strength and turned to propaganda to win the battle for hearts and minds. As it had during World War I, the federal government established a propaganda agency, the Office of War Information (OWI), to coordinate the nation's propaganda offensive. But compared with Creel's CPI and the tens of hundreds of voluntarily organized branches of the American Protective League that it spawned and supported, the OWI was underfunded and received even less interest from the public. So, while the executive branch and military continued to romance the phantom of propaganda during the war, widespread congressional and public suspicion of such efforts compelled policymakers to look for other means of strengthening soldiers' fighting faith. Education presented the best—and most democratic—alternative.[27]

Ultimately, the U.S. Army pinned its hopes on education for reasons that were at once manipulative, practical, and heartfelt. Education was a democratic form of propaganda that offered soldiers a subtle but clear affirmation of liberal values. The very freedoms that Americans were fighting for were invoked each time a soldier put pen to paper, read a book, or dropped a completed correspondence course in the mail. Further, education promised improved postwar economic prospects by providing soldiers with an avenue for skills enhancement and professional credentials. Most critically, education gave soldiers psychological strength. In short, the IE Division believed that if it used pedagogy and propaganda before, during, and after combat, American G.I.s would be better off as soldiers and citizens.[28]

For some 300,000 draftees, educational training commenced with a stint in an Army Special Training Unit literacy program. The discovery of a less than "literate America" derived from the Selective Service Administration's own examination of the draftee population and the release of confirmatory 1940 census data. Compared with previous census data, which classified as illiterate only persons with "no education whatever," the 1940 census probed further into citizens' educational backgrounds. It included the new category of functional illiterates, defined as people with fewer than four years of schooling. By expanding the definition of illiteracy in this way, the 1940 census counted 10 million Americans (and nearly 14 percent of the draftee population) as "functionally illiterate"—twice the number tallied in the 1920 census using the more restrictive definition of illiteracy.[29]

The nation's failing educational health at home boded poorly for democracy's victory abroad. The illiteracy problem crossed all regional boundaries. That the South and its black inhabitants surfaced as the nation's most educationally deprived region and people was hardly surprising. Spartan state-level funding and the lax enforcement of compulsory attendance laws in the name of Jim Crow had been the object of public scrutiny and ridicule for decades. What did surprise policymakers was the discovery that New York and Pennsylvania were home to as many functionally illiterate citizens as states south of the Mason-Dixon line. The illiteracy problem also threatened the production of war matériel and the enlistment of soldiers. As early as 1942, the U.S. Chamber of Commerce reported that half of the nation's war contractors had to reduce production because of the shortage of literate, skilled labor. Inside the army, meanwhile, the results of the Army General Classification Test (AGCT) revealed additional cause for alarm. Developed by army psychologists, the AGCT was a direct descendant of the World War I Army Alpha and Beta intelligence tests, though army officials sought to disarm their critics by describing their new multiple-choice exam as an achievement rather than intelligence test. While the difference between the two generations of exams was largely semantic, the AGCT's impact on army life was real. The War Department's insistence on "functional literacy" resulted in the rejection of some 500,000 otherwise acceptable recruits—labeled Grade V "slow learners" under the AGCT's five-tiered classification typology—during the first two years of the draft.[30]

The magnitude of the nation's illiteracy problem finally forced the army's hand. In 1943 the War Department authorized the formation of 239 Special Training Units to help Grade V recruits learn how to read at or above fourth-grade level. Some literacy instructors were pulled from the army's own ranks, but more often than not they were recruited directly from colleges and universities and lower schools. To ensure consistency from one literacy unit to another, the army organized three national training conferences to discuss instructional techniques and to distribute literacy guides. Initially the army used remaindered literacy materials from the Works Progress Administration, the Immigration and Naturalization Service, and the Civilian Conservation Corps. *Meet Private Pete: A Soldier's Reader* replaced those outmoded materials. The *Reader* was based on a functional approach to literacy that combined filmstrips with reading and writing exercises in order to connect lessons to a soldier's "daily life in the Army." The *Reader* followed the fictitious exploits of Private Pete Smith and his best friend Daffy and offered soldiers a humorous glimpse into the everyday experiences of living and working in the U.S. Army. Some Grade V's rebuffed the army's literacy training, but the overwhelming majority responded positively to it. "More than anything else," confessed one such soldier, "I want to learn how to read . . . to read letters from home . . . to know what's going on in other places . . . to read the things the other fellows do."[31]

One may reasonably question the educational value of the army's fly-by-night literacy-training experiment. Yet available evidence suggests that the army's eight-week crash course left a lasting impression on all those who experienced it. Instructors came away from the experience convinced of the educability of all citizens, regardless of race. "No great differences in learning ability between the two races were demonstrated," declared the *Journal of Negro Education*. But the best indicator of the success of the army's literacy program can be gleaned from the words of the participants. "I suge appreciate what you taught me down there, it is helpoing me in many ways," wrote a thankful recruit from Camp Blanding, Florida. A self-described "country boy" from Columbus, Ohio, had a similar experience: "When I went into the army I couldn't write . . . but as you see that I can write and by that you know that the school is Helping me." Another satisfied soldier wrote that his newfound literacy not only kept him from being prematurely discharged, it also gave him the confidence to "ask [his] wife for a divorce." A joyful parent of a recently inducted Grade V recruit contacted the executive officer of the Special Training Unit at Fort Benning, Georgia: "I thank you all for Learning My child how to read . . . I did not have time to send him to school . . . and I thank you."[32]

Few recruits who passed through Army Induction Centers during the war underwent literacy training. Introduced into basic training in June 1942, a mandatory orientation course was the usual embarkation point for the army's multilevel education program. The major aim of the program was to increase soldiers' "store of knowledge" as to why American troops were fighting in Europe and Asia. Understanding the reasons behind the conflict supposedly helped soldiers adjust more quickly to the constantly changing circumstances of global war. Failure to provide adequate knowledge about the war was cited as a key explanation for the significant increase in soldier neuropsychiatric breakdowns, which according to one report, were running 60 percent higher than during World War I when, explained an army official, soldiers "fought from fixed positions, in trenches," and could get acclimated to their surroundings. "In this war," he continued, "our men are constantly on the offensive. They fight in the open. . . . They keep moving all the time. They must keep on fighting; only until they have won a campaign can there be a let-up." As the first phase of the IE Division's education agenda, the orientation program provided new soldiers with educational and political indoctrination that military leaders hoped would ease adjustment difficulties caused by the war's constantly shifting geopolitical landscape.[33]

The orientation program developed over a period of several years, at first employing only civilian speakers and films. Based on Research Branch findings, however, the army determined that the most successful course format employed a combination of film and lecture or film supplemented by an open question-and-answer session. After various configurations of the orientation course were tested in the field, the final iteration of the program was composed of five parts: introductory phase, consisting of seven orientation films; current phase, including war information tailored to the particular needs of individual regiments; film program, addressing strategic, economic, and social issues, anchored by the *Why We Fight* film series; newsmap, a map detailing the prosecution of the war effort; and lecture series, informational presentations delivered by military experts for purposes of group discussion. As part of the orientation program, taught in classrooms outfitted with chalkboards, desks, and textbooks, every soldier received an orientation course kit and participated in sessions led by full-time orientation and education officers trained at the army's School for Special Service at Washington and Lee University in Lexington, Virginia.[34]

Special Service officers matriculated from the army's officer and enlisted ranks. Training included 192 hours of course instruction in everything from "athletics and training" to "information and education" to "military training and tactics." The War Department's program of instruction for IE personnel recommended that all Special Service officers possess "a deep conviction of the cause for which we fight, and the importance of the role of individual" and "be college graduates with backgrounds of training and experience in such fields as teaching, educational administration, government, international relations, [and] law." In reality, most of the army's fifty-five hundred Special Service officers were simply college graduates.[35]

Professional credentials mattered less in the field. Once deployed, officers used the *Guide to the Use of Information Materials*, the army's official orientation manual. According to the *Guide*, an officer's major objective was to provide soldiers with information on the progress of the war "fairly, dispassionately, and with full emphasis on its military significance to the armed forces of the U.S. and its allies." The primary function of the officer, who performed the role of a news anchor, was to transmit "facts." The scripted replies to soldiers' questions were veiled in idealized democratic language that stressed core if not fully realized American principles such as equality, freedom, and individualism. When questioned about issues of race relations in the U.S. Army, for example, the orientation officer was instructed to reply that "problems of race are a proper concern . . . so far as they affect the efficiency of the Army, no more, no less." If the officer was pressed on the issue of America's Jim Crow army, the *Guide* instructed him to add: "To contribute by act or word toward the increase of misunderstanding, suspicion, and tension between people of different racial or national origin in this country or among our Allies is to help the enemy." On the military's pronounced wartime role in a society hostile to statist decision making, officers were encouraged to articulate the U.S. tradition of small government and individual liberty by reminding soldiers that the "Army and Navy consider themselves the servants of the State and not its masters."[36]

While the *Guide* provided officers with canned responses, the military recognized that the mere presentation of facts in the absence of open discussion would not suffice for citizens accustomed to robust and unmediated verbal exchange. When prepared responses failed to satisfy soldiers' questions, orientation officers were encouraged to move off script and to use the facts about the war "as a basis for the understanding of ideas." The *Guide*'s first section began with a discussion of truth and falsehood: "To speak of truth is not enough. . . . A truth need not only be well-rounded, but the utterance of it should take account of the stresses and objectives of the moment. Truth becomes falsehood unless it has the strength of perspective." A significant development in the instructional design of the orientation program was the army's acceptance that officers needed to engage recruits in open rather than closed discussion. As in classrooms in the civilian sphere, even seemingly incontrovertible information was open for debate and discussion between teachers and students.[37]

The use of education in the maintenance of soldiers' mental health continued after basic training. It was widely accepted that initial orientation programs were more effective when followed with educational instruction close to the battlefronts in overseas camps and bases. Launched in April 1942, the U.S.

Armed Forces Institute (USAFI) correspondence program was operated jointly by the University of Wisconsin and the military with the assistance of eighty-five colleges and universities and for-profit correspondence schools. Following the approval of their commanding officers, for a nominal fee of two dollars soldiers could choose from more than seven hundred different courses offered in the USAFI course catalog, *What Would You Like to Learn?* Fields of study ranged from foreign languages to calculus, from shorthand to cost accounting, and from biology to American history. In electrical and mechanical fields, thirty-six courses were offered, while steam engineering, automobile and airplane maintenance and repair, plumbing, and steam fitting were a few of the trade courses provided. By every measure, the USAFI was one of the "largest educational endeavors ever undertaken in this country."[38]

Correspondence study accommodated the varied interests and aptitudes of the modern globe-trotting soldier. The USAFI provided two different types of correspondence courses at the high school and college levels. The first type was geared to soldiers in theaters of war with reliable postal service, where regular and rapid contact with instructors was possible. In these traditional correspondence courses, many of which were simply pulled from existing university offerings, soldiers worked closely with professors via the mail. Because many soldiers were located in theaters without efficient mail service, the USAFI educators also developed a second set of "self-teaching" courses that minimized the need for instructor contact.[39]

The USAFI's self-teaching courses permitted soldiers stationed in remote Accra, British West Africa, to set up their own student-run Army Training Center and design their own customized curriculum. At first, courses were offered in algebra, analytic and plane geometry, art, French, and German. Following the distribution of an educational survey, however, courses in college algebra, English, and Fanti (a West African dialect) were added to the curriculum. Soldiers taught many of the courses themselves in an unused officers' barrack, which housed two large classrooms, four small classrooms, a laboratory, several storerooms, and a music studio with a piano.[40]

Although the USAFI's academic offerings exceeded the needs of the army's collegiate-grade soldiers, what most men wanted was hands-on vocational training. "What I desire," wrote one soldier to the USAFI registrar, "is a course of study on some practical vocation which will assist me to earn a living, in the event of future discharge from the U.S. armed forces." Other soldiers were less certain as to what they could or should study. "Any suggestions for study are sincerely appreciated," wrote a sailor aboard the USS *Dale*. "Because of the limited time on a wartime destroyer, the most of this opportunity must be made." It is not known if either of those servicemen was among the 1.25 million students to enroll with USAFI; if he did, he had to complete and pass fifteen increasingly difficult individual lessons before sitting for a USAFI subject examination. This graduated course format afforded even mediocre students the opportunity to advance and achieve. For students talented enough to complete the required battery of courses and exams, the award of vocational certification or high school or college credit was all but guaranteed.[41]

Yet the academic strengths of "Foxhole U" were routinely undermined by individual and administrative weaknesses. Especially in overseas theaters, shortages of texts and class materials, compounded by soldiers' fleeting interest, compromised the USAFI's efforts. Not all soldiers were up to the task of fighting and learning. Adding a regional twist to the old dog-ate-my-homework excuse, an antiaircraft battery sergeant stationed in the Caribbean blamed his lack of academic progress on hungry "tropical insects": "[They] ate up all my papers," he wrote, "while I wasn't lookin' out." Additionally, the USAFI's administrative reach often exceeded its grasp. Initially, program administrators circulated texts mainly in the continental United States. As the American war effort widened to a global scale, interest in correspondence study grew rapidly, posing the challenge of shipping texts internationally. To expedite course delivery, the USAFI organized distribution centers in all nine major theaters of war, which managed to keep most of the international locations stocked with texts and materials. Still, education officers complained that soldiers' demand continually outstripped supply. "I am still somewhat confused over the plan of distribution of correspondence courses," remarked an overwhelmed education officer stationed in Brisbane, Australia. "This week we are initiating a requisition for text material for certain courses which, our first six weeks of registration indicate, will be exhausted by the time this requisition can be filled."[42]

Despite significant setbacks, soldiers exhibited creativity in completing assignments. A soldier submitting his homework quipped: "Red ink has not been used on these reports as I do not have any available and the local fox hole does not carry it in stock." Other soldiers used tin can labels and scrap paper to write on. But the most severe obstacle facing soldier-students was enemy attack. "It's awful hard to get time to do the work," admitted a soldier stationed at the Anzio beachhead in Italy. "I get into my foxhole at night, and by pulling a blanket over it and using a bit of candle, I get some work done. But when Jerry comes over, bombing and strafing, I must say my mind's not on my lesson." Although experiences with the USAFI varied widely, soldiers' interest in education was undeniable. Indeed, many G.I.s shared the excitement of one soldier stationed in Fort Jackson, South Carolina, who saw correspondence study as a tool for both self-improvement and national service: "If you have a course in mathematics, I would be interested in same, and a word of advice on my prospects of advancing myself, and at the same time being of more service to my country."[43]

As the end of war drew near, the army shifted gears to prepare soldiers for the readjustment to civilian life. Army officials speculated that after the war, soldiers would pass through "three psychological stages": celebration, letdown, and restoration. A War Department memo anticipated that symptoms would be especially acute among American prisoners of war, the majority of whom suffered from "significant psychological or attitudinal disturbances which make subsequent adjustment difficult." Experience demonstrated, however, that without an adequate substitute for combat, cases of desertion and soldier insubordination increased greatly, even among seemingly normal soldiers. Just as it had throughout the war, the army looked to education to ward off chronic soldier "let-down."[44]

The Army Education Program's (AEP) Post-Hostility Schools were organized to provide service personnel with educational opportunities throughout demobilization—the final phase of service prior to reentering civilian life. Army officials considered demobilization a critical aspect of the war effort. The Post-Hostility Schools were charged with providing all high school–educated soldiers an opportunity to enroll in courses that military leaders believed would boost soldier morale and prepare them for the inevitable emotional stresses of coming home. AEP administrators helped place several thousand specially qualified and ambitious soldiers in three-month courses at elite European institutions such as Oxford, Cambridge, and the Sorbonne. The overwhelming majority of the AEP's 500,000 participants, however, attended one of the IE Division's two thousand hastily organized but serviceable schools in England, France, Austria, and the Philippines. To ease this undertaking, the army produced 171 customized USAFI general education course curricula that covered everything from agricultural and technical to business fields. These courses were not intended to prepare the soldier solely for life as a worker but also, according to the IE Division, for life as a "citizen . . . with his own needs and interests." The program grew so quickly and was received so well that the IE Division Education Branch was forced to train an additional twenty-five thousand men as supervisors and instructors and to produce some 4 million textbooks covering 179 topics in less than 6 months.[45]

The apex of the AEP Post-Hostility School program was the organization of four Army University Centers at Shrivenham, England, and Biarritz, France, in the European theater; at Florence, Italy, in the Mediterranean theater; and at Oahu, Hawaii, in the Pacific theater. Where the army's other postwar schools relied on available USAFI courses and the initiative of individual soldiers, the administration of the Army University Centers involved the coordinated efforts of American higher education, the IE Division, and the War Department. One-half of the Army University Centers' faculty was pulled from the ranks of the standing army. The remaining instructors were civilian professors from American colleges and universities. These scholars were handpicked by Paul Packer, dean of education at the University of Iowa, and transported to France, England, and Italy on the *Queen Elizabeth* and *Queen Mary* ocean liners in the summer of 1945. Packer used *Who's Who in America* to select approximately three hundred professors to teach at the Army University Centers. Scholars populated seven academic divisions—agriculture, commerce, education, engineering, fine arts, journalism, and the liberal arts and sciences—and taught

Figure 4.2. U.S. soldiers fallout at the conclusion of opening ceremonies at the Florence Army University Center, Florence, Italy, September 7, 1945. The Army Information and Education Division operated four university centers—in the European, Mediterranean, and Pacific theaters—during demobilization. Courtesy George C. Marshall Research Library, Lexington, Virginia.

412 different courses. The only admission requirement was a high school diploma, which allowed soldiers to matriculate from all branches of the army. From Potsdam, President Harry S. Truman wired a "hearty congratulations" to mark the opening of the Shrivenham Army University Center and predicted that "thousands of our American soldiers will take advantage of the splendid educational opportunities provided." Truman was right. According to army estimates, thirty-five thousand American service personnel and hundreds of their Allied counterparts attended the Army University Centers in 1945–46, their sole year of operation.[46]

For professors and G.I.s, the experience seemed like a fitting end to a grueling war. Faculty at the Florence Army University Center claimed the students were the best they had ever taught. "The present students are more mature than the average college man," gushed one professor. "If I can get a student body like this one when I return to the States, life will be one long rest!" Faculty peppered courses with guest lecturers and day-trips to some of Italy's most storied locales. Classes in mineralogy and geology took trips to the Tyrolean Alps and Mount Vesuvius. The Florentine Observatory, where Galileo Galilei studied, was available to students enrolled in the introductory astronomy class. The department of physical sciences made good use of the Institute of Geology and Paleontology and its world-renowned collection of fossils. Education students, meanwhile, visited the original Pestalozzi School, the seedbed of the modern American kindergarten movement. A library in excess of ten thousand volumes—augmented by the substantial English-language collections at the nearby University of Florence and the national library—was cobbled together to assist students in completing their assignments.[47]

The campus life of the Florence Army University Center differed little from that of any American college. For starters, military regulations were kept to a minimum. Neither saluting nor the wearing of army uniforms was required except during the two mandatory military formations each week. Journalism students kept the university community informed with the publication of the *USCollegian*, the weekly campus newspaper. A student council was established to lobby the academic administration for better food and transportation alternatives, more sight-seeing tours and grading options. A Tuesday night lecture series featured outstanding faculty and guest speakers. The Florence Symphony Orchestra—disbanded during the war and reconstituted by the head of the music department, Robert Lawrence, a graduate of the Juilliard School and former *New York Herald Tribune* music critic—performed several concerts for the university and greater Florentine community. A full slate of intramural sport competitions was held at a nearby outdoor swimming pool and athletic stadium, dubbed the "Spaghetti Bowl" by the university's students.[48]

In other ways the Florence Army University Center was far more socially progressive than most American colleges of the time. While the majority of soldier-students were white Christian males, Jewish, African American, and Japanese American students, along with more than one hundred Women's Army Corps (WAC) members, also attended the institution. Indeed, the student council chairmanship was in succession occupied by a Japanese American, Private Isamu S. Aoki of the 442nd Regimental Combat Team, and an African American, Sergeant Harold Brown; the first student council secretary was a WAC, Technical Sergeant Jennie Kraft; and at the closing ceremonies, the outstanding athletic leader award was given to a black student from Cincinnati, Ohio, Sergeant Willard Stargel, "amid prolonged applause." It may be too much to believe that the soldier-students at the Florence Army University Center exhibited "little or no evidence of racial prejudice," as one observer claimed; but it does seem likely that the university's experiment in interracial coeducation helped students learn "to respect each other." To be sure, rounding out their tour of duty at an army university was the chance of a lifetime for many G.I.s. "The most wonderful thing has happened to me in the Army," recalled an alumnus of the Florence Army University Center, Sergeant Charles M. Northrup, of Pisgah, Iowa. Sergeant L. Laverty of the Air Corps wholeheartedly agreed: "The four weeks I spent was the best deal I ever had in the Army and all the other GIs attending the school thought so too."[49]

"I Am Deeply Concerned over the Physical and Emotional Condition of Men Returning from the War": The G.I. Bill and the Future of Democratic Citizenship

The abrupt end to the war and the decision to demobilize the European and Mediterranean theaters of operation rapidly prevented the AEP from realizing its full potential as the main vessel for soldiers' readjustment. For that, the American people, veterans, and government looked to the newly passed Servicemen's Readjustment Act of 1944—better known as the G.I. Bill of Rights.

With 2.5 million individuals discharged from military service for psychological deficiency—nearly 20 percent of whom were diagnosed with severe neuropsychiatric disabilities—the state considered the eradication of soldier maladjustment a pressing national security matter. Questions about the stability of the economy and the emotional health of returning soldiers dogged policymakers and civilians alike. Wartime opinion polls highlighted widespread anxiety about the postwar economy: 70 percent of Americans expected to be worse off after the war; 60 percent anticipated lower wages; and 75 percent expected fewer jobs. A January 1945 *Fortune* poll showed that a majority of Americans expected another major economic depression to hit within a decade. *Fortune*'s sobering finding was confirmed by a cross-sectional IE Division Research Branch study that revealed one-half of all soldiers believed the biggest challenge facing them after the war would be "the problem of earning a living." One soldier envisioned a future of "ditch digging and bread lines." Another soldier echoed that sentiment and forecast "another depression" and imagined "11 million apple salesmen" trying to eke out a postwar existence.[50]

In addition to earning a living, soldiers also worried about "making a mental readjustment to civilian life". 15 percent of the Research Branch's sample population believed that they would have "difficulty in settling down, getting over the restlessness, adjusting to a steady job, or getting over the mental effects of the war." One respondent thought he would have trouble "getting along with other people." Another soldier thought it was going to be difficult to "adjust . . . to the living customs of civilian life" and thought that it might be hard to get "familiar with the changes in the U.S. and my family and friends" since leaving for war. Many soldiers divulged more intimate concerns about the prospects of readjustment to civilian life: 10 percent of the men surveyed "expected to face marital, familial, or sexual problems of some sort" following their return home.[51] Mental health experts and popular pundits exacerbated soldiers' private fears and contributed to the public's growing concern. In his popular 1944 tome to the returning soldier, *The Veteran Comes Back*, the Columbia University sociologist Willard Waller expected American soldiers to return home "bitter," "angry," and incapable of resuming life as self-sufficient and responsible adults. What is more, "not one community in ten," observed the psychologist Alanson H. Edgerton in *Readjustment or Revolution?* "has anything approaching an adequately developed program of adjustment services." These experts predicted that lingering effects of warfare would disrupt the emotional reconnection of husbands and wives, fathers and children, possibly resulting in the spread of sexual "perversions," such as homosexuality and pedophilia.[52]

War Department self-help manuals reinforced pervasive public doubt. One such publication was the National Research Council's veterans' demobilization guide *Psychology for the Returning Serviceman*, a copy of which was provided to every soldier. In the area of parenting, for example, *Psychology for the Returning Serviceman* instructed veteran-fathers to present a balanced, well-adjusted persona to their children. In its own words: "In general, there are two conditions which lead a boy to give up the inclination to be like his father: (1) When his father is too tough and (2) when his father is too weak or ineffectual." The former parenting approach promised rebellion while the latter promised effeminacy. Only by striking a middle ground between authoritarian and permissive parenting could a veteran-father reasonably expect to succeed at the arduous task of raising a healthy, well-adjusted son. Other expert prognoses were even less sanguine. Feeling like a "stranger" to his family and friends, the returning veteran, insisted psychologist Carl Rogers, would retreat from his family in disgust, buried beneath the "deep anger and hatred that has . . . been smoldering within."[53] Harvard president James B. Conant, chair of the National Defense Research Committee and a major architect of the Manhattan Project, added to the sense of worry. In the pages of the *Atlantic Monthly* he warned that an improperly handled demobilization could "sow the seeds of a civil war."[54] Even President Roosevelt voiced concerns over the safe return and emotional welfare of American soldiers. "I am deeply concerned over the physical and emotional condition of men returning from the war," Roosevelt wrote in a letter to Secretary of War Stimson. "I wish you," he continued, "to insure that no overseas casualty is discharged until he has received the maximum benefits of hospitalization, psychological rehabilitation, and resocialization."[55]

Veterans' benefits proposals emanated from multiple venues. The American Legion and its key supporters in the Veterans Administration focused on arming federal veterans' legislation with the traditional material bounty and employment preferences embedded in past provisions. Although the Roosevelt administration supported that benefit package, it also wanted to add an education provision. President Roosevelt created two committees to study the education and training needs of the nation. The first committee was housed in the National Resources Planning Board (NRPB), but that report never saw the light of day. Congressional conservatives terminated the NRPB, along with its education study, in the closing months of 1943. A second committee chaired by Frederick H. Osborn, director of the IE Division, flew under the anti–New Dealers' radar. Its proposal, *The Armed Forces Committee on Postwar Educational Opportunities for Service Personnel*, also known as the Osborn Committee Report, was delivered to the president in July 1943.[56]

The Osborn Report served as the basis of the Servicemen's Education and Training Act, the first bill introduced in Congress regarding veterans' education benefits. Senator Elbert Thomas (D-UT), chair of the Senate Committee on Education and Labor, sponsored hearings on the would-be education act, which the American Legion subsequently expanded.[57] During the initial Thomas hearings, however, policymakers defended the veterans' education plan as it had been presented in the Osborn Report and voiced rationales that would be echoed in subsequent policy debates: first, that the nation needed a plan to make up for the deficit of college graduates caused by the war; and, second, the plan would serve as a crucial part of the government's postwar national security strategy. This was an argument for federal education policy that would endure long after World War II. "We are fighting Germany and Japan and Italy and we don't want those systems to come here," cautioned Senator Thomas. The likelihood of political instability and emotional disturbance, he said, increased as long as a veteran "is just a veteran . . . and nothing else."[58]

The quest for a capacious national security strategy alluded to by Senator Thomas in the Capitol received a much stronger public endorsement from President Roosevelt in his State of the Union Address just weeks later, on January 11, 1944. In this famous speech, Roosevelt professed his support for a "Second Bill of Rights under which a new basis of security and prosperity can be established for all—regardless of station, race, or creed." Roosevelt, looking ahead to a prosperous postwar period of audacious government action, enumerated a lengthy list of "rights" to be enjoyed by all Americans—chief among them, a right to "a useful and remunerative job"; "to earn enough to provide adequate food and clothing"; "a decent home"; "adequate medical care"; "adequate protection from the economic fears of old age, sickness, accident, and unemployment"; and, not least of all, "the right to a good education."[59]

The political barriers to this "Second Bill of Rights" were simply too high. But the categorical assistance provided to veterans under the bill of rights that Congress did pass—the G.I. Bill of Rights—nevertheless had profound policy effects then and after the war. In a departure from previous legislation that emphasized cash bonuses and survivors' pensions, usually granted to veterans or their dependents decades after returning from battle, the 1944 G.I. Bill awarded ex-soldiers immediate and comprehensive benefits covering their emotional, educational, and financial security. Signed by Roosevelt on June 22, 1944, the bill contained provisions that covered counseling, disability, and unemployment, promised up to four years of college, and provided generous low-interest

Figure 4.3. Encircled by members of the Senate and House and leaders from the American Legion and Veterans of Foreign Wars, President Franklin D. Roosevelt signs the Servicemen's Readjustment Act of 1944, better known as the G.I. Bill of Rights, June 22, 1944. Copyright Bettmann/CORBIS.

loans for financing homes, farms, and businesses. Approximately half of the nation's 16 million veterans pursued education or training under the G.I. Bill; 2.2 million did so at the college or university level. Additionally, 5.4 million veterans made use of the $20 per week unemployment insurance, while 3.8 million took advantage of the home and business loan provision.[60]

The G.I. Bill changed the way the state and its citizens thought about one another in the postwar period. This was seen especially in regard to higher education, which quickly emerged as one of the institutional embodiments of the G.I. Bill. With an estimated 1.5 million college-student school years lost to military service, and with national enrollment stuck at half its prewar level, a record windfall of veterans on college campuses precipitated an unparalleled period of expansion in American higher education. In 1947–48 veterans totaled nearly 50 percent of college students nationwide. At the University of Michigan, for example, better than half of the 20,000 undergraduates were veterans, and by 1949 nearly 2.5 million Americans were in college—1 million more students than in any single year prior to World War II.[61]

Though several university presidents agreed with Robert M. Hutchins, president of the University of Chicago, who predicted that returning soldiers would

Figure 4.4. Scenes such as this one at North Carolina State University in 1948 were replayed at campuses across the country after World War II. "Joe College" embodied the hope and promise of psychologically adjusted democratic citizenship deep into the cold war. Courtesy University Archives Photograph Collections, Special Collections Research Center, North Carolina State University Libraries, Raleigh, North Carolina.

turn American colleges into "hobo jungles," nothing of the sort occurred.[62] Rather, by most accounts veteran students in many ways improved the quality of American higher learning. Veterans were older, often married with children, and eschewed the high-jinks and "rah-rah" behavior characteristic of their younger peers. They dismissed Greek life as well as the traditions of in loco parentis, providing ample evidence that the American college was a place for "adults" as well as "children." Traditional undergraduates complained about the seriousness with which veterans approached their educations. "All they care about is their school work," fumed an exasperated undergraduate. "They're grinds, every one of them. It's books, books all the time." College administrators thought otherwise. They credited veterans for helping to cultivate a more rigorous and disciplined academic and social culture—a few even went so far as to proclaim them the "best" single cohort of students ever enrolled in American higher education.[63] By the turn of the twenty-first century, this heroic narrative was not only etched in stone, but also permeated popular culture and academic histories. Books, films and miniseries all celebrated the G.I.-Bill-wielding veteran as the heart and soul of America's so-called "greatest generation."[64]

While the G.I. Bill certainly was great for many white male veterans—the quintessential "adjusted" citizen—the legislation had a far more modest impact on other segments of the veteran population. By design the means-test for accessing the G.I. Bill was simple: a minimum of ninety days of continuous service and a discharge other than a dishonorable one. These criteria automatically barred dishonorably discharged homosexual veterans. Nothing on paper made the systematic exclusion of African Americans and females a foregone conclusion, but the G.I. Bill's decentralized administrative structure combined with entrenched, often legal discriminatory practices by banks and colleges prevented millions of Americans from tapping the benefits due them. Although many women enjoyed the privileges of the G.I. Bill by way of marriage, fewer than 3 percent of all female veterans actually made use of the legislation in their own name. And African-American veterans found the G.I. Bill's rewards still more elusive. To preserve their segregated racial order, southern Democrats fought mightily—at one point threatening to altogether derail the legislation—in order to ensure that the Veterans Administration disbursed G.I. Bill home and business loans and educational aid through private lending agencies and semiautonomous higher education institutions and training centers. This decentralized administrative approach reinforced bigoted appraisal practices in the North and South, and prevented all but the most determined African-American veterans from receiving the federally insured loans promised them. An *Ebony* study highlighted the near-insurmountable challenges of this localized distribution model, discovering that black veterans in thirteen Mississippi cities only secured 2 of the 3,229 loans approved by the Veterans Administration during the summer of 1947. One observer, himself a black veteran, commented, "To Negro veterans in Mississippi getting a G.I. loan is similar to seeking the 'The Holy Grail.'"[65]

College going proved equally challenging for black veterans. Inadequate preparatory training and racist college admission systems largely prevented African-American veterans from enrolling in the nation's elite schools, forcing them instead to pursue their educational aspirations at vocational schools or at historically black institutions of higher learning. Unfortunately, the country's small network of black colleges and universities was unprepared for the flood of veteran applicants, and an estimated twenty thousand African-American veterans were denied admission because of the lack of institutional capacity. In spite of these obstacles, and in large part thanks to the G.I. Bill, African-American colleges, consistent with the experiences of other higher education institutions, achieved double-digit enrollment increases in the postwar period, educating a record seventy-five thousand students in 1950. Many African-American veterans returned from the war convinced higher learning was necessary for full democratic citizenship.[66]

For psychological and economic reasons, state policymakers and academic leaders agreed veterans should be granted special educational opportunities as a reward for their wartime service. But soldiers were not the only Americans who served and sacrificed during the war. On the home front, the state asked Americans not only to endure the absence and death of loved ones, but also to tolerate rationing, price and wage controls, and tax increases that exacted their own emotional and financial toll. For the most part the civilian population willingly obliged the state's various demands: families planted "victory gardens," bought war bonds, curbed gasoline use, cut back on common household consumables, and deprived themselves of personal fineries, including silk and cotton. These may have been trivial burdens in comparison to those experienced by most soldiers, but that did not prevent many civilians from exiting the war convinced that they had contributed to victory and now deserved their fair share of the spoils. "Americans," one historian has concluded, "had begun during the war to look to the federal government for guarantees of growing economic opportunity, not just rescue from the Depression."[67]

In this respect the G.I. Bill proved vitally important as a policy touchstone. It whetted Americans' appetite for education and cemented a reciprocal relationship between higher education and the state that irrevocably altered both institutions in a number of ways over the course of the following decades. First, the state made both active duty education programming and the G.I. Bill permanent policy tools. Subsequent incarnations of the G.I. Bill were less bountiful. But the reformulation of military service as an extension of civilian life—replete with material and educational entitlements for service personnel—endured and permanently changed the way the U.S. armed services marketed themselves to America's young men and women. Not even the debacle of the Vietnam War, which seriously tested the state's commitment to its veterans, came close to undermining higher education's role in sustaining the citizen-soldier tradition forged in the crucible of World War II.[68]

Second, the state extended the promise of the G.I. Bill of Rights by helping elevate higher education as a right of democratic citizenship independent of military service. Policy statements crafted by the Truman administration played a pivotal role in this development. In 1947 the historic publication of the widely influential *To Secure These Rights: The Report of the President's Committee on Civil Rights* provided one of the most devastating indictments ever of racial inequality in America. The committee demanded that the federal government vigorously act to guarantee all Americans' right to safety and security, to freedom of conscience and expression, to equality of opportunity—that is, to full democratic citizenship and its privileges. The report described the persistence of racial segregation and discrimination, not only in the South but everywhere, as beyond shameful, describing in painful detail the moral, economic, and international costs of America's "history of bigotry."[69] The committee challenged the federal government to protect racial minorities against "the crime of lynching"[70] and to end discrimination in voting and employment, in housing and military service, and not least of all, in education. Here the report highlighted citizens' right to education—including higher education—as a core recommendation. Equal educational opportunity had long been a demand of civil rights activists, but their traditional focus had been on equalizing elementary and secondary rather than higher education. *To Secure These Rights* changed that.[71]

Only weeks after the release of the civil rights report, the President's Commission on Higher Education unveiled *Higher Education for American Democracy*, which advanced the state's growing claim on higher education policymaking in the postwar era. The Truman Report, as it was often called, offered a bold defense of higher education as important for the psychosocial development of the individual, for a more robust and informed public sphere, for international understanding, and for creative solutions to the nation's and the world's most vexing problems. The report reaffirmed the call of the Committee on Civil Rights for an end to segregated colleges, universities, and professional schools. And it also endorsed a bevy of other federal initiatives, including a national program of scholarships and fellowships, direct financial support for campus building projects, a new cabinet-level Department of Education, greater support of adult education, and a doubling of the nation's higher education enrollment (to nearly 5 million) within the decade.[72]

With the exception of desegregating the military, which occurred via executive order in 1948, the other promises listed in the civil rights and higher education reports remained unfulfilled until the 1960s. Even so, the egalitarian message embedded in both documents (along with the creation of the National Science Foundation in 1950) helped put higher education on the nation's political agenda in a most visible way. The belief that millions more Americans—white and black, young and old—were not only deserving but capable of at least some advanced study fueled widespread interest in the so-called "democratization" of higher education during the 1950s. The continued growth of college enrollments, the steady expansion of the junior college sector, and the introduction of educational television suggested that the government was serious about equalizing educational opportunities for all. Meanwhile, participation in the United Nations Educational, Scientific, and Cultural Organization (UNESCO) and the government's enactment of the Fulbright educational exchange program, the Point IV Program, and other broadly construed academic exchange programs revealed that the state and higher education were interested in exporting America's educational expertise to the rest of the world. By the close of World War II, American higher education had become democracy's proving ground.

But higher education was not equipped to address all veterans' adjustment challenges. That required additional state action in the form of the National Mental Health Act of 1946. The return of at least 500,000 severely mentally ill veterans, for whom educational therapy would never alone suffice, suggested that the country's dilapidated clinical care infrastructure needed to be fortified with better facilities and more practitioners.[73] William Menninger certainly believed that the psychiatric profession's battlefield victories more than justified an expanded peacetime role. "It is vividly apparent," said Menninger, reflecting on the psychiatric profession's wartime service, "that psychiatry can and must play a much more important role in the solution of health problems of the civilian."[74] The NMHA reflected Menninger's therapeutic hubris. It placed a premium on preventive treatments rather than chronic custodial care, obligating the federal government to undertake all necessary steps for the "improvement of the mental health of the people of the United States through the conducting of researches, investigations, experiments, and demonstrations relating to the cause, diagnosis, and treatment of psychiatric disorders." With a $30 million budget for programming and research, the NMHA helped university medical schools revise their medical curricula and train more mental health personnel. It also allotted the National Institutes of Mental Health (NIMH), formed in 1949, a matching grant budget of $7.5 million for dispersal to the several states for the construction of outpatient clinics. Critical as each of these provisions turned out to be, according to one leading scholar on the subject, the NMHA's long-term significance lay in its sweeping mandate which effectively conferred responsibility to the federal government for the emotional health of all Americans. Together the G.I. Bill and the NMHA affirmed the state's commitment to psychologically adjusted democratic citizenship in the postwar period.[75]

Finally, the state's vigorous promotion of higher education as a right of democratic citizenship paved the way for the redefinition and expansion of the obligations associated with that citizenship. This was embodied in the reauthorization of the conscription activities of the Selective Service Administration in 1948. Fearful that a renewed draft would again deplete the nation's intellectual reserves, educational leaders and federal policymakers secured support for generous student deferments to ensure the continued growth and prosperity of the nation's higher education sector. By equating educational service and military service, policymakers converted collegiate study into a new weapon of the nation's defense arsenal. "If America is to have a chance of winning an all-out war with Russia," stated one policymaker, "it must plan on the most effective use of its brainpower, for in manpower it is greatly outnumbered." Not everyone agreed with this assessment, and until the armed services moved to an all-volunteer force, in 1973, student deferments remained as divisive as the continuation of the draft itself. But, at the time the deferment program was implemented, there was little doubt among policymakers that American brains had helped to win the war and to secure the peace. In the span of a few years, American higher education had become a stronghold of democracy, an arbiter of citizenship, and a key institution of the emerging cold war national security state.[76]

❖❖❖

By the early years of the cold war, citizens and state policymakers agreed, albeit for different reasons, that education created prosperous, politically astute, and psychologically adjusted citizens. For the state, education produced the citizens it most wanted to have; for soldiers and veterans—especially white males—education provided a gateway to full citizenship and its attendant benefits. The university's capacity to synthesize citizens capable of coping with the interrelated political, economic, and psychological demands of cold war citizenship resonated with key opinion leaders and millions of Americans. World War II placed higher education at the center of American citizenship.

Yet the mere crafting of state education policy before and after the G.I. Bill did not inevitably lead to the twin revolutions in American higher education and democratic citizenship. Elite policymakers may have brought the state and higher education together, but it took common citizens in uncommon times to ensure that higher education would remain a core mediator between citizens and the state in the decades that followed.

Chapter 5

Educating Global Citizens in the Cold War

———————— ❖❖❖ ————————

In *The Vital Center* (1949), Harvard history professor and liberal activist Arthur Schlesinger Jr. predicted the high-stakes global dimensions of the cold war precluded resolution by conventional military means. According to Schlesinger, the combined destructive capacity of the Russian and American militaries ensured that the standoff between "free" and "totalitarian" societies would likely be won nonmilitarily, by the combatant most adept at winning the battle for the "minds and hearts of men." As the principal national institution responsible for shaping citizens' hearts and minds during the cold war, American higher education served as a vital mediating institution between citizens and the state, and as a vital weapon in the worldwide struggle against the spread of communism.[1]

Toughened up by World War II, higher education seemed ready for a new fight. This time the challenge was arguably greater than it had been in World War II. In that war the focus had been on the education of soldiers. The global dimensions of the cold war, however, expanded higher education's responsibility to encompass the education of civilians, too. In the battle for world supremacy, in which communists were allegedly plotting to overthrow America, and political radicalization was diagnosed as a psychological malady, educating the entire public to "duck and cover" as well as to "stand up and fight" was considered absolutely necessary for national survival.

By examining the state-academic partnership's effort to educate democratic citizens on and off campus, at home and around the globe, this chapter challenges the existing understanding of the cold war university. While previous studies have focused on the rise of McCarthyism, the rapid institutionalization of the federal-academic research matrix, or both, this chapter adds two new dimensions to that story. First, it explores how the global scale of the bipolar cold war drove the state to create a robust educational foreign policy to contain Soviet communism abroad. Second, it explores how the state's use of education abroad shaped the development of higher education at home, even before the National Defense Education Act of 1958. In each instance the goal was the same: to mold public opinion in order to help the United States win the cold war.

Policymakers and the general public tracked public opinion—an aggregate measure of citizens' psychological adjustment—with rapt intensity throughout the cold war. The quest for an enlightened public consensus had preoccupied presidents and college leaders since the nation's founding. But it was not until World War II that the technologies and sampling techniques employed by polling experts were reliable enough to aid the policymaking process. Opinion polling offered policymakers ready access to citizens' political beliefs in a way that not only enhanced democracy but also respected the American polity's preference for an unobtrusive central government. The scale and scope of the government was of particular concern during the cold war, when fears that America really might be turning into a "garrison state" loomed larger than ever.[2]

The belief that opinion polling could be used as a link between citizens and the state, and that educated citizens aided Washington decision makers, kept the pressure on American higher education. Studies of the relationship between attitudes and opinions, and between opinions and the state's prosecution of the cold war, indicated time and again that educated citizens represented democracy's best hope to make the world safe for freedom. The need for an informed public was captured well by cold warrior–philosopher Sidney Hook. "A democratic society," he said, "relies on the educational process to impart the knowledge and strengthen the values that sustain faith in freedom and promote wise decision on matters affecting the public welfare."[3] Educational elites had always believed that their institution trained democratic citizens of the first rank, free of self-interest, open minded, and wise. But during the cold war that belief spread far and wide as federal policymakers, college leaders, foundation officers, and corporate chiefs joined together to remake American higher education into a global institution, and to make the education of informed citizens a top priority.[4]

This mission took on new urgency during the McCarthy hysteria of the early 1950s when the fear of radical politics gripped the nation. Not only were communists allegedly embedded in the federal government, as McCarthy recklessly accused, they were also apparently serving in the armed forces. Fantastical accounts of the communist "brainwashing" of American G.I.s in Korea pointed to gaping chinks in the nation's psychological armor. If twenty-one U.S. soldiers captured in Korea could "turn commie," the American people wondered, was anybody really safe? The simultaneous publication of large-scale social scientific investigations into the nature of racial discrimination suggested right-wing political radicalization represented an equally grave threat to democracy's "vital center." Studies of brainwashed soldiers and of southern bigots seemingly offered conclusive evidence that educational deprivation caused political radicalization, and that educational interventions could prevent that radicalization.

The "problem" of political radicalization turned out to be more easily diagnosed than cured. Higher education's effort to create informed and centered citizens—whether in a college classroom or a local discussion group, or studying abroad or watching educational television from the comfort of home—generated erratic results. In all these different venues, most students showed little interest in cold war politics. Their private experiences commonly differed with officials' stated aims. "The average freshman doesn't know much about current affairs," grumbled one observer. "He can't name any specific provisions of the Taft-Hartley Bill . . . he never heard of the Politburo . . . or such public figures as Kenneth C. Royall or Karl Compton. In fact, his aloofness from such day-to-day affairs is exceeded only by that of the upperclassmen."[5] The return of "student apathy" and "childishness" during the cold war was reminiscent of the dull pre–World War II campus scene that veterans had altered between 1945 and 1950.

The change did not last. As veterans' numbers dwindled, so too did the intensity of campus political activity. In loco parentis, after a brief hiatus during the war, returned with vengeance. Students retreated to the Greek system and campus club culture. And university leaders quickly discovered the institution's traditional eighteen to twenty-one-year-old student population—three-quarters of whom could not vote—exhibited little interest in cold war politics, preferring instead the pretend politics of student government organizations.[6] Content to have a little fun, study business, cheat if necessary, and graduate to a well-paying corporate job, students avoided politics altogether. "College is still a cloister," allowed one former college instructor-turned-newspaper reporter. "The longer the average student stays in college, the less he seems to know, or care, about the day-to-day history called news."[7] Educating globally aware citizens would prove more challenging than expected during the hottest years of the cold war.

"We Are Faced with the Task of Building a Better-Informed Opinion": The Government's Global Cold War Education Strategy

American higher education exited World War II better than anyone predicted. The relocation of hundreds of émigré European scholars and scientists—including dozens of Germany's renowned physicists—to U.S. colleges and universities before the war brought inestimable prestige to those schools af ter it.[8] At the same time, the G.I. Bill pushed undergraduate enrollments to record levels. And the steady flow of federal research funding, which alone topped $2.2 billion in 1950, or nearly as much as it did during the entire war, portended high rates of investment thereafter. Flush with cash, confidence, and more students than anyone knew what to do with (3.7 million by 1960, 1.2 million more than in 1950), it is understandable why scholars have described this period as an academic golden age. Measured purely in terms of resources, it was.[9]

The same could not be said for higher education systems in war-ravaged Europe. In addition to claiming 50 million lives, World War II destroyed much of Europe's educational and cultural infrastructure. Not only had Germany's great universities been ruined—disgraced by their complicity with the Nazi regime and now depleted of much of their best young talent—Germany's brutal military conquests had also laid waste to education systems across Europe. In Poland—ground zero of Hitler's race war—thousands of professors and teachers had been killed, 50 to 90 percent of all schools and universities had been razed, and troves of books and cultural artifacts had been destroyed or stolen.[10] An American observer sent to assess Europe's postwar education system likened it to a scene from a science fiction novel. "All are familiar with H. G. Well's characterization of civilization as a continuous race between education and catastrophe. In this atomic age one is no longer considered a pessimist who suggests that we may well be on the last lap of this inexorable race."[11]

European educational rehabilitation thus emerged as a major front of the U.S.-led reconstruction effort. While the American Military Government set out to reeducate and de-Nazify former fascists and fascist sympathizers in its German Occupation Zone, a host of international nongovernmental organizations made the educational resurrection of the entire European continent a top priority. Ultimately, the newly established United Nations (UN) and its educational, scientific, and cultural organization, UNESCO, took charge of the rebuilding effort. "Wars begin in the minds of men," declared the first sentence of the UNESCO charter, and it was in the minds of men that the "defenses of peace must be constructed."[12] Unlike the failed League of Nations after World War I, the UN and UNESCO garnered strong U.S. support. Reports of Hitler's death camps, the shock of the atomic assault on Japan, and discouragement with conventional and perhaps time-worn political approaches to national and international security matters coalesced support for the fledging "world government" organization.[13] With the backing of 80 percent of American voters, in July 1946 Congress authorized U.S. involvement in UNESCO, agreeing as well to cover half its $12 million budget.[14]

UNESCO never took shape as originally imagined. Like the League of Nations before it, which was hobbled by the nonappearance of the United States, UNESCO also was burdened by the absence of a key member state. The Soviet Union's refusal to attend the London Conference, sign the charter, and join UNESCO until 1954 undermined the organization's credibility from the start.[15] That fact did not prevent the enactment of subsequent educational foreign policy among the nation's handful of lawmakers who claimed expertise in that area. Two congressmen who did were J. William Fulbright (D-AR), and Karl E. Mundt (R-SD). Their signature education policies—Fulbright's Surplus Property Act of 1946 and Mundt's Information and Educational Exchange Act of

1948—pushed the state's education policy beyond its native borders into the thick of global affairs.[16]

Personal predilections influenced Fulbright's and Mundt's policymaking. Fulbright's educational pedigree, while not pure establishment, was as close to it as well-off boys from the Ozark Mountains got in the 1920s. He graduated from the University of Arkansas, in 1925, and attended Oxford University on a Rhodes Scholarship the following year. He then earned a law degree at George Washington University. After a brief stint in the Justice Department, he returned to Arkansa in 1936, and divided his time between teaching law at his alma mater and running his family's lumber company. Three years later Fulbright retired from business permanently to teach law full time, and within months he was named president of the University of Arkansas. At thirty-four years of age, Fulbright was the youngest university president in the country.[17] Of all Fulbright's experiences, however, not one was more important to his political future than his stint as a Rhodes Scholar. The opportunity to study and travel extensively in Europe awakened Fulbright to the power of education. It was not until he journeyed abroad, he recalled, that he became truly "intellectually curious": "I was ashamed of my ignorance and lack of knowledge of literature and other things," he admitted. "Before, I had studied because it was the thing to do." By the time Fulbright graduated from Oxford his point of view had changed. Education, he now believed, could be used for personal and political transformation.[18]

In 1943, Fulbright took this vision of education with him to Washington as a freshman representative. He immediately made a name for himself as a vocal proponent of the United Nations, and, after his election to the Senate, as a key sponsor of UNESCO. In the *New York Times*, Fulbright made his position known. World War II, he wrote, forced the United States to abandon forever its isolationist tendencies. The time had arrived for America to supply "that vital spark of leadership" to prevent the world from "a return to the barbarism of those Dark Ages." To achieve enlightened rule the American people would have to let go of their "prejudices and petty provincialism." This would require time and effort, however. "It will be especially difficult for America to adjust its . . . way of thinking about its relations with foreign people, largely because we have had so little to do with them in the past."[19]

Devising a means to enhance the peaceful interaction of American and foreign citizens preoccupied Fulbright. Riding the wave of public support for UNESCO, Fulbright introduced educational exchange legislation that, he hoped, would prevent another war. "We all know that no country is far away in the age of airplanes," said Fulbright on the Senate floor. "The necessity for increasing our understanding of others and their understanding of us has an urgency that it has never had in the past."[20] Idealistic pronouncements aside, Fulbright really gathered support for the Surplus Property Act of 1946—the foundation of the Fulbright exchange program—by emphasizing its practical benefits and low administrative costs, the bulk of which would be covered by proceeds from the overseas sale of surplus American war property. Although the State Department's Office of Educational Exchange held nominal jurisdiction over the program, real decision-making authority rested with the ten-member Board of Foreign Scholarships. With the assistance of the nongovernmental Institute of International Education (IIE), which, in time, would become the State Department's proxy coordinating body for most federally sponsored exchange programs, including the Fulbright, the board selected individual and institutional participants.[21] Like the state's domestic educational programs that preceded it, the Fulbright program laundered its authority via semiautonomous, nongovernmental intermediaries such as the board, the IIE, and, of course, colleges and universities. Operating through this mix of institutions protected the program from charges of government intrusiveness in educational affairs. The plan worked. Until the passage of Fulbright's Mutual Educational and Cultural Exchange Act in 1961 (also known as the Fulbright-Hays Act), which merged all the government's educational exchange activities under one piece of legislation, his original makeshift exchange program sent 21,300 Americans abroad and helped 34,381 foreign teachers, professors, researchers, and students come to the United States.[22]

In the interim the federal government's educational exchange programming changed dramatically. The unfolding cold war crisis edged U.S. educational exchange activities in a more aggressively ideological direction. The devaluation of foreign currencies across the European continent cut the flow of foreign students to American institutions by half between 1946 and 1947, thus jeopardizing the United States' worldwide leadership in scholarship exchange.[23] More troubling, according to the State Department, was that increasing numbers of foreign students were attending tuition-free Soviet-controlled universities in Eastern Europe. Although higher education had been linked to Russian state development since the Bolshevik Revolution, American policymakers were slow to recognize the "sovietization" of East European universities as part of the Soviet Union's long-term occupation strategy. After the war, according to a leading scholar, the Soviet Military Administration, assisted by student-led "action committees," sought to remake East European universities into Marxist-Leninist "party schools" dedicated to the communist indoctrination of proletariat youth. It turned out that the results of the Soviet Union's top-down reorganization of East European higher education varied widely from one satellite to another. But at the time, the Soviet takeover of education systems in East Germany, Czech lands, Hungary, and Poland compelled American policymakers to reassess their use of education and propaganda in fighting the cold war.[24]

The United States, which gutted its propaganda apparatus after the war, would have to cram to catch up. The Soviet Union's propaganda machine was "global and total," according to government experts, and well funded—the

Figure 5.1. President Harry S. Truman, flanked by Democratic Senator J. William Fulbright of Arkansas (left) and Assistant Secretary of State William Benton (right), signs the Surplus Property Act, August 1, 1946. The act created the Fulbright Exchange Program, the distant inspiration for which was the Rhodes Scholarship that Fulbright had won twenty years before. Courtesy Harry S. Truman Library.

recipient of $1.4 billion annually by 1950.[25] Unlike the United States, every facet of Soviet life, posited the Senate Foreign Relations Committee, was disciplined by the Communist Party's Section of Propaganda and Agitation (Agitprop), which controlled the "press, printing, films, radio, belles letters, arts, sports, schools, sciences, and so forth." A massive "school system" of 300,000 propagandists-in-waiting provided Agitprop with a global army of "ideological warriors." These functionaries never engaged in "expensive methods of direct instruction," according to the government's own paranoid assessment but promulgated the Soviet position from within a wide range of institutions—everything from Soviet Friendship Societies and peace councils to the Russian Orthodox Church, trade unions, international student federations, universities, and government. They slyly targeted the weak-minded and the fanatical both using "persuasion and blackmail to open the door to infiltration" in order "to make the world safe for Stalinism." How possibly could the United States compete?[26]

The federal government, according to one historian, set aside lingering reservations about the role of propaganda in a democratic state and pursued a "total" propaganda program of its own. The state merged its propaganda operations under the banner of the U.S. Information Agency (USIA), created in 1953, which was anchored by the Voice of America radio station, a library system, and other cultural programs to spread America's own version of the "truth" about democracy to peoples around the world.[27] Additionally, state policymakers also set their sights on strengthening the arsenal of democratic propaganda tools, especially education. As it had during World War II, the state again deployed education in order to mitigate potentially deflating criticisms of its overt propagandizing. Higher education represented an ostensibly apolitical alternative to barefaced propagandizing that simultaneously met the polity's demand for a noninvasive state.[28] Unlike the Soviets, Americans had this parastate mechanism at their disposal that already had deep roots in civil society, was highly regarded as a neutral source of expertise—especially after the war— and perhaps most important, helped calm the fear that in order successfully to fight the Soviet Union, the United States would have to emulate Soviet penetration into the political economy and the lives of its citizens.

The ideological conversion of the state's education foreign policy gained momentum after a joint subcommittee of the Committee on Foreign Relations returned from a two-month European tour during the fall of 1947. Led by Senator H. Alexander Smith (R-NJ) and Representative Karl E. Mundt (R-SD), the trip awakened all twelve travelers to the full power of the Soviet's propaganda machine. On both sides of the iron curtain, the American contingent witnessed the "influence of misrepresentation, falsification, division, chaos, compromise, despair, and ultimate absorption" achieved by the Communist ideological attack.[29] Even though the Marshall Plan provided $20 billion in material aid to Western Europe, the continent teetered on the brink of enslavement.[30] Food was not enough. For while the United States had been "preoccupied . . . with feeding stomachs of people, the Soviets had concentrated on feeding their minds."[31] According to the committee's final report, the only way to fight back was for Congress to pass legislation, then languishing in the Senate, to create a more potent information and educational program in Europe and around the world. Noting that economically depressed Great Britain spent more on these activities than the United States, the group demanded a new course of action. "We are shooting with popguns and water pistols," Mundt quipped, "while those who are against us are using all the heavy artillery they can muster."[32]

No member of the subcommittee was affected more by the trip than Karl Mundt. First elected to Congress in 1938 on a staunch isolationist platform, Mundt was a committed conservative who quickly curried favor with the Republican leadership by vociferously attacking virtually all of President Roosevelt's foreign policy initiatives. In his first term he unsuccessfully fought against amending the U.S. Neutrality Acts, and, again unsuccessfully, against the administration's enactment of a peacetime draft. In 1941 the Republican leadership rewarded Mundt with a position on the prestigious House Foreign Affairs Committee, the first time a South Dakotan had been so honored.[33]

Mundt had little personal or professional experience in foreign affairs. Republican leaders appointed Mundt because they knew he would irritate Democrats. He did not disappoint. During his first year on the Foreign Affairs Committee, Mundt threw his support behind Charles Lindbergh's American First Committee while futilely rallying House opposition against the Lend-Lease Agreements and the Ship-Arming bills—against practically all of President Roosevelt's "strong arm" executive actions. Not one of Mundt's efforts succeeded. Three days after the Japanese attack on Pearl Harbor, Mundt's dismay was palpable: "Feel very tired and low tonight—to see the end of two years fighting to avert our entrance into a shooting war all kicked into a cocked hat. . . . One's mind fills up with might have beens."[34]

Mundt did not stay deflated long. After America declared war he set aside his differences with the White House and modified his isolationist views. Mundt now reasoned the only way to protect American interests in an uncertain world was to rule that world. To do so, he positioned himself as the Republican's leading expert in the area of educational foreign policy, coming out in favor of seemingly big-government initiatives like the UN and UNESCO, even as his bid to locate the UN headquarters in the Black Hills went unrequited. Mundt was no Rhodes Scholar, but he did have an energetic intellect and a genuine affection for arts and letters; as a cofounder of the National Forensic League in 1925, he also was passionate about speech and debate of all kinds. A graduate of Carleton College, prior to entering politics Mundt earned his living as a teacher, school superintendent, and college instructor. He and his wife were actively involved in the South Dakota Poetry Society and, for a time, attended a summer writers' colony at the University of Colorado. These days Mundt, who was elected to the Senate in 1948, is largely remembered for his dubious role as chairman of the Senate Subcommittee on Investigations during the Army-McCarthy hearings in 1954, and, before that, for his enthusiastic participation on the House Un-American Activities Committee from 1943 to 1948. There is no question that Mundt was always a ferocious red baiter. He sponsored or supported practically every piece of anticommunist, antisubversive legislation that wound its way through Congress during his long career. What has been lost as a result of the singular focus on Mundt the anticommunist, however, is that he also educated himself into one of the government's leading experts on educational foreign policy.[35]

Mundt was a quick study who threw himself into this role during and after World War II. He and Smith rallied support for a more capacious and overtly

Figure 5.2. A former school teacher and sometimes poet, Republican representative (and, later, senator) Karl E. Mundt of South Dakota struck a professorial pose in this 1940 headshot. Perhaps best known as a militant anticommunist, Mundt also cosponsored the Information and Educational Exchange Act of 1948, which expanded U.S. information and educational exchange activities to a global scale. LC-H22-D-8476. Courtesy Harris and Ewing Collection, Library of Congress.

anticommunist educational foreign policy on their return from Europe in November 1947. Smith, a former administrator at Princeton University and lecturer in the department of politics, had been Mundt's ally since Mundt submitted a bill to fortify the nation's existing information and education services the previous summer. Quickly passed by Mundt's House Foreign Affairs Committee and Smith's Senate Foreign Relations Committee in July 1947, the legislation aimed to strengthen the Voice of America radio broadcast, to set up information libraries in cold war battle zones, and to extend the reach of the nascent Fulbright program. It stalled in the Senate, however. Dean Acheson, the future secretary of state, at the time the undersecretary of state in charge of congressional relations, pushed Mundt's bill to the bottom of the department's legislative agenda, where it would have stayed had it not been for the American press's day-by-day coverage of the Smith-Mundt group's harrowing European tour behind the iron curtain. Front-page headlines fostered popular support for Mundt's bill. The trip, Mundt said, in a verbal jab at Acheson, "had been very much worthwhile"; it gave the group, and ultimately the entire Congress, "first-hand impressions [of the situation in Europe] impossible to obtain if we had to rely on the State Department."[36] In early January 1948, having finally secured Acheson's grudging support, Senator Smith finally brought Mundt's bill to a vote on the Senate floor; days later, President Truman signed the Information and Educational Exchange Act into law.[37]

The Smith-Mundt Act, as the legislation was popularly known, supplemented the existing Fulbright program in a number of key ways. Funded with congressional rather than foreign dollars, the new act permitted the federal government to operate educational exchange programs on a truly global scale—wherever the State Department determined a U.S. presence was needed and wanted. Relieved of the Fulbright program's crippling foreign currency requirements, exchange activities moved beyond Europe and into South America, Africa, and Asia. The act also brought new attention and funding to America's overseas information programs and paved the way for the consolidation of those programs under the USIA, the visible portion of the government's global propaganda machine. Finally, the act set the stage for an even more aggressive educational foreign policy later on. Where Smith-Mundt was a response to the Soviet Union's disinformation campaign, subsequent interventions such as Point IV, the Mutual Security Act, even the Peace Corps became cornerstones of American foreign policy itself. With two-thirds of the world believed to be underdeveloped and politically unstable, it was crucial, explained one State Department official, that the United States help "people in these [underdeveloped] areas realize that, through perseverance, hard work, and a little assistance, they can develop the means for taking care of their material needs and at the same time can preserve and strengthen their individual freedom. . . . [and] democracy."[38] Throughout the cold war, presidents acted on this idea, believing that a combination of political, military, educational, and technological interventions could effortlessly mold modern, democratic, and capitalist nations out of Third World states. In Guatemala, Iran, British Guinea, Cuba, and the Dominican Republic—until the Vietnam quagmire finally and painfully persuaded them otherwise—U.S. foreign policy planners remained deadly serious about using education and academic expertise to adjust and readjust worldwide public opinion, and entire Third World countries, in America's democratic image.[39]

This required energizing an equally strong current of domestic public opinion. After all, robust overseas support of the United States would mean little if the home-front foundered. Lester Markel of the Council on Foreign Relations captured perfectly the interrelationship between domestic and overseas opinion and the importance of fusing them to win the cold war: "We are faced with the task of building a better informed opinion," he said. "That means, on the government's part, a clear and courageous definition of its job and a new and vigorous drive to inform the nation and the world; on the part of the people, an understanding of the task and full support of it." But what was public opinion? And how exactly did education stand to improve it? Professional psychologists and opinion researchers offered answers to both questions.[40]

"An Uninformed Electorate Acts as a Drag upon the Government": Public Opinion and the Crisis of Cold War Citizenship

The rise of public opinion as a psychological technology and accepted source of political intelligence constituted one of the major triumphs of cold war social science. Military service brought prestige to an entire generation of professionally trained psychologists, sociologists, and political scientists committed to making opinion polling part of the academic and political mainstream. Political leaders, starting with President Franklin Roosevelt and his pollster Elmo Roper, played with opinion data, but almost always in private. After the war, elected officials increasingly relied on public opinion—publicly available—in their decision-making process. Among everyday citizens, meanwhile, polls of one form or another suffused the media, and "sciency" terms such as sample size, population, and margin of error became part of the nation's lexicon. Opinion researchers like Elmo Roper and George Gallup, founder of the American Institute of Public Opinion in 1935, established firms in which to ply their craft. Finally, the study of opinion polling flourished inside the cold war university. By 1950, Columbia University, the University of Chicago, Princeton University, and the University of Michigan all housed major research centers dedicated to the scientific study of public opinion.[41]

Public opinion was the aggregate expression of underlying individual attitudes shaped in a social context. The distinction between private attitudes and public opinion was important. Attitudes, the building blocks of opinion, were not directly accessible. Individuals could suppress private attitudes and thus undermine the measure of public opinion. Even when public opinion trended strongly in one direction the possibility remained that beneath the surface of opinion lurked unstable attitudes. American citizens could say one thing publicly, but believe the opposite privately. This begged the question, in the American context, where private and public realms were theoretically separate: Was it possible to bring attitudes and opinions into harmonious union?[42]

Opinion researchers argued attitudes, though deeply embedded, were malleable and could be adjusted through education and changes to the social environment. Researchers scrutinized the Russian enemy to prove this point. According to Paul Kecskemeti, a research scientist at the RAND Corporation and a member of Harvard's Russian Research Center, the Soviet Union maintained strict oversight of the entire "flow of communication . . . and content of publicly transmitted symbols" in order to erase the divide between private attitudes and public opinion. Controlled environments with limited private space, like those in the Soviet bloc, expunged all variability from the opinion-making process. In totalitarian societies attitudes and opinion were one and the same because "the mass media of communications in the totalitarian state reflect . . . a controlled and carefully fashioned body of opinion."[43] Alex Inkeles, Kecskemeti's Harvard colleague, elaborated. "All of the media of communication, including the personal address in face-to-face contact with small audiences are part of a political monopoly, precisely controlled, backed by the force of state and law," he said. "The potentialities of mass communication for exerting an influence on human attitudes and actions in the Soviet Union," Inkeles concluded, "are thus greatly magnified." By eviscerating the line between private and public experiences, totalitarian regimes were believed to have achieved an airtight public opinion.[44]

In contrast to Soviet society, in which the state hammered private attitudes into a seemingly unitary public opinion, American public opinion was pluralistic. Liberal democracy's commitment to free expression, and a strict divide between private and public life, made the achievement of a predictable public opinion much more challenging. According to pluralist theory, the dominant explanation of the American governmental process during the cold war, interest groups dominated American politics in a most salutary way. Interest groups, also called pressure groups or attitude groups, created a stable political environment in which dramatic policy shifts were rare. This belief was traceable to James Madison's *Federalist No. 10*. With remarkable prescience, Madison explained the virtues of the new republic's "factious spirit" in a geographically expansive realm: more not less factions, he argued, reduced the chances "that a majority of the whole . . . [would] . . . invade the rights of other citizens."[45] But it was political scientist Alfred Bentley's 1908 masterwork, *The Process of Government: A Study of Social Pressures*, which renewed interest in interest groups after World War II. Though generally ignored when first published, in part because Bentley, after a failed reappointment in the sociology department at the University of Chicago, made his living as a Chicago journalist rather than an academic, *The Process of Government* eventually found a wide audience. Bentley's focus on self-interested groups—"the very flesh and blood" of American politics—resonated with cold war political scientists.[46] None more so than Columbia University's David Truman whose book *The Governmental Process* echoed Bentley's in title and text. Truman celebrated group life and the centrist politics groups purportedly produced. He thought interest groups were the seedbed of the democratic opinion-making process.[47]

Other political scientists were less sure. One criticism, voiced by Theodore Lowi and E. E. Schattschneider, was that interest group access was far more circumscribed than the theory allowed. Some groups—the farm lobby, big business, and veterans groups, for example—had more influence than other groups, such as consumers, the elderly and poor, and women and African Americans.[48] Another criticism was that the particularistic aims of individual interest groups sapped democracy of its creative energy and led to gridlock. "A democratic order cannot operate indefinitely in purely segmental terms," said Edgar Lane, an editor at *Public Opinion Quarterly*, in 1956.[49] His was a commonly voiced concern. Not only did interest groups fractionalize the policymaking process, they also narrowed their members' political outlook and opinion-making skills, especially in the all-important realm of foreign affairs.[50]

Studies indicated that most citizens' political outlook was blinded by "dark areas of ignorance." A voter study of the 1950 midterm election (in which only 44 percent of eligible voters cast a ballot) identified 30 percent of voters as "totally unaware" of American foreign affairs and only 25 percent of voters "reasonably well informed."[51] A two-year study of the "information levels" of Minnesotans conducted by the *Public Opinion Quarterly*, published in 1951, likewise revealed widespread ignorance. When asked to identify "prominent personages" from the international political scene, for example, fewer than 50 percent of respondents could identify Prime Minister Clement Attlee of England, while fewer still could identify either Franco of Spain or de Gaulle of France. Minnesotans performed somewhat better when asked to identify national political leaders, but only 60 percent of respondents correctly identified Dwight D. Eisenhower, and only 30 percent George C. Marshall, two heroes of World War II. Although many respondents could give partial answers, most Minnesotans were just plain confused. "Nehru—Nehru? Let's see. I believe he's a Japanese leader of some kind."[52]

The global information gap touched all segments of the population. Although college-educated citizens exhibited the strongest sense of "citizen duty" and understanding of national and international politics (as measured in voting patterns and political participation), even they comprised a portion of the "uninformed" and "apathetic" public.[53] According to Martin Kriesberg, a political scientist at the Survey Research Center at the University of Michigan, this particular public—the uninformed public—was a main source of policy stalemate in Washington. "An uniformed electorate acts as a drag upon the government," he said. "Prejudices which fetter the ignorant and apathetic voters hang heavily upon the hands of their representatives also. Therein lies the danger."[54] A study of political apathy in Ithaca, conducted by Morris Rosenberg of Cornell University, glimpsed the mind of the uninformed. "Well, I'm not interested enough," admitted one respondent. "I don't take the time to read such matters."[55] This was the key problem. In his seminal work, *American People and Foreign Policy*, political scientist Gabriel Almond concluded most Americans lacked "intellectual structure and factual content" about the nation's foreign policy. As a result, he said, the public reacts "with formless and plastic moods which undergo frequent alteration in response to changes in events."[56]

The public's well-documented lack of political faith posed a real challenge for elites concerned about the future of democratic citizenship. The 1952 meeting of the National Conference on Citizenship made this point clear. The conference coincided with the first official observance of Citizenship Day, September 17—passed by Congress and signed into law by President Truman to commemorate the signing of the U.S. Constitution. Truman delivered the conference's keynote address. Before an audience of education, business, religious, civic, and political leaders, he proudly described the federal government's multifaceted "fight against . . . communism." The creation and expansion of the New Deal's social safety net, Truman said, had stamped out the desperate social conditions that communism needed to spread. His administration's vigorous loyalty oath campaign had purified government while the prosecution and conviction of the Communist Party's "top leadership" had helped to chase Communists from the nation's trade unions. To win the cold war, however, required more than activist government—it required an energetic and enlightened citizenry. Education, as Truman knew, had been marshaled during World War II to strengthen the psychological fortitude of soldiers before, during, and after combat. The current crisis likewise required educational warfare, if on an even larger scale: soldiers *and* citizens needed educational training to help make democracy safe. The high-school educated Truman did not need a college diploma to reach the same conclusion as most pollsters and social scientists: "Among the greatest dangers to free government in this country are lack of knowledge, lack of civic responsibility — ignorance and apathy and perversion of truth."[57]

Two education-related crises suggested the American people's educational firepower was more diminished than originally reported. The first was the alleged brainwashing of American G.I.s captured by Chinese Communist forces in the Korean War. The apparent ability of Chicom interrogators to remanufacture individual's attitudes—the raw material of public opinion—through psychosocial manipulation sent shockwaves through a country already stunned by the destructiveness of Senator Joseph McCarthy's Communist witch hunt. It was reported that the Chinese-led Korean enemy had used crude Pavlovian stimulus-response techniques to flip twenty-one American POWs into sympathetic Party drones. Though psychologists at Johns Hopkins University, George Washington University, and at the Air Force Personnel and Training Center (most of the alleged victims had been captured Air Force pilots) initially dismissed the brainwashing story, the alleged switch of American G.I.s into fellow travelers seized the country's imagination.[58]

Newspapers across the country tracked the fate of America's "Red" G.I.s. Most stories groped for answers. Why did America's soldiers crumble when confronted with psychological interrogation? Malvina Lindsay, a popular columnist for the *Washington Post*, believed the soldiers bore no responsibility: "The average captured GI likely had little mental armor with which to resist communist indoctrination. Unlike youth under authoritarian rule, he had not been drilled from an early age in any catechism of political faith."[59] Columbia psychiatrist Joost Meerloo upped the anxiety level. Based on his study of the Korean POWs, and on his understanding of the Chicom indoctrination process, no one was safe—there was, he believed, a little "turncoat in each of us." The only defense against self-betrayal, he concluded, was a good offense. Protecting citizens against "the rape of the mind" required "a deeply founded belief in democratic freedom."[60]

Additional studies strongly intimated that educational deprivation was to blame. In *U.S. News and World Report*, Major William E. Mayer, an army psychiatrist and leading expert on brainwashing, claimed "the behavior of many Americans in Korea prison camps appears to raise serious questions about American character, and about the education of Americans." He said the G.I.s lacked a clear understanding about the "duties and responsibilities of citizenship" and were unprepared to combat the psychological attack to which they were subjected. When confronted by their Chicom captors' warped version of American history, they were too paralyzed to respond. Indeed, according to Mayer, many soldiers admitted that their Chinese captors knew more about America's democratic political tradition than they did.[61]

The publication of Virginia Pasley's best-selling, Pulitzer Prize–winning book *21 Stayed* (1955) seemingly confirmed the education-brainwashing thesis. For starters, she discovered that eighteen of the twenty-one soldiers were high-school dropouts. Pasley also uncovered evidence of troubled upbringings that she speculated contributed to their acute psychological maladjustment: nineteen soldiers "felt unloved or unwanted by fathers or stepfathers" and eleven of the G.I.s came from "broken homes." Not only how they lived, but where they lived mattered to Pasley. Nineteen of the twenty-one came from from rural communities or small towns—a connection that reinforced popular notions about the provincialism, if not backwardness, of country living. In sum, the studies by Pasley and others suggested Communists were preying on the maladjustment of the American people.[62]

Ignorance lay at the heart of a second crisis in democratic citizenship: America's ongoing struggle with racial prejudice. Swedish economist Gunnar

Myrdal's *An American Dilemma: The Negro Problem and American Democracy*, published in 1944 with a grant from the Carnegie Corporation, focused new attention on the centuries-long problem of race relations in the United States.[63] Though intended for scholars and policymakers, the book somehow managed to find a broad popular readership, making the *New York Times'* "Ten Best" booklist of 1944.[64] This was surprising not only because of the utter heft of his study, but also because Myrdal blamed whites for the nation's racial troubles. Myrdal characterized race prejudice as a psychological disorder brought on by pervasive white denial—what he called their "opportunistic escape reaction."[65] Whites' ignorance of the real effects of discrimination was opportunistic, in Myrdal's estimation, because it functioned to normalize white supremacy and black inferiority. To cure the nation of its racial sickness, Myrdal supported granting full citizenship to blacks as well as embarking on "an educational offensive against racial intolerance."[66] Myrdal's faith in education was rooted to his Enlightenment belief in the "changeability of human beings" and to his confidence in educational intervention as a key instrument of social engineering.[67] According to Myrdal, education was the surest way to help blacks and whites recognize their shared stake in the "American Creed"—the color-blind democratic ideals he believed should infuse the nation's political and social institutions.[68] In the absence of an extensive national program of educational uplift and reconciliation, however, racial tension would fester, possibly worsen. "The American nation will not have peace with its conscience until inequality is stamped out, and the principle of public education is realized universally," he concluded.[69]

Ensuing social science research likewise highlighted education's role in possibly curing the psychological illness of prejudice. No work was more influential in this regard than Gordon Allport's *The Nature of Prejudice*, published in 1954.[70] Allport, a Harvard professor and one of the nation's leading social psychologists, found that sustained contact between members of different groups in educational settings was one of the best ways to forge durable interracial understanding. Allport's faith in education as a social panacea was steeled by his belief that prejudiced attitudes had no hereditary basis and could be adjusted and modified to meet new social realities. "Not only is prejudice itself learned, but so too are all of its ingredients," Allport stated. "And what is learned can, theoretically at least, be unlearned; or at least . . . prevented."[71]

This discovery was hardly new. Since the nation's founding, Americans had turned to education to create democratic citizens. And during the cold war, social scientists reaffirmed that belief, recommending education as protection against radical politics and as the best hope for strengthening the country's vital center. The stakes could not have been higher. "The real drama of American life is this race between ignorance and prejudice on the one hand, and the work of the universities on the other," noted an Oxford University professor. "Will the universities win?"[72]

"The American Citizen, Whether He Likes It or Not, Is About to Become a World Citizen": Educating "Children" for Cold War Citizenship

Competing answers to this question emanated from the highest reaches of academe and government in the immediate postwar period. The two most important of which were *General Education in a Free Society* (dubbed the Red Book because of its crimson cover), commissioned by President James B. Conant of Harvard University, released in 1945, and *Higher Education for American Democracy* (better known as the Truman Report), released two years later. The studies were similar in a number of ways. For one thing, both reports conceived of higher education in strongly ideological terms and as the key ingredient for the production of democratic citizens. For another, both reports recommended "general education"—the political and occupational training of the "whole man"—as the best way to prepare citizens for democratic life. While neither study offered a precise definition of general education, both rooted it to the liberal arts and imagined it in boldly international terms.[73]

On the specifics of this latter point the studies diverged. The authors of the Red Book, led by historian Paul Buck, limited their internationalism to the Great Books of Western civilization. The authors of the Truman Report, on the other hand, proposed a more capacious internationalism that not only extolled the greatness of Western civilization but also Western civilization's—especially America's—interaction with the rest of the world. In this respect the Truman Report represented the future of Harvard, whose faculty rejected the recommendations in the Red Book, and American higher education writ large. World War II, the cold war, and the emergence of the U.S. global education strategy helped end the political and academic isolationism of the interwar period by giving birth to what some called an "internationally-minded" university—and to what others imagined as the birth of a new breed of democratic citizen.[74] "The American citizen," declared a hopeful professor at the University of Iowa, "whether he likes it or not, is about to become a world citizen."[75]

Higher education's growing fascination with world affairs revealed itself in a number of overlapping ways in the 1950s. Elite research universities housed new interdisciplinary area and international studies centers. The shortage of trained specialists with expertise in the political, linguistic, and cultural life of Central and Eastern Europe, and especially Asia, had limited the intelligence gathering and analysis capacities of the Office of Strategic Services (OSS) during World War II. The onset of the cold war and the felt need for a more robust intelligence operation energized the federal government and the philanthropic sector after the war. The Ford Foundation funded this endeavor, investing $270 million in area studies centers at dozens of leading research universities in the 1950s.[76] "The Second World War and the post-war responsibilities of the United States as the strongest power of the free world," said Philip E. Moseley, a pioneering Russian area studies specialist and director of the Russian Institute at Columbia University, "made clear the need for the systematic and many-sided study of major world areas outside the United States and Western Europe."[77]

It also made clear the need for a more internationally vibrant undergraduate experience. Educational elites looked to Western civilization and international affairs courses to do most of this work. Western Civ, compulsory undergraduate fodder at many colleges since its introduction as War Aims at Columbia University during World War I, offered students what typically amounted to a semester-long (sometimes two) celebration of the birth of American democracy.[78] To this story of freedom's gradual triumph over tyranny was added international relations (IR) courses that purportedly examined U.S. interactions with the rest of the world. These courses also became commonplace in the wake of World War I, and like Western Civ they served as backdrops against which professors typically tracked the steady rise and expansion of American freedom in an otherwise hostile world. While hopelessly jingoistic by later professional standards of objectivity, at the time IR courses in history and political science proffered interested undergraduates a verisimilar version of the genesis of America's growing global role. This point was made well by Richard Swift, a professor of government at New York University: "What is best in Western cultural traditions can survive only if Westerners understand the values, hopes and ambitions of non-Western peoples and help them use constructively the revolutionary forces inspired by, but too often directed against, the West. Western universities must devise truly global curricula."[79]

Even institutions without IR programs or required Western Civ classes peppered their curricula with global issues and politics. A 1947 study conducted by the American Association of Teachers Colleges discovered that all but 6 of 117 teachers colleges examined either required, or planned to require, courses on international politics and problems. What Teachers Should Know About Russia, Educational Foundations of a World Community, and Pacific Relations, were just several of the courses being offered, according to the study.[80] The teacher training program at St. Johns University inaugurated a course, Communist Society, which promised students a "critical analysis of the Marxian program for the reconstruction of social institutions as visualized by the early nineteenth century Socialists, through the years to Russia as she is today."[81] Elsewhere, teachers colleges teamed with local school districts to organize regional institutes aimed at fostering global perspectives. A teacher-training workshop in Oneonta, New York, for example, focused on U.S. involvement in the United Nations, another in Montclair, New Jersey, on Sino-American relations.[82]

Over time, the spread of internationalism subtly changed how undergraduate education was packaged and taught. Linguists now insisted that foreign language fluency increased one's capacity to engage in public affairs in a more sophisticated and nuanced way. Building on instructional methods developed for military personnel in World War II, colleges adopted the so-called "Army method," emphasizing speech and oral approaches to language proficiency instead of grammar and culture.[83] The focus on speaking, pronunciation, and colloquial uses of language was encouraged by the advent of newfangled language labs replete with taped lessons and hi-fi receivers.[84] "The mantle of world leadership rests heavily on the shoulders of all American citizens," explained the chairman of the French department at the University of North Carolina. "It is not merely a matter of common sense, but also of survival, to insist on the development of skill in foreign languages."[85]

Other fields likewise promoted themselves as required training for cold war citizenship. Economic departments introduced developmental economic courses that stressed the application of capitalist economic programs in the development of Third World countries. English departments, meanwhile, emphasized "new look" approaches that urged interpersonal and small group "communication" and "discussion"—the basis of a truly healthy public opinion—rather than the rarely experienced activity of "public speaking."[86] Artists claimed that making art was "an indispensable means for achieving a democratic way of life"; geographers talked in terms of geopolitics and highlighted the well-documented "ignorance of [the] population in things geographic"; scientists and mathematicians, meanwhile, cloaked many of their activities in terms of national defense. Even religious studies professors found the cold war curriculum, which was stoked by the growing religious fervor of the American people, more welcoming than ever after decades of marginalization.[87] The struggle against "Godless Communism" made this, and the other curricular changes discussed above, possible. In the future, professors would continue to use the curriculum to confront the political challenges of their own day. Rather than celebrating the march of American capitalism and democracy in Western civilization, IR, and developmental economics classes, however, during the 1960s younger professors (pushed by skeptical students) condemned those classes as cold war relics, and retrofitted them into vehicles for the exploration of America's imperialist, racist, and sexist past.[88]

En route the engine of internationalism attempted to rev up the extracurriculum. A key development was the formation of the U.S. National Students Association (NSA), formed after a small delegation of American college students returned from a meeting of the World Student Congress in Prague, in 1946. Delegates were alarmed at the strong Communist bias of their European hosts and by the International Union of Students, the sponsoring organization. Founded at the University of Wisconsin in 1947, the NSA positioned itself as a training ground for democratic citizenship. In a student political universe suffused by in loco parentis and dominated by Greek-letter societies, the NSA represented something different. The organization's motto said it all: "Citizenship, Opportunity, Equality."[89] "It'll be our contribution to democratic training," proclaimed the association's first president, Jim Smith, a student at the University of Texas, "to make student government a laboratory of democracy."[90]

The NSA quickly achieved prominence as the largest student government organization in the country. Its membership included more than four hundred college and university student government associations and thus counted more than one-half of the country's registered students as official members (even though many students were unaware of such membership). A federation of state, regional, and national offices controlled the association and sets its policy agenda, which was backed by a number of core higher education interests, including the American Council on Education and the American UNESCO Commission.[91] Congress and the president of the United States conveyed messages of support while the Central Intelligence Agency channeled clandestine funding to the NSA starting in 1952. By the time the agency's involvement was exposed in 1967, of course, the NSA's leadership role in campus politics had been eclipsed by Students for a Democratic Society, organized in 1960 as a spinoff of the NSA and the student wing of the League for Industrial Democracy.[92]

In its heyday, however, the NSA took solidly liberal stands on some of the most divisive political issues of the day. For example, the organization's northern caucus ignored the cries of its southern members by insisting that a statement on equal educational rights—"regardless of sex, race, religion, political belief, or economic circumstances"—be written into the NSA Constitution.[93] Later, in 1951, the association strongly denounced McCarthy's communist witch hunt far more forcefully than any comparable professorial body ever did—even going so far as to celebrate Academic Freedom Day to promote First Amendment rights.[94] Still later, members of the association lent their support to the youth division of the Southern Christian Leadership Conference and actively participated in the founding of the Student Nonviolent Coordinating Committee, in 1960. All these moves contradicted the association's original claim that it would "refrain from . . . partisan political affairs," and quickly propelled the national leadership well left of the political center.[95]

While the political beliefs of the NSA leadership mirrored those of the liberal education interests that supported the organization, they did not necessarily reflect the views of many of the nation's college students who comprised the NSA's membership. In Greek-letter-dominated student government organizations, there was little evidence of interest in the issues that occupied the association's national leadership, like civil rights or academic freedom. As appendages of the Greek system and an undergraduate culture inundated with in loco parentis, most student government organizations passed the time engaging in a different kind of politics—planning homecoming, running intramural sport leagues, and organizing fraternity and sorority rush events. This was just the way the administration liked it, too, concluded a 1955 NSA study of six hundred colleges. *Student Government, Student Leaders, and the American College* painted a bleak picture of the cold war campus.[96] The study found students to be at once apathetic and hostile—indifferent to real politics on the one hand, yet mad at their administrators for cultivating an infantile environment that rewarded indifference on the other. Harry Lunn, a past NSA president, thought Greek-dominated student government was broken, perhaps beyond repair: "No real issues of educational importance occupy the thinking of most student leaders and, by and large, they have few ideas for new areas of activity."[97]

That was not for lack of trying. During the 1950s, students had opportunities to engage in more than child's play. The establishment of the United Nations encouraged universities to organize their own student-run model UN organizations. Coordinated and sponsored by the Collegiate Council for the United Nations and the American Association for the United Nations, more than three hundred campus UN chapters were in operation by the early 1950s. Similar to the real organization, student delegates represented different countries and throughout the course of the academic year discussed, formulated, and submitted position papers for the resolution of a mock international security crisis. Each spring, a weeklong gathering of delegates near the New York headquarters of the actual United Nations marked the national organization's capstone event.[98] College UN organizations sponsored festivals and special campus events during UN Day, observed in October. At Indiana University, for instance, a week of special activities celebrated the event. Faculty members were encouraged to invite students to their homes; the library set up a promotional display; the cafeteria featured a different "foreign food" every day; and the student union organized a foreign film festival. All of this, the administration hoped, would "arouse [students'] interest in international affairs." Howard E. Wilson, secretary of the education policies commission of the American Council on Education, concurred: "The undergraduate curriculum," Wilson believed, "may be supplemented and enriched by relatively serious cultural out-of-class activities bearing on foreign and international affairs."[99]

A few clubs of this kind emerged. The Association of International Relations Clubs (AIRC), founded in 1948, targeted serious students interested in "real" politics. The AIRC, with the help of the Carnegie Endowment and through the direct sponsorship of the Foreign Policy Association, hired an executive secretary to coordinate the activities of international relations clubs. By the mid-1950s there were nearly seven hundred AIRC clubs in operation.[100] Yet there was a problem: those clubs tallied preciously few members. The results of a Carnegie Endowment survey of international relations clubs found most students did not want to learn any more about foreign policy matters than they absolutely had to: fewer than 3 percent of eligible undergraduates were members of "international clubs" nationwide.[101]

Undoubtedly, the swell of anticommunist passions during the cold war limited students' participation in government and international clubs. The spread of McCarthyism in the early 1950s rendered suspect all campus political activity by both faculty and students. This was especially true of any political activity that was expressed in terms of, or channeled through, either international contexts or international organizations. International governmental and nongovernmental organizations—including the State Department and its foreign service personnel; the United Nations; the Carnegie Endowment for International Peace; international affairs institutes, such as the Asia Institute; area studies experts, notably the nation's leading authority on Central Asia, Owen Lattimore; and even organizations that operated primarily in a global arena, such as the U.S. Army—became special targets of the House Un-American Activities Committee and Senator McCarthy. Although few academics were ever convicted of being Communists, perhaps as many as six hundred careers at the secondary and college level were ruined by the mere accusation.[102] The fear of being accused, and the ill effect it could have on a career, was enough to create a "world of . . . silence" on universities, as the leading historian on the topic has aptly put it. During the cold war, politics was a dangerous business, and many institutions and individuals kept quiet.[103]

Yet higher education was never completely smothered. Students and faculty sought to make the world their classroom despite the specter of McCarthyism. Drawing inspiration from the Fulbright program and other federally sponsored exchange acts, study abroad became an increasingly favored way of doing so. Promoted vigorously on and off college campuses, foreign exchange, according to a leading scholar, served as an important, if underappreciated, gauge of "American imperial power in the twentieth century."[104] Especially during the cold war, when participation in study abroad began climbing rapidly. By 1960, the IIE—which coordinated student exchanges, including the Fulbright program, on behalf of the federal government—reported fourteen thousand U.S. students studying abroad and twice that traveling overseas for noncredit educational purposes. When combined with the roughly sixty-five thousand foreign citizens (forty-eight thousand of whom were students) then coming to the United States on official educational assignment from Asia, Latin America, Europe, Africa, and the Middle East, it was true American higher education really did span the globe.[105]

While the state relied on intermediaries such as the IIE to import and export students to and from U.S. soil on official federal assignments, many more undergraduate study abroad programs were coordinated by professors and students themselves. The NSA's Office of International Student Affairs emerged as the nation's leading study abroad organization of this type. That it was run by and for students led to the organization's numerous administrative problems. In the summer of 1950, for example, the association chartered a Norwegian ocean liner named the Svalbard to transport students from New York to Rotterdam. Round-trip fare was $310 per passenger and included dormitorylike accommodations, including a lecture series and language lessons. The U.S. Coast Guard cancelled the trip, however, when it deemed the Svalbard unsafe. Had it not been for the intervention of President Truman, who let the students travel on the General C.C. Ballou, a U.S. Navy transport ship, the students would have been stranded.[106]

Figure 5.3. American universities served as destinations of choice for students from around the world during the cold war. In this image Fulbright Scholars from Pakistan take a break from their studies at the University of Wisconsin to have some fun in the snow, February 1962. Courtesy University of Wisconsin-Madison Archives.

Travel glitches notwithstanding, college administrators and national policy-makers believed study abroad created globally aware democratic citizens. Walter H.C. Laves, a professor of government at Indiana University and a representative of the Education and International Affairs Committee of the American Council on Education, described the importance of study abroad to a congressional appropriations subcommittee, in 1957. Laves urged the committee to continue funding the State Department's Educational Exchange Program, which offered leadership and financial backing not only for the council, but also for university study abroad initiatives. Funding was essential for two reasons, according to Laves: first, because universities had invested "heavily in international educational activities" since World War II; and, second, because educational exchange was "not a luxury" but a critical facet of "national security."[107]

Laves elaborated on the council's Leaders and Specialists Program, which delivered foreign political leaders to American universities, to make his point. In thousands of towns and cities the program benefited visiting dignitaries and host institutions as well as the wider community. Laves quoted a few of the "hundreds of letters and newspapers clippings" he had collected to highlight the program's effectiveness. One community member wrote: "All of us learned much regarding [the visitor's] people, their customs, their problems and their aspirations." The foreign dignitary responded in kind: "My time with you was short but it was long enough to have a lasting impact. Thank you, again, for this rich and never-to-be-forgotten experience."[108] The *Monroe Advertiser*, published in the small town of Forsyth, Georgia, opined just days before welcoming a foreign delegation of its own: "When the first of the visiting Leaders from other countries arrives in Forsyth Tuesday evening international relations will depend to some small degree on this community."[109]

Other studies, however, suggested that more organic encounters between American college students and foreigners did not always result in a mutually satisfactory outcome. A research report on France issued by the IIE, in 1956, discovered American students rarely shared the same study abroad "goals" as their educational sponsors. Among university leaders, the most frequently expressed goal was "to promote international understanding," followed by "to develop friends and supporters for the United States," and third, "to contribute to the economic, social, or political development of other countries."[110] In contrast, students betrayed deeply private motives for studying abroad. Based on the evaluation of more than six hundred student essays, 75 percent of students wanted to study abroad for "professional or educational advancement," and not because of any concern for improved international relations. Of the top six reasons listed in order of frequency, in fact, all of them stressed personal rather than political rationales. Aside for professional reasons, more students wanted to study abroad for pure "adventure" (23 percent), and for the opportunity "to be one's self" (17 percent) than they did because they hoped for "better Franco-American relations" (15 percent). The gap between students' and policymakers' expectations, researchers concluded, was sufficiently large to be a "concern."[111]

A closer examination of American students' recollections of studying abroad helps to explain this disconnect. A female graduate student in English literature, for instance, thought an outside French field would increase her employment prospects back in the States: "I decided to make my specialty outside of English that of French literature. That way I'll also have better bargaining power when I want a raise once I get established." Another student, who had "dreamed of living in Paris since [he] was a Sophomore," believed by immersing himself in French culture he "could learn more of permanent benefit . . . than [he] could acquire any other way." Another student, who aspired to be an artist, said he wanted to study abroad "mainly" because of the "atmosphere of freedom" and to be "himself" in a place where "nobody asks why he's different as long as he isn't hurting others." Still, other students expressed no real motive at all: "I came along," confessed one student, "mainly for the ride." As for strengthening international relations, the study found that most students thought it was "too vague" a goal "for any but the most idealistic." "Improving international good will is all well and good," said a student, "but just what in the hell does it mean?"[112]

Most travelers, it would seem, just wanted adventure and excitement—a good time. Bernard D. Pechter, a student at University of Illinois who traveled on a NSA-sponsored trip to Europe, described his time abroad as "not only educational . . . [but] also fun." He recalled parties in every country and savored the chance to meet students and socialize—"exchanging songs, games, and dancing"—everywhere he went.[113] Another student, Mary Ann Sigmund of Mt. St. Vincent College, remembered her NSA-sponsored study abroad experience, in 1955, as a "holiday in Europe." Her eight-day voyage was "filled with hours in the sun, listening to Jazz Concerts or Chamber Music provided by student groups, dancing under the stars, and just the right amount of intellectual stimulus." After docking in the Netherlands, she spent a few "gay days in Paris," hopped a train to Venice, next went to Vienna, and then to Germany, where she spend two weeks with her family before returning home.[114] In both instances their study abroad experiences were highly personal matters seemingly bereft of political meaning.

The experiences of foreign students in the United States also veered far afield of official policy goals. Similar to their American counterparts, a majority of foreign students travelled abroad for nonpatriotic reasons. According to a study by the IIE, foreign students' main reason for coming to the United States was "to advance . . . personal and professional development." Foreign policy justifications that tied study abroad to national security policy were lost on many foreign visitors.[115]

More troubling were reports that, while a majority of foreign students enjoyed their time on American soil, a small but significant number of nonwhite foreign students were repulsed by the experience. A study of one hundred exchange students from India indicated that studying in the United States actually diminished their opinion of the "American way of life." Before arriving in the United States fully 89 percent of Indian students admired their host nation: "I was enamored of American democracy," said one student typical of this cohort. "I had a burning desire to go to a country which I believed was the leader of Today and Tomorrow."[116] After living in the United States for four months, however, only 22 percent remained favorably inclined toward their host nation. Students traced their disillusionment to two sources: political apathy and racial prejudice. "American democracy is ineffective because . . . the ordinary people have little to say in government," admitted a troubled Indian student. "American is not a democracy, as evidenced in racial prejudice," submitted another. A majority of Indian students left American feeling "completely shattered," according to one respondent, "because of the discrepancy between [America's] ideals and its practices."[117]

African students confirmed that assessment at all-black American institutions where the reality of "segregation and discrimination" was their biggest challenge.[118] While some of these visitors and their African-American peers used the experience to cultivate a nascent pan-African political consciousness, others just felt letdown.[119] One student who did transferred from Jackson College in Mississippi to Hampton University in Virginia, believing interracial relations would improve north of the "deep South." He was sadly disappointed to find segregation alive and well "in Virginia and even in Washington, DC." Having seen enough, the student decided there was only one thing left to do: "finish my studies to return home where I can be free."[120]

"To Train Well-Balanced Citizens and Leaders": Educating "Adults" for Cold War Citizenship

The capricious results of efforts to shape students' political outlooks during the cold war did not deter university administrators. With the help of foundation leaders they pressed ahead with even more grandiose educational projects to reach the "adult" public and adjust its opinions. Experimenting with ways to tap the adult education market turned out to be one of the biggest education initiatives of the entire era. Adult learners (aged twenty-five-years and older) had always represented a niche within the American higher education. Since the late nineteenth century, extension divisions and correspondence schools—whether operated by the Department of Agriculture, the U.S. Army, or independently by schools themselves—had provided millions of adults with practical educational opportunities. But the surprising academic success of veterans under the G.I. Bill, buoyed by the optimistic assessment of adult educability embedded in the Truman Report, persuaded many university administrators to go after a larger swath of the estimated 50 million "adults" living in the United States in 1950.[121]

The only problem was that no single, existing delivery mechanism was up to the task of handling even a sliver of the enormous adult market.[122] Correspondence study was a well-established method, and so too the blossoming two-year junior college system and its 540 public and private institutions.[123] Following the passage of federal "manpower" training legislation by the Kennedy administration, the junior college sector would assume de facto responsibility for the adult market, becoming the fastest growing segment of the higher education sector by the end of the century. But during the early cold war it remained unclear exactly how all the nation's adult learners were to be reached. A new approach was needed to connect citizens to the state.

The Ford Foundation emerged as the necessary link. The Ford's leadership in this regard was unexpected. Founded in 1936 as a family charity and tax shelter, the Ford Foundation, in contrast to the Carnegie Fund and the various Rockefeller foundations, was known for its parochialism (it exclusively served Michigan) and stinginess. The death of Henry Ford in 1947, at the age of ninety-two, permitted the Ford to remold its image as well as the image of its namesake. There was plenty of money to do both. Ford's massive bequest instantly made it the richest philanthropic organization in the world. Moreover, the team of planners hired to manage the "new" Ford Foundation by Henry Ford II, Ford's grandson and head of the Ford Motor Company, shared none of its founder's well-known isolationist and xenophobic views.

In fact, the new generation was enthusiastically internationalist. Paul G. Hoffman, the former head of the Studebaker Corporation and chief administrator of the Marshall Plan, became the foundation president. He surrounded himself with former Marshall Plan and Truman administration officials, many of whom had ties to the Committee on Economic Development, a Washington-based business lobby, formed in 1942, to cultivate corporate support for U.S. aid to Europe and Asia. Once ensconced at the Ford's headquarters in White Plains, New York, Hoffman's team conceived its mission as they had previous ones: to make the nation and the world safe for democracy through education and economic development.[124] Their charge was outlined in the *Report of the Study for the Ford Foundation on Policy and Programs*, released in 1949, and framed in psychosocial terms typical of the period. The presence of untold millions of "maladjusted" and "uneducated," at home and around the globe, declared the report, required a comprehensive educational counterattack "to train well-balanced citizens and leaders able to participate intelligently and constructively in the society in which [they] live."[125]

The Ford Foundation moved in two complementary directions to achieve this goal, awarding funds for the training of elite area study experts on the one hand, and for the training of informed citizens on the other. The Ford's citizenship training program fell under the auspices of the Fund for Adult Education (FAE), created in 1951. Hoffman named his friend and associate C. Scott Fletcher director. A former Studebaker vice president and member of the Committee on Economic Development, at the time of his appointment Fletcher was president of Encyclopedia Britannica Films, and a leading light in the emerging field of "new educational media." An Australian by birth, Fletcher's various corporate and foundation activities had taken him all over the world. In the course of his travels, and perhaps owing to his father's work as a night school instructor for the Workers Educational Association in Brisbane, Fletcher developed an interest in adult education, in "organizing and training large groups of adults to enable them to attain important local, state or national goals."[126]

The FAE offered Fletcher the chance to blend his expertise in business management, education, and mass communications—and in a big way. During his presidency, between 1951 and 1961, Fletcher distributed $150 million for the promotion and development of mass communication-based adult education programs.[127] He turned the FAE into a laboratory for democratic citizenship, sponsoring educational programs that ranged from the familiar to the fantastic. Collaborating with leaders from the telecommunications industry, government, and higher education, Fletcher built human and technological networks for adult study-discussion and the nation's first experiment with noncommercial educational television. At a conference on Workers' Education at Penn State

University, in 1955, and at countless other venues like it, Fletcher expounded on education's role in protecting American democracy. "One of the major goals in the field of adult education," declared Fletcher, "is to find ways to satisfy the need of American adults for programs which are designed specifically to stimulate and assist them to think independently and critically, to grow in knowledge and wisdom, and to accept with a mature sense of responsibility positions of trust in civic, national, and international affairs." That is, by using all the tools of public opinion making—printed matter, radio, television, and group discussion—Fletcher hoped to improve the public's opinion-making skills.[128]

Fletcher believed in "new media," but was not blinded by it. The people's and higher education's fear of a Soviet-style command and control education system held his wildest fantasies in check. To navigate the narrow pass between democracy and dictatorship, Fletcher and his team of educators infused all the FAE's programs with trusted democratic educational techniques. The FAE's programs incorporated "study and discussion"—the quintessentially American approach to small group deliberation and debate that had undergirded the federal forum program in the 1930s. "Group discussion relates the individual and the society," explained Fletcher. "It is best suited to those issues concerning which differences of opinion are widest, and a friendly discussion of emotionally charged issues exemplifies 'the agreement to disagree agreeably,' which makes self-government possible."[129] This approach, claimed Fletcher, imparted critical psychological and political benefits to all participants, especially the discussion leader. "When a person assumes the role of the discussion leader," he continued, "an interesting psychological change takes place. As a participant, he is concerned mainly with his own improvement. As a well-trained discussion leader . . . his viewpoint shifts . . . he learns how the democratic skills of a good discussion leader can be applied with effectiveness in the home, on the job, and in voluntary organizations, whether they be local, national or international in character."[130]

The operation of the FAE's core programming reinforced Fletcher's faith in democratically organized small-group study and discussion. For example, the American Foundation for Political Education Program relied completely on study and discussion to explore units on world politics, U.S. foreign policy, and Russian foreign policy, among others.[131] The Film Discussion Project took a similar approach but augmented print media with film in order to energize the discussion. Anchored by Fletcher's own *Encyclopedia Britannica :American Statesman* film series, the main goal of the project was to improve adults' understanding of the nation's "great political leaders," including Franklin, Jefferson, and Lincoln. At the conclusion of each film, participants took turns leading discussion, cribbing from a list of prepared questions to get things moving. Questions included: "How did Franklin harmonize his love for America with his love for the whole world?" Or: "Was Lincoln right in his view that the President himself can decide when to assume his emergency powers?" Like John

Studebaker's New Deal forums and Frederick Osborn's World War II army education programs, Fletcher regarded the small group as the lifeblood of democratic life and citizenship.[132]

Second, the FAE cultivated supports at the grassroots. The commitment to local control was evidenced by the Test Cities Project, which awarded action grants of twenty-five thousand dollars to thirteen different communities around the country. Awardees spent their grants in different ways. In San Bernardino, California, for example, participants formed a partnership with local newspapers, radio stations, libraries, and junior colleges; in Akron, they created an educational program explicitly for senior citizens; and in Kansas City, they merged with twenty-eight local "Great Books" discussion groups (the Great Books Foundation had opened in 1947) already in operation.[133] Fletcher understood all too well that when it came to educational planning and delivery, whether for high school students, collegians, or adults, the American people preferred local input and control.[134]

By far, however, Fletcher's promotion of educational television (ETV) represented the Ford Foundation's most ambitious undertaking. The National Association of Educational Broadcasters' (NAEB) drawn-out battle for noncommercial radio bandwidth in the 1930s suggested that the FAE's quest for noncommercial television would be equally if not more daunting. At that time, commercial interests, led by the Columbia Broadcasting Station (CBS), prevailed on the Federal Communication Commission (FCC) to delay the allocation of noncommercial educational radio channels for nearly a decade. This struck a severe blow to the NAEB and its land-grant college member institutions, whose engineers had helped fine tune radio technologies and whose agricultural extension divisions imagined, and occasionally realized, radio as a mechanism for cheap, effective rural instruction and informational delivery. The cause of educational television presented the NAEB and the entire higher education community with a shot at redemption.[135]

After World War II the NAEB and a number of schools in the Midwest and South with strong extension traditions plowed ahead in the name of noncommercial educational television. The Institute for Education by Radio and Television (IERT) at Ohio State University became a leader in ETV research and development—a test site for the exploration of on-campus closed-circuit telecasting and televised extension programming for broadcast to homes across the land. The University of Michigan opened its "video university" in the fall of 1950 with the help of the IERT. *University Television Hour* aired every Sunday on WWJ-TV of the *Detroit News*. The first two segments offered viewers a smattering of "academic" and "how-to-do" instruction followed by a final promotional segment that showed "the University of Michigan at work." Successful students took examinations and some even earned "certificates of instruction."[136] Within a few years, upward of ninety colleges and universities were offering televised "home-study" programs via local commercial stations.[137]

Figure 5.4. University of Michigan faculty film a segment of the *University Television Hour*, which aired Sunday mornings on WWJ-TV in the early 1950s. Courtesy Media Resources Center Records, 1948–87, box 33, folder 3, Bentley Historical Library, University of Michigan.

New York City was home to a number of adventuresome commercial educational shows during the decade. In 1958, WCBS-TV began early morning broadcasts of *Sunrise Semester* in collaboration with New York University. The first for-credit segment was *Comparative Literature 10*, taught by a professor of romance languages. Critics praised the professor's "native histrionic talent," particularly his ability to speak "without notes," and the "attractive book-lined setting."[138] Media critic Jack Gould of the *New York Times* dubbed it "college in pajamas" and declared it "a refreshing and civilized hit."[139] A year later WNBC-TV, with a grant from the Ford Foundation, premiered a direct-competitor, for-credit educational offering, *Continental Classroom*. The first installment was entitled *Physics for the Atomic Age*, taught by physicist Harvey E. White of the University of California, Berkeley. A veteran of the Manhattan Project and consultant to the Atomic Energy Commission, White devoted his first lecture to Newton's Laws of Motion. Standing in front of three chalk-covered blackboards, White used a toy truck to explain the relationship between force, mass, and acceleration.[140] Simulcast on over 140 affiliate stations and to students at 250 different colleges, producers claimed the show was the "largest 'class' in the history of American education."[141] *Continental Classroom* aired for three years.

Commercial courses such as these, relegated to the nether regions of the programming schedule, reinforced the belief among ETV purists that the medium's full potential would only be realized through noncommercial channels free of ruinous competition and counterprogramming. That this cause was advanced by Frieda B. Hennock, an FCC commissioner, proved doubly ironic. The FCC had initially disregarded educational radio in the 1930s, and Hennock had not expressed any interest in educational television prior to arriving in Washington in 1948. At the time of her confirmation as the FCC's first female commissioner, Hennock was a policymaker in search of a policy issue. ETV became that issue. A 1950 *McCall's* article likened Hennock's advocacy of ETV to a "single-handed crusade."[142] The religious allusion was appropriate. Hennock had converted to ETV while attending an IERT meeting at Ohio State University in her first year at the FCC, in 1949. "It was here," she later revealed, "that many of my ideas concerning educational-TV were born."[143] At every turn, Hennock stressed the interrelationship between ETV, democracy, and national security. "My purpose is to rekindle the flame of the educator's excitement," she said. "I urge our educational community to get into television immediately." At the annual meeting of the Community Institute, Hennock implored her audience to think about the ways in which television, if properly used, could spread "knowledge, enlightenment and culture" and make "every American a student of international affairs." Hennock passionately believed ETV would protect American democracy from the spread of Soviet communism. In a speech to the Adult Education Council, she made this point patently clear: "In advocating [ETV], I believe I am advocating the preservation of our sacred American heritage."[144]

In the summer and fall of 1951, Hennock presided over ETV hearings at the FCC. Friendly witnesses from a host of educational institutions testified, framing their support in terms of democracy promotion and national security. The president of Miami University in Oxford, Ohio, said: "As a state-supported, land-grant institution Miami is dedicated to serve the citizenry to the full extent of our facilities. For well over a century and a quarter, young men and women have been coming to the Miami campus seeking that knowledge. . . . Now, in television, we realize the opportunity for reversing . . . this process. We can go out to the people." The president of the Ohio Education Association, J. D. Blackford, highlighted the defense preparedness benefits of educational television: "In the event of actual warfare, a television station, operated by the people who know and understand the problems of instructing boys and girls, can be a tremendously vital force in developing morale and meeting disaster." The president of Southern Illinois University lent his support in much franker terms: "The area of Carbondale, Illinois, is known to be one of the most back-ward areas of the United States, and in need of the greatest development." On April 14, 1952, the FCC set aside 242 channels (later increased to 258) for non-commercial educational television.[145]

That same year the FAE created the Educational Television and Radio Cen-ter (ETRC) to nurture ETV. Publicly, officials described the ETRC as the coun-try's "fourth network." But this was not completely accurate as the network did not produce original content. Rather, the ETRC, which moved to the Uni-versity of Michigan in 1954, served as a national programming clearinghouse and ETV consulting firm. The ETRC purchased original programming from local stations and charged a licensing fee to distribute prints-by-mail to affili-ates, a practice known as "bicycling." The goal, according to ETRC's director of information, was to ensure a rich mix of "integrated and balanced" content from across a number of geographic regions and subject areas—"History and Civilization, The Individual and Society, Public Affairs, Literature and Philoso-phy, Music, The Arts, The Natural and Physical Sciences, Child Interests, and Youth Interests." The ETRC favored "lecture-type" or "group discussion" for-mats in which content was "objectively" relayed in a didactic if not dry manner by ETV's small but distinguished cast of "stars," including atomic scientist Dr. Edward Teller, chemist Dr. Glen Seaborg, and baby expert Dr. Benjamin Spock. All this was according to script. "While programs must be of sufficient interest to catch and hold the attention of a potential audience, their basic reason for being must be to educate," declared ETRC president H. K. Newborn. "In prac-tice this has meant that although entertainment values, humor and other such factors can be utilized wherever possible, they must be the means to an end and should never predominate."[146]

The creation of noncommercial educational television stations was slowed by fiscal, administrative, and technological problems. First, a new television sta-tion cost at least $250,000 to build, and usually much more. The FAE's matching grant program defrayed some of the expense, but not enough. State govern-ments and universities still needed to foot most of the bill. This complex fund-ing system led to complicated administrative arrangements at many stations, whose licenses were held by independent boards or a single state government agency but operated by universities and colleges. Located at the crossroads of state-society relations, land-grant institutions became a favorite home for ETV stations in the Midwest and South where the tradition of university extension had especially deep roots.[147] In Wisconsin, for example, WHA-TV was licensed to an independent committee but placed under the "complete control" of the University of Wisconsin. A similar arrangement was worked out in North Carolina where WUNC-TV was authorized by the state legislature but run by a consortium of three schools: UNC-Chapel Hill, the state flagship; North Carolina State College, in Raleigh; and UNC-Greensboro, a women's college.[148]

Figure 5.5. From left to right, University of Houston president Walter W. Kemmerer, FCC commissioner Frieda B. Hennock, and chair of the University of Houston's Board of Regents, Hugh Roy Cullen, celebrate at the 1953 dedication gala for KUHT Public Television, the first noncommercial public station to begin broadcasting in the United States. Courtesy KUHT Archive Collection, University of Houston Libraries' Special Collections.

Finally, regardless of whether an ETV station was operated by a university or another semiautonomous public agency, precious few citizens actually tuned in during the 1950s. Half of the forty ETV stations operating by decade's end were assigned Ultra High Frequency (UHF) channels. This presented a problem for viewers, the vast majority of whom owned televisions that were only equipped to receive programming on the Very High Frequency (VHF) range of the broadcast spectrum. On top of everything else, ETV access required viewers to spend an extra $75 for a UHF converter box.[149]

Stations did open despite all these hurdles. The very first to do so was the University of Houston's KUHT in June 1953. President Walter W. Kemmerer insisted the investment was well worth it. Using educational television the university could reach more students, at a lower per unit cost, than was possible using traditional classroom instruction, saving the institution an estimated $10 million.[150] More important, according to KUHT's station manager, the venture promised a return of a sort that could not be measured in mere dollars and cents: "We at KUHT believe that the preservation of democracy depends on an informed electorate. To this end we are devoting all our efforts in bringing to an ever-increasing audience programs concerned with information, education, and the humanities. Educational television may prove to be the best friend democracy has."[151]

The friendship took years to develop. On campus, students found televised instruction less interesting, harder to follow, and more alienating than traditional classroom formats. Most professors also rejected the idea of educational television, if for largely erroneous reasons. They feared surveillance by nosy administrators and voiced concerns about academic freedom and the possibility of "technological unemployment."[152] Their more rational colleagues dismissed doomsday scenarios yet still raised legitimate pedagogical concerns: "You can't ask television a question," griped one professor, "you can't debate it!"[153] Off campus and in households around the country, ordinary adults apparently found the brave, new world of ETV to be a complete bore. The small audience who watched was select, not mass; well to do, not poor; and overwhelmingly white and college educated. In other words, most Americans tuned out ETV and tuned in the entertainment and news offerings of the "big three" commercial networks instead. Sitcoms, soap operas, and game shows dominated the ratings wars, monopolizing ever-larger chunks of the public's leisure time. *I Love Lucy*, *Gunsmoke*, *Dragnet*, and *Your Show of Shows* were watched weekly by tens of millions of Americans in the 1950s. And when Americans wanted news, they kept the dial pegged to one of the commercial networks' evening news broadcasts, not ETV. ETV programs like *President's Press Conference*, *Science Reporter*, and *Eliot Norton Reviews* never generated the same excitement or numbers of viewers as the commercial networks' shows did.[154]

In spite of nonexistent ratings, ETV never faded to black, of course. The ETRC continued operation into the 1960s, thanks in large measure to the federal government, which boosted ETV's ill-defined profile with the passage of the National Defense Education Act of 1958. The final act in ETV's two-decade run occurred in 1967, however, when President Lyndon B. Johnson signed the Public Broadcasting Act.[155] At the White House ceremony, Johnson did not mention the Ford Foundation or its then-obscure Fund for Adult Education, which ceased operations in 1961. Nor did he speak directly about the cold war origins of educational television. Yet Johnson certainly extolled public broadcasting in words familiar to Fletcher—who had helped organize the Carnegie Corporation's Commission on Educational Television in 1965, whose final report provided a blueprint for the legislation Johnson signed—and his cadre of Ford program officers.[156] "Educational television" Johnson promised, "will be carefully guarded from Government or from party control. It will be free, and it will be independent." He continued, apparently unaware or unconcerned about ETV's rocky past, optimistically forecasting that the legislation's seminal achievement, the Corporation for Public Broadcasting, would help turn the nation into "a replica of the old Greek marketplace, where public affairs took place in view of all the citizens."[157] Three years on the American people finally gazed into the future of informed citizenship that had been more than two decades in the making. In 1970 the Public Broadcasting Service (PBS) made its national debut broadcasting to "viewers like you" on the vestiges of the old ETV network. This history was not completely forgotten. Just months later, C. Scott Fletcher and the defunct Fund for Adult Education received their due. The NAEB, whose university member institutions, together with the Ford Foundation, had helped guide ETV through its formative first decade, awarded Fletcher its Distinguished Service Award "in recognition of his outstanding contribution to educational broadcasting."[158]

"Essential and Necessary to . . . National Survival": The National Defense Education Act of 1958

During the 1950s, the bipolar global cold war changed American higher education. The battle for worldwide hegemony compelled the institution to assume a more global outlook better suited for the creation of cold war citizens. Perhaps more important, the cold war electrified popular and political support on behalf of the most important piece of federal education legislation since the G.I. Bill of 1944—the National Defense Education Act of 1958 (NDEA).[159]

Although it is primarily remembered as an emergency elementary and secondary education act, in fact the NDEA authorized nearly $1 billion in federal emergency aid to fortify every rung of the nation's educational ladder from elementary to graduate school. As is well known, educational anxieties over the Soviet Union's successful launch of its Sputnik rocket on October 4, 1957, set the stage for this legislative breakthrough. Fears of falling militarily, psychologically, and intellectually behind the Russian enemy roused the federal government, and the American people, to action. Proposals for increased federal funding for the nation's education system had been circulating around the Capitol for nearly two decades, but it took the Sputnik crisis to secure the political support needed to move the legislation through Congress. The handful of liberals who inhabited the "small world of education politics," as one leading historian on the topic has described it, seized their opportunity to increase federal support for elementary, secondary, and higher education.[160] Two friends from Alabama, Representative Carl Elliott (D-AL) and Senator Lister Hill (D-AL), both of whom served on the education subcommittees in their respective chambers, coauthored the Democrats' education bill. Longtime allies, Elliot had worked for Hill before winning office, both men were racial moderates and shared a commitment to improving the dilapidated educational infrastructure of their home state and region. The bill they crafted closely resembled the administration's bill sponsored by Senator H. Alexander Smith (R-NJ), no stranger to educational policymaking.[161] The final NDEA legislation combined elements from both bills, clearing the legitimacy barrier because legislators agreed with Elliot's assertion that the NDEA—and the federal involvement that it beckoned—was "essential and necessary to . . . national survival."[162]

National defense imperatives may have made the passage of the NDEA easier, but it was hardly automatic. Congressional debate dragged on for a year as stakeholders sought to determine how increased federal support would comport with the age-old tradition of local control in elementary and secondary educational matters. One source of resistance flowed from the White House. President Eisenhower harbored reservations about extending the government's reach into the nation's public schools despite the recommendations of his own education task force, the Committee on Education Beyond High School, which supported more federal involvement in elementary and secondary education. A second source of resistance flowed from Elliot's and Hill's more ardently segregationist chamber colleagues. They were still seething over the Supreme Court's 1954 *Brown* decision that had ended legal segregation in public education. Coming just four years after the court's 1950 rulings in *Sweatt v. Painter* and *McLaurin v. Oklahoma State Regents* had put segregated graduate and professional education on notice, southerners had good reason to believe that the NDEA might lead to greater federal involvement in all walks of southern life, not just education. That did not occur—at least not immediately. "Judge" Howard W. Smith (D-VA), chairman of the all-powerful House Rules Committee, through which all bills had first to pass, made it well known any control but local control would not do. Title I of the NDEA made this point loud and clear: "The States and local communities have and must retain control over and primary responsibility for public education."[163] Eisenhower, torn by federal intervention of any sort, in any domestic arena, concurred. The goal of the NDEA, he carefully explained, was not to "inject the Federal government into education in a massive or dominating role," but to correct "certain deficiencies in education which handicap . . . national security."[164] Federal dominance over education policymaking would, in time, come. But this was never preordained. Sold as a temporary emergency measure, not a permanent realignment in federal and state governance, the NDEA won over enough skeptics who believed that training linguists, mathematicians, and scientists was a national security priority worth supporting.[165]

In contrast to the debate that attended the K-12-related aspects of the NDEA, hearings on the legislation's higher education provisions were remarkably tame. Emotions did run high over Elliot and Hill's proposal for federally funded college scholarships, which, if enacted, would have provided a small group of especially promising math, science, and language students with a free education. It was struck from the final legislation by conservatives from both parties who regarded the provision as little more than a handout by another name and thus too great an extension of federal power.[166] Emotions also ran high over the NDEA's "loyalty oath" provision, modeled on the various loyalty oath provisions that had been installed in both government and in higher education since the late 1940s and the eruption of the cold war. A by-product of the anticommunist frenzy of the period and of the national security rationales used to justify the NDEA in the first place, the oath requirement demanded individuals to swear allegiance to the United States as a condition of accepting a defense loan or fellowship, the NDEA's main higher education provisions. Twenty-nine institutions protested the loyalty oath (later repealed in 1962) on academic freedom grounds, but the vast majority of institutions embraced the NDEA, oath and all.[167] Despite the surge in academic freedom violations during the McCarthy hysteria in the early part of the decade, by 1958, perhaps in part because of McCarthy's alcohol-fueled death the year before, most university leaders were willing to let bygones be bygones. Moreover, by the late 1950s their institutions had become dependent on the state's largess, if not fully trusting of the state itself. Since the New Deal, higher education had been immersed in national policymaking and a major recipient of federal aid for veterans, for building projects, and for national defense research and development work in many fields, especially in science, engineering, and medicine. What the NDEA did instead was permanently institutionalize a host of initiatives that higher education had been pursuing with and without steady external support since the end of World War II. The legislation's first appropriation provided $32 million for the improvement of language and area studies centers; $20 million for additional research into high-tech educational delivery systems, such as television and radio; $15 million for vocational education; and $5 million for National Defense Graduate Fellowships for elite graduate training in math, science, and the foreign languages. Considered in this light, the NDEA deepened higher education's relationship with and dependence on the state without dramatically altering it.[168]

In still other ways, however, the NDEA marked a key turning point in the federal-academic partnership. First, the NDEA refocused federal legislators' interest in educational politics and policymaking, shifting their gaze from the international to the national and to the relationship between the two. The increased capacity of the House Committee on Education and Labor, which handled education-related policy, bears this point out. Prior to 1958, the committee, chaired by Representative Graham Barden (D-NC), was arguably the least productive standing committee on Capitol Hill. This changed under the energetic chairmanship of Barden's successor, Representative Adam C. Powell Jr. (D-NY), who turned Education and Labor into one of the busiest congressional committees by the early 1960s.[169] Second, the NDEA expanded the federal government's capacity to administer education policy, delivering lasting changes to the Office of Education, housed since 1953 within the Department of Health, Education, and Welfare. The number and complexity of the NDEA's new administrative demands forced the Office of Education to adapt on the fly. The office's staff increased from 589 in 1958 to 900 the following year, remaking it, as the commissioner from those years later recalled, "from the 97 pound weakling of the world of education into a robust organization."[170] In short, the passage of the NDEA attracted a whole generation of legislators to the limitless possibilities of education policymaking, persuading many of them that education might be the best way to build a truly great society.

Finally, and most significant of all, the NDEA introduced federal loans to American students and their families. From a long-range perspective, the NDEA's $295 million student loan provision would have the greatest impact on American higher education, previewing a future in which college access would increasingly turn on borrowed money. Even at the time of the passage of the NDEA, the importance of the loan program was well understood. From the get-go, according to one leading historian, the loan provision exceeded "all other programs in its institutional reach, number of participants, and dollars spent."[171] Building on the state's support for veterans—the model adjusted citizen—the NDEA now extended that support to a new class of deserving citizens who pledged to strengthen democracy by going to college. The federal government granted individual institutions up to a $250,000 annually for student-loans, covering 90 percent of each loan with a 10 percent institutional match, which could also be borrowed from the government. Loans were earmarked initially for students pursuing math, science, and language fields deemed crucial to national security but were in fact distributed to students proportionally across all undergraduate fields, thereby turning what was theoretically categorical aid into general aid. Individual students could borrow up to a thousand dollars per year, at an interest rate of 3 percent, repayable over ten years, with partial loan forgiveness options available to graduates who taught for five years in a public school. In 1957, the year before the passage of the NDEA, 80,000 students borrowed $13 million from college student-loan funds; in 1961, 115,000 students borrowed four times that amount thanks to the infusion of NDEA money. Or, to put it another way, the NDEA's student loan program helped 630 of the 1,400 participating higher education institutions establish student loan programs on their campuses for the first time.[172] Nationwide, an estimated 1.5 million students used an NDEA loan to go to college between 1959 and 1969, when the NDEA's core higher education provisions were either terminated or absorbed by the Higher Education Act of 1965.[173]

Before the Higher Education Act turned the federal government into the nation's preferred student aid lender, recipients of NDEA student loans let their appreciation be known. Letters poured into the Office of Education. Students admitted that in the absence of a National Defense Education Loan, they would not be able to attend school. "My family could not have sent me to college without this loan," explained a student. Another recipient thought the loan program was "one of the finest things that has happened to educational assistance." An engineering student at Clarkson College, in Potsdam, New York, said, "I am truly grateful that I was born in a country where the government shows such a true interest in its citizens."[174] But were the country's citizens truly interested in their government? Did they understand the stakes of the cold war conflict and the role the state expected educated citizens to play in winning it? At the start of the cold war these questions had been rhetorical. By the end of the 1950s they were not.

❖❖❖

In the 1950s, educational elites dedicated the better part of a decade to the education of globally aware democratic citizens. They believed education was the foundation of an enlightened public consensus. And by wrapping American higher education in the flag during the cold war, they transformed the institution and garnered greater federal and foundation support for the education of average citizens.

Yet politicians' and university leaders' efforts to prepare a better-informed and more vigilant citizenry was not entirely—or at least obviously—successful. College students and adults remained shockingly aloof on and off campus. They avoided international clubs and activities at alarming rates, preferring instead the pretend politics of student government, or better yet, no politics at all. The undergraduate experience remained moored to the Greek system and all the fun and games the system held in store.

By comparison, study abroad offered a glimmer of hope. Excited by the possibility of seeing the world, students enthusiastically lined up to do so in the 1950s. Promoted as a way to make the world safe for democracy, study abroad did not quite meet those haughty expectations. American students relished their overseas adventures, to be sure, but the aims of their travels were more than parochial—they were personal. Like veterans after World War II, cold war collegians had their own ideas about the real benefits of an education: some wanted a change of scenery, others anonymity, and still others, good times. Foreign students' motivations were just as varied. Some came to the United States for professional credentials, others for pleasure, and some in search of democracy. But those who did were often disappointed by what they found. Pervasive inequality and segregation (whether by law or custom) undercut American society's—and higher education's—promise of freedom.

Higher education's high-tech venture into the adult education marketplace was likewise mixed. Spurred by the availability of new media, techno-proselytizers imagined using television to connect with and shape the American people's political beliefs. The development of ETV marked the apogee of this foundation-academic-government nexus, the most recent extension of higher education's ongoing effort to reach deep into the heart of the polity. ETV, as had agricultural extension and the federal forum program before it, represented democracy's newest hope for the cultivation of a vital political culture. Few Americans watched ETV, however, and instead kept the dial pegged on the "big three" commercial broadcasting networks and all the escapist pleasures they had to offer.

When all was said and done, creating informed citizens turned out to be far more difficult than educational elites originally assumed it would be. With more than a decade's worth of educating America's "children" and "adults" for cold war citizenship, neither higher education nor the government had much to show for it. In *The American Voter* (1961), political scientist Angus Campbell and his colleagues at the University of Michigan's Survey Research Center, saw little if any evidence of an emergent informed citizenry. Having scoured a decade's worth of voting data, Campbell and company concluded the distance between citizens and the state had grown as wide as ever: "The typical voter has only a modest understanding of the specific issues and may be quite ignorant of matters of public policy. . . . The stakes do not seem to be great enough for the ordinary citizen to . . . make himself well informed politically."[175]

PART III

Diversity

Chapter 6

Higher Education Confronts the Rights Revolution

—————— ❖❖❖ ——————

By 1960, California embodied the future of American higher education, and Clark Kerr, the balding, bespectacled president of the University of California, embodied California's approach. In that year Kerr achieved international acclaim as designer of the Master Plan, which readjusted California's system of universities, and state and junior colleges. Hailed a technocratic triumph, the California system's new mission was to readjust millions of students. Using high school grade point averages (and soon, the SAT) to determine admission, and by charging no tuition, only fees, the Master Plan guaranteed all Californians a shot at higher education. Like the NDEA and the G.I. Bill before it, the plan boldly reaffirmed higher education's place as a key mediating institution between citizens and the state.[1]

Kerr continued reimagining the institution in *The Uses of the University* (1963). Here Kerr declared the arrival of a new university that resembled closely his own beloved Berkeley. He called it a multiversity. Forged during the World War II era and the great transformation in state-academic relations that accompanied it, the multiversity was an amalgamation of institutional types. It combined the German commitment to research, the British to teaching, and the American to mass access and practical utility. To Kerr, the multiversity was a "city of infinite variety" where competing groups of administrators and faculty, students and their families, business leaders and government officials pursued crosscutting endeavors variously related to the production and consumption of "the university's invisible product, knowledge"[2]

Kerr painted a generally optimistic picture of the multiversity. A trained labor economist who brokered hundreds of labor disputes before entering academic administration, Kerr was a diehard pluralist who remained committed to group theory and the multiversity model he believed it helped run.[3] Yet he also observed the multiversity's human costs—and pluralism's limits. In theory the pluralist multiversity promised boundless "freedom" to all its citizens; in practice this rarely occurred. Different groups battled it out for scarce resources within the university. There were winners and losers. For students, the multi-

Figure 6.1. The "Master Planner," University of California president Clark Kerr (front, center), at the height of his power, with President John F. Kennedy, and directly behind them, Emeritus President Robert B. Sproul, Charter Day Ceremony, Memorial Stadium, Berkeley, California, March 23, 1962. Courtesy Bancroft Library, University of California, Berkeley.

versity was a "confusing place" filled with "refuges of anonymity"; for faculty, research ruled, not teaching, and increasingly "fractionalized" disciplinary lines meant fewer shared "topics of conversation at faculty clubs"; and for administrators, continuous intergroup conflict required constant oversight and attention. At the end of the day, life in the "city of intellect" was like life in any old city. "Some get lost in the city," said Kerr, "some rise to the top within it; most fashion their lives within one of its many subcultures."[4]

Less than a year later, Kerr's worst fears were realized. In the fall of 1964, the Berkeley free speech movement (FSM) mobilized to challenge his administration's McCarthy-era ban on student political activity. The FSM was the beginning of the end for Kerr, who was fired by Governor Ronald W. Reagan three years later. Following closely and inspired by Freedom Summer, the FSM not only showed that student unrest was on the move, but also that the multiversity's glow had begun to dim. Mario Savio, a Freedom Summer veteran who became the reluctant head of the FSM, compared the university to a "machine" and implored his fellow Berkeley students "to put your bodies upon the gears and upon the wheels, upon the levers, upon all the apparatus . . . to make it stop."[5]

Savio's denunciation of the multiversity was not unique to Berkeley. Midway across the country, a similar grievance had been lodged two years earlier by the Students for a Democratic Society (SDS), in their signature treatise, the "Port Huron Statement," drafted by University of Michigan graduate student Tom Hayden. Like other members of the nascent New Left, Hayden's political education had taken him west and south. He spent a summer with members of SLATE, an independent student organization that had won control of Berkeley's Greek-dominated student government in the late 1950s, before joining the Student Nonviolent Coordinating Committee (SNCC) in a summer voter registration drive. Those experiences awakened Hayden to the thrilling possibilities of political action and to the depressing realities of the modern university—a bureaucratic menace awash in "alienation" and "apathy," as he put it in the "Port Huron Statement." According to Hayden, the psychological tools and techniques of in loco parentis—freshman week, orientation courses, dormitory living, and the psychological clinic—originally deployed in the 1920s to help students adjust to college had become barriers to liberation. The "business-as-usual" academic experience, Hayden wrote, offered students "no real conception of personal identity except one manufactured in the image of others." It was a stupefying institution, Hayden believed, "a place of mass affirmation of the Twist, but mass reluctance toward the controversial public stance. Rules are accepted as 'inevitable,' bureaucracy as 'just circumstances,' irrelevance as 'scholarship,' selflessness as 'martyrdom,' politics as 'just another way to make people, and an unprofitable one, too.'" In the opinion of these critics, the modern university was the antithesis of a democracy—a psychologically oppressive place dominated by self-interested factions, the embodiment of all that was wrong with American life and politics.[6]

The political and psychological perils of mass higher education galvanized student activists. In this respect, Savio, Hayden, and others were influenced by leading 1950s social critics, including David Riesman, William H. Whyte, and C. Wright Mills, who loathed the spirit-breaking "massification" of American life and worried about the long-term prospects of a society consisting of lonely crowds of organization men manipulated from above by power elites. These criticisms resonated with students, many of whom had come to think of the university in a similar fashion—as yet another bureaucracy in a social and political "system" governed by little else. The university was really an appendage of the state, they claimed, a key "machine" in the nefarious "military-industrial complex" that had to be stopped. Throughout the remainder of the decade, students at campuses across the country tried in a variety of ways to do just that.

Students never stopped the machine. But they did change the politics of American higher education in the 1960s, proving once and for all that education and politics were both personal. Higher education's relationship to what by decade's end would be known as "personal politics," and later identity politics, had been presaged during World War II and the cold war when the differences between students' and policymakers' expectations for educated citizenship first surfaced. Policymakers supported widened educational access for instrumental purposes that rarely meshed with students' more personal pursuits. Social science research identified this disconnect in the 1950s: the divergence between attitudes and opinions—between what citizens believed privately and declared publicly—raised serious doubts about higher education's capacity to create enlightened democratic citizens. The rise of campus unrest a few years later, and then for the rest of the 1960s, all but confirmed this finding. Higher education's ability to adjust and readjust citizens for democratic life had become anything but a sure thing.

Almost as soon as the university's epitaph was written it had to be revised. By the mid-1970s, a new understanding of higher education emerged, one that prized the rights-bearing educated citizen and embodied her identity through a new variant of pluralist politics known as diversity. Forged during the turbulent 1960s and 1970s, a combustible mix of radical ideas and the existential call to action ironically forged a diversity-based framework that met administrators' need for order and students' need for liberation—ironic because the student movements of the early 1960s explicitly rejected pluralist politics only to return to them by decade's end, if in a different and more personal way. They may have been reluctant pluralists, but they were pluralists nonetheless.

This chapter documents this dramatic shift and locates its origins in the interplay between and among federal higher education policy, the campus wings of the minority rights revolution, and psychological thought. First, I trace the policy origins of student diversity to the Johnson administration's War on Poverty, revealing how the pursuit of equal opportunity led to the discovery of diversity. Next, I explore the various intellectual justifications used to promote diversity as a cure for the new maladjustment of the New Left: alienation. Finally, I examine the political origins of curricular diversity by following the rise of two of the major campus identity groups of the late 1960s: the black power and the women's liberation movements. Even though they counted Freud as one of their most maligned enemies, these movements embedded post-Freudian psychological assumptions at the very heart of their intellectual core and ensured that psychological understandings of what it meant to be an educated citizen would define both campus and national politics into the 1980s and beyond.

"We Need a Negro as a Symbol of Liberalism": The 1965 Higher Education Act and the Policy Origins of Student Diversity

President Lyndon B. Johnson's War on Poverty ushered in an unparalleled period of federal involvement in education policy. Over the course of his presidency, Johnson signed sixty major education bills that dramatically expanded existing federal commitments to education and introduced new ones.

Figure 6.2. Lyndon B. Johnson and his students pose for their class photo, Welhausen School, Cotulla, Texas, 1928. Image 28-13-4, Courtesy LBJ Library and Museum.

He spoke often of wanting to be the nation's first "education president," and in many ways he was.[7]

While the Johnson administration's transformation of elementary and secondary education has been well documented by scholars, comparatively little is known about its equally remarkable accomplishments in the higher education arena.[8] Johnson supported innovative policies that upped the federal government's involvement in virtually every aspect of the nation's colleges and universities. He authorized the wider geographic dispersal of federal research dollars and crafted and signed laws that increased federal aid for facilities construction, student assistance, and the support and development of historically black and junior colleges. Between 1963 and 1966, federal aid to colleges increased from $1.4 billion to $3.7 billion, and by the end of the decade federal support for all levels of education had surged to $12 billion annually, half of which flowed to higher education. His record in the area of education policy was, and remains, unparalleled.[9]

Johnson's commitment to education was genuine. Unlike John F. Kennedy, who, for a variety of reasons—his Catholicism, his novice legislative skills, his preoccupation with foreign rather than domestic affairs—was never able to deliver a new education policy, Johnson truly believed in the power of education to change citizens' lives.[10] A 1930 graduate of Southwest Texas State College at San Marcos, he taught at a Mexican-American neighborhood school in Cotulla, Texas, to help finance his education. The experience left a lasting impression on him. As president, he reminisced how he never forgot "the faces of the boys and girls in that classroom . . . [and] . . . the pain of realizing . . . then that college was closed to practically every one of those children because they were too poor."[11]

Johnson's faith in education and in activist government became even more pointed during his service in behalf of the New Deal—the major source of Johnson's own political education. In 1935, after four years spent teaching high school in Texas and then working on Capitol Hill, he was appointed the Texas state director of the National Youth Administration (NYA). The youngest state-level NYA director in the country, Johnson quickly distinguished himself. He gained national acclaim, and the accolades of the Roosevelt administration he adored, by turning his program, in the words of his NYA superior, into "one of the best programs with the most universal and enthusiastic public support of any state in the Union."[12] Johnson created a number of novel NYA projects that deftly combined hard work with self-improvement, including the construction of new roadside parks and the formation of a free network of "freshman college centers" to teach young people too poor to attend school full time. "Those NYA experiences were valuable to me," remarked Johnson in his memoirs, "suggesting some of the solutions we were searching for [in the 1960s]."[13]

Johnson put his faith in education to the test when he declared an unconditional War on Poverty. Launched in 1964 as the main plank of his reelection platform, the War on Poverty veered away from income transfer programs, focusing instead on service transfers and training—on the creation of what he and his political allies effusively described in shorthand form as "opportunity." Johnson, like FDR before him, hated the idea of dependency, believing handouts sapped recipients' desire for independence. Opportunity, on the other hand, was a proven American value that comported well with Johnson's own New Deal-inspired political worldview.[14]

Johnson's commitment to opportunity was energized by widespread enthusiasm in behalf of the academic enterprise and the "knowledge revolution" it was fueling. From the social sciences, in particular, two emergent theories suggested education might be the government's secret weapon in the fight against poverty and unemployment. First, from economics, human capital theory lent academic heft to the longstanding assumption that social investments in education paid handsome dividends. Advanced by economists primarily affiliated with the University of Chicago, human capital theorists had the ear of Johnson's Council of Economic Advisers who agreed education was probably the most expeditious way to eradicate poverty in all its forms.[15] Johnson actually never spoke publicly about human capital theory per se. But there is no doubt he believed educational investments in poor people yielded political and financial profit. "One thousand dollars invested in salvaging an unemployable youth today can return $40,000 or more in his lifetime," said Johnson in his 1964 State of the Union Address.[16]

Second, from social psychology, culture of poverty theory recommended fighting poverty by distributing educational opportunity rather than redistributing wealth. Originally developed by University of Illinois anthropologist Oscar Lewis in the late 1950s, culture of poverty theory cast deprivation as a transmittable psychopathological disease handed down from one generation to the next.[17] Because Lewis's research was conducted in Mexico, and Mexican families served as his subject, his theory did not resonate widely with American readers until after it was repackaged by sociologist Michael Harrington in his groundbreaking bestseller *The Other America* (1962). Estimating the poor population at between 40 and 50 million, and encompassing inhabitants from Appalachia to the inner-city, Harrington memorably described the poor as "internal exiles"—all but invisible to politicians and middle-class Americans—possessed of their own language, habits, and customs, indeed, their own "psychology."[18] According to one leading scholar, by popularizing a cultural interpretation of poverty in which maladjusted, urban dwelling, matriarchal African-American families were the prime culprits, Harrington's work helped psychologize human privation, persuading mainstream liberals, such as Johnson, that the poverty problem was amenable to educational prescriptions for rehabilitation.[19] "Every child must be encouraged to get as much education as he has ability to take," Johnson declared, echoing the fundamental tenets of such an approach, in 1965. "We want this not only for his sake—but for the nation's sake. Nothing matters more to the future of our country . . . for freedom is fragile if citizens are ignorant."[20]

Within a few years new counterresearch would emerge to challenge the foundational assumptions that underlay both human capital and culture of poverty theory. The Coleman Report and the Moynihan Report leveled especially devastating blows against the supposedly irredeemable "black family," suggesting to many skeptical policymakers the limits of using education as a weapon against poverty. But during the golden first two years of Johnson's presidency—prior to the wide circulation of that counterresearch and before urban riots and Vietnam ended his dream of building a great society—he moved confidently on the domestic front, shepherding legislation through Congress that revitalized the state's commitment to educating citizens. In the summer of 1964, two pieces of legislation firmly moored equality to opportunity, setting the stage for the passage of decisive higher education legislation the following year. First, the Civil Rights Act of 1964, which outlawed discrimination in employment and accommodations, also transformed higher education. Title VI banned discrimination based on "race, color, or national origin" by any institution that received federal funds, which encompassed practically all colleges and universities.[21] This financial enticement lent some much-needed momentum to the integration of southern higher education after *Brown*. Officials tried every gimmick to delay integration, particularly at private institutions, which claimed amnesty from *Brown*. The moral push of the civil rights movement combined with the monetary pull of federal civil rights legislation finally ended the impasse. And by 1965 every public flagship university in the South except Louisiana State counted at least one black student among its undergraduate population. Up and coming elite private schools such as Duke, Emory, Rice, Tulane, and Vanderbilt, whose leaders desired national greatness for their institutions, grudgingly followed suit.[22]

Second, the Economic Opportunity Act of 1964 created a host of antipoverty education programs, including Head Start, the Job Corps, and Volunteers in Service to America (VISTA). These programs provided preschoolers and unemployed adults with compensatory education opportunities and hands-on job training, and gave idealistic young people of all backgrounds the chance to join their government in the fight against poverty. While less publicized, the act also touched higher education. It revived the government's long-defunct federal work-study program, originally initiated during the New Deal, and created brand new student support programs, anchored by Upward Bound (later transferred to the Office of Education), to help poor but capable high school students prepare for college.[23]

Johnson's gamble on antipoverty programming paid off at the polls. His landslide reelection over Senator Barry Goldwater (R-AZ) in 1964 breathed new life into the New Deal coalition and helped congressional Democrats to their largest majorities since 1938. The election of sixty-five freshmen Democratic congressmen, many of whom had run on activist government platforms, assured Johnson of the comprehensive federal education legislation he desired.[24] Still glorying in his triumph, in January 1965 Johnson challenged Congress to help more young people—especially poor young people—go to college. Demanding nothing less than "full educational opportunity," he urged the legislature to "start where men who would improve their society have always known they must start—with an educational system restudied, reinforced, and revitalized."[25]

The Higher Education Act (HEA) of 1965 marked the culmination of the Johnson administration's fight for educational opportunity. Crafted by a White House task force and passed after the more controversial Elementary and Secondary Education Act, the HEA easily made its way through Congress. Representative Adam C. Powell Jr. (D-NY), chair of the House Education and Labor Committee, and Representative Edith Green (D-OR) and Senator Wayne Morse (D-OR), each head of the subcommittee on education in their respective chambers, managed the bill. Though Powell would later depart Congress in disgrace in 1970 after a series of political scandals, Green and Morse continued to provide consistently liberal support in behalf of higher education policymaking well into the Nixon years.[26]

The eight-title act absorbed the state's existing higher education programs and added a multitude of new ones.[27] Administered by the Office of Education, the $2.7 billion act extended federal authority to every sector of the nation's higher education system. One title provided land-grant institutions with aid to pursue antipoverty urban extension programs; two titles offered financial assistance that covered brick-and-mortar projects and faculty development programming; and another title created the Teachers Corps to train teachers

Figure 6.3. President Lyndon B. Johnson, with Lady Bird Johnson looking on, at his alma mater, Southwest Texas State College, signing the Higher Education Act, November 8, 1965. Image C844-7-WH65, Courtesy LBJ Library and Museum.

for work in impoverished areas of the country. Two remaining titles covered student financial aid and funding to strengthen so-called "developing institutions"—the country's 123 predominantly black colleges and universities.[28] It was in these final two areas—funding for historically black colleges and universities (Title III) and for student aid (Title IV)—where the act moved most creatively to equalize educational opportunity and to fight poverty.

Title III sought to help predominantly black-serving institutions, which enrolled 60 percent of the nation's 158,000 black collegians, overcome years of racist neglect. The title provided aid for general operating expenses and for the establishment of cooperative arrangements between "developing" black institutions and "established" white ones.[29] Edith Green sponsored Title III. A former school teacher and education lobbyist, she claimed the Fulbright program as her main inspiration for the developing institutions provision, which created a domestic exchange program that sent "senior scholar[s]" and students between top-tier research universities and black colleges to improve academic quality and to strengthen interracial relations.[30] Green also could have cited the just-passed Area Redevelopment Act of 1961, the Manpower Development and Training Act of 1962, and the Vocational Education Act and Higher Education Facilities Act of 1963 as evidence of the federal government's conviction that education could cure poverty.[31] This entire stream of education and training legislation was guided by the same antipoverty/human capital rationales that animated the HEA, and thus owed much to the confluence of international and domestic policymaking during the cold war. In the 1950s, the state exported academic experts and students to strengthen democratic institutions in postcolonial, Third-World battle zones. The civil rights movement and War on Poverty at home, however, shifted the state's attention to the economic development and adjustment of one of America's most neglected groups—African Americans.[32]

The HEA targeted the development of the country's historically black colleges and universities through intranational partnerships with leading research universities in thirty-eight different states.[33] One of the best known Title III exchange programs existed between Hampton Institute in Virginia and Cornell University. The arrangement stipulated the exchange of administrators, teachers, and students between both schools. In practice, however, the exchange program was a one-way street, requiring Hampton personnel to travel to Ithaca to undertake advanced study and research, but demanding little from Cornell in return. "It [is] relatively easy to schedule these [tenured Cornell professors] as lecturers or as consultants for a day or two," confessed English professor Hugh Gloster, then Hampton's dean of faculty and soon-to-be-named president of Morehouse College, in Atlanta, "but hard to do so for a regular or summer term." This created some tensions between Hampton and Cornell. Though the president of Cornell heralded the partnership as one of "joint enrichment," Gloster was less sanguine. Choosing his words carefully, he admitted, "One problem is the assumption by certain university personnel that predominantly Negro colleges are uniformly inferior."[34]

Like the global educational exchange programs of the 1950s that sent American faculty and students to developing countries around the world, the domestic exchange of black and white students and teachers under the auspices of Title III generated unanticipated outcomes. While the avowed goal was to strengthen democracy by creating better schools and more racially tolerant citizens, whether this occurred was far from certain. The very idea of sending faculty and students from developing to established institutions struck many African-American educators as reinforcing the very intellectual and material disparities the program was intended to overcome—or worse.[35] Many faculty and students never returned after visiting elite northern institutions. An administrator at Tuskegee Institute, which had a longstanding cooperative arrangement with the University of Michigan, said, "Michigan takes most of our best faculty. Even though their faculty is very helpful and capable, we need our best faculty at Tuskegee."[36]

Predominantly white universities like Michigan also cherry picked their partner schools' best students. Rufus Clement, the president of Atlanta University, denounced the "brain drain" and blamed white universities for causing it. "These people go down there and say, 'We need a Negro as a symbol of liberalism,'" Clement told a meeting of the National Council of Churches. "If they take the cream of our student crop they leave us poor indeed."[37] Though a slow but steady influx of white students to predominantly black colleges made up some of the gap, many black administrators believed the process of "reverse integration," by offering access to students of lesser ability, actually benefited white rather than black institutions.[38] Hugh Gloster, then president at Morehouse College, reflected on these changes in black higher education during the 1960s with mixed feelings. Though the strongest black colleges were "better centers of teaching and learning than ever," Gloster later wrote, by the 1970s most black colleges teetered on the brink of disaster, "involved in a struggle for existence in which only the fittest will survive."[39]

While Title III increased the amount of contact between black and white faculty and students, it was the financial aid provision of the HEA, Title IV, which really propelled the diversification of American higher education. It included a four-part package of financial aid options. The first two were rolled over from previous acts. The HEA incorporated the work study provision from the Education Opportunity Act of 1964 as well as the direct student loan provision from the NDEA—the former provided needy students with the chance to work toward their degree; the latter provided students enrolled in national-defense-related fields of study (i.e., foreign languages, math, and science) with subsidized loans and loan forgiveness options. These were familiar reciprocal aid mechanisms that offered students funding in return for service.[40]

Two additional student aid options included in Title IV were brand new initiatives: grants and guaranteed student loans for all students regardless of academic major. Democratic leaders, led by Representative Powell, agreed to a Guaranteed Student Loan Program for the middle-class—guaranteed because the federal government insured the loans on behalf of the private banks and lending agencies that financed them—in order to garner Republican support for federal aid to students with "exceptional financial need." Democrats considered the guaranteed loan provision a small price to pay for the achievement of federal grants for needy students. In the end, both parties got their wish.[41]

It is difficult to overstate the importance of the HEA's financial aid title. Liberal Democrats and education interest groups had lobbied for need-based aid since the G.I. Bill had revealed the benefits of expanded access. It took the War on Poverty to make it happen. The creation of Education Opportunity Grants (the official name of the federal scholarship program) extended the possibility of collegiate access to untold millions of students, not just veterans and students enrolled in national-defense-related fields of study, without any reciprocal obligations. Where the G.I. Bill and the NDEA increased educational opportunities for specific categories of citizens in exchange for past or future service, the HEA, what the *New York Times* described as a "natural extension of the G.I. Bill," now held out the promise of the same to everyone else.[42]

The HEA embraced an expansive notion of student aid to ensure broad access. After all, the availability of vast new sums of money would achieve little in the absence of a larger pool of qualified students. Government data revealed that while 1.4 million of the nation's 2.7 million high school graduates entered college in 1964, the remaining 1.3 million, half of whom were black and poor, did not enroll because of the lack of funds, or academic preparation, or both.[43] In order to level the academic playing field, Title IV earmarked funds for the development of compensatory education, counseling, and student recruitment programs to help talented but poor students prepare for the academic and emotional adjustments of college life.[44]

Upward Bound emerged as the HEA's main college preparatory program. Directed by Richard T. Frost, vice president of Reed College, it debuted in the summer of 1966 at 250 colleges and universities around the country. Twentythousand students were selected to participate in the eight-week program. A traditional academic core was augmented by cultural programming, psychological counseling, and self-esteem building classes.[45] Project directors believed the combination of remedial and therapeutic interventions helped students overcome the psychological as well as social conditions of poverty.[46] "The [counselors]," explained a student at the Mercer College Upward Bound program, in Macon, Georgia, "try to open your mind and help you discover for yourself what you want to be."[47]

Most participants were black and poor, but seats were filled by poor and middle-class whites, too. This was deliberate. Since the 1950s, psychologists had argued that the classroom was the best venue in which to work through racial differences. Some students thought so: "I was guilty of judging people mostly on looks," said a white student from Macon, Georgia. "Upward Bound has changed all that in helping me see beyond the exterior."[48] Others disagreed. Arezell Brown had a very different experience interacting with white students at her Upward Bound program at Mercy College, near Detroit, Michigan. Brown expressed dismay at her white peers' inability to get past racial stereotypes. "Three of the white girls . . . kept a record player in the lounge and they'd often call us down and ask us to teach them to dance," said Brown.[49]

Despite some pockets of congressional opposition, strong support from instructors and students—to say nothing of the program's low cost—ensured Upward Bound's survival.[50] Robert G. Jeffrey, an assistant program director at Murray State University in Kentucky, told the *Paducah Sun-Democrat* he was "thoroughly convinced that there is definitely a place and need in our society for future Upward Bound projects."[51] Jerome Holland, president of Hampton Institute from 1960 to 1970, felt the same way. After reviewing the uniformly positive results of his school's Upward Bound program, Holland raved: "The Upward Bound program will not only be a very important recruitment instrument for our college, but our college will gain status in the local communities because we are concerned about the culturally disadvantaged youth."[52] Holland's optimism was warranted. Studies conducted by the Office of Education revealed that the program succeeded at helping poor students develop the skills they needed to attend college. Data collected between 1965 and 1968 found that 65 to 80 percent of Upward Bound participants entered college and that 75 percent of those entering remained in college, though not all of them until graduation.[53]

A major reason for the success of Upward Bound was that increasing numbers of colleges were organizing their own compensatory recruitment and education programs to increase the admission and retention of poor black students. Officials at selective and nonselective institutions organized compensatory programs in the early 1960s at a rapid rate. The University of North Carolina, for example, created a special summer visitation program to attract black students from across the state. Appalachian State University, meanwhile, developed a "high risk student admissions program" that offered students ongoing academic and psychological remediation services during the freshman year. And the University of Florida organized a similar program called the Critical Year Program, which provided "professionally trained personnel to aid the student with academic and personal problems," according to an administrator. Taking their cue from the War on Poverty and the HEA, administrators across the country organized remediation services to help poor, often ill-prepared students ready themselves for the scholastic and emotional tests of college life.[54]

This was not the first time administrators had deployed special services programs for students. Although few if any administrators made the connection in the 1960s, the model for this compensatory organizational model dated back to the 1920s when the personnel perspective first penetrated American higher education. Personnel specialists' belief in malleable personhood and institutions drove the adoption of personalized recruitment and freshmen week programs, of orientation and remedial education courses, and of campus psychological clinics to help maladjusted white students stay in school. This personalized approach to student management offered administrators broad authority over the physical, academic, and psychological well being of their charges. It also laid the groundwork for a flexible admissions process that could be tailored to suit the admissions needs of practically any reasonably qualified applicant. Critics disingenuously pointed to the extension of the personnel perspective in the 1960s as evidence of special treatment for blacks and other minority groups. What few remembered was that colleges and universities had been providing variations on the same services and admissions benefits to ill-prepared white students for decades. The seed of the affirmative action wars of the 1970s was planted in the 1920s, when college officials followed the lead of expert psychologists' theories of human and organizational development to create a therapeutic living and learning environment for all students.

The HEA transformed American higher education. The act doubled the federal government's annual higher education budget, while the triumvirate of opportunity enhancing student aid tools included in it—work study, direct and guaranteed loans, and need-based grants—changed the way college administrators crafted student bodies and how all students financed their educations. By 1975, a total of 1.5 million students (out of a total enrollment of 11 million) received aid via a direct loan, work study, or Basic Educational Opportunity Grant (then known as a Pell Grant); and another million students helped finance their education with a federally guaranteed student loan from a bank or credit union. The availability of $1.7 billion in federal student aid helped triple black student enrollment between 1968 and 1978, pushing it above a million for the first time in the mid-1970s. In sum, the HEA created the structural preconditions for the onset of diversity by giving admissions personnel access to a truly diverse student population (see appendix A.3).[55]

This fact was apparent to many administrators much earlier. In 1967, Ivy League administrators reported their institutions were moving toward a new concept in admissions known as "student diversity."[56] This marked a departure away from the old geographic diversity, dominant since the dawn of the century, and its lily white patina. The moral and legal force of the civil rights movement and the War on Poverty had left them no choice. The quest for opportunity that had been the hallmark of the Johnson administration's education policy-making was institutionalized on campus as a program committed to cultivating diversity. John T. Oslander, admissions director at Princeton University, one of the least socioeconomically and racially diverse institutions in the country, explained the sudden shift in perspective this way: "It's not the place they're from, really, but rather some sense of a different background that we're looking for."[57]

"The Uncommitted":
Alienated Youth and the Promise of Diversity

In 1967, when Oslander predicted diversity would be the future of American higher education, the most turbulent campus conflicts of the era were still a year away. The FSM at Berkeley in the fall of 1964 revealed the same peaceful tactics used by the interracial civil rights movement could be effectively deployed by college students to achieve institutional reform. For the next three years, prior to the violent blowouts of 1968 student protestors "generally proceeded in this [FSM] spirit of non-violence," according to the federal government's study on campus unrest.[58] Not without some justification, then, did Oslander and other administrators believe "student diversity" held the key to improving college life and to curing the new maladjustment of the 1960s: "alienation."

During the 1950s, the idea of alienation permeated American society. Among leading conceptions of alienation, one was attributable to orthodox Marxism, another to the Christian existentialism of Karl Bonhoffer and Paul Tillich, and still another, to the work of the New York City writers' community known as "the Beats."[59] However contextualized at midcentury, alienation was used to convey the utter loneliness of living and working in a mass society of gray flannel, button-down conformism. Social scientists likewise studied the nature of alienation with great interest and, not surprisingly, defined it as the opposite of adjustment—a psychological idea ingrained within the social scientific imagination. In *The Lonely Crowd* (1950), for example, Harvard's David Riesman defined alienation—what he also called "anomie"—as the mirror opposite of adjustment and traced its origins to the growing chasm between individuals and the large-scale "institutional forms" they inhabited.[60] A year later, Columbia's C. Wright Mills published *White Collar*, in which he named the interlocking bureaucratic network of "institutional forms"—the government, big business, the media, and the university, chief among them—responsible for alienating the "Little Man," the college-educated white collar worker, "who is acted upon but who does not act, who works along unnoticed in somebody's office or store, never talking loud, never talking back, never taking a stand."[61]

At the time, Mills and Riesman cut against the grain of mainstream sociological thought dominated by Riesman's Harvard colleague, Talcott Parsons.[62] Parsonian structural-functionalism posited the proliferation of large-scale, vertically integrated institutions, such as universities, as key markers of a modern, industrial society. Borrowing from German political-economist Max Weber's work on bureaucracies, Parsons and his acolytes in Harvard's Department of Social Relations (contra Mills and Riesman) took a more or less optimistic view of large-scale organizations. Partly this was because Parsons's work ducked any examination of the human experiences of individuals in bureaucratized settings, but also because he was convinced that bureaucratic organizations evidenced a society at a structurally advanced "stage of development." Bureaucratic institutions seamlessly adjusted and readjusted human activity, Parsons believed, and thus helped maintain political and social cohesion.[63]

Grumblings from intellectual insurgents like Mills and Riesman notwithstanding, the performance of big business and higher education seemingly vindicated Parsons's convergence theory. This was especially true of higher education, which had symbolized the adjustment regime since World War II. But the consensus around higher education's capacity to produce adjusted citizens started to crack in the late 1950s when studies of public opinion revealed intense political apathy among students and the general public both. In this respect, the locus of administrators' and policymakers' concern with college students shifted from one decade to the next. While apathetic college students posed the central problem of the 1950s, it was higher education's overly engaged and politically active students who posed the major threat in the 1960s. This was first glimpsed during the FSM. According to the Berkeley Faculty Senate report on the uprising, *Education at Berkeley: Report of the Select Committee on Education* (1966), "scholastically able young people" with the highest grades were the main culprits in the siege of Sproul Hall.[64] Though subsequent investigators would dispute this claim, there was no denying that many of the era's most combustible protests occurred at the nation's most elite colleges. This persuaded some observers that the nation's best-educated students, who disproportionately derived from highly educated households, were the most susceptible to political radicalization.[65]

At Berkeley, protesters set their sights on the complete reformulation of the university. Their pursuit of "free speech" and an end to the ban on student political activity served as an opening wedge into what became an extended critique of the multiversity itself. The hope and promise of a more individualized education model during the 1920s eventually succumbed to climbing enrollments after World War II. In the 1950s, enrollments grew from 2.3 to 4 million, and continued to grow in the 1960s, reaching 8.6 million students by decade's end.[66] Berkeley followed a similar trajectory: by 1965 the total campus enrollment was just shy of 28,000, making it one of the biggest—and, according to the FSM, one of the most alienating—multiversities in the world.[67]

The FSM leadership took careful notes. What they determined was that Berkeley was academically as well as socially alienating. Inside the classroom, according to Savio, Berkeley's huge lectures and crowds of nameless, faceless students and faculty resulted in "a distorted education . . . destructive of human values."[68] It was a factory, he claimed, whose organization replicated the impersonal hierarchical structure of its military-industrial patrons.[69] Things were equally miserable outside the classroom, where the doctrine of in loco parentis ensured Berkeley undergraduates would be treated like children. A spring of 1965 FSM position paper made this point clearly when it reminded students they were "powerless" because "the university assumes the role of the parent."[70] Echoing G. Stanley Hall, the FSM acknowledged students occupied the ambiguous middle ground of human development known as adolescence. "In our society, students are neither children nor adults," the paper continued. "As a result, students are more or less outside of society, and in increasing numbers they do not desire to become a part of the society."[71] Conversely, the administration's position on students' proper role was not ambiguous at all. Martin Meyerson, who replaced Edward Strong as Berkeley chancellor in the midst of the FSM upheaval, reminded an alumni gathering that "your students are your charges. . . . They are practically your children."[72] Sometimes children misbehaved, the *Report of the Select Committee* concluded later, blaming the FSM uprising on the "anti-rational aspects of student thought" and "the anti-intellectual stance of the non-conformist students."[73]

Figure 6.4. From atop a campus police cruiser, Mario Savio, the leader of the Berkeley free speech movement, addresses his fellow students, Sproul Plaza, October 1, 1964. Courtesy Bancroft Library, University of California, Berkeley.

The belief that college students were prone to alienation dated back to the 1920s, but gained renewed vigor in the late 1950s thanks to the work of Yale social psychologist Kenneth Keniston. One of the country's foremost experts on alienation, Keniston's work probed the alienation of white, male college students—the supposed prototype for adjusted citizenship. Admitting alienation was neither a modern nor exclusively American phenomenon, Keniston's work sought to understand why so many well-off, white young people were so disenchanted.[74] The alienation of the "impoverished and the rejected [i.e., black people] rightly concerns us, but it does not puzzle us as much as the alienations of the average, affluent, adjusted American, nor the estrangements of the fortunate, talented, and privileged."[75] Why were college students alienated, wondered Keniston, when there was no obvious reason for them to be?

The Uncommitted: Alienated Youth in American Society (1965) was Keniston's answer to this question. What he discovered was not exactly novel. Mass society—and all its middle-class suburban trappings—was to blame for the "new alienation."[76] Alienated youth, Keniston determined, shared the common experience of being raised in white-collar suburban households dominated by overbearing, possessive mothers and emotionally distant, cold fathers. Anxious about the adult unhappiness that surrounded them, they consequently sought to avoid, or at least delay, adulthood for as long as possible. Having equated adulthood with submission to others—whether a spouse, or a corporation, or the government—the alienated pursued every means to "escape their pasts and avoid their futures." They lived an "uncommitted" existence in the here and now, free of external demands, removed from history, comforted by childish fantasies of "infantile fusion."[77]

At the center of this childish universe was the modern university. It was, Keniston believed, a key propagator of the alienated worldview.[78] Shaped by the customs of in loco parentis and the personnel perspective, the modern university left students in suspended animation between childhood and adulthood. Originally conceived to protect students from maladjustment in the 1920s, the therapeutic university—its endless parade of adjustment courses, orientations, and psychological interventions—had become a chief purveyor of it. "College students are normally prone to become excessively dependent on advisers, counselors, and even psychotherapists," Keniston observed, "who at best duplicate the role of the 'good mother' [alma mater] by exploiting their patients' involvement with them in order to promote their eventual disengagement."[79] At worst, higher education was a "bad mother" [malus mater], or at least an overbearing one, which encouraged childlike behaviors and narcissistic tendencies that delayed students' ability to forge lasting commitments beyond the self.

To solve this problem, Keniston recommended higher education embrace "social diversity" to counteract the "backward pulls of childhood."[80] The belief diversity could transcend the dislocations of modern bureaucratic life, creating genuine community, dated back to the first two decades of the twentieth century. Philosophers Horace Kallen and Randolph Bourne argued that more harmonious social relations hinged on retooling political pluralism in cultural terms. Keniston also turned to interest group pluralism—"extended from [group] politics to the individual"—and injected it with a psychological twist.[81] He implored educational leaders to promote "a new social diversity based not on region, ancestral origin, class, or race, but on the special accomplishments, potentials, talents, and vital commitments of each individual." By "vital commitments" Keniston meant those beliefs held dear by each individual. They could be political commitments or something else entirely. It did not matter. What did matter was whether individual students felt free to express their personal and political commitments with others on a voluntary basis. Keniston's clinical training inclined him toward focusing on the individual not the group, even though soon enough the focus on diversity would shift perceptibly and irreversibly in that direction, a point he hinted at toward the end of *Uncommitted*: "A society of whole men and women must, then, be a society which encourages diversity," Keniston concluded.[82]

By 1965, college administrators had the tools at hand to do just that. The 1964 Civil Rights Act had barred discrimination while the HEA offered administrators new tools to foster diversity. What remained an open question was whether diversity would really change the campus environment, strengthen the bonds of commitment between students and administrators, and bring an end to alienation. The Berkeley case offered one possible answer. During the height of the FSM, in the 1964–65 academic year the number of students who sought psychological counseling declined 20 percent from the previous year's record high. A similar pattern was revealed at Harvard College later. Apparently the emotionally debilitating effects of in loco parentis were relieved whenever students committed themselves to organized political action. Was protesting itself liberating? Or had students begun to challenge the whole adjustment framework embedded in the modern bureaucratic university? The answer to both questions turned out to be yes.[83]

"I Have Some Identity That I Intend to Preserve": Black Power Remakes Diversity

Two concurrent political and intellectual trends infused the idea of diversity with moral and theoretical legitimacy that helped to prepare the way for its future application. The first of these was the civil rights movement whose leaders linked diversity with Myrdalian egalitarian integrationism. In 1963, Dr. Martin Luther King Jr. famously championed this "color-blind" vision as the surest path to a "beloved community" when he famously dreamed of a time when his "four little children . . . [would] . . . not be judged by the color of their skin but the content of their character."[84] A year later, in his book *To Be Equal*, Whitney Young, the executive director of the National Urban League, articulated this same goal in terms of diversity. "I hope that we will be able to create the kind of society wherein people will have to apologize for sameness—for an all-white school or neighborhood or church—because this would be an indication of their immaturity, their lack of sophistication and security. We want a society where people will boast of diversity and the fact that their churches, their businesses, their schools and their neighborhoods are like little United Nations."[85]

Interest group pluralism served as a second legitimizing force. During the cold war, pluralism's chief attraction, according to its many adherents, was that it created a stable and predictable political environment—a "vital center"—

since opposing interests cancelled one another out. For Clark Kerr and other academic leaders weaned on interest group theory, this seemed like a near-perfect politics for American higher education, too. The idea that diverse student groups could inhabit the same space, jockey for advantage without creating any net disadvantage, resonated with college administrators who thought higher education offered the best hope for incorporating blacks into the American mainstream.[86] This conviction was practically hegemonic until the late 1960s. Indeed, as Spellman College sociologist George Napper recalled, in 1973: "The question of black students' proceeding along assimilationist-integrationist sanctioned avenues of success, using education as the primary vehicle, was never a real issue."[87]

But few anticipated diversity might aggravate campus discord rather than soothe it. In this respect the widespread faith in the socially and politically pacifying power of racial integration and pluralist politics proved utterly naïve. Both theories, as critics as different as Malcolm X and E. E. Schattschneider argued, incorrectly assumed that all groups were equal and had similar degrees of access to, and exerted the same influence on, the governmental process. In fact, different groups exercised different levels of influence. As in Washington so too on campus: white student groups had more power and influence than black student groups. This realization came late to college leaders who believed passionately in higher education's self-regulating pluralist framework and in education's capacity to create adjusted citizens irrespective of race or gender.

Black students were not so easily fooled. The longer they spent at predominantly white institutions the more convinced they became that those schools were designed to meet the intellectual and personal needs of their white peers. The case of Cornell University, site of some of the most violent, racially charged protests of the era, is instructive. Like so many other predominantly white universities at the time, Cornell's leadership endeavored to increase its population of black undergraduates in the early 1960s. And in 1963, Cornell's new president, James A. Perkins, a staunch racial liberal and former executive director of the Carnegie Institute, launched the Committee on Special Education Projects (COSEP) to manage the integration process. Initially administrators imagined they could treat and cure black students' alienation using the same combination of techniques administrators at Cornell (and elsewhere) had been using to adjust white students since the 1920s. They created compensatory admissions, remedial courses, and special living arrangements, and they hired a black educational psychologist named Gloria Joseph as an assistant dean and academic counselor to serve Cornell's growing black student body. One student recalled how Joseph helped black students overcome the academic, social, and psychic difficulties of attending a predominantly white institution: "Gloria was our adviser, our counselor, our mentor, our everything."[88] With Joseph at the helm, the COSEP rapidly increased black-student numbers at Cornell from 8 to 250 between 1963 and 1969.[89]

The COSEP had a much more challenging time creating a racially harmoni-ous campus than it did recruiting black students. Black students' adjustment to Cornell proved far more volatile than administrators ever expected as ra-cial tensions simmered on and off campus in the early 1960s before exploding by decade's end. Dormitory disputes involving Malcolm X posters and the mer-its of "soul music" boiled over.[90] In the latter incident the white student went unpunished while the black student was given a "psychiatric suspension," the underlying assumption that the battle over the radio dial was precipitated by the black student's psychological problems rather than the white student's rac-ism.[91] Confrontations such as these were commonplace. A perceptive student speculated as to why this was the case. Though she thought administrators were genuinely interested in creating "a multicultural experience" in the dorms, what they failed to account for was "people's ignorance about other cultures."[92]

This was particularly true off-campus. Away from the university's tightly controlled living environment, in the private, overwhelmingly white world that was the undergraduate Greek system was where blacks learned the true extent of Cornell's covert, institutionalized racism. In October 1966, Phi Delta Theta, an all-white fraternity, charged blacks but not whites to attend a house party. News of the incident traveled fast through the ranks of the recently formed Afro-American Society (AAS), eventually finding its way to Gloria Joseph, who immediately took it to the *Cornell Daily Sun*, the student newspaper. In the story that followed, Joseph asserted that the fraternity episode demon-strated "the contrast between overt discrimination which is condemned in the United States and . . . a more subtle form which usually goes unpunished."[93] The university's own investigation later corroborated Joseph's account, lending credence to her assertion that covert racism—Cornell's institutionalized racial attitudes—posed the greatest threat to campus race relations.

The forcefulness with which Cornell's black students made themselves heard in the fall term of 1966 was the result of more than growing numbers. Ear-lier that summer, Howard University graduate Stokely Carmichael, the newly elected president of SNCC, unveiled a new slogan at a rally in Greenwood, Mississippi: "Black Power!" Overnight, black power redefined the mainstream, interracial civil rights movement and its goal of political and legal rights. Frus-trated by the procedural focus of the old movement, Carmichael's call for the formation of black-only economic, social, and political institutions proved par-ticularly seductive to young blacks in search of a faster track to liberation.[94]

In *Black Power* (1967), Carmichael staked out black power as both a cultural and political project in which the attainment of the latter depended on the suc-cess of the former.[95] First, blacks needed a new historical self-understanding, or "identity." This new sense of self was necessary in order to crack the "covert, individual attitudes of racism" embedded in the "white power structure."[96] Re-tracing the long arc of black oppression from slavery to "institutional racism" was required, Carmichael argued, before blacks could move to the second stage:

Figure 6.5. Phi Delta Theta, shown here in their 1967 Cornellian Yearbook photograph, was the scene of a racial incident that convinced members of Cornell's Afro-American Society that predominantly white universities such as Cornell were steeped in racist attitudes. Courtesy The Cornellian.

political action.[97] Though Carmichael is often remembered for advocating force to "make . . . positions known," force was not his favored tactic.[98] Rather, he thought interest groups—what he called "independent party groups"—offered blacks the best hope for the achievement of real power in America's "pluralistic society."[99] Carmichael explained: "Black Power recognizes . . . the ethnic basis of American politics as well as the power-oriented nature of American politics. Black Power therefore calls for black people to consolidate behind their own, so they can bargain from a position of strength."[100]

Carmichael's interest group strategy captured the attention of black college students. Especially at predominantly white institutions, blacks discovered that the doctrine of in loco parentis was not only infantilizing and alienating but also racist. Examined through the lens of black power, the hated parent-child relationship more closely resembled that of a master and slave, or colonizer and colonized. Delivered to campus by well-meaning white administrators, many black students expressed feelings of profound disillusionment with the white academic and social experiences that greeted them. They discovered the painful truth that the white higher education system did not—in fact, could not—empower them because the entire institution was skewed against them, so much so that it corroded their very identities. To be sure, routine social slights and assumed intellectual inferiority by many white students seemed to back up Carmichael's claim that "integration [was] a subterfuge for the maintenance of white supremacy."[101]

Black students responded by organizing racially separatist identity groups to fight for their educational "rights" and to win collective liberation.[102] Ironically, while black radicals rejected pluralist politics as racist, they took the initial steps that would lay the groundwork for the pluralist solution that came to dominate American higher education—they created identity groups that would soon enough be supported by identity-based institutions. At the time, the existing Greek-dominated extracurricular system provided blacks with the only officially sanctioned administrative structure in which to do so. Long regarded as a site for "sandbox politics" and beer drinking, the extracurricular club culture served up more than fun and games for politically engaged students in the 1960s. At Cornell University, for example, black students founded the AAS in early 1966, to work in tandem with Gloria Joseph's COSEP. Like most other student-run clubs used to fill extracurricular free time, the AAS's modest mission was to formulate programs on the "history of black people . . . and to initiate and support programs which are devoted to the eradication of the social, economic, and psychological conditions which blight black people."[103] Initially interracial, it became exclusively black and increasingly radical after the emergence of black power in 1966. The AAS's commitment to black power coalesced around the Phi Delta Theta confrontation that fall, which remade the organization into a hub for black power politics at Cornell for the rest of the decade.

The AAS conditioned the ways in which blacks framed their political demands and mobilized for action. Originally a student-club appendage of the COSEP, the AAS quickly outgrew its subordinate role, becoming a safe space where students shared their personal experiences. "We really had stimulating conversations," recalled one student. "A part of it was socializing, seeing everybody. . . . Another part of it was political: we were developing in what the world was, what was our position in the universe, and we helped each other make sense." Through discussion and personal exploration AAS members became "aware of who we were, what our history was, and for many of us, this was the first time we were being exposed to this."[104] A 1969 COSEP promotional piece characterized black students' struggle over the meanings of "blackness" and the "subtleties of racism" in academe as a necessary outgrowth of "a minority group on campus that is not only growing larger but increasingly concerned with establishing a sense of identity and racial pride."[105]

Having already unmasked the institutional racism entrenched in the Greek system, black students shifted their critique to the hidden racial attitudes in the undergraduate curriculum. At Cornell this first occurred in the spring semester of 1968, in Economics 103—Economic Development. From the start of the class, wrote three AAS members in an official complaint, the professor's discussion of economic development was dashed with "institutionalized, or covert racism, that type by which attitudes of white superiority are perpetuated." The professor reflexively equated "economic development" and "Western civilization" in such a way that "assumed . . . that the rational decision involved in economics, and the study of economics as such is solely the product of Western man."[106] The students' accusation escalated tensions that, according to the leading scholar on the subject, set in motion a chain of events culminating with black students' takeover, in April 1969, of Willard Straight Hall, the main administration building. A hundred black students, armed with guns and belts of ammunition, barricaded themselves in the hall to protest "covert racism" on campus and to gain greater autonomy for the black studies program established seven months before.[107]

Nationally visible black leaders had long alleged that higher education's curriculum was racist to the core. Malcolm X often spoke about the need for blacks to learn history and their integral place in it. "You have to have a knowledge of history no matter what you are going to do," intoned Malcolm X from the pulpit at the Abyssinian Baptist Church in Harlem, New York, in 1963. "The thing that has made the so-called Negro in America fail, more than any other thing, is your, my, lack of knowledge concerning history."[108] Stokely Carmichael advanced a similar argument. "Our concern for black power addresses itself directly to this problem," he said, in the fall of 1966, "the necessity to reclaim our history and our identity from the cultural terrorism and depredation of self-justifying white guilt."[109]

Lesser-known black student groups, such as the Black Student Alliance at Yale (BSAY), voiced the most penetrating critiques of white higher learning. Founded in 1966 by members of the Yale Discussion Group on Negro Affairs, the BSAY first achieved renown at the "Yale Symposium on Black Studies in the University" in May 1968.[110] Convened only weeks after the King assassination, the event led to the creation of the country's first accredited undergraduate black studies major and to the opening of the Yale Afro-American Cultural Center in the defunct Chi Psi fraternity, which BSAY members irreverently called "the House."[111] The event also attracted more than a hundred representatives from three dozen colleges along with national media coverage that offered average Americans an up-close look at the racial order of the modern university. In published conference proceedings and subsequent interviews BSAY members expounded on their assertion that Yale, like other predominantly white universities, was not only "white" but "anti-black."[112] The implicit aim of higher learning at Yale, they claimed, was to scrub blacks students of their black identity in preparation for life in a white, middle-class world.[113]

BSAY members elaborated on their alienation, on their feelings of "being lost in a sea of whiteness." Armstead Robinson, a cofounder of BSAY, had arrived to Yale in the fall of 1964 by way of the racially divided public schools of his hometown of Memphis. One of fourteen black students admitted that year, at the time Yale's largest class of black students ever, Robinson observed little difference between his old southern haunts and his new school. He felt "separated" and profoundly "lonely" outside the classroom as well as in it. "Courses were designed for the white people," recalled Robinson, "and we couldn't find courses that had anything to do with us."[114] Raymond Nunn said this lack was extra devastating as the available education that was offered was "geared to make [us] as white as possible."[115] Nothing in the current organization of the institution, charged Donald Ogilvie, was applicable to "the experience . . . of black people."[116] To remedy the situation, they all agreed, Yale needed to offer courses that were really "relevant" to black people's lives. This was the only way in which black students would come to understand they have a "cultural identity." "We refuse to come here and lose our blackness," declared Robinson. "I have some identity that I intend to preserve."[117] Robinson really meant it. After graduating from Yale in 1969 with honors in history, he went on to graduate study under the tutelage of Eugene Genovese at the University of Rochester. He eventually joined the faculty at the University of Virginia in 1981, where he served as the founding director of the Carter G. Woodson Institute for African-American and African Studies until his death in 1995.[118]

Using education to retrieve personal and group identity emerged as a main goal of the black power movement's campus wing. The existing curriculum, insisted critics like Robinson, devoted to the intellectual traditions and ideas

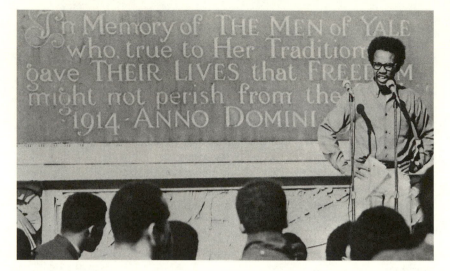

Figure 6.6. Black Student Alliance at Yale (BSAY) leader and future University of Virginia historian Armstead Robinson rallying support on behalf of black studies, Hewitt Quadrangle, March 1968. In December, following meetings with members of the BSAY, the Yale College faculty approved an undergraduate major in Afro-American Studies—the first accredited major of its kind in the country. Yale Class Book (1969), Manuscripts & Archives, Yale University.

of Western civilization, actively divorced black students from themselves and their heritage. Elliott Moorman, a prominent member of Princeton's Association of Black Collegians, wrote in the *Saturday Review*, "The actual curriculum of most predominantly white universities *is* an Anglo-American studies program: the study of the culture and heritage of the American ideal as it has unfolded in the several disciplines—American politics, history, sociology, music, drama, the life sciences."[119] At the University of Wisconsin, the racially mixed faculty-student Committee on Studies in Instruction in Race Relations reached a similar conclusion: "The important role of Afro-Americans in the shaping of these United States has been seriously ignored and quite often distorted in the curricula of this and other universities."[120]

In Madison and elsewhere, black students reframed existing understandings of black psychological maladjustment to uncover the ways in which the modern university systematically obliterated their identity. The concept of identity crystallized in the work of the German émigré psychoanalyst Erik Erikson. A 1933 graduate of the Vienna Psychoanalytic Institute, Erikson's interest in identity formation was more than academic. The product of an extramarital affair, Erikson, born in 1902, never knew the real identity of his biological father, a mystery, according to his chief biographer, that haunted him his entire life. When he became an American citizen, he changed his name from Homberger (his mother's second husband's surname) to Erikson, an explicit acknowledgment of identity's protean nature.[121]

Stateside, Erikson honed his craft at leading university and veterans' hospitals. In the course of working with soldiers at San Francisco's Mt. Zion Veterans' Rehabilitation Clinic during World War II, he coined the term with which he would forever be linked—"identity crisis." He postulated most bouts of maladjustment were caused by the "lost sense of personal sameness and historical continuity" wrought by wartime service. Transported to distant lands and then thrust into combat, Erikson contended, even outwardly well-adjusted soldiers felt "their lives no longer hung together—and never would again." After the war, Erikson continued refining his theory, eventually concluding "identity crises" were not only situational but also developmental. They were especially common—maybe inevitable—in young adults. The adolescent ego, aware of the past but unsure of the future, easily overloaded and lost the ability to integrate the self's place in a changing world.[122] Erikson's formulation of identity as dynamic and historically contingent suffused expert as well as popular understandings of personhood throughout the postwar period.[123]

By 1968, members of the nascent Association of Black Psychologists (ABPsi) had latched onto the idea of identity to explain black alienation. Formed at the annual meeting of the American Psychological Association (APA) in 1968, the ABPsi catalyzed black psychologists' own quest for a more powerful professional identity. Clinical psychologist Joseph White of the University of California, Irvine, helped organize the ABPsi and its fifty-eight original members.[124] The realization the white-dominated psychology profession, and its "Anglo middle class frame of reference," had been misdiagnosing African Americans for decades forced White and his fellow black psychologists to act. In his seminal "Toward a Black Psychology," published in *Ebony* in 1970, White pleaded with the white psychology establishment to leave black psychologists—and black people—alone. The development of "a comprehensive theory of black psychology," White argued, required a true understanding of the real "black experience"—an experience fundamentally shaped by nearly four centuries of Euro-American society's psychological and physical oppression of black people.[125] In due course, the formation of ABPsi and the study of black identity, according to a leading scholar, "made it clear that psychological identity was multifaceted and that psychological knowledge was locally situated."[126]

White's diagnosis of the black identity crisis, variations of which appeared in countless other works, was widely accepted in large part because it was not entirely new. "It is a peculiar sensation, this double-consciousness, this sense of always looking at one's self through the eyes of others, of measuring one's soul by the tape of a world that looks on in amused contempt and pity," wrote W.E.B.

Du Bois in his elegiac meditation, *The Souls of Black Folks* (1903).[127] "The history of the American Negro is the history of this strife—this longing to attain self-conscious manhood, to merge his double self into a better and truer self."[128] Sixty years later, black thinkers and activists from Joseph White to Malcolm X, from Carmichael to the BSAY leadership, seized on Du Bois's original insight into the psychological agony of divided selfhood. Instead of referencing the old language of adjustment and integration, which inferred adapting to a normative white conception of selfhood and institutions, they embraced identity. Identity gave blacks—and all those who chose to use it—a new personalized template for self-liberation. Indeed, it was the key to opening the door to political acceptance, economic independence, and social respect.

In so doing, black power challenged the idea that mere student diversity—the simple act of racial mixing—could overcome the racial divide between and among students. For diversity to work it not only had to address the personal needs of individuals and groups, it also had to change the very system that negotiated between individuals and groups. In both cases, advocates of black power sought to harness the most precious resource available at the university—education. By harnessing "black knowledge," and creating black studies, black students believed they could undo the knot of alienation, transforming themselves and society. "Most [white] people think all we want to do is learn a little history for the sake of our pride and walk around in dashikis," said L. F. "Skip" Griffin, the president of the Afro Association at Harvard, in 1969. "We want to understand the system so we can go about changing it."[129]

"Black College": Black Studies Institutionalizes Diversity

In the late 1960s, educational elites and black students alike regarded black studies as the best approach to changing the system.[130] Violent uprisings at schools across the country forced some administrators to create courses and programs on the fly, but at most schools the mere threat of violence served as impetus enough for most officials to justify doing so.[131] By the early 1970s, sometimes with seed money from the philanthropic sector, most of the time without it, nearly five hundred schools had established black studies departments, centers, programs, or classes.[132]

Black studies innovators drew inspiration from a number of contemporaneous academic developments. One was the emergence of internationally focused courses and interdisciplinary area studies programs during the 1950s.[133] The internationalization precedent resonated with black studies supporters who needed to build programs fast, wanted to create "relevant" knowledge outside the established white disciplines, and were committed to connecting the African-American experience with the experiences of other oppressed peoples around the world.[134] Working between the disciplines and pulling professors and knowledge germane to the Pan-African movement from existing departments seemed like the best recipe for programmatic as well as intellectual liberation.

The spread of student-run "experimental education" programs provided a second important precedent. Student-led education had always been an unadvertised part of organized higher education. But the Vietnam War and the civil rights struggle spiked students' demand for alternative educational formats. After President Johnson ramped up troop levels in Vietnam in the spring of 1965, faculty and students at the University of Michigan organized the first teach-ins. Perhaps three thousand students participated in the lectures and discussions that lasted through the night of March 24. And in the following weeks some thirty-five other schools held teach-ins, culminating in Vietnam Day at Berkeley in May, attended by ten thousand students.[135]

Teach-ins begat more teach-ins, which eventually led to institutionalization in experimental colleges and then in the official curriculum. "Free universities" materialized at some thirty institutions, including San Francisco State College (SFSC).[136] Organized by students in 1966, the aim of the college, according to its founder Michael Vozick, was "not only to teach subjects that are not given in the universities, but to explore new ways of learning."[137] At SFSC, student-run courses deployed unconventional formats and delved into topics such as sex, psychedelic drugs, the Vietnam War, and race relations not offered in the official curriculum.[138] It was against this backdrop of incessant curricular experimentation that more formal programs in black studies took root at SFSC—where the battle over black studies claimed two presidential administrations and led to frequent school closing between 1967 and 1969—and elsewhere. If a course on French New Wave Cinema was relevant to the curriculum, reasoned black studies innovators, then a course on Black Thought, with readings by Frederick Douglass, Richard Wright, and Dr. Martin Luther King Jr., should be relevant too.[139]

The push for formal programs and departments went into high gear after the King assassination in April 1968. That summer and the following fall, colleges and universities organized programs and approved courses at a prodigious rate. Howard University's program was representative of the best programs, offering minors and majors and a mix of courses exploring the history and culture of black people. The aim of the program was to place African Americans in time, to recover their past heritage in order to make the present more meaningful. The director of the Howard program, Gregory Rigsby, conceived it as more than "a mere addition to the traditional Liberal Arts College," but as the foundation of a truly "Black College"—even at predominantly black schools like Howard, created after the Civil War, whose curriculum embodied the ideas and institutions of Western civilization. A real black college, Rigsby said, would focus exclusively on the black experience and the production and dissemination of black knowledge.[140]

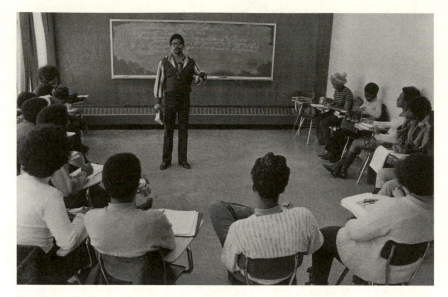

Figure 6.7. Professor Chestyn Everett teaching a seminar in the Africana Studies Program at Cornell University, January 1971. Courtesy Division of Rare and Manuscript Collections, Cornell University Libraries.

Yet the rush to gain a foothold in black studies led to a highly uneven developmental pattern. Predominantly white, research-intensive institutions—home to the most successful programs—created whole graduate and undergraduate degree programs, enticing the best faculty from predominantly black colleges with promises of better pay and resources.[141] At less prestigious schools, meanwhile, the organization of black studies programs was hindered by a lack of trained faculty and resources. At these institutions black studies programs were programs in name only, often including no more than a course or two on African-American literature and history.[142] "The only process involved in setting up black studies courses in most institutions up to the moment," confessed Atlanta University professor Richard A. Long, in 1968, "has been the assembling of materials in the manner in which this is done for other courses, sticking the label 'black' on it, and opening the door to the classroom. What is not fully appreciated is that the materials available for the most part are worthless."[143]

His claim was not unfounded. Reports of hastily constructed courses and poorly trained faculty circulated widely, putting the field on the defensive from the start.[144] The biggest problem was the dearth of appropriately trained professionals. At Stanford University, for example, administrators admitted to judging potential black studies professors on their teaching ability and "classroom charisma" rather than scholarly promise. Often times the only available faculty were graduate students and advanced undergraduates.[145] Other institutions went in a completely different direction. At Kent State University, The Black Experience was taught by a "neighborhood faculty." A self-described "graduate" of the Ohio Penal System, Raymond Broaddus, a thirty-three-year-old convicted felon, served as the instructor of record. The course was designed around "rap sessions" between students and black residents from Broaddus's Akron neighborhood.[146] This was an extreme but not uncommon example of relevance run amuck. Stories such as these harmed the black studies cause, and probably contributed to the less-than-stellar enrollment figures reported at many schools.

Fierce battles over the future of black studies broke out between and among white and black administrators, professors, students, and activists. The debate turned on the issue of integration versus segregation—also known as the "autonomy question."[147] Sociologist Nathan Hare nominally led the black separatists. After being fired from Howard University for his participation in student protests, he was hired as the first coordinator of the black studies program at San Francisco State College in the spring of 1968, a position he held briefly until being summarily fired the following year. A teacher and mentor to Stokely Carmichael and Claude "H-Rap" Brown, Hare thought white faculty members were incapable of teaching black studies, and that they must be kept away. Black professors should emphasize black referents, use black-authored materials, and actively pursue "both ideological and pedagogical blackness."[148] In Hare's opinion, this represented the only way for students to foster a real "identity with the black community."[149]

A number of notable old-guard civil rights leaders and presidents at predominantly black colleges criticized the black power movement and black studies. Having dedicated their personal and professional lives to advancing civil rights through interracial cooperation and established political and legal channels, they considered black studies a step backward. "We feel," said Roy Wilkins, the sixty-seven-year-old executive director of the NAACP, the nation's largest civil rights organization, "that any effort to set up a black studies departments which would be wholly autonomous . . . represents setting up a Jim Crow school."[150] Stephen J. Wright, director of the United Negro College Fund, predicted that autonomy of the sort advocated by Hare would "only lead to an intensification of the kind of hatred that will help destroy the nation and the myriad opportunities for Negroes."[151]

Some faculty expressed concerns about the long-term fallout of black studies on the university's supposed production of disinterested research. Martin Kilson, a professor of government at Harvard, and himself an African American, supported black power and the "politicization of ethnicity," but drew the line at black studies.[152] "I don't believe a university is a place to train ideological cadres," he said. "If it becomes politicized you can forget the university as a place where learning and scholarship are pursued."[153] Yale historian C. Van Woodward, a southern-born white, agreed blacks deserved "academic atten-

tion," but dismissed the call for autonomy. "I don't believe in a color qualification for teaching. That's neither possible nor desirable," he said. Cornell government professor Allan Sindler highlighted what he saw as the central paradox
of the situation. "The black students seem to be saying two things at the same
time," said Sindler. "'We are part of this community' and 'We do not want to be
part of this community.' Many white faculty are bewildered."[154]

Finally, prominent social scientists considered the push for autonomy—evidenced in black studies but also in the wider black community—anathema to
the achievement of tolerance and interracial harmony. The most outspoken
critic was Kenneth B. Clark, a professor of psychology at City College of New
York, whose work on segregation and black "self-hate" had helped persuade
the Supreme Court to ban segregation in public schools in 1954. Following
the formation of the black-only Afro-American Studies Institute at Antioch
College, Clark, who was black, insisted there was "no evidence to support the
contention that the inherent damage to human beings . . . on the basis of race is
any less damaging when demanded or enforced by [blacks] then when imposed
by [whites]." Segregation brought psychic harm to both blacks and whites, he
said, and was also illegal.[155]

Within several years the fight for autonomy was superseded by more pressing administrative and financial concerns. Generally low enrollments and the
fight for scarce resources forced perhaps half the original black studies programs to close by the 1980s.[156] Among those that endured, directors focused on
survival rather than separation, realizing that traditional institution-building
mechanisms and disciplinary alliances were the keys to long-term success.[157]
The creation of professional organizations and scholarly research organs, like
the *Journal of Black Studies*, first published in 1970, and the *Journal of Black
Psychology*, four years later, provided a viable model. So, too, did the penetration of the study of African Americans into the established disciplines. The
history profession proved especially receptive. Black history courses (typically
taught by white instructors, since as late at 1970 less than 1 percent of all
doctorates were awarded to African Americans) grew in number and variety
while African-American history and the history of race emerged as fecun subfields.[158] This work built on "a new, assertive, particularist consciousness" that
reflected the essence of black power itself. Where older scholars such as John
Hope Franklin and C. Van Woodward's work trended toward "integrationist
optimism," newer historians took a more critical stance. They emphasized racial difference by searching for and finding ample evidence of black resistance
and autonomy—that is, black identity—in both slavery and freedom.[159]

The irony was thick. From an institution-building standpoint racial autonomy was a dead end, yet the study of race proved a professionally rewarding
one for scholars who pursued it. To dwell on the rise and troubled institutionalization of black studies, however, misses the main point: black students' claim
they had a "right" to an education that included the exploration of black iden-

tity changed how all students measured the personal and political returns of a college education. After black students achieved their right to black studies, other identity groups organized to claim their place in the college curriculum and a louder voice in campus politics.

"Women's Studies Is in a Lot of Ways—Consciousness Raising": Diversifying Diversity

Women staged the largest revolt. That they did was somewhat surprising. Unlike blacks, who were virtually invisible on college campuses (except at black-serving institutions) until the mid-1960s, women had been a fixture for more than a century. Nationally, between coordinate colleges, single-sex and coeducational institutions, women earned nearly 45 percent of all bachelor degrees and comprised 20 percent of all faculty. Yet their numbers did not translate into demonstrable power, and in many respects women were second-class citizens on and off campus.[160]

The women's liberation movement endeavored to change women's citizenship status. Two loosely federated strands of the women's movement crisscrossed and strengthened one another, eventually circling back to the university by decade's end. A first strand consisted of female politicians and professional women who organized women's lobby organizations to focus (male) politicians' attention on a host of long-neglected women's issues: employment and salary equity; birth control and abortion rights; and education and childcare. This liberal feminist coalition (which would soon throw its support behind the doomed Equal Rights Amendment) was led by the National Organization of Women (NOW), founded in 1966 to ensure the enforcement of Title VII of the 1964 Civil Rights Act banning sex discrimination in employment. The act's failure to extend antidiscrimination protection to women in higher education galvanized the Women's Equity Action League (WEAL)—an offshoot of NOW founded in 1968 by female academics—whose main goal was to close the act's sex discrimination loophole. A second, more radical strand, emanated from the male-dominated mass student movements of the mid-1960s, was closely linked to college campuses, and sought liberation, not just equality. For the tens of thousands of women students and faculty who joined this fight, their goal was to identify and dismantle the male supremacist power structure that permeated American society and institutions, including higher education.[161]

The women's movement was highly decentralized. The primary organizing tool used to connect all its disparate strands was the consciousness-raising group (CR)—"leaderless, structureless" small groups where women discussed and analyzed their secret experiences in preparation for political action.[162] CR groups, sometimes called "rap groups," quickly spread after 1968 thanks to the growing network of women's organizations and to the media's mounting interest in women's liberation. The poet-activist Robin Morgan described women's liberation occurring whenever "three or four friends or neighbors decide to meet regularly over coffee and talk about their personal lives . . . in the cells of women's jails, on the welfare lines, in the supermarket, the factory, the convent, the farm, the maternity ward, the street corner, the old ladies' home, the kitchen, the steno pool, the bed."[163]

CR was more organized than this, if only slightly. Guidelines sketched out by the film editor and radical feminist Kathie Sarachild—a New Left veteran and a founding member of the New York Radical Women—circulated at women's liberation meetings in New York and Chicago, spreading from there to other urban centers and to college towns.[164] The goal of CR was to help women understand that their personal problems were not individual problems amenable to private solutions, but social and structural problems experienced by all women that demanded political action. During CR sessions women spoke freely on a host of personal, previously secret topics—"husbands, lovers, privacy, sex, loneliness, role-playing in the home, our children, our parents, our daily routines," as one participant recalled. By discussing their common experiences of oppression in small, female-only groups, participants gained insight into patriarchy's power over their personal and political lives. "It was like opening up a whole new world," recalled Sarachild. "I was talking with other women and learning things I had never known before."[165]

CR's utility stemmed from its easy transportability and because it infused politics with educational insight and therapeutic possibility. Of course, radical feminists—whether they viewed female oppression as an outgrowth of material or sexual relations—considered CR a political mobilizing technique, nothing more. They located CR's origins in the Chinese Communist Revolution, when Mao's army permitted "liberated" peasants to "speak bitterness" about the wrongs that had been perpetrated against them.[166] While technically true, most rank-and-file liberal feminists' understanding of the CR process was shaped by more familiar political motifs. None was more important than "participatory democracy," reintroduced to a new generation of Americans by Students for a Democratic Society (SDS) in their signature 1962 political treatise, the "Port Huron Statement." Participatory democracy, SDS believed, would reinvigorate a polity severely dispirited by secretive interest group politics and elite decision making. Ironically, though SDS bemoaned group politics, it nevertheless remained beholden to groups—what it called communities—united not by race, class, region, or pecuniary self-interest but shared experience. It was in experiential communities where "private problems" were recast as political issues and resolved through participatory democracy.[167]

The implicit gesture toward "personal politics" in the "Port Huron Statement" literally migrated to the women's movement, flourishing there in more radical fashion than it ever had in SDS. As activist-turned-historian Sara Evans has documented, it was in SDS and other male-dominated student movements that many future feminists first experienced the crippling effects of male domination.[168] In SNCC and SDS both, women were shunted into supporting administrative roles and publicly demeaned. An SDS pamphlet, for instance, likened "the system" to a "woman"—"you've got to fuck it to make it change."[169] Fed up, women responded in kind. "Fuck off, left," wrote ex-New Leftist Shulamith Firestone, in 1969. "You can examine your navel by yourself from now on."[170] Joined by bands of sisters, like Casey Hayden, Mary King, and Jo Freeman, Firestone and other disaffected leftists broke with the male-dominated left, taking with them a belief in participatory democracy that was all but indistinguishable from consciousness raising. CR's component parts—sharing, analyzing, and abstracting private experiences to mobilize for political action—meshed with participatory democracy's goal to personalize American politics.[171]

The CR process was also educational. By excavating and sharing individual experiences, participants used it to uncover their personal histories and true identity. This view was articulated most forcefully by Florence Howe, a CUNY Graduate School professor and early women's studies innovator, whose remarkable scholarly and organization-building work on behalf of women's studies later propelled her to the presidency of the Modern Language Association in 1973. She first came to CR during her stint as a SNCC Freedom School teacher-volunteer in 1964. Howe joined hundreds of northern white volunteers in Mississippi to teach blacks about their rights as citizens. They used unconventional practices intended to enhance democracy. Students and teachers sat together in circles, on the floor, rather than at rigidly organized desks typical of a traditional school. The curriculum, which emphasized black history and culture, drew directly from students' everyday experiences living under of Jim Crow. Students were encouraged to divulge stories of their individual experiences of oppression in order to jumpstart class discussion. The goal was to help the students realize, in Howe's words, "that they [had] knowledge of value to themselves and others."[172] This highly personalized approach to learning left a lasting impression on Howe, and other teacher-volunteers, who departed Mississippi with new CR-inspired teaching methods later used to "[turn] the women's movement into a teaching movement."[173]

Finally, the CR process was therapeutic. This was most controversial, and many radical women's groups dismissed that accusation. Radical women's groups, like the New York Redstockings, flatly rejected the claim that CR was just another name for therapy, declaring in their widely circulated 1969 Manifesto: "CR is not therapy." The authority of therapeutic interventions, they contended, rested on the faulty assumption that male-female relationships were "purely personal."[174] "I am greatly offended that I or any other woman is thought to need therapy in the first place," wrote another Redstocking, Carol Hanisch, in her signature polemic, "The Personal is Political," published underground shortly after the Manifesto. "Women are messed over, not messed up! We need to change the objective conditions, not adjust to them." In Hanisch's opinion there was no such thing as a truly personal problem—every problem had a material basis and was about power, plain and simple.[175] In this fashion, the transformation of the personal into the political—begun in SDS and SNCC and transferred to the black power and women's movements—was all but complete.

Feminists' hostility toward therapy stemmed from received understandings about therapeutic interventions and the kinds of people who needed them. Here the person and ideas of Sigmund Freud loomed large. Among liberal and radical feminist thinkers, Freud's psychoanalytic theory exemplified how patriarchal knowledge systems contributed to female oppression. Freud's ideas, albeit diluted for a mass American audience, had lent the guise of scientific certainty to longstanding assumptions about women's innate inferiority that exhausted the first-wave women's movement in the 1920s. This point was broadcast to a wide audience by Betty Friedan, in her groundbreaking, best-selling feminist tome, *The Feminine Mystique* (1963). A psychology major at Smith College who later studied briefly under Erik Erikson, Friedan spelled out the ways in which "the problem with no name" was energized by "Freudian thought." In her opinion, Freud's premise that anatomy was destiny—that women's psychosexual development was skewed as a result of "penis envy" and the "feminine Oedipal attitude" (named the "Electra Complex" by Carl Jung)—was flawed. Female inferiority was not predestined but socially constructed by patriarchal ideologies and institutions.[176] "The core of the problem for women today is not sexual," wrote Friedan, Freud clearly in her sights, "but a problem of identity—a stunting or evasion of growth that is perpetuated by the feminine mystique."[177]

Later, radical-feminist thinkers targeted the adjustment regime to describe Freudianism's role in derailing women's quest for liberation since the 1920s. Shulamith Firestone's Marxist-inspired tract, *The Dialectic of Sex* (1970), was the most intellectually adventuresome and important work to do so. In her analysis, as Freudianism suffused clinical therapy and the social sciences during the interwar period, it became increasingly mechanistic in the hands of crudely trained American practitioners who turned it into yet another "applied" field. It was in this context that Freudianism was "regroomed for its new function of 'social adjustment,'" explained Firestone, "to wipe up the feminist revolt." Transmitted via print matter, therapists, and the patriarchal social science disciplines, Freudianism became the ideological foundation of an "artificial sex-role system" in which "adjustment" meant accepting "the reality in which one finds oneself" regardless of how misogynistic that reality might actually be.[178] "The revolt of the underclass (women) and the . . . restoration to women of ownership of their own bodies," Firestone concluded, applying the capitalist fetish with property to the body proper, was the only way to destroy the adjustment regime that controlled the most intimate dimensions of women's lives.[179] Women needed secure reproductive rights and new reproductive options in order to break the shackles of male oppression. According to Friedan and Firestone, Freud had sidetracked the first-wave women's movement. It was critical, then, to derail Freudian interpretations and the therapeutic enterprise itself.

Yet the women's liberation movement never really succeeded in escaping its therapeutic imprimatur. One reason was prosaic. CR's small-group format often resembled a group therapy session.[180] The other reason was more complicated and emerged from the institutional decentralization, professional expansion, and intellectual fragmentation of psychology in the 1960s. The passage of the 1963 Community Mental Health Act, an extension and refinement of the federal government's role as emotional caretaker of the nation originally outlined in the 1946 National Mental Health Act, was most important. It decentralized psychological care, previously dominated by state-run asylum facilities, transferring it to new, locally run community outpatient facilities and treatment centers.[181] The act's definition of community care was ambiguously defined and changed constantly over the next several decades. At the time, however, the explicit nod toward "community" appealed especially to young, newly trained practitioners who were inspired by the activist spirit of the era but skeptical of their ability to use their training to heal psychic pain and dislocation. A tide of antiprofessional critiques—led by French philosopher Michel Foucault and Hungarian-born psychiatrist Thomas Szasz, both of whom indicted psychological knowledge as a tool of social control—made increasing numbers of psychologists, especially women, wonder whether their professional training cured human suffering or caused it.[182]

Some feminists acted on their concerns. At the annual meeting of the APA in 1969, a contingent of feminist psychologists formed the Association for Women in Psychology (AWP). Following in the tracks of the ABPsi, formed the year before by black psychologists, the AWP and its thirty-five (female and male) founding members aimed to make known women's second-class treatment within psychology. The association focused on expunging the commonplace sexism of the male-dominated profession and on stopping the proliferation of sexist psychological knowledge that enabled sexist behavior to occur in the first place. Starting in 1972 the association promoted "feminist therapy"—therapeutic techniques developed by and for women—to counteract patriarchy's hegemony over psychological knowledge and institutions.[183] The following year, an AWP-inspired task force report to the APA leadership resulted in the creation of the APA's Division of the Psychology of Women (Division 35). The division—which because of its official ties to the APA irked some members of the more loosely organized AWP, despite the groups' overlapping mission and membership—became the center for research on feminist psychology and therapy, and home to *Psychology of Women Quarterly*, the field's leading journal, first published in 1976.[184]

Beyond the APA's ambit, in San Francisco, Chicago, New York, and Boston, self-identified radical therapists organized "therapy collectives" to remake psychological knowledge from the bottom up. Professionally, they sought alternative certifications and increased autonomy from the medical school-university system that monopolized the training and placement of psychologists; practically, they sought to change how patients accessed and understood the therapy they received. To achieve both objectives radical therapists reformulated the therapeutic encounter as a social rather than individual process in which society itself was the problem, and liberation from the white, middle-class adjustment regime the cure.[185] An article in *The Radical Therapist*—the movement's principal mouthpiece—expounded on this point: "Therapy is change, not adjustment. This means change—social, personal, and political. When people are fucked over, people should help them fight it, and then deal with their feelings. A 'struggle for mental health' is bullshit unless it involves changing this society which turns us into machines, alienates us from one another and our work, and binds us into racist, sexist, and imperialist practices."[186] By rejecting adjustment and accepting liberation, radical therapists helped to translate psychological knowledge into political terms that challenged rather than accommodated the white, middle-class status quo.

In time, these feminist alternatives to patriarchal psychological knowledge freed feminists to reconcile CR's therapeutic means and political ends. Doing so was not necessarily easy. The belief that therapy led to narcissistic self-annihilation, not political action, was difficult to overcome. Marilyn Zweig, an assistant professor of philosophy at the University of Florida and member of the Gainesville Women's Liberation Group, offered this contorted explanation: "Although we are not a therapy group and do not try to resolve personal problems of individual women, we want to study ways to make the conditions of all women better so that individual women should have fewer problems. In the long run, then, each of us can hope that the group will help to make a better life for her personally."[187] Pamela Allen, a CR proselytizer from San Francisco, struck something of a middle ground in her popular book *Free Space*, describing CR as a political act that coincidentally felt good. "The total group process is not therapy because we try to find the social causes for our experiences. . . . But the therapeutic experience of momentarily relieving the individual of all responsibility for her situation does occur and is necessary if women are to be free to act."[188] In the end, feminists across a wide political spectrum decided that CR could be political and therapeutic.

All of CR's animating features—political action, education, and personal liberation—became synthesized within the women's movement's campus wing. Feminists pursued two main objectives. First, they set their sights on ending discriminatory hiring and admissions practices that they claimed had eroded women's role in higher education since the 1920s. WEAL gathered copious data that revealed an "industry-wide pattern" of sex discrimination, eventually filing suit under Executive Order 11375, signed in 1967, which banned sex discrimination in federal employment and by federal contractors and subcontractors, including higher education.[189] Many of the nation's top colleges and universities were implicated, including Harvard, Wisconsin, Michigan, Columbia, Minnesota, and Chicago, and the entire state college systems in California, Florida, and New Jersey. "Women have taken the first long step on the hard and rocky road of equal opportunity," said Bernice Sandler, chairperson of WEAL's Federal Contract Compliance Committee and the mastermind of the organization's legal strategy, "The American campuses will never be the same."[190]

This was an understatement. In addition to ending higher education's sexist employment practices, the women's movement's second objective was to expose the blatant sexism that ordered women's experiences inside and outside the college classroom. The doctrine of in loco parentis exacted an especially heavy toll on women, whose social and academic conduct was closely scrutinized by male peers, faculties, and administrators. Women were subject to special dormitory regulations, curfews, and dress codes. Their academic options were often limited to so-called feminine fields of study, like education, social work, home economics, and nursing. And across the masculine, Eurocentric curriculum, faculty relied on patriarchal knowledge and authoritarian pedagogical techniques that signaled female students' second-class status.[191] "The traditional curriculum," wrote historian Barbara Sicherman, "while assumed to be blind to sex, only confirmed the woman student's conscious or unconscious conviction that women were inferior to men, that their achievements were virtually non-existent, or, if noted at all, distinctly second rate. It told her in addition that only as a wife and mother could she be completely fulfilled."[192] That was why Betty Friedan wanted to enact "a national educational program, similar to the G.I. Bill" to release the "untapped reserves of women's intelligence in all the professions." Her generation had "wasted" their college years pursuing "M-R-S Degrees," or so the joke went, preparing for a "career" of marriage and motherhood. Friedan was not laughing. "The only point in educating women," wrote Friedan in the closing chapter of *The Feminine Mystique*, "is to educate them to the limit of their ability."[193]

Women's feelings of alienation ran deep everywhere—at coeducational universities but also at coordinate colleges and at single sex institutions, where the spatial separation of the sexes, even when chosen voluntarily, seemed to contribute to women's intellectual and emotional estrangement. "I fight to be recognized in class," said a female student at Douglass College of Rutgers University, "and if I'm a success, the teacher thinks I must be an exception to the female race."[194] A student at Sarah Lawrence College admitted her past education had not given her "any sense of heritage or anyone to identify with, with the exception of Betsy Ross." Her outlook improved after she enrolled in a women's history course and "found [herself] ... within a historical perspective."[195] At the University of Wisconsin, coeducational since the nineteenth century, a student shared her frustrations in detail: "In classes, I experienced myself as a person to be taken lightly. In one seminar I was never allowed to finish a sentence. ... Invariably, I was called by my first name while everyone else was called Mr. All in all, I was scared, depressed."[196]

Women's documented misery was not typically due to a lack of numbers. At a majority of institutions female students nearly equaled, and sometimes outnumbered, males (see appendix A.2). Rather, women's sense of alienation was caused by the utter lack of respect and recognition they suffered in and outside the classroom. This was the conclusion of a study sponsored by the Russell Sage Foundation, which blamed institutionalized patriarchy as the root of women's problems: "At both the undergraduate and graduate level women students are often subjected to a concentrated dosage of materials formulated by and filtered through an exclusively male perspective."[197] Writer and gay activist Adrienne Rich went a step further, denouncing the "man-centered university" as "an insidiously exploitive environment for women."[198]

Feminists looked to women's studies to loosen patriarchy's iron grip on higher education. Some feminists, like Rich, wanted complete freedom from male interference and urged the creation of autonomous programs and classes. Most academic feminists, however, supported a more modest agenda. The "hard lessons" of black studies offered women's studies innovators a cautionary example.[199] Rather than expend valuable capital on complete organizational and intellectual autonomy, as had blacks, female strategists focused on creating interdisciplinary programs and classes to occupy the space between the rigid, patriarchal borders of the male-dominated disciplines.[200] Here women banked on a key asset unavailable, then and later, to black studies pioneers: their relative strength in faculty and student numbers. This advantage allowed women to create standing caucuses within mainstream professional associations—like the APA, the Modern Language Association (MLA), and the American Historical Association—that ensured female members access to professional power and authority later on. At the time, it also allowed women to form ad hoc national bodies to help guide the nascent women's studies movement into being. The MLA's Commission on the Status of Women, established in 1969, was among the most influential of these groups, coordinating the collection and distribution of women's studies syllabi, reflections, and testimonials from across the disciplines. Published under the title *Female Studies*, the ten-volume work reveals in stunning detail the influence of CR on the organization of early women's studies courses and programs.[201]

One of the contributors was University of Wisconsin historian Gerda Lerner. Whether founding one of the first programs in women's history at Sarah Lawrence College, or serving as president of the Organization of American Historians, Lerner spent her professional career working to further women's place in the American history profession. Lerner's biography is helpful here. Born in 1920 and raised in an upper-middle-class Jewish family in Vienna, Austria, Lerner was an academically and politically precocious youth. She was a top student at her Gymnasium and attracted, at a young age, to antifascist politics. After being jailed by the Gestapo, in 1938, she immigrated to the United States in 1939 with the help of her then-boyfriend's relatives. Together they settled in New York, married, but quickly divorced. Six weeks after ending that relationship, Lerner met and eventually married the theater writer and director Carl Lerner. She followed him to Hollywood. There she filled her time as a new mother, a part-time writer, and as an active member of Los Angeles's Communist underground. She became a Party member in 1946 and two years later helped to organize the Los Angeles chapter of the Congress of American Women, a Popular Front feminist organization. In 1949, the Lerners moved back to New York City, at which point she decided to pursue her long-postponed college education. After collecting a bachelor's at the New School, she enrolled in the history graduate program at Columbia University in 1963.[202] Her dissertation-turned-book, *The Grimke Sisters of South Carolina: Rebels against Slavery* (1967), was an instant classic that established her as a powerful voice in the budding field of women's history.[203]

In graduate school, Lerner discovered that it was impossible to separate her personal life and political beliefs from her intellectual pursuits. Her personal experience, perhaps as much or more than her professors or peers, shaped how she studied the past and the meanings she derived from it. She recalled "testing what I was learning against what I already knew from living." Mining the past in search of women's history, Lerner realized that her personal life—as a Jewish immigrant, political activist, historian, and woman—was the decisive factor in how she approached her work. "I never accepted the need for separation of theory and practice," she recalled, in 2005. "My passionate commitment to Women's History was grounded in my life."[204]

This discovery crystallized in her the relationship between history and identity. Indeed, by studying history, Lerner changed her identity, eventually breaking from her Marxist past, in the mid-1980s, after several decades of private struggle.[205] The pain of this decision and of her lifetime of "various transformations" was chronicled in her 2002 autobiography, *Fireweed*.[206] In the work's opening line, Lerner described the "breaks, the fissures" of her life: "I've had too many—destruction, loss, then new beginnings." Yet her story ended on a hopeful note, revealing the liberating power of her own history and perhaps all history. After a lifetime of contemplating the history of women, Lerner concluded by applying that history to her own life, "The fact is that I combine all these elements of my life, and I think I have finally found the wholeness that embraces contradictions, the holistic view of life that accepts multiplicity and diversity, a view that no long demands a rigid framework of certainties."[207]

Well before her public confessions, however, Lerner was excitedly probing the possibilities of history's role in women's liberation. In her contribution to *Female Studies*, in 1972, Lerner reflected at length on the therapeutic power of women's history in women's lives:

> Most girls, by the time they reach college, have been accustomed to "failure," to sub-ordinating their curiosity, initiative and particularly their own female reactions and feminine insights, to the standards imposed by the dominant culture. They actually

Figure 6.8. History professor Gerda Lerner (seated on the left, wearing glasses) leading a graduate seminar in women's history at Sarah Lawrence College, 1972. Photo by Gary Gladstone.

"turn off" the essential parts of their personality and force upon themselves a separation of feelings and thoughts, of intellectual performance and being. This alienation is true to some extent for all people in our culture, but it is particularly true for girls and young women. Feminist Studies must attack this division of self at its roots. This is simply a fancy way of saying that consciousness-raising is an integral part of teaching Feminist Studies. Before women can study Feminist Studies with any effectiveness, they must come to grips with their own deep-seated anxieties, tensions and uncertainties in regard to their femininity. They can do this only by learning that what they have considered to be personal agony and traumas are really societally conditioned problems.[208]

Based on her life experiences, Lerner thought the study of history could help women discover their true identity—one free from imposed, patriarchal definitions. After all, if femininity—what in a few years would be known simply as gender—really was historically constructed and conditioned, as Lerner and others claimed, then why not use history to construct it anew?[209]

By all indications, first-generation women's studies instructors considered the reconstruction of female identity an important goal. What this meant as a practical matter differed from one instructor to another. In time, however, a number of therapeutic pedagogical practices, bearing more than a family resemblance to CR, became indelibly linked to the field. One was the transformation of the teacher into a "clarifier, a translator, a resource" instead of an authority figure; another was the use of small-group discussion and democratic deliberation; and still another was the reliance on journal writing, where students divulged the secrets of their private lives.[210] As a private form of CR, journal writing was believed to be an effective way of continuing the process of self-discovery outside the classroom, of melding theory and practice. "I consider the journal as potent a political tool as the activist group project," said Florence Howe, "for it fosters confidence in a necessary skill, as well as the significant growth of consciousness about one's own and others' lives."[211] Many students agreed. Amanda Kissin, a freshman at Barnard College, said that Sexuality in Literature affected her "personally" and drew her closer to the larger women's struggle: "The course gives me a nice sense of being part of it. I know that it's not just my own neurotic perception." Beryl Kaplan, a classmate enrolled in Determinants of Sex, was more specific. "Education is a basic foundation for any kind of movement," she explained. "Women's studies," she concluded, "is in a lot of ways—consciousness raising."[212]

Students found their new women's studies courses ripe with possibilities for intellectual and personal emancipation. "I've never been as interested in academics," explained Ella Kusnetz, a student at Cornell University. "Female studies is a new reference, I have some identity now as a woman."[213] A student at San Diego State College, birthplace to one of the first women's studies programs, described her experiences in women's studies as nothing short of revolutionary. "Ultimately [women's studies] is an organizing tool, getting a woman to realize her own oppression so she can deal with it."[214] English professor Elaine Showalter of Douglass College at Rutgers University reported that her courses had actually emboldened some students to divorce their husbands. "Although their husbands threaten me, I can't feel it was my fault," she explained. The readings and discussion helped them make this decision on their own, "sensitizing women to the political and cultural aspects of their lives."[215]

Some male faculty and students predictably cried foul at the institutionalization of women's studies. They ran with anecdotal accounts of gender bias and outright discrimination in women's studies classrooms to advance their case. They derided it as a "fad course." And they claimed it fragmented and politicized a college curriculum already in disarray.[216] "Black studies is divisive enough," protested a humanities professor, "Female studies would inevitably be aimed toward political goals, which I am far from sharing."[217]

Complaints such as these persisted but went largely unheeded. After decades of intellectual and emotional neglect, women, like blacks, were finally given their due. In 1976, the National Advisory Council on Women's Educational Programs counted 270 programs and 15,000 courses being offered by 1,500 different higher education institutions.[218] One year later, female faculty from 500 different institutions gathered together in San Francisco to found the National Women's Studies Association, to this day the field's main professional body.[219]

By that point, however, identity-group mobilizing had reached a fever pitch. Following the lead of blacks and women, other identity groups—Asians and Latinos, in particular, but also Native Americans—began demanding a right

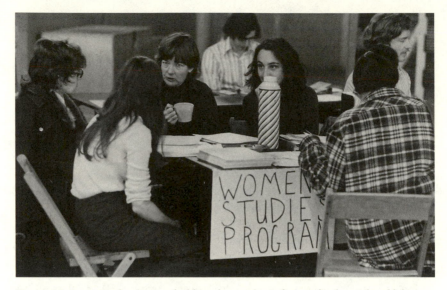

Figure 6.9. Jennie Farley (center, holding the mug), professor of industrial and labor re-lations and cofounder of the Women's Studies Program at Cornell University, talks with a group of students at the program's registration desk, January 1973. Courtesy Division of Rare and Manuscript Collections, Cornell University Libraries.

to an education of their own, too.[220] The combination of student body and re-gional demographic patterns determined what classes and programs were in-stituted where. Here the federal government again helped to make this hap-pen. The 1965 Immigration Act ended the discriminatory quota system of the 1920s, which had cutoff immigration flows from most parts of the world and limited the total number of new immigrants to 5 million between 1930 and 1965. After the quota plan was lifted immigration exploded. An estimated 28 million immigrants—a majority of whom derived from Asia (26 percent) and Latin America (46 percent)—came to the United States during the final three decades of the century, contributing greatly to the remarkable diversification of America—and American higher education—already well underway.[221] In the last quarter of the twentieth century, minority enrollment climbed from 15 to nearly 30 percent of the national total.[222] And while minority students were unevenly spread across the higher education sector, disproportionately concen-trated in two-year and in less-prestigious four-year institutions, the diversifica-tion that occurred was still profound, particularly compared to the pre-1965 period (see appendix A.3).[223]

White men did not passively sit back and watch from the sidelines. They mobilized to meet the diversity juggernaut head-on. First, following a dip in membership in the 1960s, fraternities regained popularity in the 1970s, this time fortified by stronger political organizations.[224] The College Republican National Committee and the Young Americans for Freedom were the two most powerful conservative student groups, and each built solid constituencies in these years that shaped the future of the Republican Party. Conservative political operatives Lee Atwater and Karl Rove, direct-mail expert Richard Viguerie, Senator and Vice President Dan Quayle, and antitax activist Grover Norquist all cut their political teeth in one or both organizations during college.[225] Second, white-ethnic students also got in on the action, claiming that the prevailing adjustment regime had likewise robbed them of their difference, their identity. President Richard M. Nixon's courtship of white working-class ethnics in his 1972 reelection campaign helped energize these efforts. So did his support for the 1972 National Ethnic Heritage Studies Act, which provided $2.5 million in federal aid for the development of ethnic studies (and black studies) programs.[226] Courses grew rapidly as Italian, Irish, Greek, Polish, and German studies—complete with rallying cries of "Italian Power" and "Polish is Beautiful"—found especially supportive environments at immigrant-heavy urban institutions in New York, Buffalo, Detroit, and Chicago.[227]

The influence of black studies was profound. It went beyond mere sloganeering to shape the ways in which ethnic studies organizers justified the very existence of their programs. Ethnic identity, like black identity, was worth discovering and preserving, they claimed, "no longer . . . considered something to get rid of as quickly as possible."[228] The search for a usable past and a new identity originally launched by blacks, then women, once set free, proved uncontainable. "I guess blacks legitimated cultural diversity," surmised Father Andrew Greeley, a sociologist and director of the Center for the Study of American Pluralism at the University of Chicago, in 1973. "Once that was considered all right, they legitimated it for everybody."[229]

In what became a predictable pattern, identity groups decried their exclusion from the curriculum and administrators granted reparations by making room for them in it. Professor Isao Fujimoto captured the essence of this political dynamic when he described the birth of Asian-American studies at the University of California, Davis: "Students from all over are interested in getting classes started. Whenever there are concentrations of Asians, there are attempts to push for Asian-American studies classes." Fujimoto's colleague, George Kagiwada, thought that improved relations between students and administrators marked a profound shift in how each regarded the other: "The climate is quite different. . . . You don't have this line of open challenge to the system as such. Rather, [students] have developed a kind of acceptance of the system."[230]

Students' acceptance of the "system" no doubt derived from the creation of a more diverse college curriculum. The additive approach to curricular maintenance seemed like democracy in action, satisfying students and administrators. In 1971, at City College of New York, where the ethnic studies department included programs in Jewish, Asian, Puerto Rican, and African-American studies, President Robert E. Marshak admitted to the managerial upside of curricular diversity at large bureaucratic institutions like his: "I hope as a result of the creation of these departments there will be a general relaxation on the campus and that these departments will enable students to achieve an ethnic or group identity, about which they feel so strongly."[231] After years of strife, by the early 1970s university administrators had finally gleaned a mission for the university that would both satisfy internally generated demands and "readjust" its long-standing commitment to crafting democratic citizens for the national, increasingly global world that they would graduate into.

"G.I. Bill for Everybody": Diversity and the Rights-Based Reconstruction of the Educated Citizen

By the early 1970s, the quest for diversity helped to forge a new rights-based understanding of the educated citizen. Students had won the right to an education all their own—an education that offered access to one's historical self and identity. But the creation of the rights-bearing educated citizen was not alone the product of the political mobilization of black and women student groups and of the waves of identity groups that followed. The simultaneous changes in the political and legal citizenship status of students also contributed to this makeover, convincing students their newly earned educational rights and privileges were just several of the rights now available to them in the post-1960s era.

No change was more important than the long-anticipated passing of in loco parentis. Nineteenth- and twentieth-century case law had defined higher education as a privilege—not a right—which could be revoked absent cause or a fair hearing because, according to this view, there was no disadvantage suffered from lost opportunities to which there was no inalienable right.[232] The landmark *Dixon v. Alabama Board of Education* (1961) decision overturned the right-privilege tradition at public institutions.[233] The Fifth Circuit Court agreed the summary expulsion of several Alabama State College students for their participation in an off-campus lunch counter sit-in had violated their due process rights under the Fourteenth Amendment. Subsequent court rulings upheld students' procedural rights in cases involving disciplinary and, if to a lesser degree, academic dismissals, eventually extending to students at private institutions, whose leaders thought their students should also be granted equivalent procedural safeguards.[234] The case law highlighted another important rationale for the shift in students' status as rights-bearing citizens: the widespread acceptance higher education was of inestimable financial benefit to individuals and society. That each degree earned appreciably increased earnings and occupational status confirmed that college really was more than child's play.[235] By 1968, as one judge put it, "the college does not stand, strictly speaking, in loco parentis to its students."[236] The age-old distinction between educating "children" and "adults" was rendered obsolete. All students were now adults whether they acted their age or not.

Three years later, the court-ordered change in students' status as rights-bearing citizens was further steeled by the ratification of the Twenty-sixth Amendment, which lowered the voting age from twenty-one to eighteen for all local, state, and federal elections. Proposals to lower the voting age had been making the rounds on Capitol Hill since World War II, but not until the late 1960s and the radicalization of the antiwar movement did political and popular support finally coalesce. Conservatives and antiwar liberals agreed lowering the voting age was in their respective best interests: for Republicans, including President Nixon, doing so meant allaying the antiwar movement and thus ending the war in Vietnam on their terms; for Democrats it meant collecting a majority of the "youth vote" and widening their electoral base. While neither of these assumptions proved entirely accurate, at the time they were enough to energize Congress and the legislatures of the several states to approve the measure in overwhelming fashion. Despite lingering doubts about the qualifications of the radical, albeit statistically small, student activist community, most policymakers agreed young people deserved the right to join the ranks of the nation's voters. Students, after years of chanting "old enough to fight, old enough to vote," had at last been deemed old enough to do both. [237]

The following year the state strengthened its commitment to college going with the Education Amendments of 1972.[238] With campus order at last restored, education policymakers sought to extend the educational rights of women, the poor, and all students originally laid out in the Higher Education Act. First, Title IX prohibited sex discrimination by any higher education institution receiving federal aid, thereby closing the sex discrimination loophole in Title VI of the Civil Rights Act. Representative Edith Green (D-OR), one of the original architects of the Higher Education Act, with the help of Senator Birch Bayh (D-IN), shepherded the ban through Congress. No "women's libber," Green was a moderate who believed ardently in equality of opportunity and had grown wary of higher education's "backward treatment of its working women." Although Title IX was primarily intended to remedy inequities in female professors' compensation and in student admissions, in practice it had far-reaching implications for all aspects of university life—from the professoriate and student services to athletics—covering as it did "any education program or activity."[239]

Second, the Education Amendments altered the ways in which the state packaged and delivered financial aid to all students—the needy as well as the better off. The original legislation channeled aid to institutions, not individuals, and relied on aid officers to compile "aid packages" using a combination of work-study, grants, and loans. The amended legislation kept these existing campus programs, but augmented them with portable market-driven mechanisms that moved the federal government's role in student finance to an approximation of its present-day form. The legislation created the Student Loan Marketing Association (Sallie Mae) to better coordinate the guaranteed student-lending activities of private banks. The public-private partnership turned into a lucrative one for lenders. While it lasted (the guaranteed loan program was terminated in 2010), participating banks reaped guaranteed rates of return on the money they loaned while the government assumed all the risk.[240] Within two decades the government's various subsidized and un-subsidized, direct and guaranteed loan programs dwarfed all other sources of student aid, totaling nearly $25 billion annually, or 50 percent of all available aid, by the mid-1990s (see appendix A.4).[241]

At the time, the loan provision was something of an afterthought. Congress and the media hailed the Basic Educational Opportunity Grant Program (BEOG) as the more important policy development. The BEOG, renamed the Pell Grant in 1980, was the brainchild of Senator Claiborne Pell (D-RI), who succeeded Wayne Morse of Oregon as chair of the Senate Subcommittee on Education in 1969—since the late 1950s and the enactment of the NDEA, the main policy incubator for federal higher education legislation. Best known for his work against deep-sea nuclear testing and in favor of metric conversion and high-speed mass transit, Pell's only noteworthy education-related accomplishment was his successful sponsorship of the National Endowment for the Humanities in 1965. Now, seven years later, he assumed his new subcommittee chairmanship determined to make college going, in his own words, "a matter of right."[242] An entitlement program that guaranteed assistance, Pell wanted the grant to become the foundation on which all students would finance their educational careers—a "G.I. Bill for everybody."[243] Students applied directly to the federal government via the Free Application for Federal Financial Aid (FAFSA); grants were determined by subtracting an applicant's "Family Contribution" from the government's $1,400 maximum award. Although its purchasing power eroded in time, forcing students to make up the difference with evermore loans, when initially passed the Pell Grant could be counted on to cover up to half the cost of attendance at many schools, as it was intended to do.[244] Collectively, the Education Amendment's ban on sex discrimination, and its provision of portable federal loans and grants advanced students' rights in remarkable ways.

The final act in the state's rights-based reconstruction of educated citizenship occurred with the repeal of the draft and the move to an all-volunteer force in 1973. In the works for a number of years, the end of conscription helped muffle an already quiet student antiwar protester community. More important, it decoupled the longstanding relationship between national service and education that had been so instrumental to the enactment of federal higher education policy since World War II. The perennial dilemma of educational versus military service that was tangled up in the thicket of the Selective Service Administration's educational deferment program was finally laid to rest. Though soldiers continued to receive educational benefits in exchange for service after 1973, for civilians, service to their country (or their community or school, for that matter) was no longer required—unless they felt like it. They could enlist in the armed forces, seek admission to college, or do something—anything—else. Campuses were calm, students relieved. The worst of the turmoil had ended, and with it the heroic age of reciprocity between citizens and the state.[245]

❖

Lest there be any doubt about the change in citizenship that had occurred, a year later the state passed the 1974 Family Education Rights and Privacy Act (FERPA). Little noted by anyone at the time, just another amendment to the recent spate of educational amendments, the law granted students eighteen and older privacy rights previously furnished to their parents: "The permission or consent required of and the rights accorded to the parents of the student," the law declared, "shall thereafter only be required of and accorded to the student."[246] Regardless of who paid the tuition bill, from then on parents would have to request permission from their children to access grades or any other records found in their personal file.

The new regard for privacy rights embedded in the law was symptomatic of the larger shift toward personal experience chronicled in this chapter. In an effort to overcome their own alienation and achieve transcendent selfhood, blacks and women excavated their private lives and experiences and discovered that politics and education were personal. The yearning for existential self-understanding—what students, then and later, called "identity"—resulted in a new rights-based conception of democratic citizenship that was intimately connected to an energetic pluralist politics known as diversity. "Students don't think of themselves as students anymore," declared a campus leader in an article on the "student mood" published in the *Chronicle of Higher Education*, in the spring of 1976. "They think of themselves as citizens getting an education."[247]

This was supremely ironic. At the very instant higher education finally succeeded at imbuing students with a sense of citizenship, citizenship was rewrapped in a bundle of group and personal rights, with few if any reciprocal obligations. Citizenship had become personalized, and, like higher education and politics, it would never be the same.

Chapter 7

Conclusion
The Private Marketplace of Identity
in an Age of Diversity

———————— ❖❖❖ ————————

By the mid-1970s, the state's four-decade-long citizenship education project had come full circle. As this book has chronicled, beginning in the Great Depression, the state played an active if obscured role supporting higher education and extending its reach deeper into the life of the people than ever before. After World War II the state's involvement became much more visible. The enactment of groundbreaking federal legislation revolutionized college going in the United States. The G.I. Bill, the National Defense Education Act, and the Higher Education Act expanded educational opportunity to increasing numbers of Americans—to veterans, to students in defense-related fields of study, and then to everyone else. Believing that higher education created psychologically adjusted citizens capable of fulfilling the duties and obligations of democratic citizenship, the state coordinated and funded this remarkable expansion, transforming higher education into a key mediating institution between citizens and the state.

This argument reconfigures the dominant historical narrative of the twentieth-century state-academic partnership. Existing scholarship focuses on the rise of the research matrix and the impact of university experts in American government. But the birth of "big science" is not the only story worth telling—and as the education of tens of millions of Americans attests, it might not even be the most important. After World War I new psychological understandings of human and organizational development became embedded within the university structure in ways that ultimately changed how citizenship was defined. Higher education's promise was first glimpsed during the Great Depression. But its full potential as a tool of statecraft was not truly realized until World War II, when the state deployed education to build better soldiers and rewarded veterans with generous education benefits in exchange for their wartime sacrifices. This reciprocal conception of educated citizenship endured until the

1960s, before being eclipsed by a rights-based citizenship model that did not require service to the state. Led by the black power and the women's liberation movements, and the throng of subsequent identity groups that followed in their wake, students turned the politics of American higher education to their own ends. They claimed that education and politics were personal and the discovery of identity the gateway to true liberation. It was out of this storm of rights-based, identity-group introspection and political action that the current-day idea of diversity was born.

Diversity offered a new and powerful way to conceive of citizenship, politics, and American higher education after 1975. It emerged as the defining idea of the contemporary university at the same time that the state-higher education partnership collapsed. Like so many relationships gone bad, this one fell apart over money matters and broken promises, and led to a new relationship between the university and the state, one that critics charged was forged "on the rebound." Identity politics, heuristically founded and organizationally nurtured on college campuses, became the model emulated by hundreds of interest groups that infiltrated Washington, DC—a variant of interest group politics best described as pluralism on steroids. Identifying the economic, political, and psychological causes of the breakup—and the new decentralized, market-driven, identity-based framework that replaced it—is the task of this concluding chapter.

"I've Seen Some Pretty Poor Products Come out of Those Colleges": Economic Decline and Psychological Maladjustment Revisited

At the very instant the state-higher education partnership reached its height, it crumbled to the ground. A year after the passage of the Pell Grant in 1972—a "G.I. Bill for everybody"—the bottom fell out of the economy and along with it the close relationship between higher education and the state. The OPEC oil embargo revealed the structural weaknesses of a U.S. economy already overburdened by the rising costs of the Great Society and Vietnam War. When plentiful sources of cheap oil evaporated, it drove the economy into a freefall, the likes of which had not been seen since the Great Depression. Between 1973 and 1975, unemployment rose from 5.7 to 7.5 percent and inflation doubled to 12.4 percent as economic growth stalled—a vexing set of economic circumstances known as "stagflation." The net impact on American higher education was profound, bringing to a screeching halt the sector's post-1945 golden age.[1]

The writing had been on the bathroom-stall wall since the late 1960s when a "cost crisis" in higher education was first revealed. Across the country, institutions were confronted by "grave financial trouble . . . that threatens their very existence," according to *Time*.[2] Within a few years, Earl Cheit, a professor of business administration at the University of California, Berkeley, declared a "new depression in higher education" had arrived.[3] Enrollments leveled off in the early 1970s and then fell in the 1975–76 academic year for the first time since 1951. Federal research funding, which reached its apogee in 1967–68, also waned, declining modestly in real terms over the course of the 1970s.[4] A difficult challenge lay in absorbing all the new costs associated with the growth in research infrastructure—for graduate fellowships and stipends, overhead, construction costs and maintenance, insurance, and health benefits. In these areas most institutions found themselves operating in the red. Faced with less purchasing power and rapidly rising costs, colleges and universities did just about the only thing they could do to make up the difference: they passed the burden on to students. Beginning in the early 1970s, annual tuition increases averaged more than double the rate of inflation, and the cost borne by students almost doubled in real terms in the two decades that followed. Federal grants and work-study helped the neediest, but not nearly enough. And by decade's end the future of college going was, in a word, borrowed. Loans helped increasing numbers of families and their students pay the tuition bill. Today's high-cost/high-aid model of student finance grew out of the economic downturn of the 1970s when record inflation forced average Americans to borrow more money than ever to live *and* to learn.[5]

To be sure, higher education had faced economic and wartime challenges earlier in the twentieth century. But now, unlike during the Great Depression, World War II, and the cold war, the state was reticent to help. In many ways, the lack of federal support was simply a dollars-and-cents issue. The recession of 1973–75 severely constrained the federal government's fiscal options. While the state had thrown money at higher education in the past, it now balked at doing so for the simple fact that there was less money to throw around. High unemployment and runaway inflation reduced worker productivity and greater global competition, especially from Asia, eroded America's competitive economic advantages, pushing the gross national product to a virtual standstill in the 1970s, after years of remarkable growth. But even if there had been surplus funds to save higher education, it is unlikely that the government would have come to the rescue. After all, most of the really big policy questions had already been answered by the mid-1970s. Segregation was outlawed; coeducation ruled; well-defined federal guidelines had brought uniformity and structure to academic hiring; the curriculum and student body had become more diversified than ever; and thanks to the triumvirate of federally supported aid mechanisms—grants, work study, and loans—students had greater educational opportunities than ever before. What more could the state do?

Indeed, many policymakers and average citizens thought that the state had already done far too much. With the tragedy of Vietnam and a decade worth of campus violence to show for it, many policymakers and educational leaders believed the partnership was exhausted. Criticisms showered down on faculty and students as doubts about higher education's production of cutting-edge research and of democratic citizens gained momentum. Not only scientists who had conducted and profited from weapons research but also academics in fields from medicine to the humanities came under intense scrutiny. Policymakers who had previously lavished attention on higher education now jealously withheld it. Senator Ted Kennedy (D-MA) advocated cutting funding for the National Institutes of Health, calling it a "sacred cow." His chamber colleague, Claiborne Pell (D-RI), architect of the Pell Grant, showed less patience with professors than he had students. Eleven years after sponsoring the legislation that created the National Endowment for the Humanities, in 1965, Pell suggested disbanding it. "We cannot justify the expenditure of taxpayers' money in support of the humanities," Pell said, "if the tendency of the program is to proliferate volumes of humanistic studies in university libraries, just for academic humanists to read."[6] Conservatives pressed harder still. Republican Senator Robert Baumann (R-MD) sponsored legislation that, had his colleagues approved it, would have given Congress veto power over any of the fourteen thousand grants awarded annually by the National Science Foundation. Conservatives scored their share of victories, too. Disturbed by academic scientists' lack of support for the Vietnam War, President Richard Nixon stopped awarding the National Science Medal, ignored his science adviser, abolished the Office of Science and Technology, and refused to convene, then terminated, the President's Science Advisory Committee, an active Executive Office body since the Eisenhower administration.[7] "The scientific-technological elite . . ." reported Daniel Greenberg, author and publisher of the Washington-based newsletter, *Science and Government Report*, "has fallen from political grace as has no other group."[8]

Except for college students, whose stock kept sinking lower the longer the 1960s dragged on, finally hitting rock bottom in May 1970.[9] After President Nixon announced the U.S. invasion of Cambodia, furious student protests erupted across the country. A few turned tragic. On May 4 the Ohio National Guardsmen shot and killed four white students at Kent State University. Ten days after that, Mississippi state police shot and killed two black students at Jackson State College, triggering additional protests, and even more violence, elsewhere. By May's end, police forces had been summoned to dozens of colleges and National Guardsmen mobilized in sixteen states as campuses burned. Later that summer, in August, four radical antiwar demonstrators blew up the Army Mathematics Research Center at the University of Wisconsin. The blast destroyed "Army Math," damaged dozens of other buildings, and left three people wounded and one post-doctoral researcher dead. Events such as these convinced many observers that higher education had become a breeding ground for political radicalism, not democratic citizenship. In the fall, the FBI's "most wanted" list was overrun with "young radicals"—so many that the bureau expanded its list from the usual ten to sixteen mug shots. The *Chronicle of Higher Education* remarked on this discomfiting turn: "Gone are the days when the FBI's most-sought-after criminals were middle-aged, male hatchet-killers, wife-murders, and rapists, as they were less than a decade ago."[10] Additional acts of senseless terrorism by the Weather Underground and other marauding bands of violent young people fueled antiacademic sentiment everywhere. More than a few parents were afraid to let their children even go to college. "My son is 17 and I don't want him to go," confessed one nervous mother, a resident of the Chicago suburbs. "In the last eight years I've seen some pretty poor products come out of those colleges."[11]

Students had their defenders, of course. After all, most students remained politically middle-of-the-road and far from far-left wing. The final report of The *President's Commission on Campus Unrest*, released in the fall of 1970, reminded readers "that only a minority of the students involved in most campus protests are tactical extremists, and that the vast majority of student protests, even in 1970, have been well within the American tradition of lawful protest."[12] A subsequent study by the American Council on Education discovered that of the 9,408 protests in 1970, only 731 involved the police and arrests.[13] Contrary to conventional wisdom, most protests were peaceful. This fact made what followed all the more difficult to understand: after winning the right to vote at eighteen, students suddenly, and quite inexplicably, lost interest in voting. Many political observers assumed that the country's 26 million 18-to-25-year-old voters might turn the 1972 general election and propel Democratic challenger Senator George McGovern of South Dakota to victory. Yet less than half of the potentially eligible "youth vote" actually cast ballots—a figure lower than for older voters. McGovern was pummeled along with college students' reputation. Dismal turnout, a trend that continued for the rest of the century, compelled the editors of the *New York Times* to conclude: "Youth as such are not a cohesive political category . . . they are less, not more, politically active than their elders."[14] Did this make students lesser citizens? Many thought the answer to that question was an unqualified yes.

Not even veterans, once the very embodiment of the adjusted citizen, escaped unscathed. Vietnam veterans enjoyed little of the fanfare that had greeted World War II veterans on their return from battle. Though the state reauthorized the G.I. Bill twice during the Vietnam War, the actual benefits were approximately half as generous as they had been in World War II.[15] Still more troubling was the perception that Vietnam veterans were ungrateful and perhaps unworthy of better treatment and of greater rewards. Media portrayals of the Vietnam veteran as an unpatriotic, drug-addicted, pathological misfit with post-traumatic stress disorder became standard fare.[16] Such portrayals had a corrosive effect, irreparably severing the link between education and adjustment that had defined democratic citizenship since World War II. Olin Teague (D-TX), the chairman of the House Committee on Veterans Affairs, made no effort to hide his contempt for the nation's newest crop of veterans, defending his position on limiting benefits to "disadvantaged soldiers." "My main mission," said Teague, a World War II veteran who had built his political career on veterans, "is to keep the nuts and kooks from messing up the greatest school program ever devised."[17] Lost amid all the vitriol, however, was a truly startling fact: despite the paucity of benefits and public support, a proportionally greater percentage of Vietnam-era veterans (6.8 million out of 10.3 million eligible) used the educational benefit at a college or university than did any previous veteran population, including that of World War II.[18]

"The Distinct Identity Groupings on Campus, Once Institutionalized, Found Reasons to Remain Distinct": Personalizing Politics

What happened? By the mid-1970s, three changes to the state-academic partnership had become manifest. First, the higher education economy was in shambles with the macroeconomy. The full recovery of one or both seemed unlikely anytime soon. Second, the old consensus around adjusted citizenship lay in ruins, crushed beneath the weight of incongruous definitions of identify and a divided psychology profession whose diverse membership no longer shared the same assumptions about psychology's power to adjust and readjust individuals and institutions.[19] The rise of feminist therapy and black therapy and the spread of radical therapies of all kinds—from Timothy Leary's LSD-laced "psychedelic consciousness movement" and Arthur Janov's "primal scream therapy" to the whole New Age "human potential movement"—revealed just how far professional psychology had moved beyond the adjustment paradigm. That this happened was not surprising. The concept of adjustment had always been a narrowly defined ideal-type scarcely realizable in practice. Students, young and old, whether consuming knowledge in a traditional classroom setting, or by way of some other experimental medium or alternative venue, were never just empty vessels. And try as they may, educational elites never really figured out how to use education to manufacture the outputs they wanted. Built on a normative conception of selfhood rooted to white male, middle-class values and institutions, the quintessential adjusted citizen was for a short while embodied by the World War II veteran: "Joe College." As a prototype, however, it was destined to disappoint, and it did— black and female students made sure of it.

Finally, the politics of American higher education and the American state changed profoundly after the 1960s.[20] The civil rights movement started it all. It thrust black and white college students, along with millions of "local people," into the thick of American politics for the first time.[21] It was *the* event of a lifetime. Organizations like the Student Nonviolent Coordinating Committee (SNCC) and the Congress for Racial Equality (CORE) closed the gap between the self and society and infused political action with profound meaning. "This was how SDS [Students for a Democratic Society] was born as well, much of SDS," recalled Tom Hayden, one of its founders. "I started in the South, not in Ann Arbor; I spent two years in the South."[22] Inspired and awed by what they witnessed, the New Left, with SDS at its core, sought to emulate the nonviolent direct-action tactics of the civil rights movement; and, for a time, they did. But when SDS lost patience with trying to "name that system . . . and change it," as SDS president Paul Potter put it in 1965, and moved to destroy "the system" entirely, all hope for "One Big Movement"—interracial, cross-class and coeducational —was destroyed with it.[23] "The spectacle of the post-SDS factions hurling incomprehensible curses at one another was not inviting to newcomers," lamented SDS veteran Todd Gitlin, Potter's immediate predecessor. The "turn to violence and mindless disruption," Gitlin explained, destroyed the New Left and scattered its members among a multitude of groups, each with its own narrow agenda.[24] This was bitterly ironic. The New Left had explicitly rejected interest group politics as secret politics, as antidemocratic politics—as a "politics without publics."[25] Yet this was exactly the type of politics that resurfaced with a vengeance by decade's end. Having failed to create a mass movement to "change the world," students were faced with group politics or oblivion. They chose the former and called it identity.[26]

The dissolution of the New Left into a mishmash of distinct identity groups was not an isolated event—a result of overly idealistic, temperamental, and hormonal college students failing to get along. The same fractionalizing phenomenon was recapitulated across the polity as previously hardened political orderings crumbled into more and more complex arrangements of interests. The root cause was the rapid expansion of government—and of citizens' interaction with government—since World War II.[27] New politics triggered new policies. This dynamic interaction spawned allied interests to support and administer key programs on behalf of various constituencies. In Washington, the Congressional Black Caucus became a locus of agenda-building for African Americans, while the National Organization of Women (NOW) served a similar function for female representatives and senators. Across the policy spectrum an identical pattern of disaggregation and reconsolidation occurred as well. In health care, for example, Medicare and Medicaid helped to splinter the medical lobby, dispersing support among a host of interests from doctors and insurance companies to medical schools and local health boards. In education, the enactment of the Elementary and Secondary Education Act of 1965 (ESEA) energized teachers unions, especially the National Federation of Teachers and the National Education Association, to national prominence. And in the area of environmental policy, the creation of the Environmental Protection Agency, in 1970, followed two years later by the Clean Water Act, heightened the profile of groups like the Sierra Club and the Wilderness Society and persuaded millions more Americans to live "green." Higher education, as this book has demonstrated, followed a similar developmental course. Between World War

II and the 1960s, state action aimed at increasing opportunity, access, and affordability succeeded wildly, but not before unwittingly generating a host of unexpected and increasingly consequential feedbacks for the state and higher education both.[28]

Group mobilizing and countermobilizing occurred at an alarming rate during the 1960s and 1970s. According to one student of the subject, it brought "many formerly quiescent elements of the population into closer contact with the nation's political leaders."[29] Whether public, voluntary, or profit making, groups pressed for action not at the local or state but national level. In the trade and professional association arena alone, for instance, a majority of the biggest and most powerful relocated to the nation's capitol, to say nothing of the scads of public interest groups, like Ralph Nader's consumer group Public Citizen, founded in 1971, which followed closely behind. Like the civil rights movement, these groups relied on a combination of methods—class-action law suits; referenda and initiatives; and good, old-fashioned electoral politics—to advance their agendas. Most were "liberal" groups. NOW, Planned Parenthood, Common Cause, and the American Association of Retired Persons, to name but a few, gravitated to a Democratic Party known for accommodating discrete interest groups—like labor unions and farmers' organizations—since the New Deal. Arguably the most influential interest groups migrated to Washington from the other side of the political aisle. The National Rifle Association, the Family Research Council, the National Right to Life Committee, the Moral Majority, and other evangelical Christian groups forged a powerful New Right coalition that reinvigorated the Republican Party and propelled Ronald Reagan into the White House in 1980.[30]

Then and later, the upsurge in group mobilizing struck a number of scholars as decadent and narcissistic, possibly ruinous to the American political order.[31] Other critics found it paradoxical. Chief among this group of skeptics was political scientist Hugh Heclo. He questioned the long-term prospects of a political system in which a "radically pluralized" public demanded more from government while trusting government less—a political order glommed together by mutual distrust and anxious attachment that Heclo later described as "postmodern."[32] The 1960s made a jumbled mess of state-society relations: Vietnam, urban decline, campus violence, Watergate, and the economic recession signaled the end of America's post–World War II era of abundance and of the American people's abundant faith in government. Party memberships fell as the number of independent voters climbed and average Americans mobilized in new, self-interested, and highly personal ways.[33] Drawn together by a shared, often traumatic, experience or some other involuntary marker of identity, rights-conscious identity groups steered American politics into "previously nonpolitical terrains: sexuality, interpersonal relations, lifestyle, and culture."[34] There can be no doubt that the public's profound distrust of government pointed it toward group politics—especially the politics of personal identity.

Overlooked in the rush to embrace this new skepticism was a more enduring basis for the revolution in group politics during the 1970s: the public's increased trust in itself. Higher education's widening jurisdiction over the public
sphere after World War II powered this revolution. It was on college campuses
where the personal and the political intersected and identity was nourished
and grown. It was a fecund environment. "The distinct identity groupings on
campus," wrote Todd Gitlin, no friend he to identity politics, "once institutionalized, found reasons to remain distinct. They radiated savoir faire and solidar-
ity. They seemed to offer the satisfactions of intellectual companionship and
political passion at the same time—a heady mixture."[35]

In fact, higher education's new role in forging students' personal identities was really a continuation and extension of a role it had always performed.
Well before the diversification of higher education in the 1960s turned politics
and education personal, the institution had been instrumental in shaping the
professional identities of its overwhelmingly white, middle-class student body.
The advanced credentials received by those students easily translated into occupationally based interest groups after graduation—so effortlessly, in fact, that
higher education's dominant role in politicizing professional guilds of doctors,
lawyers, accountants, engineers, businessmen, and teachers hardly required
comment. There was no reason for it to be otherwise: these overwhelmingly
white male, occupationally affiliated professional groups, used to influencing
the policymaking process in insular confines, dominated America's pluralist
politics before the 1960s. These older groups remained strong as ever after the
1960s, but they faced more competition from personal identity groups well-
versed in "personal politics." A decade of sit-ins, teach-ins, and protests—of
black studies, women's studies, and ethnic studies of all kinds—had a cumula-
tive political effect. Blacks, females, Asians, Latinos, Native Americans, gays
and lesbians and other historically underserved, underrepresented student
groups discovered that personal, not just professional, identity could be a powerful tool for political work.[36]

The case of Supreme Court Justice Sonia Sotomayor illuminates this point
well. Sotomayor entered Princeton University in 1972—only the third class to
include women. In her first year, Sotomayor spent her time buried in books.
But as a sophomore, she became more active in campus politics. Sotomayor
became the chief spokesperson for Princeton's small Puerto Rican community,
occasionally serving as President William Bowen's personal adviser on "Hispanic issues." No functionary, Sotomayor organized and cochaired Princeton's
first Puerto Rican student group (Acción Puertorriqueña), which became a
hub for Latino student life more generally; in 1974, the organization drafted
and filed with the Department of Health, Education, and Welfare an official
discrimination complaint that helped change recruitment and hiring practices
at Princeton. In her third year, she enrolled in Princeton's first Puerto Rican
studies seminar and grew enthralled by her heritage and history. She graduated
summa cum laude with an A.B. in history, writing her senior thesis on Luis Mu-

ñoz Marin, Puerto Rico's first democratically elected governor. Her dedication revealed much about her college experience: "To my family, for you have given me my Puerto Rican-ness." The following fall she enrolled in Yale Law School.[37]

The intermingling and politicization of students' professional and personal identities complicated the ways in which identity was defined on and off campus. Where identity had previously been gleaned by what you did for a living, it now begged a more probing analysis in which how you felt, what you believed, where you were from, the way you looked, the clothes you wore, who—or what—you loved, and whether you had been addicted, victimized, traumatized, or abused mattered as much if not more. African Americans and women had long known this painful truth, of course, since race and gender were the two most impervious markers of identity—and now so did the rest of the country. The old male-dominated political regime of party politics and occupational interest groups was forced to accommodate a whole range of new personal and group demands. Feminist Kate Millet forecast this shift in her book *Sexual Politics* (1970). As to whether the relationship between the sexes was "political," Millet replied: "The answer depends on how one defines politics. This essay does not define the political as that relatively narrow and exclusive world of meetings, chairmen, and parties. The term 'politics' shall refer to power-structured relationships, arrangements whereby one group of persons is controlled by another."[38] By the 1980s, millions of Americans of every political persuasion knew the answer, too. They had learned it in college.[39]

"As Diverse as This Nation of Many People": Privatizing Citizenship

It was only a matter of time before higher education's role in and reliance on group politics, especially the role of affirmative action in higher education admissions policies, became a hotly contested political issue in its own right. The personnel perspective that emerged in the 1920s—which had been used to admit *and* exclude applicants—adapted easily to the diversity imperatives foisted on (and, in many cases, welcomed by) higher education after the passage of the Civil Rights Act of 1964 and the Higher Education Act of 1965. In an effort to right past wrongs and equalize educational opportunity, admissions directors and equal employment opportunity representatives wrote antidiscrimination policies into their hiring and admission practices. Some of these policies went beyond the federal requirements, erasing the line between opportunity and advantage already blurred by the proliferation of minority student recruitment programs and compensatory educational courses, and by minority counseling programs and dormitory facilities—"special services" also provided to white students that some white students and their parents now cited as proof of "special treatment" for minorities. Perhaps this was inevitable. In a political and educational universe rife with internecine battles for individual and group advantage, where students fought for a limited number of seats in college and for even fewer jobs afterward, affirmative admissions and hiring policies became a source of extraordinary controversy as the 1970s dragged on and the economy continued to stagnate. There was no way to satisfy everyone. Supporters claimed that historically underrepresented groups had a "right" to higher education; well-organized white, middle-class opponents responded in kind. The former clung desperately to the idea of "group opportunity"; the latter to the idea of individual "merit."[40]

Eventually the Supreme Court was forced to choose a side in the affirmative action debate. In the epochal *Regents of the University of California v. Allan Bakke* decision (1978), the court's split decision turned on yet a third idea: diversity.[41] At issue in the case was the admission policy of the Medical School at the University of California, Davis. The respondent, Allan Bakke, asserted he had been a victim of "reverse discrimination" and unjustly rejected because of the medical school's policy reserving sixteen seats for minority candidates. Justice Lewis F. Powell wrote the lead opinion in two sharply divided 5–4 decisions that banned quotas, thereby granting Bakke retroactive admission to Davis Medical School, but upheld "race or ethnic background" as a constitutionally protected "element—to be weighed fairly against other elements—in the admissions process." Citing an amicus brief submitted by Columbia University, Harvard University, Stanford University, and the University of Pennsylvania—one of the record fifty-eight submitted to the court in advance of its deliberations—Powell agreed a "diverse student body" created an "atmosphere of 'speculation, experiment and creation.' " Higher education, he concluded, must be "as diverse as this nation of many people."[42]

Powell's was far from the last word. Affirmative action melded with a cluster of other divisive issues—the reeling economy, high taxes, and a stretched social safety net—to propel California Governor Ronald W. Reagan (R-CA) to the White House two years later. His difficult history with the California higher education system well known, Reagan's victory sent shockwaves throughout the higher education sector. As governor he had managed California's public colleges and universities with an iron fist, orchestrating the firing of Clark Kerr, establishing martial law on campuses up and down the state, and taking a hard line with students and faculty both.[43] Reagan's campaign pledge to shrink "big government"—to slash spending and taxes, to dismantle the Department of Education, and to unleash the free market—seemingly promised tough times ahead for "big education." After Reagan assumed the presidency, many in higher education predicted that all the gains of the past twenty years would be washed away. Said the director of financial aid at the University of Massachusetts, Amherst: "The 1980s will mark the end of the dream of access, choice and retention for low-income and minority students."[44] Higher education braced for the worst—permanent funding cuts, executive orders abolishing affirmative action, a freeze on lending, and the end of the Pell Grant.

The doomsday scenarios never materialized. After Reagan's victory the state broke with, but did not break, higher education by speeding up the decentralization process begun in the early 1970s. The government set free the free-market by cutting taxes, deregulating the economy, and granting the governments of the several states greater control in administering federally funded social programs. Doctrinaire free market beliefs—once limited to a small bloc of neoclassical economists and antigovernment libertarian political thinkers—seized the imaginations of both major parties, especially the GOP, as well as average Americans everywhere. By the early 1980s, the idea that government which governed least governed best reshaped national governance, and the American people's expectations of government, for the rest of the century and beyond.[45]

In due course, the free market ideology that suffused Washington after 1980 "trickled down" to the marketplace of ideas.[46] Temporary cuts in federal aid for students and research gave way to a series of market-driven policies that irrevocably privatized the burdens and benefits of college going.[47] First, the federal government altered its role in sponsored research by granting institutions greater incentive to pursue and profit from cutting-edge research discoveries. This was the accomplished with the Patent and Trademark Amendments of 1980, better known as the Bayh-Dole Act, which transferred the patent rights for federally funded research discoveries from the government to higher education. A boom in academic patents along with the creation of dozens of university-based research incubators to develop, market, and profit from that research followed. Although criticized at the time by humanities professors least likely to produce or benefit from marketable research, Bayh-Dole transformed the research agendas of budding fields like biomedicine, computer science, and engineering. In the long run, the hope that financial inducements would boost research productivity and thus encourage private funding for that research proved accurate. By the end of the 1990s, licensing revenues collected from patented discoveries exceeded $675 million annually. "In the decades of the 1980s and 1990s," according to one expert, "American universities literally transformed themselves. Responding to changes in federal policy . . . and the lure of the marketplace, they . . . made forays into the private economy by commercializing their own discoveries."[48]

Second, the federal government recalibrated the trajectory of its financial aid programming. The rapid shift from grants to loans was the most profound development. The first move in this direction occurred in 1978—at the front edge of the Reagan Revolution—with the passage of the Middle Income Student Assistance Act aimed at placating middle-income families and students who were too poor to afford college outright but too wealthy to qualify for Pell Grants.[49] The legislation significantly liberalized the availability of federally subsidized loans for middle-class families and students by lifting the income ceiling for guaranteed, low-interest loans. Soaring interest rates made the government's terms more than attractive as borrowing shot up by 60 percent in real terms in just three years. And by the mid-1980s, loans had become students' ticket to college, reversing the original intent of the Higher Education Act, which had imagined grants serving that role. Steadily escalating costs across the entire higher education sector, exacerbated by state-government disinvestment in public higher education, increased the need for federally backed direct and guaranteed loans of all types—particularly for low- and middle-income students. As tuition climbed so did students' and families' borrowing habits, which increased from $9 to $37.5 billion annually in the last two decades of the twentieth century, with the fastest growth occurring after the Higher Education Act Amendments of 1992 significantly liberalized access to unsubsidized loans (see appendix A.4).[50]

The Taxpayer Relief Act of 1997 added yet another market-driven dimension to the federal government's loan-based aid strategy that further neglected the country's neediest college hopefuls. The Lifetime Learning Credit and the Hope Scholarship were promoted by the Clinton White House as a broad national investment in higher education access. In reality, however, these tax expenditures represented a $40 billion middle-class entitlement program that did nothing for impoverished students and their families whose yearly income disqualified them for the credit.[51] The slight uptick in Pell Grant funding fell well short of making up the difference and farther still from the Pell Grant's original mandate to cover up to half the cost of attendance at a public college or university.[52] Testifying before Congress in 2000, one of the nation's leading experts on student aid explained the historic significance of the government's movement away from grants and toward loans. "Above all, the drift toward a system that relies on student debt to finance higher tuition," said Lawrence E. Gladieux, the executive director for policy analysis at the College Board, "has turned the original commitment to equal opportunity on its head."[53]

Finally, the devolution of the state-academic partnership led to the privatization of educated citizenship itself. In a dramatic departure from the heyday of that partnership examined in this book, after Reagan's election the state's interest in higher education, and in using higher education to mold a one-size-fits-all democratic citizen, all but disappeared. Even as the federal government continued to pump billions of dollars into student aid and tax credits and deductions of one form or another, it did so with few clear expectations for much, if anything, in return. This was particularly true in the area of educated citizenship. Once the beacon light of democracy, the educated citizen had become a free agent, working within a free market, whose primary allegiance was to herself and to the cultivation of a well-rounded professional *and* personal identity. According to one leading scholar, higher education became "a setting where individuals acted out their private dramas of personal fulfillment and ambition."[54] Whatever sense of higher purpose once attached to higher learning was now lost. Students made their own meaning out of the education they received. Some students continued to serve their school, or community, or government with intense passion; other students focused more on serving themselves. The choice was theirs to make. In an era when the government asked less and less of citizens, higher education and the state asked less and less of students. The market had become the vehicle of higher education—career training and identity formation students' favorite destinations. "The result," mused historian Thomas Haskell in 1984, "is a situation of unprecedented confusion about the proper content of a university education and about the purposes of the university itself."[55]

In retrospect, state policymakers clearly agreed: fed up with higher education's unpredictable outputs, they turned their attention to the reform of elementary and secondary education. The first inkling of such a move appeared after the enactment of the Elementary and Secondary Education Act (ESEA) in 1965. After 150 years of "local control" that was truly local, the ESEA granted the state a far greater stake in K-12 policymaking than it had ever before enjoyed.[56] The state's involvement grew rapidly as the issues of desegregation and suburbanization—race and taxes—became inextricably intertwined with academic achievement and economic development.[57] By the mid-1970s, heated controversies over court-ordered busing and suburban sprawl turned elementary and secondary education politics into a national debate of increasing electoral significance. Alarmed by a widening "achievement gap" between and among different students, and by America's diminished economic standing in the world, increasing numbers of political leaders—encouraged by parent groups and educational reformers housed in Washington "think tanks"—concurred that elementary and secondary education was broken and needed to be fixed.[58]

A Nation at Risk: The Imperative for Educational Reform (1983) broadcast a market-based reform agenda to a wide audience. Commissioned by Education Secretary Terrance H. Bell, and coordinated, ironically enough, by the very Department of Education that Reagan had pledged to abolish, the study foreshadowed the general contours of America's coming educational politics. Like so many other educational jeremiads, the study was full of doom and gloom. "Our nation is at risk," read the first line. From there the findings went downhill quickly: "We report . . . the educational foundations of our society are presently being eroded by a rising tide of mediocrity that threatens our very future as a Nation and a people." Numerous "indicators of risk" pointed to major problems: 23 million adults were functionally illiterate and average student achievement based on SAT, math, and science test scores had been in steady decline since 1963. In response, the commission recommended getting back to basics, longer school days, greater teacher preparation, and the creation of "rigorous and measurable" academic performance standards. If the country failed to act, the study warned, America's global economic and military leadership would be jeopardized. "If only to keep and improve on the slim competitive edge we still retain in world markets, we must dedicate ourselves to the reform of our educational system. Learning is the indispensible investment required for success in the 'information age' we are entering."[59]

A Nation at Risk resulted in few immediate changes to the federal government's educational policy agenda. But in the long-run it profoundly altered the ways in which politicians, school officials, and concerned citizens understood educational reform. During the 1990s, a broad-based, bipartisan reform coalition took root. Encouraged by presidents George H.W. Bush and Bill Clinton, the coalition sought reforms that would increase academic rigor and improve academic results in order to strengthen America's global competitiveness. Its crowning achievement was President George W. Bush's 2002 No Child Left Behind Act (NCLB). NCLB's focus on "standards" and "accountability" and "annual yearly progress"—on testing and still more testing—cemented the state's control over K-12 education policy and presented a whole new generation of policymakers with the tantalizing possibility of using education to adjust the country's youngest citizens for life in a democracy.[60]

"A Cultural, Racial, and Ethnic Diversity That Will Be Greater Than We Have Ever Known Before": The Triumph of Diversity

Left to the whims of the marketplace, higher education's diversity-based academic and organizational structure grew stronger in the last two decades of the twentieth century. It was bolstered by developments in the corporate and voluntary sectors both. In 1987, the Hudson Institute released the widely influential study *Workforce 2000*. The thrust of the report was that America's corporate sector needed to adjust its managerial techniques to better meet the needs of its increasingly diverse workforce.[61] Personnel management gurus like R. Roosevelt Thomas Jr. dubbed this "managing diversity." In an influential *Harvard Business Review* article, he argued ethnic, gender, and racial diversity represented a renewable source of corporate energy, creativity, and innovation. "Unlike affirmative action, which was considered a social, moral and legal responsibility," Thomas explained to the *New York Times*, from the Morehouse College headquarters of his American Institute for Managing Diversity, "managing diversity is a business issue."[62] The idea spread. In 1991, the first meeting of the National Diversity Conference convened in San Francisco. Human resource and equal employment opportunity officers from more than fifty corporations and twenty government agencies took part. They soon discovered diversity to be an expedient way not only to talk about but also to deal with workforce "difference." Smitten, corporate personnel officers turned diversity management into a key source of professional power.[63] By the mid-1990s, a survey of fifty Fortune 500 companies found that 70 percent had organized diversity management programs.[64] The "diversity industry," reported the *New Republic*, had become a multimillion dollar business within American business.[65]

But it was higher education where the diversity framework became most entrenched—and most controversial. Conservatives and progressives relived the

1960s all over again, taking sides on a host of "cultural" and "lifestyle" issues dominated by sexual orientation, religion, abortion rights, race, and gender. These identity debates were triggered by a number of sources. The loss of a cohesive "American identity" at the twilight of the cold war was one factor. Without an enemy to demonize—a proverbial "other"—many Americans felt lost. Another factor was the growing menu of identity options available to Americans after the 1960s. The plethora of identities available for the taking—to be tried on, then revealed, and, if need be, discarded—raised fresh questions about whether an all-encompassing "American identity" could be, or even should be, defined. "In those nether years," Tom Englehardt has perceptively written, "bursts of triumphalism yoyo-ed with unease and self-doubt, with the angry, divisive politics of resentment as well as with roiling identity and culture wars."[66]

On campuses firefights erupted over the curriculum, speech codes, and of course, affirmative admissions—in other words, over the very meaning of diversity itself. Though we remember best the battle cries of diversity's enemies—e.g., Allan Bloom, Dinesh D'Souza, Charles Murray, Pat Buchanan, Lynne Cheney, William Bennett, Rush Limbaugh—there is little doubt as to which side won the war. In the late 1980s and 1990s, diversity pervaded higher education. From admissions and student life into the core of the disciplines themselves, administrators and faculty discovered that diversity effectively conveyed the organizational, intellectual, and human complexity of the contemporary university and the society it served. The growth of academic centers, the formation of interdisciplines and whole new hybrid majors infused every segment of higher education from two-year junior colleges to research universities. To wit, the numbers of campus-based Native American and Latino groups doubled during this time while the number of gay and lesbian groups tripled; and at many institutions diversity went from a voluntary extracurricular option to an involuntary curricular requirement.[67] By the early 1990s, nearly half of all four-year colleges and universities required students to take a multicultural general education course in order to graduate.[68]

The institutionalization of a pluralist framework in which identity was channeled through the prism of diversity occurred nationwide. Administrators led this "quiet revolution," having learned that granting identity groups a piece of the curriculum and an organizational base from which to operate (commonly overseen by an assistant dean, or faculty advisor, or both) was worth the effort.[69] Many students thought so. Often accused of political apathy, students mobilized identity groups to gain recognition and respect when they had to. Admittedly, this did not occur that frequently. At many schools, administrators and professors acted preemptively in the name of diversity by gently encouraging the diversification of the curriculum and supporting the formation of allied student clubs and associations. At those institutions where diversity was threatened or actively blocked, student groups organized nonviolent direct-action protests in order to advance their agendas. Far more often than not, students were pleased with the results. Like most Americans since the 1970s, college students got politically energized on an issue-by-issue basis, especially if that issue intersected with their identity or sought to thwart diversity.[70]

Nowhere was the diversity regime put to the test more than at the University of Michigan. In 1988, Michigan's new president James J. Duderstadt launched a strategic planning group to identify the various ways in which diversity could be cultivated and sustained and to pinpoint its related academic and social benefits. A professor of nuclear engineering and a past dean of the College of Engineering and provost at Michigan, Duderstadt seemed, on paper, an unlikely social engineer.[71] Simmering racial tensions on campus and his genuine commitment to diversity, however, forced him to act. Two years worth of interviewing faculty and students and of assessing Michigan's academic offerings and social climate resulted in the "The Michigan Mandate: A Strategic Linking of Academic Excellence and Social Diversity." Unveiled in 1990, later revised and updated, the mandate provided a blueprint for diversity management at Michigan and elsewhere. In bold strokes, the mandate declared that "the leadership of the University of Michigan is firmly convinced that our institution's ability to achieve and sustain a campus community recognized for its racial, cultural, and ethnic diversity will in large part determine our capacity to serve successfully our state and nation and the world in the challenging times ahead."[72] The mandate summarized how Michigan—and American higher education more broadly—had adapted to previous challenges as a way to justify its new mission. The nation was becoming "a truly multicultural society," American life "internationalized," and the economy "knowledge intensive."[73] The world was changing in all these ways and the University of Michigan needed to change with it. Predicting "a cultural, racial, and ethnic diversity that will be greater than we have ever known before," the mandate outlined a strategic vision to meet this challenge head on.[74]

In so doing, the mandate also linked pluralism to diversity and thus the past to the present. Though *diversity* was definitely the preferred term, Duderstadt and his collaborators also used *pluralism*. In describing an early meeting of the committee, for example, Duderstadt noted how it became "clear that a central issue confronting us as an institution and a society is to take action to better reflect the growing pluralism of American society both in the diversity of the people . . . and in our intellectual activities."[75] Later, under the section "Missions and Goals," this connection was reinforced more strongly, when the mandate declared that one of its chief aims was to "build . . . an environment that seeks, nourishes, and sustains diversity and pluralism."[76] The close proximity of these terms was no mere coincidence. Pluralism had always been the root of diversity, as the Michigan Mandate made patently clear.

There was a critical difference, however, between the old pluralism and the new diversity. The diversity regime was strategic and proactive rather than reactive and ad hoc. It sought to prevent campus turmoil by building and maintain-

Figure 7.1.   University of Michigan president James J. Duderstadt, 1995. During his presidency from 1988 to 1996, Duderstadt committed Michigan to a far-reaching—and controversial—institution-wide diversity initiative known as the Michigan Mandate. Courtesy box 3, News and Information Services, Photo Series D, Faculty and Staff Portraits, 1946–2006, Bentley Historical Library, University of Michigan.

ing a vast network of personnel services and curricular innovations within the university's core structure: affirmative action student and faculty recruitment and retention programs, the creation and support of allied advocacy organizations, and the further diversification of the curriculum.[77] Only a multifaceted approach of this sort would achieve the "long-term systemic change," as Duderstadt later put it, that the University of Michigan aspired to. "We foresaw the limitations of focusing only on affirmative action—that is, on access, retention, and representation. We believed that without deeper, more fundamental institutional change these efforts by themselves would inevitably fail."[78]

By most accounts, the University of Michigan made significant progress under the Michigan Mandate. Within five years, minority representation in the student, faculty, and staff ranks had more than doubled and minority graduation rates had also increased significantly.[79] Moreover, the idea of diversity attracted broad support from across the campus in large measure because it could be used strategically in almost any context and by any group. Not all groups were thrilled with the results of Duderstadt's diversity agenda, which by 1995 had expanded to include women and gender; and in due course, the University of Michigan was besieged by antiaffirmative-action forces, led by the Center for Individual Rights (CIR), a well-financed conservative public litigation firm. Fresh off its win against affirmative action at the University of Texas Law School in 1996, and buoyed by the passage of California's Proposition 209 in the same year, which banned affirmative action in public institutions, including public colleges and universities, the CIR set its sights on the University of Michigan.[80] In 1997 the CIR filed one discrimination suit against the undergraduate College of Literature, Arts, and Sciences; another against the Law School.[81]

Both suits eventually ended up on the Supreme Court's docket in 2003—the first time the Court agreed to hear a case on the constitutionality of affirmative admissions since *Bakke*.[82] Like *Bakke*, the *Michigan Cases*, as the two cases were colloquially known, initiated passionate debate. Record numbers of amicus briefs poured in from business, the U.S. military, and from colleges and universities—nearly a hundred in all. And, again, like *Bakke*, the final outcome of the *Michigan Cases* hinged on the constitutionality of diversity. In a new twist, however, the psychological research used to defend diversity in the *Michigan Cases* now highlighted diversity's educational as well as social benefits. Not only did a diverse student body create tolerant citizens, claimed the university, backed by the expert findings of Michigan psychology and women's studies professor Patricia Gurin, it created smarter citizens better equipped to cope with the realities of living and working in an increasingly diverse society and world.[83] Although the court ruled against Michigan's undergraduate admissions practices in a 6–3 decision, in a separate 5–4 decision, it sided with the Law School, thus upholding *Bakke*. The court ruled that race, or any other applicant characteristic or attribute, for that matter, could be used as a "plus factor" in admissions. "Today," wrote Justice Sandra Day O'Connor, on behalf of the majority, "we hold that the Law School has a compelling interest in attaining a diverse student body."[84]

That one of the most conservative judiciaries of the last century again found race to be a "compelling state interest" in university admissions decisions was by far the ruling's most important outcome. But the court's endorsement of racial diversity in admissions—and the media's singular focus on it—scarcely captured the extent to which the idea of diversity had really suffused higher education. Aside from shaping the student body, the idea of diversity also shaped

Figure 7.2. The Michigan Mandate stirred up passionate debate over the role of diversity in higher education. In this photo, taken on February 23, 1998, University of Michigan students mobilize to defend diversity against anti–affirmative action forces, led by the Center for Individual Rights, which had recently filed two discrimination lawsuits against the university. In 2003 these lawsuits were the basis of the Supreme Court's *Michigan Cases* ruling, which upheld the constitutionality of diversity in college admissions. Copyright Najlay Feanny/CORBIS

the organization of knowledge, the structure of the extracurriculum, and perhaps most important, how academic administrators and faculty sought to convey the economic, social, and political value of higher learning to the diverse publics their institutions served—publics that increasingly doubted affirmative action but professed to value and support diversity. In short, diversity was more than an idea; it had become a lived experience of millions of Americans and a core value of large-scale public and private organizations, especially colleges and universities. And since the 1960s, educating students in the name of diversity has been what American colleges and universities do. Not convinced? Access any college or university webpage and somewhere on that page will be a diversity link. Follow it and enter a world of myriad diversity policies and procedures, initiatives and programming, advocacy groups and allied organizations. These are the politics of American higher education in the twenty-first century.

Yet there remains an open question: For how much longer? A more voluminous pluralism, diversity, like its predecessor, is also historically contingent. Where the old pluralism purported to recognize all groups but really only provided access for and responded to a select few, today's diversity model seeks to remedy all grievances. This is fine in economic flush times when adding programs and staff is easily achieved; it is more challenging in economic hard times when climbing student debt (twenty-four thousand dollars on average, per student, in 2009)[85] and student graduation rates range wildly between selective, elite institutions on the one hand, where virtually all students finish, and nonselective, broad access institutions on the other, where most students do not.[86] At a time when institutions are cutting programs, not adding them, and students are piling up ever more debt while taking longer to graduate, that is if they graduate at all, it is worth considering: Might the diversity regime really be on the ropes?

I wouldn't bet on it. Over the course of the last century, the development of American higher education occurred in unison with the development of the American state. Each institution became increasingly big, powerful, and dependent on the other, forging a mutually reinforcing relationship buffeted by cataclysmic wars, economic challenges, and mass social movements. Along the way, higher education became a powerful parastate capable of exerting preponderant influence over the American people's understanding of themselves and of the state—and world—in which they lived. Existing at the fringes of American life at the start of the twentieth century, higher education became a state within the state by the end of it, a mirror image of the decentralized, flexible, competitive, and diverse interest group political order that created it and that nurtures it still. Now enrolling upward of 18 million students—young and old, from the United States and around the globe—American higher education's diverse mix of public, private, and for-profit two- and four-year institutions permeate the physical and digital landscape both, reaching deeper into students' lives than ever before. A mediator between citizens and the state in the twentieth century, higher education now wields its own influence largely absent the state's direct, hands-on involvement. Federal money for research and financial aid remains, but by conscious design and historical happenstance the felt presence of the state in most students' lives barely registers at all. At the dawn of the twenty-first century, the state is at once everywhere and nowhere on the American campus, and higher education's authority over who should be admitted and what students should learn—indeed, over the very terms of democratic citizenship—has become its alone to decide.

Appendix

A Graphical Portrait of American Higher Education in the Twentieth Century

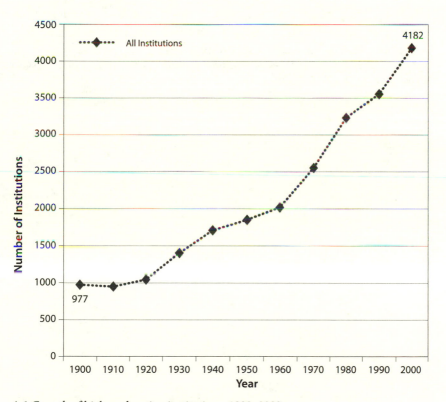

A.1 Growth of higher education institutions: 1900–2000

T. D. Snyder, *120 Years of American Education: A Statistical Portrait* (Washington, DC: NCES, 1993); T. D. Snyder and S. A. Dillo, *Digest of Education Statistics, 2009* (Washington, DC: NCES Publication No. 2010013, 2010).

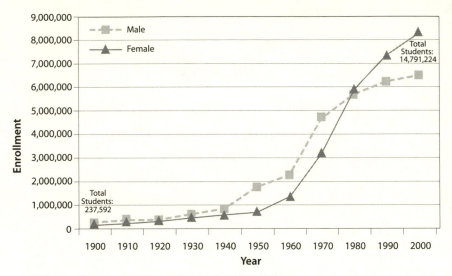

A.2 Higher education enrollment by gender: 1900–2000
T. D. Snyder and S. A. Dillo, *Digest of Education Statistics, 2009* (Washington, DC: NCES Publication No. 2010013, 2010).

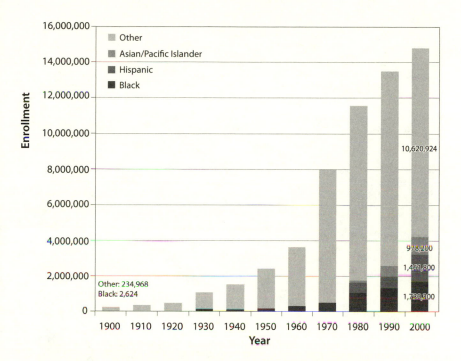

A.3 Higher education enrollment by ethno-racial classification: 1900–2000

V. A. Clift, "Higher Education of Minority Groups in the United States," *Journal of Negro Education* 38 (summer 1969): 291–302.

W.E.B. Du Bois and A. G. Dill, ed., *The College-bred Negro American: Report of a Social Study Made by Atlanta University under the Patronage of the Trustees of the John F. Slater Fund; with the Proceedings of the 15th Annual Conference for the Study of the Negro Problems, Held at Atlanta University, on Tuesday, May 24th, 1910* (1910; Atlanta, GA: Atlanta University Press, 2010).

M. D. Jenkins, "The National Survey of Negro Higher Education and Postwar Reconstruction: The Resources of Negro Higher Education," *Journal of Negro Education* 11 (July 1942): 382–90.

F. McCuistion, "The Present Status of Higher Education of Negroes," *Journal of Negro Education* 3 (July 1933): 379–96.

T. D. Snyder and S. A. Dillo, *Digest of Education Statistics, 2009* (Washington, DC: NCES Publication No. 2010013, 2010).

U.S. Census Bureau, *Statistical Abstract of the United States, 1978*, retrieved from U.S. Census Bureau website: http://www2.census.gov/prod2/statcomp/documents/1978-01.pdf.

Note: Hispanic and Asian/Pacific Islander enrollment data are not available from NCES prior to 1976.

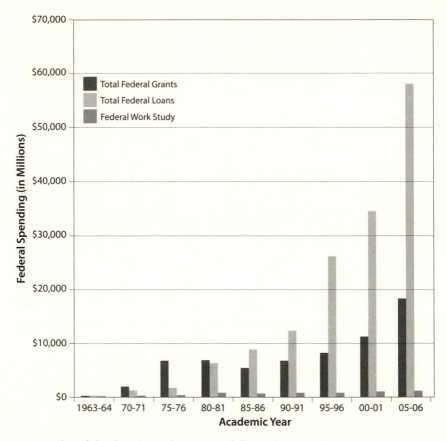

A.4 Trends in federal student aid in current dollars: 1963–64 to 2005–6
The College Board, Trends in Student Aid 2009, retrieved from the College
Board website: http://www.trends-collegeboard.com/student_aid/1_1_total_aid_c.html
?expandable=1.

Notes

❖

Acknowledgments

1. He was president from 1990 to 1995.

2. Richard Hofstadter, "Columbia University Commencement Address," 1968, in *American Higher Education Transformed, 1940–2005*, ed. Wilson Smith and Thomas Bender (Baltimore: Johns Hopkins University Press, 2008), 384.

Chapter 1
Introduction: The Politics of American Higher Education in the Twentieth Century

1. On the rise of research, see Laurence R. Veysey, *The Emergence of the American University* (Chicago: University of Chicago Press, 1965); Roger L. Geiger, *To Advance Knowledge: The Growth of American Research Universities, 1900–1940* (New York: Oxford University Press, 1986); Roger L. Geiger, *Research and Relevant Knowledge: American Research Universities since World War II* (New York: Oxford University Press, 1993); Stuart W. Leslie, *The Cold War and American Science: The Military-Industrial-Academic Complex at MIT and Stanford* (New York: Columbia University Press, 1993); Bruce Hevly and Peter Galison, ed., *Big Science: The Growth of Large-Scale Research* (Stanford: Stanford University Press, 1992); Rebecca S. Lowen, *Creating the Cold War University: The Transformation of Stanford* (Berkeley: University of California Press, 1997); Hugh Davis Graham and Nancy Diamond, *The Rise of American Research Universities: Elites and Challengers in the Postwar Era* (Baltimore: Johns Hopkins University Press, 1997); Margaret Pugh O'Mara, *Cities of Knowledge: Cold War Science and the Search for the Next Silicon Valley* (Princeton: Princeton University Press, 2005); and Jonathan R. Cole, *The Great American University: Its Rise to Preeminence, Its Indispensible National Role, Why It Must Be Protected* (New York: Perseus, 2009). On the professions, see Mary O. Furner, *Advocacy & Objectivity: A Crisis in the Professionalization of American Social Science, 1865–1905* (Lexington: University Press of Kentucky, 1975); Magali Sarfatti Larson, *The Rise of Professionalism: A Sociological Analysis* (Berkeley: University of California Press, 1977); Thomas L. Haskell, *The Emergence of Professional Social Science: The American Social Science Association and the Crisis of Authority* (Urbana: University of Illinois Press, 1977); and Dorothy Ross, *The Origins of American Social Science* (New York: Cambridge University Press, 1991). On the "prominstrative state," see Brian Balogh, "Reorganizing the Organizational Synthesis: Federal-Professional Relations in Modern America," *Studies in American Political Development* 5 (1991): 119–72; and Brian Balogh, *Chain Reaction: Expert Debate and Public Participation in American Commercial Nuclear Power, 1945–1975* (New York: Cambridge University Press, 1991).

2. For two exceptions, see Mark R. Nemec, *Ivory Towers and Nationalist Minds: Universities, Leadership, and the Development of the American State* (Ann Arbor: University of Michigan Press, 2006), which focuses on the period between the Civil War and World

War I and looks exclusively at the role of university presidents; and Shelia Slaughter, "Academic Freedom and the State: Reflections on the Uses of Knowledge," *Journal of Higher Education* 59 (May–June 1988): 241–65.

3. For an introduction, see Peter B. Evans, Dietrich Rueschemeyer, and Theda Skocpol, ed., *Bringing the State Back In* (New York: Cambridge University Press, 1985); Meg Jacobs, William J. Novak, and Julian E. Zelizer, ed., *The Democratic Experiment: New Directions in American Political History* (Princeton: Princeton University Press, 2003); and Karen Orren and Stephen Skowronek, *The Search for American Political Development* (New York: Cambridge University Press, 2004). On state building as an institutional phenomenon, see Stephen Skowronek, *Building a New American State: The Expansion of National Administrative Capacities* (New York: Cambridge University, 1982); and Brian Balogh, *A Government Out of Sight: The Mystery of National Authority in Nineteenth-Century America* (New York: Cambridge University Press, 2009).

4. On the theoretical dimensions of APD, including discussions of space, time, and institutions, see Orren and Skowronek, *Search for American Political Development*; Paul Pierson, *Politics in Time: History, Institutions, and Social Analysis* (Princeton: Princeton University Press, 2004); James March and Johan Olson, "The New Institutionalism: Organizational Factors in Political Life," *American Political Science Review* 78 (1984): 734–49; and Hugh Heclo, *On Thinking Institutionally* (Boulder, CO: Paradigm, 2008).

5. On parastates, see Eldon J. Eisenach, *The Lost Promise of Progressivism* (Lawrence: University Press of Kansas, 1994), 18; and Balogh, *Government Out of Sight*. For works on the American state suggestive of this approach, see, for example, Skowronek, *Building a New American State*; William Novak, *The People's Welfare* (Chapel Hill: University of North Carolina Press, 1996); Ellis W. Hawley, *The New Deal and the Problem of Monopoly: A Study in Economic Ambivalence* (1966; Princeton: Princeton University Press, 1995); Ellis W. Hawley, *The Great War and the Search for Modern Order: The American People and their Institutions, 1917–1933* (New York: St. Martin's Press, 1973); and Barry D. Karl, *The Uneasy State: The United States from 1915 to 1945* (Chicago: University of Chicago Press, 1983). Hugh Heclo does not use the term, but described a similar phenomenon when he discussed the role of "intermediary organizations" in the operation of the post–World War II federal government, what he called "government by remote control." See Hugh Heclo, "Issue Networks and the Executive Establishment," in *The New American Political System*, ed. Anthony King (Washington, DC: American Enterprise Institute Press, 1978), 87–124, esp. 92–93.

6. Balogh, *Government Out of Sight*.

7. This literature is especially rich in the social policy arena. See, for example, Christopher Howard, *The Hidden Welfare State: Tax Expenditures and Social Policy in the United States* (Princeton: Princeton University Press, 1997); Jacob S. Hacker, *The Divided Welfare State: The Battle Over Public and Private Social Benefits in the United States* (New York: Cambridge University Press, 2002); Jennifer Klein, *For All These Rights: Business, Labor, and the Shaping of America's Public-Private Welfare State* (Princeton: Princeton University Press, 2003); and Andrew J.F. Morris, *The Limits of Voluntarism: Charity and Welfare from the New Deal through the Great Society* (New York: Cambridge University Press, 2009).

8. Thomas D. Snyder, ed., *120 Years of American Education: A Statistical Portrait* (Washington, DC: NCES, 1993), 76–77.

9. On the expansion of higher learning in the new nation, see Daniel Walker Howe, *What Hath God Wrought: The Transformation of America, 1815–1848* (New York: Oxford University Press, 2007), 446–82; and Jennings L. Wagoner, *Jefferson and Education* (Chapel Hill: University of North Carolina Press, 2004). On the role of land grants, see Harold M. Hyman, *American Singularity: The 1787 Northwest Ordinance, the 1862 Homestead and Morrill Acts, and the 1944 G.I. Bill of Rights* (Athens: University of Georgia Press,1986); Peter S. Onuf, *Statehood and Union: A History of the Northwest Ordinance* (Bloomington: Indiana University Press, 1987); and Roger L. Williams, *The Origins of Federal Support for Higher Education: George W. Atherton and the Land-Grant College Movement* (University Park: Penn State University Press, 1991), 11–54.

10. E. E. Schattschneider, *Politics, Pressures, and the Tariff: A Study of Free Private Enterprise in Pressure Politics, as Shown in the 1929–1930 Revision of the Tariff* (New York: Prentice Hall, 1935), 288.

11. On feedback and path dependence, see, for example, Theda Skocpol, *Protecting Soldiers and Mothers: The Political Origins of Social Policy in the United States* (Cambridge, MA: Belknap Press of Harvard University Press, 1992); Paul Pierson, "When Effect Becomes Cause: Policy Feedback and Political Change," *World Politics* 45 (July 1993): 595–628; and Paul Pierson, "Increasing Returns, Path Dependence, and the Study of Politics," *American Political Science Review* 94 (June 2000): 251–67.

12. Joseph F. Kett, *The Pursuit of Knowledge under Difficulties: From Self-Improvement to Adult Education in America, 1750–1990* (Stanford: Stanford University Press, 1994).

13. The difference between "public" and "private" institutions has always been blurred. See John R. Thelin, *A History of American Higher Education* (Baltimore: Johns Hopkins University Press, 2004), 70–73; and Harold T. Shapiro, *A Larger Sense of Purpose: Higher Education and Society* (Princeton: Princeton University Press, 2005), 5–6.

14. For a few of the best known works in this genre, which gets larger with each passing semester, see, for example, Allan Bloom, *The Closing of the American Mind: How Higher Education Has Failed Democracy and Impoverished the Minds of Today's Students* (New York: Simon and Schuster, 1987); Dinesh D'Souza, *Illiberal Education: Race and Sex on Campus* (New York: Basic Books, 1991); and Roger Kimball, *Tenured Radicals: How Politics Has Corrupted Higher Education* (New York: Harper and Row, 1990).

15. See, for example, Sheila Slaughter and Larry L. Leslie, *Academic Capitalism: Politics, Policies, and the Entrepreneurial University* (Baltimore: Johns Hopkins University Press, 1997); David L. Kirp, *Shakespeare, Einstein, and the Bottom Line: The Marketing of Higher Education* (Cambridge, MA: Harvard University Press, 2003); and Bill Readings, *The University in Ruins* (1996; Cambridge, MA: Harvard University Press, 1999).

16. This point has been made best by Roger L. Geiger, *Knowledge* and *Money: Research Universities and the Paradox of the Marketplace* (Stanford: Stanford University Press, 2004); and Derek Bok, *Universities in the Marketplace: The Commercialization of Higher Education* (Princeton: Princeton University Press, 2003).

17. On the benefits of universities to doing so, see John Connelly, *Captive University: The Sovietization of East German, Czech, and Polish Higher Education, 1945–1956* (Chapel Hill: University of North Carolina Press, 2000), 7–9. On the benefits of policy history more generally, see Julian E. Zelizer, "Clio's Lost Tribe: Public Policy History Since 1978," *Journal of Policy History* 12.3 (2000): 369–94; and Donald T. Critchlow, "So-

cial Policy History: Past and Present," in *Federal Social Policy: The Historical Dimension*, ed. Donald T. Critchlow and Ellis W. Hawley (University Park: Penn State University Press, 1988), 9–31.

18. Christopher Lasch, *Haven in a Heartless World: The Family Besieged* (New York: Basic Books, 1977); Christopher Lasch, *The Culture of Narcissism: American Life in an Age of Diminishing Expectations* (New York: W. W. Norton, 1978); Jackson Lears, *No Place of Grace: Antimodernism and the Transformation of American Culture, 1880–1920* (New York: Pantheon Books, 1981); Jackson Lears, "From Salvation to Self-Realization: Advertising and the Therapeutic Roots of the Consumer Culture, 1880–1930," in *The Culture of Consumption: Critical Essays in American History, 1880–1980*, ed. Jackson Lears and Richard Wightman Fox (New York: Pantheon Books, 1983), 1–38; and Jackson Lears, *Rebirth of a Nation: The Making of Modern America, 1877–1920* (New York: Harper Collins, 2009).

19. Ellen Herman, *The Romance of American Psychology: Political Culture in the Age of Experts* (Berkeley: University of California Press, 1995); James H. Capshew, *Psychologists on the March: Science, Practice, and Professional Identity in America, 1929–1969* (New York: Cambridge University Press, 1999).

20. On the history of adjustment, see Donald S. Napoli, *Architects of Adjustment: The History of the Psychological Profession in the United States* (Port Washington, NY: Kennikat Press, 1981); and Ed Gitre, "America Adjusted: Conformity, Boredom, and the Modern Self, 1920–1980" (Ph.D. diss., Rutgers University, 2008). For a critique of the white male, middle-class dimensions of adjustment, see C. Wright Mills, *The Sociological Imagination* (New York: Oxford University Press, 1959), 90–91. As Mills explained, in his typically irreverent tone,

> The type of person who is judged to be ideally "adjusted": . . . is the ethical opposite of "selfish." He thinks of others and is kindly toward them; he does not brood or mope; on the contrary he is somewhat extrovert. . . . He is in and of and for quite a few community organizations. If not an outright "joiner," he certainly does get around a lot. Happily, he conforms to conventional morality and motives; happily, he participates in the gradual progress of respectable institutions. His mother and father were never divorced; his home never cruelly broken. He is "successful," at least in a modest way. . . . He does not scramble after the big money. Some of his virtues are very general, and then we cannot tell what they mean. But some are very specific, and then we come to know that the virtues of the adjusted man of local milieu correspond with the expected norms of the smaller, independent middle class verbally living out Protestant ideals in the small towns of America. (*Imagination*, 91)

21. Skowronek, *Building a New American State*, ix.

22. The standard history charting the professional ascendance of psychology and therapy, and of the social sciences more generally, has emphasized the "social control," antidemocratic uses of psychology and therapeutic techniques to the exclusion of all others. See, for example, Ross, *Origins of American Social Science*; Andrew J. Polsky, *The Rise of the Therapeutic State* (Princeton: Princeton University Press, 1991); William Graebner, *The Engineering of Consent: Democracy and Authority in Twentieth-Century America* (Madison: University of Wisconsin Press, 1987); and Daryl Michael Scott, *Contempt* and *Pity: Social Policy and the Image of the Damaged Black Psyche, 1880–1996*

(Chapel Hill: University of North Carolina Press, 1997). In contrast, this book builds on a countercurrent historical literature that emphasizes professional psychology's connection to, and promotion of, liberal democratic politics and institutions. See, for example, Nikolas Rose, *Inventing Our Selves: Psychology, Power, and Personhood* (New York: Cambridge University Press, 1996); Katherine Pandora, *Rebels within the Ranks: Psychologists' Critique of Scientific Authority and Democratic Realities in New Deal America* (New York: Cambridge University Press, 1997); Doug Rossinow, *The Politics of Authenticity: Liberalism, Christianity, and the New Left in America* (New York: Columbia University Press, 1998); Peter Sheehy, "The Triumph of Group Therapeutics: Therapy, the Social Self, and the Triumph of Liberalism, 1900–1960" (Ph.D. diss., University of Virginia, 2002); Ian A. M. Nicholson, *Inventing Personality: Gordon Allport and the Science of Selfhood* (Washington, DC: American Psychological Association, 2003); Catherine Gavin Loss, "Public Schools, Private Lives: American Education and Psychological Authority, 1945–1975" (Ph.D. diss., University of Virginia, 2005); Brian Balogh, "Making Pluralism 'Great': Beyond a Recycled History of the Great Society," in *The Great Society and the High Tide of Liberalism*, ed. Sidney M. Milkis and Jerome M. Mileur (Amherst: University of Massachusetts Press, 2005), 145–79; and Sarah E. Igo, *The Averaged American: Surveys, Citizens, and the Making of a Mass Public* (Cambridge, MA: Harvard University Press, 2007). For the classic defense of psychology as a handmaiden of liberal democratic politics, see Gordon W. Allport, "The Psychologist's Frame of Reference," *Psychological Bulletin* 37 (Jan. 1940): 1–27. Ellen Herman's influential study on the impact of psychology on American life and politics since World War II posits that psychology's net effect was mixed, contributing to personal emancipation on the one hand while increasing the likelihood of social control on the other. See Herman, *Romance of American Psychology.*

23. Veysey, *Emergence of the American University*, 119.

24. The concept of citizenship—whether defined in social-cultural, economic, or constitutional-legal terms—has guided an enormous number of scholarly works in many fields of American history in recent years. See, for example, John Bodnar, ed., *Bonds of Affection: Americans Define Their Patriotism* (Princeton: Princeton University Press, 1996); Rogers M. Smith, *Civic Ideals: Conflicting Visions of Citizenship in U.S. History* (New Haven: Yale University Press, 1997); Linda K. Kerber, *No Constitutional Right to Be Ladies: Women and the Obligations of Citizenship* (New York: Hill and Wang, 1998); Cecilia Elizabeth O'Leary, *To Die For: The Paradox of American Patriotism* (Princeton: Princeton University Press, 1999); Gary Gerstle, *American Crucible: Race and Nation in the Twentieth Century* (Princeton: Princeton University Press, 2001); and Lizabeth Cohen, *A Consumers' Republic: The Politics of Mass Consumption in Postwar America* (New York: Knopf, 2003). Yet the role of education—especially higher education—in demarcating the bounds of twentieth-century citizenship has been largely overlooked in the literature. For two exceptions, see Michael Schudson, *The Good Citizen: A History of American Civic Life* (New York: Basic Books, 1998); and Suzanne Mettler, *Soldiers to Citizens: The G.I. Bill and the Making of the Greatest Generation* (New York: Oxford University Press, 2005).

25. George W. Rightmire, "The Floundering Freshman," *Journal of Higher Education* 1 (April 1930): 185.

26. Howard R. Tolley, "The Farmer, the College, the Department of Agriculture—Their Changing Relationship," in *Proceedings of the Association of Land-Grant Colleges*

and Universities: Fiftieth Annual Convention, ed. William L. Slate (Northampton, MA: Metcalf, 1936), 70.

27. Sgt. Fred J. Bahler to USAFI Registrar, 18 April 1943, exhibit K, "Minutes of the Meeting of the Advisory Committee for the United States Armed Forces Institute," 26–27 June 1943, box 49, entry 16, Records of Joint Army/Navy Boards and Committees, NARA (College Park, MD).

28. Gilbert Bailey, "Picture of a Postwar Camp," *New York Times,* 21 Dec. 1947, MS14.

29. "Identity" has often been used interchangeably with the concept of citizenship and Americanization. Scholars from a number of different subfields have deployed it promiscuously in the last ten years. The foundational literature has focused on the formation of a dominant, white, Anglo-Saxon conception of "American identity," tracking the interplay between and among immigration, racial politics, and public policy, with a particular emphasis on the 1920s. See, for example, John Higham, *Strangers in the Land: Patterns of American Nativism, 1860–1925* (1955; New Brunswick: Rutgers University Press, 2002); Gerstle, *American Crucible*; Smith, *Civic Ideals*; O'Leary, *To Die For*; Bodnar, *Bonds of Affection*; Mae M. Nai, *Impossible Subjects: Illegal Aliens and the Making of Modern America* (Princeton: Princeton University Press, 2004); and Carl Bon Tempo, *Americans at the Gate: The United States and Refugees During the Cold War* (Princeton: Princeton University Press, 2008). Another strand of the literature has privileged the concept of "Whiteness," offering a more cultural interpretation of identity. See, for example, Grace Elizabeth Hale, *Making Whiteness: The Culture of Segregation in the South, 1890–1940* (New York: Pantheon Books, 1998); and David R. Roediger, *Working toward Whiteness: How America's Immigrants Became White* (New York: Basic Books, 2005). Still, a third strand has looked at identity from the standpoint of eugenics and the rise of racial science. See, for example, Daniel J. Kevles, *In the Name of Eugenics: Genetics and the Uses of Human Heredity* (New York: Knopf, 1985); and Wendy Kline, *Building a Better Race: Gender, Sexuality, and Eugenics from the Turn of the Century to the Baby Boom* (Berkeley: University of California Press, 2001). My approach is different. I focus on the psychological dimensions of identity—defined as the sum total of an individual's life experiences—stressing the connections between and among identity, education, and interest group mobilizing in the post-1960s United States. My thinking in this regard has been shaped by political scientist Hugh Heclo's work on the rise of "radical interest group pluralism" and "issue groups" in the late 1970s and 1980s. See Heclo, "Issue Networks and the Executive Establishment," in *New American Political System,* ed. King, 87–124; and Hugh Heclo, "The Sixties' False Dawn: Awakenings, Movements, and Postmodern Policy-making," in *Integrating the Sixties: The Origins, Structures, and Legitimacy of Public Policy in a Turbulent Decade,* ed. Brian Balogh (University Park: Penn State University Press, 1996), 34–63. Helco takes a negative stance toward the rise of such groups. For an affirmative position, see Balogh, "Making Pluralism 'Great,'" in *Great Society and the High Tide of Liberalism,* ed. Milkis and Mileur; and Balogh, *Chain Reaction.* On "identity politics" or "personal politics," see Sara M. Evans, *Personal Politics: The Roots of Women's Liberation in the Civil Rights Movement and the New New Left* (New York: Knopf, 1979); Robin D.G. Kelley, "'We Are Not What We Seem': Rethinking Black Working-Class Resistance in the Jim Crow South," *Journal of American History* 80 (June 1993): 75–112; and Amy Gutmann, *Identity in Democracy* (Princeton: Princeton University Press, 2003).

CHAPTER 2

REORGANIZING HIGHER EDUCATION IN THE SHADOW OF THE GREAT WAR

1. David M. Kennedy, *Over Here: The First World War and American Society* (New York: Oxford University Press, 1980); Christopher Capozzola, *Uncle Sam Wants You: The Politics of Political Obligation in America's First World War* (New York: Oxford University Press, 2008).

2 Carol S. Gruber, *Mars and Minerva: World War I and the Uses of Higher Learning in America* (Baton Rouge: Louisiana State University Press, 1975), 213–52, esp. 228; Kennedy, *Over Here*, 45–92; and Roger Geiger, *To Advance Knowledge: The Growth of American Research Universities, 1900–1940* (New York: Oxford University Press, 1986), 94–107.

3 Gruber, *Mars and Minerva*, 213–52.

4 Ellen W. Schrecker, *No Ivory Tower: McCarthyism and the Universities* (New York: Oxford University Press, 1986), 20–22.

5 Gruber, *Mars and Minerva*, 237.

6 For other works on the 1920s, see Paula Fass, *The Damned and the Beautiful: American Youth in the 1920s* (New York: Oxford University Press, 1977); David O. Levine, *The American College and the Culture of Aspiration, 1915–1940* (Ithaca: Cornell University Press, 1986); and Julie A. Reuben, *The Making of the Modern University: Intellectual Transformation and the Marginalization of Morality* (Chicago: University of Chicago Press, 1996).

7 Thomas D. Snyder, ed., *120 Years of American Education: A Statistical Portrait* (Washington, DC: NCES, 1993), 75, 78–80.

8 On the middle class and the American college, see Burton J. Bledstein, *The Culture of Professionalism: The Middle Class and the Development of Higher Education in America* (New York: W. W. Norton, 1976).

9 "College Records Broken," *Washington Post*, 22 Dec. 1927, 6.

10 For national dropout data during the 1920s, see Arthur J. Klein, "Survey of Land-Grant Colleges and Universities," *Office of Education Bulletin*, no. 9 (Washington, DC: GPO, 1930), 281.

11 Laurence Veysey, *The Emergence of the American University* (Chicago: University of Chicago Press, 1965), 356–60.

12 Robert C. Angell, *The Campus: A Study of Contemporary Undergraduate Life in the American University* (New York: D. Appleton, 1928), 43.

13 Ralph M. Stogdill, "An Undergrad Searches for an Education in College," *School and Society* 32 (20 Sept. 1930): 378–79.

14 Donald S. Napoli, *Architects of Adjustment: The History of the Psychological Profession in the United States* (New York: Kennikat Press, 1981), 30.

15 Morris Viteles, *Industrial Psychology* (New York: W. W. Norton, 1932), 33.

16 On the rise of a "culture of personality," see Warren I. Susman, "Personality and the Making of Twentieth-Century Culture," in *New Directions in American Intellectual History*, ed. John Higham and Paul Conkin (Baltimore: Johns Hopkins University Press, 1979), 212–26. In higher education specifically, see John S. Brubacher and Willis Rudy, *Higher Education in Transition: An American History: 1636–1956* (New York: Harper & Row, 1958), 317–38; and Sol Cohen, *Challenging Orthodoxies: Toward a New Cultural History of Education* (New York: Peter Lang, 1999), 203–26; and Fass, *Damned and the Beautiful*.

17 On the administrative reorganization of the modern university in the 1920s, with a focus on the role of religion, see Reuben, *Making of the Modern University*, 230–266.

18 Ronald Steel, *Walter Lippmann and the American Century* (New York: Vintage Books, 1980), 76–79.

19 Franz Samelson, "Putting Psychology on the Map: Ideology and Intelligence in the Alpha and Beta Tests," in *Psychology in Its Social Context*, ed. Allan R. Buss (New York: Irvington, 1979), 106.

20 On personnel theory in American business, see David F. Noble, *America by Design: Science, Technology, and the Rise of Corporate Capitalism* (New York: Knopf, 1977), 257–320; Sanford M. Jacoby, *Employing Bureaucracy: Managers, Unions, and the Transformation of Work in American Industry, 1900–1945* (New York: Columbia University Press, 1985), 127–40; and Lizabeth Cohen, *Making a New Deal: Industrial Workers in Chicago, 1919–1939* (New York: Cambridge University Press, 1990), 159–212. Quote in Viteles, *Industrial Psychology*, 25.

21 Jacoby, *Employing Bureaucracy*, 144–45.

22 Daniel J. Kevles, "Testing the Army's Intelligence: Psychologists and the Military in World War I," *Journal of American History* 55 (Dec. 1968): 569–71; Edmund C. Lynch, *Walter Dill Scott: Pioneer in Personnel Management* (Austin: Bureau of Business Research at University of Texas, 1968), 32–33; W. V. Bingham, "Army Always on Lookout for Specialists," *New York Times*, 14 April 1918, SM3.

23 Walter Van Dyke Bingham, "Walter Van Dyke Bingham," in *A History of Psychology in Autobiography*, IV, ed. Edwin G. Boring (Worchester: Clark University Press, 1952), 11.

24 On the American flight from pure psychology, see John M. O'Donnell, *The Origins of Behaviorism: American Psychology, 1870–1920* (New York: New York University Press, 1985).

25 On the founding and early work of the Bureau of Salesmanship Research, see Leonard W. Ferguson, "Bureau of Salesmanship Research," *The Heritage of Industrial Psychology* 5 (Hartford, CT: Finlay Press, 1963).

26 Lynch, *Walter Dill Scott*, 15–23.

27 Bingham, *History of Psychology in Autobiography*, IV, 14.

28 War Department, *The Personnel System of the United States Army: A History of the Personnel System*, 2 vols. (Washington, DC: Department of the Army, 1919), I, 143. On Louis B. Hopkins's background in industrial research, see L. B. Hopkins, "Personnel Research at Northwestern University," *Journal of Personnel Research* 1 (Oct.–Nov. 1922): 277–78.

29 War Department, *Personnel System of the United States Army*, I, 143–52. Additional cards and scales were developed for senior officers, too. On the development of the Officer's Qualification Card and the Officer Rating Scale, see, ibid., 543–58, 559–80; "Card Index Drafted Men," *New York Times*, 20 Sept. 1917, 2; and Kevles, "Testing the Army's Intelligence," 572–81. Quote in Bingham, "Army Always on Lookout for Specialists," SM3.

30 War Department, *Personnel System of the United States Army*, I, 671. For a complete roster of the Committee on Classification of Personnel in the Army, see ibid., 671–77.

31 On the fallout between Scott and Yerkes, see Richard T. Von Mayrhauser, "The Manager, the Medic, and the Mediator: The Clash of Professional Psychological Styles and the Wartime Origins of Group Mental Testing," in *Psychological Testing and American Society: 1890–1930*, ed. Michael M. Sokal (New Brunswick: Rutgers University Press, 1987), 128–57. On Yerkes' appointment to the Sanitary Corps, see Leonard W. Ferguson, "Psychology and the Army: Examining Recruits," *Heritage of Industrial Psychology* 8 (Hartford, CT.: Finlay Press, 1963), 107; Kevles, "Testing the Army's Intelligence," 570–71; and Joel L. Spring, "Psychologists and the War: The Meaning of Intelligence in the Alpha and Beta Tests," *History of Education Quarterly* 12 (spring 1972): 5.

32 Kevles, "Testing the Army's Intelligence," 574–81; John Carson, "Robert M. Yerkes and the Mental Testing Movement," in *Psychological Testing and American Society*, ed. Sokal, 76; Stephen Jay Gould, *The Mismeasure of Man* (New York: W. W. Norton, 1996), 225–26.

33 "Army's Classification Work Exhibit," *Wall Street Journal*, 31 March 1919, 7.

34 Robert M. Yerkes, ed., *Psychological Testing in the United States Army* (Washington, DC: U.S. Army Personnel Research Office, 1921).

35 Ruth Strang, "Trends in Educational Personnel Research," *Personnel Journal* 10 (Oct. 1931): 179–88.

36 Carl C. Brigham, *A Study of American Intelligence* (Princeton: Princeton University Press, 1923), cited and discussed in Gould, *Mismeasure of Man*, 254–60.

37 Ibid., 261.

38 Ibid., 262.

39 Gary Gerstle, *American Crucible: Race and Nation in the Twentieth Century* (Princeton: Princeton University Press, 2001), 81–127; Mae M. Ngai, *Impossible Subjects: Illegal Aliens and the Making of Modern America* (Princeton: Princeton University Press, 2004), 21–55.

40 Robert M. Yerkes, "What Is Personnel Research?" *Journal of Personnel Research* 1(May 1922): 59.

41 Kevles, "Testing the Army's Intelligence," 580.

42 Ellen C. Lagemann, *An Elusive Science: The Troubling History of Education Research* (Chicago: University of Chicago Press, 2000), 92–93.

43 Ibid., 93; David Tyack, *The One Best System: A History of American Urban Education* (1974; Cambridge, MA.: Harvard University Press, 1996), 177–255, esp. 183; Kurt Danziger, *Constructing the Subject: Historical Origins of Psychological Research* (New York: Cambridge University Press, 1990), 110–17.

44 R. L. Duffus, "New Methods Remaking Old Colleges," *New York Times*, 15 Jan. 1928, 79.

45 Michael C. Johanek, ed., *A Faithful Mirror: Reflections on the College Board and Education in America* (New York: College Board, 2001). In fact, according to Duffus, "New Methods Remaking Old Colleges," 79, the College Board actively campaigned against the adoption of intelligence tests in higher education.

46 Harold Wechsler, *The Qualified Student: A History of Selective Admissions in America* (New York: Wiley, 1977), 240–43; Nicholas Lemann, *The Big Test: The Secret History of the American Meritocracy* (1999; New York: Farrar, Straus and Giroux, 2000), 27–41.

47 "Declares Colleges Are for the Masses," *New York Times*, 30 Sept. 1922, 25.

48 Levine, *American College and the Culture of Aspiration*, 164.

49 Arthur J. Klein, "Higher Education: Biennial Survey, 1922–1924," *Bureau of Education Bulletin*, no. 20 (Washington, DC: GPO, 1926), 11–12. On the quest for a strong correlation coefficient, see David Segel, "Prediction of Success in College," *Office of Education Bulletin*, no. 15 (Washington, DC: GPO, 1934), 1–76, esp. 69; Wechsler, *Qualified Student*, 247–49; and Miriam C. Gould, "Theoretical and Practical Dilemmas in Personnel Research," *Annual Meeting of the National Association of Deans of Women* (Washington, DC: The Association, 1928), 98–99.

50 Geiger, *To Advance Knowledge*, 131.

51 John J. Coss, "Introduction," in *Five College Plans*, ed. Herbert E. Hawkes (New York: Columbia University Press, 1931), 1. While total revenues climbed dramatically in the twentieth century, fund sources displayed a relatively stable pattern: the proportion of revenues from tuition and fees was 24 percent in 1909–10 as well as in 1989–90. See Snyder, ed., *120 Years of American Education*, 71.

52 On the Ivy League's shift toward selective admissions, see Jerome Karabel, *The Chosen: The Hidden History of Admission and Exclusion at Harvard, Yale, and Princeton* (2005; New York: Mariner, 2006); Marcia Graham Synnott, *The Half-Opened Door: Discrimination and Admissions at Harvard, Yale, and Princeton, 1900–1970* (Westport, CT: Greenwood Press, 1979); and Harold Wechsler, "The Rationale for Restriction: Ethnicity and College Admissions in America, 1910–1980," *American Quarterly* 36 (winter 1984): 643–67.

53 Karabel, *Chosen*, 87, 107.

54 Klein, "Higher Education: Biennial Survey, 1922–1924," 5–6.

55 Joseph V. Hanna, "Student-Retention In Junior Colleges," *Journal of Educational Research* 22 (June 1930): 1–8; Elise Murray, "Freshman Tests in the Small College," *Journal of Applied Psychology* 7 (Sept. 1923): 258–76; Grover H. Alderman, "Failures among University Freshmen," *Journal of Educational Research* 16 (Nov. 1927): 254–56; Luther Sheeleigh Cressman, "Maladjustments between High Schools and Colleges Due to Difference in Aims and Methods and Suggested Corrections," *Journal of Educational Sociology* 3 (March 1930): 389–401, esp., 390; Ivan A. Booker, "Reducing Withdrawals," *Journal of Higher Education* 4 (May 1933): 249; Klein, "Higher Education: Biennial Survey, 1922–1924," 10; J. R. Sage, "Freshman Mortality," *Bulletin of the American Association of Collegiate Registrars* 2 (Baltimore: AACR, 1926): 56; Jay Carroll Knode, *Orienting the Student in College: With Special Reference to Freshman Week* (New York: Columbia University Teachers College, 1930), 21; "Editorial," *Journal of Higher Education* 2 (Jan. 1931): 48. Dropout rates changed very little during the twentieth century as enrollments climbed from hundreds of thousands to millions of students. See, for example, John Summerskill, "Dropouts from College," in *The American College: A Psychological and Social Interpretation of Higher Learning*, ed. Sanford Nevitt (New York: Wiley, 1962), 627–57; and Vincent Tinto, *Leaving College: Rethinking the Causes and Cures of Student Attrition* (Chicago: University of Chicago Press, 1987).

56 Lynch, *Walter Dill Scott*, 34–42; Richard Gillespie, *Manufacturing Knowledge: A History of the Hawthorne Experiments* (New York: Cambridge University Press, 1991), 31; "Psychology to Fit the Job to the Man," *New York Times*, 17 Feb. 1922, 1; Michael M. Sokal, "The Origins of the Psychological Corporation," *Journal of the History of the Behavioral Sciences* 17 (1981): 54–67.

57 James. R. Angell, "Reasons and Plans for Research Relating to Industrial Personnel," *Journal of Personnel Research* 1 (May 1922): 1.

58 Lynch, *Walter Dill Scott*, 34–42; Walter Dill Scott and Robert C. Clothier, *Personnel Management: Principles, Practices, and Point of View* (Chicago: McGraw-Hill, 1923), 1–18.

59 On Elton Mayo and the Hawthorne Studies, see Aubrey C. Sanford, *Human Relations: Theory and Practice* (Columbus, OH: Merrill, 1973), 30–34.

60 Gillespie, *Manufacturing Knowledge*, 25–27; Scott and Clothier, *Personnel Management*, 8; Lynch, *Walter Dill Scott*, 13–14.

61 Jacoby, *Employing Bureaucracy*, 137.

62 Kennedy, *Over Here*, 287–95; Christopher Capozzola, "The Only Badge Needed Is Your Patriotic Fervor: Vigilance, Coercion, and the Law in World War I America," *Journal of American History* 88 (March 2002): 1354–82; Beverly Gage, *The Day Wall Street Exploded: A Story of America in its First Age of Terror* (New York: Oxford University Press, 2009); Jacoby, *Employing Bureaucracy*, 171–73.

63 On the possibilities of such a relationship, see W. V. Bingham, "Student Personnel Service and Industrial Research," *Journal of Personnel Research* 2 (June 1923): 55–64.

64 James Capshew, *Psychologists on the March: Science, Practice, and Professional Identity in America, 1929–1969* (New York: Cambridge University Press, 1999), 1.

65 "American College Personnel Association, Eighth Annual Conference," *Personnel Journal* 10 (June 1931): 53–57.

66 Louis B. Hopkins, "Personnel Procedure in Education: Observations and Conclusions Resulting from Visits to Fourteen Institutions of Higher Learning," *Educational Record* 7 (Washington, DC: American Council on Education, 1926): 3–5.

67 Ibid.

68 Herbert E. Hawkes et al., "The Student Personnel Point of View: A Report of a Conference on the Philosophy and Development of Student Personnel Work in College and University" (Washington, DC: American Council on Education, 1937).

69 Hopkins, "Personnel Procedure in Education," 5, 95.

70 "President Speaks of College Life to New Students," *Ohio State Lantern*, 26 Sept. 1921, 1.

71 Dorothy Ross, *G. Stanley Hall: The Psychologist as Prophet* (Chicago: University of Chicago Press, 1972), 339; Joseph F. Kett, *Rites of Passage: Adolescence in America, 1790 to the Present* (New York: Basic Books, 1977), 215–21.

72 Hopkins, "Personnel Procedure in Education," 15–16.

73 On the Common Law and in loco parentis, see *Blackstone's Commentaries on the Laws of England, Book 1, Ch. 16: Of Parent and Child*, 441, available at http://www.yale.edu/lawweb/avalon/blackstone/blacksto.htm (accessed 18 Aug. 2008).

74 On the nineteenth century case law, see William M. Beaney, "Students, Higher Education, and the Law," *Denver Law Journal* 45 (Special 1968): 513–14.

75 *Gott v. Berea College* (156 Ky. 376, 161 S.W. 204 [1913]), cited in Roy Lucas, "The Right to Higher Education," *Journal of Higher Education* 41 (Jan. 1970): 56.

76 AAUP Declaration of Principles available at http://www.aaup.org/NR/rdonlyres/A6520A9D-0A9A-47B3-B550-C006B5B224E7/0/1915Declaration.pdf (accessed 23 Feb. 2009). On the Committee's neglect of *Lernfreiheit* and student freedom, see Walter P. Metzger, "Profession and Constitution: Two Definitions of Academic Freedom in America," *Texas Law Review* 66 (June 1988): 1265–1322.

77 On student resistance to parental rules, see Fass, *Damned and the Beautiful*.

78 Quote in William W. Van Alstyne, "The Tentative Emergence of Student Power in the United States," *American Journal of Comparative Law* 17 (summer 1969): 409–10.

79 All cases in Lucas, "Right to Higher Education," 55–64; and Van Alstyne, "Tentative Emergence of Student Power in the United States," 410–11.

80 Ibid.

81 Leo Strauss, "Liberal Education and Responsibility," in *Education: The Challenge Ahead*, ed. C. Scott Fletcher (New York: W. W. Norton, 1962), 51.

82 William W. Van Alstyne, "The Demise of the Right-Privilege Distinction in Constitutional Law," *Harvard Law Review* (1968): 1439–64; Lucas, "Right to Higher Education."

83 On the limits of parental power under in loco parentis, see *Blackstone's Commentaries on the Laws of England, Book 1, Ch. 16: Of Parent and Child*, 441, available at http://www.yale.edu/lawweb/avalon/blackstone/blacksto.htm (accessed 8 Aug. 2008.) Judge Blackstone wrote, "The tutor or schoolmaster . . . has such a *portion* of the power of the parent," but not all of it (emphasis in original my own).

84 On the role of "natural affection" and its absence under in loco parentis, see *Lander v. Seaver*, 32 Vt. 114, 76 Am.Dec. 156, cited in C. Michael Abbott, "Demonstrations, Dismissals, Due Process, and the High School: An Overview," *School Review* 77 (June 1969): 131–33; and Jenny Shaw, "In Loco Parentis: A Relationship Between Parent, State, and Child," in *Education and the State: Politics, Patriarchy, and Practice*, ed. Roger Dale et al. (Sussex, UK: Falmer Press in association with The Open University Press, 1981), 257–68. For the legal meanings of in loco parentis, paternal power, and affection, see Walter A. Shumaker and George Foster Longsdorf, ed., *Cyclopedic Law Dictionary* (Chicago: Callaghan, 1922), 515, 681, 749.

85 On the college as an alma mater with parentlike duties and obligations to care and to love its students, see Frederick Rudolph, *The American College and University: A History* (1962; Athens: University of Georgia Press, 1990), 86–109; and Helen Lefkowitz Horowitz, *Alma Mater: Design and Experience in the Women's Colleges from Their Nineteenth-Century Beginnings to the 1930s* (New York: Ballantine, 1984).

86 Herbert E. Hawkes, "Fundamental Values in Personnel Work," in *Provision for the Individual in College*, ed. William S. Gray (Chicago: University of Chicago Press, 1932), 22; Charles Franklin Thwing, "New Trend In Colleges Stresses Personal Need," *New York Times*, 7 June 1925, XX11.

87 James C. Littlejohn, "Personal Rating Systems," *Bulletin of the American Association of Collegiate Registrars* 1 (Baltimore: AACR, 1925): 208.

88 On the early personnel community, see Klein, *Survey of Land-Grant Colleges and Universities*, 420; and George F. Zook, "The Administration of Student Personnel Work," *Journal of Higher Education* 3 (Oct. 1932): 349–54.

89 Oscar H. Werner, *Every College Student's Problems* (New York: Boston, Silver, Burdett, 1929), 58.

90 On the secularization of the academy, see Reuben, *Making of the Modern University*; and George M. Marsden, "The Soul of the American University: A Historical Overview," in *The Secularization of the Academy*, ed. George M. Marsden and Bradley J. Longfield (New York: Oxford University Press, 1992), 9–45.

91 "Columbia Enrolls 10,000: Including Summer School, University Will be Largest in World," *New York Times*, 26 Sept.1919, 27.

92 Dorothy Ross, *The Origins of American Social Science* (New York: Cambridge University Press, 1991).

93 On the shift from character to personality, see Gordon W. Allport, *Personality: A Psychological Interpretation* (New York: Henry Holt, 1937); Ian A.M. Nicholson, "Gordon Allport, Character, and the 'Culture of Personality,' 1897–1937," *History of Psychology* 1 (1998): 52–68; and Ian A.M. Nicholson, *Inventing Personality: Gordon Allport and the Science of Selfhood* (Washington, DC: American Psychological Association, 2003), esp. 73–102, 133–62.

94 J. B. Johnston, "Methods of Improving Scholarship in the College of Liberal Arts," *National Association of Deans of Women*, 12th Yearbook (1925), 149.

95 "Report of the Sub-Committee on Personality Measurement," *Educational Record* 9 (July 1928): 53–64, esp. 53; Frank O. Holt, "Securing a More Highly Selected Student Body at the University of Wisconsin," in *Provision for the Individual in College*, ed. Gray, 45.

96 David A. Robertson, "Personnel Methods in College," *Educational Record* 8 (Washington, DC, 1927): 319.

97 Clyde Furst, "College Personnel Requirements," ibid., 308.

98 Hopkins, "Personnel Procedure in Education," 11–13. According to Hopkins, "Most of these institutions are conscious of the unreliability of these ratings but continue to use them because they are better than any other device which is known" (ibid., 13).

99 Ibid., 13–14.

100 Charles Franklin Thwing, "New Tendencies Seen in College Education," *New York Times*, 8 June 1924, XX16.

101 On the rise of selective admissions and the exclusion of Jewish applicants, see Karabel, *Chosen*, 13–136, esp. 128–36. Karabel's functionalist interpretation of personality does not delve into the wartime origins of personality. Nor does it tie personality to the personnel movement. I think higher education gravitated to personality for numerous reasons, of which the desire to exclude certain students was but one.

102 Louis B. Hopkins, "Personnel Work at Northwestern University," *Journal of Personnel Research* 1 (Oct.–Nov. 1922): 286.

103 "Character Records are Kept of Students," *Washington Post*, 6 June 1924, 20.

104 Littlejohn, "Personal Rating Systems," 213.

105 Ernest H Wilkins, "Freshman Week at the University of Chicago," *School Review* 32 (Dec. 1924): 746.

106 Knode, *Orienting the Student in College*, 89.

107 Mary Frazer Smith, "Freshman Week," in *Proceedings of the American Association of Collegiate Registrars* (2–4 April 1924): 190–97; Knode, *Orienting the Student in College*, 31.

108 Thwing, "New Tendencies Seen in College Education," XX16.

109 Ibid; Knode, *Orienting the Student in College*, 15–17, 55–57, 134,187; C. C. Little, "Freshman Week," *School and Society* 24 (18 Dec. 1926): 765–66.

110 H. M. Ellis, "Freshman Week at the University of Maine," *School and Society* 24 (24 July 1926): 110–11.

111 "Committee Meets to Discuss Success of Freshman Week," *Ohio State Lantern*, 6 Oct. 1927, 1.

112 Knode, *Orienting the Student to College*, 181; Klein, "Higher Education: Biennial Survey, 1922–1924," 10.

113 Charles Tabor Fitts and Fletcher Harper Swift, *The Construction of Orientation Courses for College Freshmen* (Berkeley: University of California Press, 1928), 149.

114 Ibid., 197.

115 Ibid., 196.

116 Ibid., 196, 180–82.

117 Ibid., 169.

118 Snyder, ed., *120 Years of American Education*, 80; Leonard V. Koos, "Recent Growth of the Junior College," *School Review* 36 (April 1928): 256–66.

119 Levine, *American College and the Culture of Aspiration*, 162–84, quote on 177.

120 Chauncey S. Boucher, "Curriculum Provision for the Individual in the University of Chicago," in *Provision for the Individual in College*, ed. Gray, 102.

121 John B. Johnston, "The Junior College of the University of Minnesota," in *Provision for the Individual in College*, ed. Gray, 111, 118; Levine, *American College and the Culture of Aspiration*, 164, 167–68.

122 "Special Honor Course Favored For Colleges," *New York Times*, 22 March 1925, 6; "The Community's Stake in the Brilliant Student," *Annual Meeting of the National Association of Deans of Women* (Washington, DC: The Association, 1924), 116; Frank Aydelotte, "Honors Courses at Swarthmore," in *Five College Plans*, ed. Coss, 59–61; Brubacher and Rudy, *Higher Education in Transition*, 264; Helen Lefkowitz Horowitz, *Campus Life: Undergraduate Cultures from the End of the Eighteenth Century to the Present* (1987; Chicago: University of Chicago Press, 1988), 112–14.

123 Robert C. Angell, *A Study in Undergraduate Adjustment* (Chicago: University of Chicago Press, 1930), 50.

124 Angell, *Campus*, 38.

125 Ibid., 36–37.

126 Leo Rosten, "Harold Lasswell: A Memoir," in *Politics, Personality, and Social Science in the Twentieth Century: Essays in Honor of Harold D. Lasswell*, ed. Arnold A. Rogow (Chicago: University of Chicago Press, 1969), 1.

127 William B. Munro, "A Self-Study of College Teaching," *Journal of Higher Education* 9 (Dec. 1932): 462. For an overview of the problem, see J. O. Creager, "The Preparation of the College Teacher," *Journal of Educational Sociology* 6 (Oct. 1932): 67–77.

128 F. J. Kelly, "The Training of College Teachers," *Journal of Educational Research* 14 (Nov. 1927): 333.

129 Archie M. Palmer, "Educating the Educators," *Journal of Higher Education* 1 (June 1930): 334–38.

130 Munro, "A Self-Study of College Teaching," 462.

131 Merle I. Protzman, "Student Rating of College Teaching," *School and Society* 34 (20 April 1929): 514.

132 For a model examination of the relationship between research technique and disciplinary formation, see Robert E. Kohler, *From Medical Chemistry to Biochemistry: The Making of a Biomedical Discipline* (New York: Cambridge University Press, 1982). On the growth of graduate education in the 1920s, see Bernard Berelson, *Graduate Education in the United States* (New York: McGraw-Hill, 1960), 24–32.

133 James L. Shulman and William G. Bowen, *The Game of Life: College Sports and Academic Values* (Princeton: Princeton University Press, 2001), 6–10.

134 On the emergence of Greek life and rates of student participation in it, see Horowitz, *Campus Life*, 111–12, 132. On Wilson as president at Princeton, see Veysey,

Emergence of the American University, 241–49. On Wilson's ill-fated attempt to abolish Princeton's eating clubs, Veysey wrote: "In short, Wilson worked to abolish the eating clubs at Princeton in order that the university might be turned into a single gigantic eating club (albeit of a somewhat more intellectual orientation)" (246).

135   Angell, *A Study in Undergraduate Adjustment*, 64.

136   Richard H. Edwards, *Undergraduates: A Study of Morale in Twenty-Three American Colleges and Universities* (New York: Doubleday, Doran and Co., 1928), 23.

137   Rufus H. Fitzgerald, "Personal Adjustments in Relation to Living Conditions," in *Provision for the Individual in College*, ed. Gray, 189.

138   Brubacher and Rudy, *Higher Education in Transition*, 327.

139   Fass, *Damned and Beautiful*, 119–67. Fass contends the "peer society" was formulated by students and existed largely independent of the administration, while I think that society was carefully shaped by the actions of administrators and faculty.

140   Horowitz, *Campus Life*, 98–150.

141   Edwards, *Undergraduates*, 91–127.

142   O. Myking Mehus, "Academic Achievement of College Students in Different Kinds of Extra-curricular Activities," *Journal of Educational Sociology* 9 (Dec. 1935): 56.

143   O. Myking Mehus, "Extracurricular Activities and Academic Achievement," *Journal of Educational Sociology* 6 (Nov. 1932): 143–49; George F. Dunkelberger, "Do Extracurricular Activities Make for Poor Scholarship?" *Journal of Educational Sociology* 9 (Dec. 1935): 215–18; F. Stuart Chapin, "Research Studies of Extracurricular Activities and Their Significance in Reflecting Social Change," *Journal of Educational Sociology* 4 (April 1931): 491–98.

144   Edwards, *Undergraduates*, 124.

145   Frank Aydelotte, *Bulletin of the National Research Council: Honors Courses in American Colleges and Universities* 7 (Jan. 1924): 6.

146   On the recognition of student clubs and teams, see Horowitz, *Campus Life*, 118–19.

147   "No College Suicide Wave Is Shown by Statistics," *Washington Post*, 12 June 1927, SM8; "Student Suicides Stir Interest of Scientists," *New York Times*, 20 Feb. 1927, XX5; "Student a Suicide, 26th Since Jan 1," *New York Times*, 9 March 1927, 27.

148   "Two More Youthful Students Commit Suicide," *New York Times*, 12 March 1927, 6.

149   "Educator Explains Student Suicides," *New York Times*, 31 Jan. 1927, 20; "Student Suicides Stir Interest of Scientists," *New York Times*, 20 Feb. 1927, XX5; "Lays Suicide Toll to Machine Age," *New York Times*, 21 March 1927, 22; "Wesleyan Head Urges More Spirit," *New York Times*, 20 June 1927, 8.

150   Cohen, *Challenging Orthodoxies*, 203–26; Harold W. Bernard, "College Mental Hygiene—A Decade of Growth," *Mental Hygiene* 24 (July 1940): 413–18; Zoe Emily Leatherman, *A Study of the Maladjusted College Student* (Columbus: Ohio State University Studies, 1925), 12–13; E. L. Stogdill, "The Maladjusted College Student—A Further Study with Results," *Journal of Applied Psychology* 8 (Oct. 1929): 440–41; "Form Anti-Suicide Club," *New York Times*, 18 Feb. 1927, 23; "Student Collapses Laid to Colleges," *New York Times*, 26 April 1925, E1; Ethel Kawin, "Adjustment in the School and College Situation," *Review of Educational Research* 10 (Dec. 1940): 426.

151   E. G. Williamson and D. G. Patterson, "Co-ordinating Counseling Procedures," *Journal of Higher Education* 5 (Feb. 1934): 75–79; Stogdill, "The Maladjusted College

Student—A Further Study With Results," 440–50; Sydney Kinnear Smith, "Psychiatry and University Men: A Study of 300 Cases on the Psychiatric Service of the University of California," *Mental Hygiene* 12 (Jan. 1928): 38–47.

152 "Psychology Clinic Will Give Help on Student Problems," *Ohio State Lantern*, 15 Jan. 1925, 1.

153 Heather Munro Prescott, "Using the Student Body: College and University Students as Research Subjects in the United States during the Twentieth Century," *Journal of the History of Medicine* 57 (Jan. 2002): 3–38.

154 Daniel Katz and Floyd Allport, *Students' Attitudes: A Report of the Syracuse University Reaction Study* (New York: Craftsman Press, 1931), 88–89.

155 Tinto, *Leaving College*; John M. Braxton, ed., *Reworking the Student Departure Puzzle* (Nashville: Vanderbilt University Press, 2000).

156 Duffus, "New Methods Remaking Old Colleges," 79.

CHAPTER 3

BUILDING THE NEW DEAL ADMINISTRATIVE STATE

1. Letter to FDR, 19 March 1933, Education: Jan.–Sept. 1933 file, box 1, Official File 107, FDR Library (Hyde Park, NY).

2. See, for example, Martin J. Finkelstein, *The American Academic Profession: A Synthesis of Social Scientific Inquiry since World War II* (Columbus: Ohio State University Press, 1984), 26–27; William E. Leuchtenburg, *Franklin D. Roosevelt and the New Deal, 1932–1940* (New York: Harper and Row, 1963); Alan Brinkley, *The End of Reform: New Deal Liberalism in Recession and War* (New York: Knopf, 1995); and Barry Dean Karl, *Executive Reorganization and Reform in the New Deal* (1963; Chicago: University of Chicago Press, 1979). For a revisionist intellectual history, see Edward S. Shapiro, "Decentralist Intellectuals and the New Deal," *Journal of American History* 58 (March 1972): 938–57.

3. See, for example, Robert Kargon and Elizabeth Hodes, "Karl Compton, Isaiah Bowman, and the Politics of Science in the Great Depression," *ISIS* 76 (1985): 301–18; Larry Owens, "MIT and the Federal 'Angel': Academic R&D and Federal-Private Cooperation before World War II," *ISIS* 81 (1990): 188–213; Daniel J. Kevles, *The Physicists: The History of a Scientific Community in Modern America* (New York: Knopf, 1978); Rebecca S. Lowen, *Creating the Cold War University: The Transformation of Stanford* (Berkeley: University of California Press, 1997), 17–42; and Roger L. Geiger, *Research and Relevant Knowledge: American Research Universities since World War Two* (New York: Oxford University Press, 1993).

4. For one exception, see Ronald Story, "The New Deal and Higher Education," in *The New Deal and the Triumph of Liberalism*, ed. Sid Milkis and Jerome M. Mileur (Amherst: University of Massachusetts Press, 2002), 272–96. To make his case for the importance of the New Deal, Story conflates the New Deal and World War II by using Franklin Roosevelt's presidential tenure (1933–45) as an organizing frame. While this approach permits Story to showcase the depth of the Roosevelt administration's commitment to higher education policymaking, it obscures the real differences in motive and intent, and in political and interest group alignments that distinguished each period.

5. On New Deal state building, see Ellis W. Hawley, *The New Deal and the Problem of Monopoly: A Study in Economic Ambivalence* (1963; Princeton: Princeton University Press, 1995); Gerald D. Nash, *The Crucial Era: The Great Depression and World War II,*

1929–1945 (1979; New York: Waveland Press, 1992); Barry Dean Karl, *The Uneasy State: The United States from 1915–1945* (Chicago: University of Chicago Press, 1983); Steve Fraser and Gary Gerstle, ed., *The Rise and Fall of the New Deal Order, 1930–1980* (Princeton: Princeton University Press, 1989); James T. Patterson, *Congressional Conservatism and the New Deal: The Growth of the Conservative Coalition in Congress, 1933–1939* (Lexington: University of Kentucky Press, 1969); and Jason Scott Smith, *Building New Deal Liberalism: The Political Economy of Public Works, 1933–1956* (New York: Cambridge University Press, 2006). My thinking on the influence of America's laissez-faire tradition on New Deal state building has been shaped by Ellis W. Hawley, "The New Deal State and the Anti-Bureaucratic Tradition," in *The New Deal and Its Legacy: Critique and Reappraisal*, ed. Robert Eden (New York: Greenwood Press, 1989), 77–92.

6. See, for example, Bruce Schulman, *From Cotton Belt to Sunbelt: Federal Policy, Economic Development, and the Transformation of the South, 1938–1980* (New York: Oxford University Press, 1991); Ira Katznelson, *When Affirmative Action Was White: The Untold History of Racial Inequality in Twentieth-Century America* (New York: W. W. Norton, 2005); and Patterson, *Congressional Conservatism and the New Deal.*

7. Brinkley, *End of Reform.*

8. On higher education's public purpose, see Scott J. Peters, *Democracy and Higher Education: Traditions and Stories of Civic Engagement* (East Lansing: Michigan State University Press, 2010).

9. Theodore Saloutos, *The American Farmer and the New Deal* (Ames: Iowa State University Press, 1982), 3–14, esp. 12–13; Anthony J. Badger, *The New Deal: The Depression Years, 1933–40* (London: Macmillan, 1989), 14–15.

10. Wayne D. Rasmussen and Gladys Baker, *The Department of Agriculture* (New York: Praeger, 1972), 22.

11. Philip Kinsley, "79 Farmers Held by Troops: Iowa Extends Martial Law," *Chicago Daily Tribune*, 2 May 1933, 5; James O. Babcock, "The Farm Revolt in Iowa," *Social Forces* 12 (March 1934): 369–73.

12. On the farm lobby, see John Mark Hansen, *Gaining Access: Congress and the Farm Lobby, 1919–1981* (Chicago: University of Chicago Press, 1991).

13. Badger, *New Deal*, 150–52.

14. Ibid., 73–75; Wayne D. Rasmussen, Gladys L. Baker, and James S. Ward, *A Short History of Agricultural Adjustment, 1933–75* (Washington, DC: Economic Research Service, U.S. Dept. of Agriculture, 1976), 1–2. The AAA was passed on 12 May 1933; the NIRA on 16 June 1933. On the success of the Agricultural Adjustment Administration and the failure of the National Recovery Act, see Kenneth Finegold and Theda Skocpol, *State and Party in America's New Deal* (Madison: University of Wisconsin Press, 1995).

15. H. A. Wallace, "More Purchasing Power for Farmers," *Extension Service Review* 4 (May 1933): 33.

16. Hansen, *Gaining Access*, 39.

17. Jan Choate, *Disputed Ground: Farm Groups that Opposed the New Deal Agricultural Program* (Jefferson, NC: McFarland, 2002), 131–33; Badger, *New Deal*, 149–50. Peek and Wallace had a contested relationship; see Saloutos, *American Farmer and the New Deal*, 155. On Henry C. Wallace's unfulfilled push for agricultural reform in the Harding administration, see Rasmussen and Baker, *Department of Agriculture*, 16–17.

18. On the failures of the 1920s, see Hansen, *Gaining Access*, 26–77. The USDA eventually created programs to redistribute agricultural surpluses to the neediest Americans;

see Rachel Louise Moran, "Consuming Relief: Food Stamps and the New Welfare of the New Deal," *Journal of American History* 97 (March 2011): 1001–22.

19. Rasmussen and Baker, *Department of Agriculture*, 26.

20. Donald H. Grubbs, *Cry from the Cotton: The Southern Tenant Farmers' Union and the New Deal* (1971; Fayetteville: University of Arkansas Press, 2000), 18.

21. Edmund deS. Brunner and E. Hsin Pao Yang, *Rural America and the Extension Service: A History and Critique of the Cooperative Agricultural and Home Economics Extension Service* (New York: Bureau of Publications, Teachers College, Columbia University, 1949), 81.

22. Badger, *New Deal*, 155–57; Murray R. Benedict, *Can We Solve the Farm Problem? An Analysis of Federal Aid to Agriculture* (New York: Twentieth Century Fund, 1955), 90–91.

23. Rasmussen and Baker, *Department of Agriculture*, 27–28. On Wallace's decision, see William J. Block, "The Separation of the Farm Bureau and the Extension Service," *Illinois Studies in Social Sciences* 47 (1960): 15; Badger, *New Deal*, 157–58.

24. For the number of land-grant colleges and universities, which included 17 all-black institutions, see Arthur J. Klein, *Survey of Land-Grant Colleges and Universities* (Washington, DC: GPO, 1930), v. Enrollment data in Arthur J. Klein, "The Rise of the Land-Grant Colleges and Universities," *School Life* 16 (Jan. 1931): 83.

25. Wayne D. Rasmussen, *Taking the University to the People: Seventy-five Years of Cooperative Extension* (Ames: Iowa State University Press, 1989), 22–23; Rasmussen and Baker, *Department of Agriculture*, 3–20; Alice M. Rivlin, *The Role of the Federal Government in Financing Higher Education* (Washington, DC: Brookings Institution, 1961), 21–26. For an overview of the entire period, see Roger L. Williams, *The Origins of Federal Support for Higher Education: George W. Atherton and the Land-Grant College Movement* (University Park: Penn State University Press, 1991), esp. 87–198. Political scientist Dan Carpenter has persuasively argued that the USDA became a de facto "university" in the first two decades of the twentieth century; see Carpenter, *The Forging of Bureaucratic Autonomy: Reputations, Networks, and Policy Innovation in Executive Agencies, 1862–1928* (Princeton: Princeton University Press, 2001), 212–54. The USDA's relationship to higher education was further enhanced by the creation of the Graduate School of the Department of Agriculture in 1921. See Paul Kaufman, "The Graduate School of the Department of Agriculture," *Journal of Higher Education* 11 (June 1940): 287–92.

26. On the differences between the instructional techniques of the USDA and the land-grant colleges, see Roy V. Scott, *The Reluctant Farmer: The Rise of Agricultural Extension to 1914* (Chicago: University of Chicago Press, 1970), 138–169.

27. Joseph Cannon Bailey, *Seaman A. Knapp: Schoolmaster of American Agriculture* (New York: Columbia University Press, 1945), 96; Scott, *Reluctant Farmer*, 208.

28. Bailey, *Seaman A. Knapp*, 132.

29. Lawrence Goodwyn, *The Populist Moment: A Short History of the Agrarian Revolt in America* (New York: Oxford University Press, 1978), 29–35.

30. On Knapp's agent preferences, see Scott, *Reluctant Farmer*, 213–16.

31. Bailey, *Seaman A. Knapp*, 177–78, quote on 202.

32. Ibid., 204–5.

33. Ibid., 213.

34. Ibid., 206.

35. Ibid., 211.

36. After Knapp's death in 1911, his son and successor at the USDA, Bradford Knapp, loosened the rules governing the selection of agents, which opened the door for land-grant graduates; see Scott, *Reluctant Farmer*, 227. On the particulars of the act, see ibid., 288–13, esp. 307–11.

37. Figures in Rasmussen, *Taking the University to the People*, 72; Gladys Baker, *The County Agent* (Chicago: University of Chicago Press, 1939), 61; C. W. Warburton, "County Agents—Today and Tomorrow," *Extension Service Review* 6 (July 1935): 81.

38. On the role of interest groups in extending the USDA's political authority, see Carpenter, *Forging Bureaucratic Autonomy*, 291. For a more reductive view of the Farm Bureau as "captor" of the USDA and the land-grants, and ultimately of all New Deal agricultural policy, see Grant McConnell, *The Decline of Agrarian Democracy* (Berkeley: University of California Press, 1953).

39. On the Farm Bureau, see Christiana McFadyen Campbell, *The Farm Bureau and the New Deal* (Urbana: University of Illinois Press, 1962), 3–13; Baker, *County Agent*, 15–24; Brunner and Yang, *Rural American and the Extension Service*, 68–71.

40. Rasmussen, *Taking the University to the People*, 77–80. On the early partnership between the county agent and the Farm Bureau, see M. C. Burritt, *The County Agent and the Farm Bureau* (New York, 1922).

41. McConnell, *Decline of Agrarian Democracy*, 53.

42. "A Message to all County Agents," *Extension Service Review* 6 (July 1935): 97.

43. Badger, *New Deal*, 158–59; Saloutos, *American Farmer and the New Deal*, 67–68; A. A. Myers, "County Adjustment Campaigns," *Extension Services Review* 4 (March 1934): 125.

44. R. E. Hughes, 1933 Narrative Report, *Annual Narrative and Statistical Reports from State Offices and County Agents: Georgia* (Washington, DC: NARA, 1951), film, roll 58 of 149.

45. T. B. Manny, "The Conditions of Rural Life," *American Journal of Sociology* 40 (May 1935): 721.

46. Baker, *County Agent*, 70; Ralph K. Bliss, *History of Cooperative Agriculture and Home Economics Extension in Iowa—The First Fifty Years* (Ames: Iowa State University Press, 1960), 167. Contact data in C. W. Warburton, "County Agents—Today and Tomorrow," *Extension Services Review* 6 (July 1935): 96.

47. Theodore Saloutos and John D. Hicks, *Agricultural Discontent in the Middle West, 1900–1939* (Madison: University of Wisconsin Press, 1951), 491.

48. On these and other alleged county agent transgressions, see Campbell, *Farm Bureau and the New Deal*, 85–102; Block, "The Separation of the Farm Bureau and the Extension Service," 25–28; and Baker, *County Agent*, 100.

49. Saloutos and Hicks, *Agricultural Discontent in the Middle West*, 491.

50. Baker, *County Agent*, 94–97; Campbell, *Farm Bureau and the New Deal*, 70–76.

51. 1935 Director's Report, Narrative Report, *Annual Narrative and Statistical Reports from State Offices and County Agents: New York* (Washington, DC: NARA, 1951), film, roll 51 of 90.

52. Baker, *County Agent*, 38.

53. Brunner and Yang, *Rural America and the Extension Service*, 133–34; Earl A. Flansburgh, "What is a Farm Bureau," in 1935 Narrative Report, *Annual Narrative and Statistical Reports from State Offices and County Agents: New York* (Washington,

DC: NARA, 1951), film, roll 51 of 90. On an agent's affiliation with the land grant, see H. C. Sanders, *The Memoirs of a County Agent* (Baton Rouge: Louisiana State University Printing Office, 1983), 1.

54. N. D. McRainey, 1934 Narrative Report, *Annual Narrative and Statistical Reports from State Offices and County Agents: Georgia* (Washington, DC: NARA, 1951), film, roll 69 of 149; George M. Briggs, 1934 Narrative Report, *Annual Narrative and Statistical Reports from State Offices and County Agents: Wisconsin* (Washington, DC: NARA, 1951), film, roll 23 of 49; Sanders, *Memoirs of a County Agent*, 1.

55. On the failed efforts the 1880s and 1890s, see Goodwyn, *Populist Moment*.

56. On Roosevelt's decision making, see assorted items in Land Grants 1933–37 file, box 1, Official File 381, FDR Library; Senator quote in Letter to FDR, 21 April 1933, ibid; and Story, "New Deal and Higher Education," in *New Deal and the Triumph of Liberalism*, ed. Milkis and Milieur, 276. On New Deal funding for the Extension Service, see Baker, *County Agent*, 79–81, esp. 80n14; and Brunner and Yang, *Rural America and the Extension Service*, 202. On the Farm Bureau's influence and the land-grant colleges' support of it, see McConnell, *Decline of Agrarian Democracy*, 82, 164–65.

57. Julian E. Zelizer, *On Capitol Hill: The Struggle to Reform Congress and Its Consequences, 1948–2000* (New York: Cambridge University Press, 2004), 22–25; Ira Katznelson, "Limiting Liberalism: The Southern Veto in Congress, 1933–1950," *Political Science Quarterly* 108 (summer 1993): 283–306.

58. On the Bankhead family, see Jack B. Key, "John H. Bankhead, Jr. of Alabama: The Conservative as Reformer" (Ph.D. diss., Johns Hopkins University, 1966); and the congressional biographies available at http://bioguide.congress.gov.

59. Quote in *Memorial Services for John Hollis Bankhead*, 80th Cong., 1st sess., Washington, DC: 1949, 55.

60. Key, "John H. Bankhead, Jr., of Alabama," 1–3.

61. Ibid; Saloutos, *American Farmer and the New Deal*, 126, 164–65, 176–77, 196–97; *Memorial Services for John Hollis Bankhead*, 72–77; Hal Steed, "Cotton Country Pins Hopes on New Measure of Control," *New York Times*, 22 April 1934, XX3.

62. Funding data in U.S. Congress, Senate, Committee on Agriculture and Forestry, *Authorize Additional Appropriations to Provide for the Further Development of Cooperative Extension Work*, 77th Cong., 1st sess., 31 March 1941, 1–3.

63. Rivlin, *Role of the Federal Government in Financing Higher Education*, 63–64; Baker, *County Agent*, 145–50; Brunner and Yang, *Rural America and the Extension Service*, 202; Walter J. Greenleaf, "The Colleges," *School Life* 21 (Sept. 1935): 22; U.S. Congress, Senate, Committee on Agriculture and Forestry, *Hearings on S. 2228*, 74th Cong., 1st sess., 28–29 March 1935, 30, 41–42.

64. Extension Director, 1935 Narrative Report, *Annual Narrative and Statistical Reports from State Offices and County Agents: New York* (Washington, DC: NARA, 1951), film, roll 51 of 90.

65. McConnell, *Decline of Agrarian Democracy*, 82.

66. Baker, *County Agent*, 82

67. Floyd W. Reeves et al., *The Advisory Committee on Education: Report of the Committee* (Washington, DC: GPO, 1938), 146.

68. Adam D. Sheingate, *The Rise of the Agricultural Welfare State: Institutions and Interest Group Power in the United States, France, and Japan* (Princeton: Princeton University Press, 2001), 115.

69. On the "broker state," see Hawley, *New Deal and Problem of Monopoly*; and, for a similar argument that examines the New Deal's role in the "redistribution of power" to new "groups," see Samuel H. Beers, "In Search of a New Public Philosophy," in *New American Political System*, ed. Anthony King (Washington, DC: American Enterprise Institute Press, 1978), 9–13. On the continued importance of county agents on the planning committees, see Dale Clark, "The Farmer as Co-Administrator," *Public Opinion Quarterly* 3 (July 1939): 488.

70. Paul H. Landis, "The New Deal and Rural Life," *American Sociological Review* 1 (Aug. 1936): 600.

71. E. R. McIntyre, *Fifty Years of Cooperative Extension in Wisconsin, 1912–1962* (Madison: University of Wisconsin Press, 1962), 133–34.

72. Arthur O. Levine, *American College and the Culture of Aspiration, 1915–1940* (Ithaca: Cornell University Press, 1986), 187.

73. Charles Riborg Mann, *Report of the National Advisory Committee on Education*, 2 vols. (Washington, DC: National Government Publication, 1931); "Conference on Crisis in Education," *School Life* 18 (Feb. 1933): 101–3.

74. Rupert Wilkinson, *Aiding Students, Buying Students: Financial Aid in America* (Nashville: Vanderbilt University Press, 2005), 107–8.

75. AAUP, *Depression, Recovery and Higher Education* (New York: McGraw Hill, 1937), 137.

76. "Higher Education in 1933–34," *School Life* 19 (June 1934): 212–13; Levine, *American College and the Culture of Aspiration*, 186; "Colleges Bear Up Despite the Slump," *New York Times*, 3 June 1932, 12; "Campus Gayety Hit By Effect of Slump," *New York Times*, 3 Oct. 1932, 19.

77. AAUP, *Depression, Recovery and Higher Education*, 137.

78. Wilkinson, *Aiding Students, Buying Students*, 97–110.

79. Madge I. McGlade, "College on $5 per Week," *School Life* 18 (April 1933): 151; "Cutting the Campus Bill," *New York Times*, 26 Feb. 1933, XX6; "Students' Morale Held Undermined," *New York Times*, 4 Nov. 1934, N5.

80. "College Gives Free Soup," *New York Times*, 5 March 1933, N2.

81. "Students to Aid Their Fellows with a Loan Fund at Boston," *New York Times*, 22 Nov. 1931, 77.

82. Dorothy Woolf, "Loans to Students on Business Basis," *New York Times*, 5 Oct. 1930, E7.

83. "Columbia Student Aid at Record With $487,000 Advanced in Year," *New York Times*, 22 May 1932, N1.

84. Clyde Beals, "Working Students Hit by Depression," *New York Times*, 12 Oct. 1930, E7.

85. "Student Jobs Scarce," *New York Times*, 26 Oct. 1930, N17. Henry Beaumont, "A Mirror of the Times," *Journal of Higher Education* 9 (Oct. 1938): 373–74; Margaret Ruth Smith, "Student Aid," *Journal of Higher Education* 7 (Jan. 1936): 29–35. On the creation of university employment offices, see Wilkinson, *Aiding Students, Buying Students*, 106–7.

86. Sanford Winston, "Selected Factors Affecting Student Adjustment," *Journal of Educational Sociology* 13 (May 1940): 547.

87. Samuel Haig Jameson, "Certain Adjustment Problems of University Girls," *Journal of Educational Sociology* 13 (Feb. 1940): 249–90, quotes on 251, 154.

88. Theophile Raphael et al., "Mental Hygiene in American Colleges and Universities," *Mental Hygiene* 22 (April 1938): 221–36.

89. Richard A. Reiman, *The New Deal and American Youth: Ideas and Ideals in a Depression Decade* (Athens: University of Georgia Press, 1992), 31–55; John W. Studebaker, "Dilemma of Youth," Radio Transcript (NBC, 9:30 p.m., 30 April 1935), 1936 Meeting Minutes file, box 15, Charles W. Taussig Papers, FDR Library; William Trufant Foster, "Psychological Factors in Business Depression," *New York Times*, 10 Jan. 1932, XX12.

90. Harold Seidman, "How Radical Are College Students?" *American Scholar* 4 (summer 1935): 326.

91. James Wechsler, "Ferment in the Colleges," *New Republic* 84 (16 Oct. 1935), 266–68.

92. Helen Lefkowitz Horowitz, *Campus Life: Undergraduate Cultures from the End of the Eighteenth Century to the Present* (Chicago: University of Chicago Press, 1987), 184.

93. Seidman, "How Radical Are College Students?" 327.

94. "Youth in College," *Fortune* 13 (June 1936), 100. On left-wing student groups during the 1930s, see Robert Cohen, *When the Old Left was Young: Student Radicals and America's First Mass Student Movement, 1929–1941* (New York: Oxford University Press, 1993).

95. "One-Sixth on Dole Are Aged 16 to 25," *New York Times*, 18 Nov. 1935, 19; National Youth Administration, "Facing the Problems of Youth" (Washington, DC: GPO, 1936), NYA Pamphlets and Leaflets file, box 9, Charles W. Taussig Papers, FDR Library.

96. Betty and Ernest K. Lindley, *A New Deal for Youth: The Story of the National Youth Commission* (New York: Viking Press, 1938), 6–9.

97. Howard M. Bell et al., *Youth Tell Their Story: A Study of the Conditions and Attitudes of Young People in Maryland between the ages of 16 and 24* (Washington, DC: American Council on Education, 1938), 104.

98. David M. Kennedy, *Freedom from Fear: The American People in Depression and War, 1929–1945* (New York: Oxford University Press, 1999), 144–45.

99. "NYA Conference of State Directors, Washington, DC, 19–31 May 1936," 32–36, Meetings, Minutes — 1936 file, box 15, C.W. Taussig Papers, FDR Library; Howard W. Oxley, "CCC Camp Education: Guidance and Recreational Phases," *Office of Education Bulletin*, no. 19 (Washington, DC: GPO, 1938), 1–23. On the relationship between education and work in the CCC, see Catherine Turner, "'A Gentleman Is No Sissy': Reading, Work, and Citizenship in the Civilian Conservation Corps," in *Education and the Culture of Print in Modern America*, ed. Adam R. Nelson and John L. Rudolph (Madison: University of Wisconsin Press, 2010), 150–72.

100. "What They Said at Minneapolis," *School Life* 18 (April 1933): 143.

101. Letter to FDR, 23 Dec. 1933, Education: Jan.–March 1934 file, box 1, Official File 107, FDR Library.

102. Levine, *American College and Culture of Aspiration*, 195–96; Reiman, *New Deal and American Youth*, 59–60.

103. Rivlin, *Role of the Federal Government in Financing Higher Education*, 20.

104. Smith, *Building New Deal Liberalism*, 1–2.

105. Rivlin, *Role of Federal Government in Financing Higher Education*, 98–100.

106. Reiman, *New Deal and American Youth*, 55–73; Timon Covert, "Federal Aid," *School Life* 20 (Sept. 1934): 6–7. For a copy of Hopkins's memo unveiling the FERA work-study plan, see Memo from Harry H. Hopkins to State Emergency Relief Admin-

istrations, 2 Feb. 1934, Personal Letter 1934 (Zook, George F.), box 606, Papers of Elea-nor Roosevelt, FDR Library.

107. Levine, *American College and the Culture of Aspiration*, 197–98.

108. Fred J. Kelly and John H. McNeely, "Federal Student Aid Program," *Office of Edu-cation Bulletin*, no. 14 (Washington, DC: GPO, 1935), 1-12; Thomas D. Snyder, ed., *120 Years of American Education: A Statistical Portrait* (Washington, DC: NCES, 1993), 76-77.

109. Patterson, *Congressional Conservatism and the New Deal*, 19–22.

110. V. O. Key Jr., *Southern Politics in State and Nation* (New York: A.A. Knopf, 1949), 19–20.

111. Jennings L. Wagoner, *Jefferson and Education* (Chapel Hill: University of North Carolina Press, 2004).

112. Lowen, *Creating the Cold War University*, 31; "Colleges to Get US Funds for Students Listed," n.d., 1934 NYA-Student Relief File (1 of 3), box 18, RG 2/1/2, Special Collections, University of Virginia, hereafter SCUVA (Charlottesville, VA); Letter to George F. Zook, 26 May 1934, ibid.

113. Letter to Harry F. Byrd, 28 April 1934, ibid; Letter to Harry Hopkins, 14 May 1934, ibid; Letter to W. A. Smith, 13 Nov. 1934; ibid. On Newcomb, see Virginius Dab-ney, *Mr. Jefferson's University: A History* (Charlottesville: University of Virginia Press, 1981), 137–41

114. Chance Stoner, "Campus Life," in Studs Terkel, *Hard Times: An Oral History of the Great Depression* (New York: Pantheon, 1970), 348–49.

115. "NYA Financial Report — 1935–1936," 1936 NYA Student Relief Office File (3 of 3), box 18, RG 2/1/2, SCUVA.

116. Letter to C. H. Kauffmann, 3 March 1934, file B, Personnel and Application Files, Records and Correspondence for Student Part-Time Jobs and Loans SCUVA; Let-ter to Kauffmann, 20 March 1933, file A, ibid.

117. Letter to J. L. Newcomb, 5 March 1934, file F, ibid.; Letter from Kauffmann to Parent, 9 March 1934, ibid; Letter to Kauffmann from Student, 21 Aug. 1935, file M, ibid. Selection criteria in letter from Kauffmann to Newcomb, 29 Oct. 1934, 1934 NYA Student Relief Office File (1 of 3), box 18, RG 2/1/2, SCUVA.

118. On Wilbur's original refusal of student aid, see Lowen, *Creating the Cold War University*, 31. All other quotes in NYA: Report of the Administration and Operation of the Program, 32-36, 41, NYA Reports, April 1936 file, box 10, Charles W. Taussig Papers, FDR Library.

119. On the rollback of the New Deal, see Brinkley, *End of Reform*, 140–42. On LBJ, the NYA, and his early House career, see Robert A. Caro, *The Years of Lyndon Johnson: Path to Power*, 3 vols. (New York: Knopf, 1982), I, ch. 1. On the revival of the federal work-study program during Johnson's presidency, see James L. Sundquist, *Politics and Policy: The Eisenhower, Kennedy, and Johnson Years* (Washington, DC: Brookings Insti-tution, 1968), 142–45.

120. Lizabeth Cohen, *Making a New Deal: Industrial Workers in Chicago, 1919–1939* (1990; New York: Cambridge University Press, 1993), 289.

121. "A Step Forward for Adult Civic Education," *Office of Education Bulletin*, no. 16 (Washington, DC: GPO, 1936), 2.

122. On Zook, see Donald R. Warren, *To Enforce Education: A History of the Found-ing Years of the United States Office of Education* (Detroit: Wayne State University Press, 1974), 179. On Studebaker, see Frank Ernest Hill, "Back to 'Town Meetings,'" *New York*

Times Magazine, 15 Sept. 1935, SM9. For the best examinations of the forum movement, see David Goodman "Democracy and Public Discussion in the Progressive and New Deal Eras: Form Civic Competence to the Expression of Opinion," *Studies in American Political Development* 18 (fall 2004): 81–111; and William Keith, *Democracy as Discussion: Civic Education and the American Forum Movement* (Lanham, MD: Lexington Books, 2007).

123. Webster Peterson, "A National Forum Plan," *New York Times*, 30 Sept. 1934, XX5.

124. For Studebaker's inspirations, see John W. Studebaker, *Choosing Our Way: The Story of the Forum Program* (Washington, DC: GPO, 1938), 2–7; Frank Ernest Hill, "Back to 'Town Meetings,'" *New York Times Magazine*, 15 Sept. 1935, SM9; and Joseph F. Kett, *The Pursuit of Knowledge under Difficulties: From Self-Improvement to Adult Education in America, 1750–1990* (Stanford: Stanford University Press, 1994), 38–40, 160–65. On Iowa and the importance of the land-grant movement, see Earle D. Ross, *Democracy's College: The Land-Grant Movement in the Formative Stage* (Ames: Iowa State College Press, 1942).

125. John W. Studebaker, *The American Way: Democracy at Work in the Des Moines Forums* (New York: McGraw-Hill, 1935), 4–5.

126. Studebaker, *American Way*, 61, 80–84, 91; Office of Education, "Education for Democracy: Public Affairs Forums," *Office of Education Bulletin*, no. 17 (Washington, DC: GPO, 1936), 16.

127. John W. Studebaker and Chester S. Williams, *Forum Planning Handbook* (Washington, DC: Office of Education, 1939), 17.

128. Studebaker, *American Way*, 45–47; "How to Conduct Group Discussion," Aug. 1935, Federal Forum Project, 1931–1941, box 1, Records of the Office of Education, RG 12, NARA (College Park, MD). For a complete list of all the participating discussion leaders from the first two years of the Des Moines Forum Program, see *American Way*, 135–47. On the importance of college-educated discussion leaders, see Goodman, "Democracy and Public Discussion in the Progressive and New Deal Eras," 94.

129. Goodman, "Democracy and Public Discussion in the Progressive and New Deal Eras," 94.

130. Warren, *To Enforce Education*, 179. On the history of the Office of Education, see Darrell Hevenor Smith, *The Bureau of Education: Its History, Activities, and Organization* (Baltimore: The Johns Hopkins Press, 1923); and Harry Kursh, *The United States Office of Education: A Century of Service* (Philadelphia: Chilton Books, 1965). On the creation of the Department of Education, in 1979, see Beryl Radin and Willis Hawley, *The Politics of Federal Reorganization: Creating the U.S. Department of Education* (New York: Pergamon Press, 1988). On the political weakness of the Office and Department of Education, see also Lynn Dumenil, "'The Insatiable Maw of Bureaucracy': Antistatism and Education Reform," *Journal of American History* 77 (Sept. 1990): 499–524.

131. Studebaker, *American Way*, 67. On the basic services provided by the Office of Education, see Kursh, *United States Office of Education*, 40–50.

132. Reiman, *New Deal and American Youth*, 112–18.

133. Webster Peterson, "A National Forum Plan," *New York Times*, 30 Sept. 1934, XX5.

134. "Proposes to Set Up 10,000 Open Forums," *New York Times*, 25 April 1935, 14.

135. "Cure for Reds Told to Rotary by Studebaker," *Washington Post*, 30 April 1935, 15.

136. "Studebaker Warns of a Dictatorship," *New York Times*, 30 June 1935, N1.

137. Rev. John Evans, "Federal 'Free Forums' Under Educators' Fire," *Chicago Tribune*, 24 April 1935, 18.

138. Memo from Studebaker to FDR, 25 Aug. 1935, Interior Department, Office of Education, 1933–35 file, box 12, Official File 6G, FDR Library; Memo from Studebaker to FDR, 30 Aug. 1935, ibid.

139. Memo from Studebaker to FDR, 3 Sept. 1935, ibid.; Office of Education, "A Step Forward for Adult Education," 4–28. See also William Graebner, *The Engineering of Consent: Democracy and Authority in Twentieth-Century America* (Madison: University of Wisconsin Press, 1987), 101–102.

140. "History of the Federal Forum Project," 1941, 1–10, Federal Forum Project, 1936–1941, box 5, Records of the Office of Education, NARA; Goodman, "Democracy and Public Discussion in the Progressive and New Deal Eras," 92.

141. "History of the Federal Forum Project," 1941, 1–10, quote on 2, Federal Forum Project, 1936–1941, box 5, Records of the Office of Education, NARA.

142. On the NDAC Fargo Forum, see Frank L. Eversull, "The Public Forum and the College," *Journal of Higher Education* 11 (May 1940): 242–46. On Eversull's educational background and presidency, see "Biography," North Dakota State College Archives, available at http://www.lib.ndsu.nodak.edu/archives/recordsandpapers/rg3/3-10.htm (accessed 16 March 2009). All national forum participation data in "History of the Federal Forum Project," 1941, 1–10, Federal Forum Project, 1936–1941, box 5, Records of the Office of Education, NARA.

143. Memo from Studebaker to FDR, 16 Nov. 1936, Interior Department, Office of Education, 1933–35, box 12, Official File 6G, FDR Library. Studebaker never again pressed for a Department of Education. After fourteen years as commissioner, Studebaker decided politics and education were a bad fit: "If a Secretary of Education were to participate in presidential cabinet conferences and were privy to all the administration secrets and partisan conflicts, he'd be pretty much cast as part of the politics and perhaps become embroiled in it. It would be difficult for a Secretary of Education to avoid getting involved and to refuse getting involved in politics." (Kursh, *United States Office of Education*, 137).

144. John Dale Russell, "The Evolution of the Present Relations of the Federal Government to Education in the United States," *Journal of Negro Education* 7 (July 1938): 244–55.

Chapter 4
Educating Citizen-Soldiers in World War II

1. Servicemen's Readjustment Act of 1944 (G.I. Bill of Rights), Pub. L. No. 78-346, 58 Stat. 284. The literature on the G.I. Bill is large and growing. See, for example, Davis R. B. Ross, *Preparing for Ulysses: Politics and Veterans during World War II* (New York: Columbia University Press, 1969); Keith W. Olson, *The G.I. Bill, the Veterans, and the Colleges* (Lexington: University Press of Kentucky, 1974); Michael J. Bennett, *When Dreams Came True: The G.I. Bill and the Making of Modern America* (Washington, DC: Brassey's, 1996); and Theda Skocpol, "The G.I. Bill and U.S. Social Policy, Past and Future," *Social Philosophy and Policy* 14 (1997): 95–115. For accounts of the G.I. Bill that address its intersection with postwar race and gender constructions, see David H. Onkst, "'First

a Negro . . . Incidentally a Veteran': Black World War Two Veterans and the G.I. Bill of Rights in the Deep South, 1944–48," *Journal of Social History* 31 (spring 1998): 517–43; Kathleen Jill Frydl, *The G.I. Bill* (New York: Cambridge University Press, 2009); Ira Katznelson, "Public Policy and the Middle-Class Racial Divide after the Second World War," in *Social Contracts under Stress: The Middle Classes of America, Europe, and Japan at the Turn of the Century*, ed. Olivier Zunz, Leonard Schoppa, and Nobuhiro Hiwatari (New York: Russell Sage Foundation, 2002), 157–77; Lizabeth Cohen, *A Consumers' Republic: The Politics of Mass Consumption in Postwar America* (New York: Knopf, 2003), 137–46; Suzanne Mettler, *Soldiers to Citizens: The G.I. Bill and the Making of the Greatest Generation* (New York: Oxford University Press, 2005); and Margot Canaday, "Building a Straight State: Sexuality and Social Citizenship under the 1944 G.I. Bill," *Journal of American History* 90 (Dec. 2003): 935–57.

2. On higher education's preemptive wartime mobilization, see I. L. Kandel, *The Impact of the War upon American Education* (Chapel Hill: University of North Carolina Press, 1948), 12-40. For an updated account, see Charles M. Dorn, *American Education, Democracy, and the Second World War* (New York: Palgrave Macmillan, 2007).

3. On the psychological profession's embrace of adjustment leading up to World War II, see James H. Capshew, *Psychologists on the March: Science, Practice, and Professional Identity in America, 1929–1969* (New York: Cambridge University Press, 1999), 98–99. On the rise of psychology's policymaking authority, see Ellen Herman, *The Romance of American Psychology: Political Culture in the Age of Experts* (Berkeley: University of California Press, 1995); and Eva S. Moskowitz, *In Therapy We Trust: America's Obsession with Self-Fulfillment* (Baltimore: Johns Hopkins University Press, 2001).

4. On the history of the opinion survey, see Sarah E. Igo, *The Averaged American: Surveys, Citizens, and the Making of a Mass Public* (Cambridge, MA: Harvard University Press, 2007).

5. On the loneliness and banality of military service, see Paul Fussell, *Wartime: Understanding and Behavior in the Second World War* (New York: Oxford University Press, 1989), esp. 72–80.

6. John Kenneth Galbraith, *American Capitalism: The Concept of Countervailing Power* (Boston: Houghton Mifflin, 1956), 63–83, esp. 63; George Q. Flynn, *The Draft, 1940–1973* (Lawrence: University Press of Kansas, 1993), 34; Hadley Cantril, "Present State and Trends of Public Opinion," *New York Times*, 11 May 1941, E3; Leonard War, "America and the Widening War—A Survey of Present Sentiment," *New York Times*, 1 June 1941, E5; Turner Catledge, "Our Eventual Entry in the War Expected at Capital," *New York Times*, 13 July 1941, E3; "Apathy in War Effort Traced to Many Causes," *New York Times*, 24 Aug. 1941, E8; Frank H. Kluckhohn, "Public Morale Viewed as a Defense Problem," *New York Times*, 31 Aug. 1941, E8; Hanson W. Baldwin, "Maneuvers Show Army's Faults and Virtues," *New York Times*, 23 Sept. 1941, E3.

7. On the morale problem, see Herman, *Romance of American Psychology*, 48–81. On the Morale Branch, see Cyril O. Houle et al., *The Armed Services and Adult Education* (Washington, DC: American Council on Education, 1947), 15–19. On George C. Marshall at Virginia Military Institute (VMI) and through World War I, see Mark A. Stoler, *George C. Marshall: Soldier-Statesman of the American Century* (Boston: Twayne, 1989), 15–48.

8. On Marshall at VMI, see William Frye, *Marshall: Citizen Soldier* (New York: Bobbs-Merrill, 1947), 44–64, esp. 61. On his interwar career, see Stoler, *George C. Marshall*, 49–67. On Elihu Root's reforms—namely the Army Reorganization Act (1901), the

Index

General Staff Act (1903), and the Militia Act (1903)—see Stephen Skowronek, *Building a New American State: The Expansion of National Administrative Capacities, 1877–1920* (New York: Cambridge University Press, 1987), 212–47.

9. On the Morale Branch reorganization, see Houle et al., *Armed Services and Adult Education*, 15–19; Brig. Gen. Wade H. Haislip, assistant chief of staff, "Memorandum for the Chief of Staff: Creation of a Separate Branch of Military Morale," 3 March 1941, Historical File of the Research Branch, 1941–1945, box 969, entry 89, Records of the Office of the Secretary of Defense, RG 330, NARA (College Park, MD); and Henry L. Stimson to Adjutant General, "Reorganization of the Morale Division of the Office of the Adjutant General," memo, 8 March 1941, ibid. On Frederick Osborn, see H. I. Brock, "Army's Morale Builder," *New York Times Magazine*, 7 Sept. 1941, 12, 19; and Daniel J. Kevles, *In the Name of Eugenics: Genetics and the Uses of Human Heredity* (Cambridge, MA: Harvard University Press, 1999), 175–76. On the professional training of the Research Branch's personnel, see Peter Buck, "Adjusting to Military Life: The Social Sciences Go to War, 1941–1950," in *Military Enterprise and Technological Change: Perspectives on the American Experience*, ed. Merritt Roe Smith (Cambridge, MA: MIT Press, 1985), 212–16. For the opinion surveys, see Samuel A. Stouffer et al., *The American Soldier: Adjustment during Army Life* (Princeton: Princeton University Press, 1949), 12. The other three volumes of the *Studies in Social Psychology in World War II* series are Samuel A. Stouffer et al., *The American Soldier: Combat and Its Aftermath* (Princeton: Princeton University Press, 1949); Carl Hovland et al., *Experiments in Mass Communication* (Princeton: Princeton University Press, 1949); and Samuel A. Stouffer et al., *Measurement and Prediction* (Princeton: Princeton University Press, 1950).

10. "History of the Army Research Branch to 1 Feb. 1946," n.d., 3, Historical File of the Research Branch, box 970, entry 89, Records of the Office of the Secretary of Defense, NARA. On Stimson's distrust of propaganda, see Allan M. Winkler, *The Politics of Propaganda: The Office of War Information, 1942–45* (New Haven: Yale University Press, 1978), 44–45. On George Creel, see David M. Kennedy, *Over Here: The First World War and American Society* (1980; New York: Oxford University Press, 2004), 74–75.

11. "History of the Army Research Branch to 1 Feb. 1946," 3–11. On the differences between George Gallup's polls and the surveys developed by Rensis Likert and Samuel A. Stouffer, see Jean M. Converse, *Survey Research in the United States: Roots and Emergence, 1890–1960* (Berkeley: University of California Press, 1987), 72–74, 114–27, 154–61, 166–67. On Marshall's crucial support for the activities of the Research Branch, see Stouffer et al., *American Soldier*, vii, 13.

12. *What the Soldier Thinks* 1 (Dec. 1942): 3; "History of the Army Research Branch to 1 Feb. 1946," 11–18.

13. *What the Soldier Thinks* 1 (Dec. 1942): 3, 8–9, 11–13.

14. Ibid., 18–19; Stoffer et al., *American Soldier*, 59–60; *What the Soldier Thinks* 2 (Aug. 1943): 3, 29–31, 34–35. On the relationship between soldiers' education level and psychoneurotic breakdowns, see Norman Q. Brill, "Station and Regional Hospitals," in *Neuropsychiatry in World War II: Zone of Interior*, 2 vols., ed. Robert S. Anderson (Washington, DC: Office of the Surgeon General, Dept. of the Army, 1966), I, 255–95, esp. 270.

15. *What the Soldier Thinks* 2 (Aug. 1943): 28–29; Stouffer et al., *American Soldier*, 70–71

16. Stouffer et al., *American Soldier*, 68–69; *Higher Education: Semimonthly Publication of the Federal Security Agency* 1 (1 March 1945): 3.

17. Stouffer et al., *American Soldier*, 68, 70; *What the Soldier Thinks* 1 (Dec. 1942): 36–39, 44–48.

18. For the Research Branch's professional aspirations, see Buck, "Adjusting to Military Life," 203–52. On soldiers' reading habits, see John Jamieson, "Books and the Soldier," *Public Opinion Quarterly* 9 (autumn 1945): 320–32. *What the Soldier Thinks* 1 (Dec. 1942): 54–55, 58–59, 62–63, 64–65; *What the Soldier Thinks* 2 (Aug. 1943): 74–75; *Prelude to War*, dir. Frank Capra and Anatole Litvak (U.S. War Department, 1942); Stoler, *George C. Marshall*, 25; *What the Soldier Thinks* 2 (Aug. 1943): 88.

19. On the treatment of shell shock during World War I, see Nathan G. Hale, *The Rise and Crisis of Psychoanalysis in the United States: Freud and the Americans, 1917–1985* (New York: Oxford University Press, 1995), 17–19. On the wartime development of educational therapeutics, see, for example, Salomon Gagnon, "Is Reading Therapy?" *Diseases of the Nervous System* 7 (July 1942): 206–12; George S. Stevens, "Education and the Control of Alcoholism," *Diseases of the Nervous System* 8 (Aug. 1942): 238–42; Lewis Barbato, "The State Mental Hospital—An Educational Center," *Diseases of the Nervous System* 9 (Sept. 1945): 269–75; and W. B. Brookover, "Education in the Rehabilitation of Maladjusted Personalities," *Journal of Educational Sociology* 20 (Feb. 1947): 332–40. On the Menninger Clinic study, see Peggy Ralston, "Educational Therapy in a Psychiatric Hospital," *Bulletin of the Menninger Clinic* 4 (March 1940): 41–50; and William C. Menninger, "Experiments with Educational Therapy in a Psychiatric Institution," *Bulletin of the Menninger Clinic* 6 (March 1942): 38, 43, 44. For a history of the clinic, see Lawrence J. Friedman, *Menninger: The Family and the Clinic* (New York: Knopf, 1990). On the changes in American psychiatry wrought by World War II, see Hale, *Rise and Crisis of Psychoanalysis in the United States*, 185–299.

20. Kyle Crichton, "Repairing War-Cracked Minds," *Colliers* (23 Sept. 1943), 22–23, 54; Harry L. Freedman, "The Mental-Hygiene-Unit Approach to Reconditioning Neuropsychiatric Casualties," *Mental Hygiene* 29 (1945): 269–302, esp. 270; Walter E. Barton, "The Reconditioning and Rehabilitating Program in Army Hospitals," *American Journal of Psychiatry* 101 (March 1945): 610; "Hospital Returns 85% to the Front," *New York Times*, 23 July 1944, L6.

21. Benjamin Shephard, *A War of Nerves: Soldiers and Psychiatrists in the Twentieth Century* (Cambridge, MA: Harvard University Press, 2003), 332-34.

22. Stouffer et al., *American Soldier*, 60. On the army's recasting itself as a school, see, for example, Philip Wylie and William W. Muir, *The Army Way: A Thousand Pointers for New Soldiers Collected from Officers and Men of the U.S. Army* (New York: Farrar and Rinehart, 1940), 1–6; War Department, *Army Life* (Washington, DC: U.S. Department of War, 1944), esp. 79–82; and Fussell, *Wartime*, 52–65.

23. Benjamin Fine, "Ignorance of U.S. History Shown by College Freshman," *New York Times*, 4 April 1942, A1; "American History Survey," *New York Times*, 4 April 1942, E10; Allan Nevins, "Why We Should Know Our History," *New York Times Magazine*, 18 April 1943, 18, 25.

24. On the army's specialized training program, see Kandel, *Impact of War upon American Education*, 155–56; and V. R. Cardozier, *Colleges and Universities in World War II* (Westport, CT: Praeger, 1993), 19–51.

25. On the Oct. 1943 reorganization, see Houle et al., *Armed Services and Adult Education*, 23–24; and Jack Edward Pulwers, "The Information and Education Programs

of the Armed Forces: An Administrative and Social History, 1940–1945" (Ph.D. diss., Catholic University of America, 1983), 191–97.

26. Marshall to General Surles, 30 Dec. 1943, in *The Papers of George Catlett Marshall*, 5 vols., ed. Larry I. Bland (Baltimore: Johns Hopkins University Press, 1981), IV, 221–25. On Marshall's bouts with depression, see Stoler, *George C. Marshall*, 28–29, 86–87.

27. On differences between democratic and enemy propaganda, see War Department, *G.I. Roundtable Series: What Is Propaganda?* (Washington, DC: U.S. Department of War, 1944), 1–17. On restraints placed on propagandizing, see Winkler, *Politics of Propaganda*, esp. 38–72; and Brett Gary, *The Nervous Liberals: Propaganda Anxieties from World War I to the Cold War* (New York: Columbia University Press, 1999), esp. 15–54.

28. Charles Hurd, "The Army, After Several Experiments, Finds A Way to Interest and Instruct Soldiers," *New York Times*, 27 Aug. 1944, E9. On the state's decision to use education and propaganda, see Neil Minihan, "History of the Information and Education Division," 1973–1976, 1–3, Frederick Osborn Papers, American Philosophical Society, hereafter APA (Philadelphia, PA).

29. Lewis B. Hershey et al., *Selective Service in Peacetime: First Report of the Director of Selective Service* (Washington, DC: GPO, 1942), 174; Eli Ginzberg, *The Uneducated* (New York: Columbia University Press, 1953), 17; Kandel, *Impact of the War upon American Education*, 41–45; W. F. Russell, "Way Is Pointed To Cut Illiteracy," *New York Times*, 21 June 1942, D5. On the 1940 census and prior incarnations, see Samuel Goldberg, *Army Training of Illiterates in World War II* (New York: Bureau of Publications, Teachers College, Columbia University, 1951), 15n36; and Sanford Winston, *Illiteracy in the United States* (Chapel Hill: University of North Carolina Press, 1930), 9.

30. According to the Chamber of Commerce, New York had 1,020,000 poorly educated, functionally illiterate citizens, while Pennsylvania had 696,000. See Thomas F. Reynolds, "Army Will 'Reclaim' 250,000 Men Rejected for Illiteracy," *Washington Post*, 30 May 1942, 7. On the AGCT, see Nicholas Lemann, *The Big Test: The Secret History of the American Meritocracy* (1999; New York: Farrar, Straus and Giroux , 2000), 53–54; and Terry H. Anderson, *The Pursuit of Fairness: A History of Affirmative Action* (New York: Oxford University Press, 2004), 29–30.

31. Goldberg, *Army Training of Illiterates in World War II*, 150–69; Ginzberg, *Uneducated*, 69–71; Goldberg, *Army Training of Illiterates in World War II*, 194–95; Paul Witty, "What the War Has Taught Us about Adult Education," *Journal of Negro History* 14 (summer 1945): 293–98, esp. 295; "Illiteracy Classes Fail: North Carolina Official Says Rejected Draftees Fail to Attend," *New York Times*, 7 June 1942, 38; *Meet Private Pete: A Soldier's Reader* (Washington, DC: U.S. Armed Forces Institute, 1944); Paul Witty and Samuel Goldberg, "The Use of Visual Aids in Special Training Units in the Army," *Journal of Educational Psychology* 35 (Feb. 1944): 82–90; Paul Witty, "Some Uses of Visual Aids in the Army," *Journal of Educational Sociology* 18 (Dec. 1944): 241–49. For more on the Special Training Units, see Paula S. Fass, *Outside In: Minorities and the Transformation of American Education* (New York: Oxford University Press, 1989), 115–55.

32. Joseph Schiffman, "The Education of Negro Soldiers in World War II," *Journal of Negro Education* 18 (winter 1949): 23; Goldberg, *Army Training of Illiterates in World War II*, 269–73; Ginzberg, *Uneducated*, 133.

33. Houle et al., *Armed Services and Adult Education*, 131; Frederick R. Barkley, "Most 'Shell Shocked' Cases Now Cured at the Front," *New York Times*, 28 Nov. 1943, E6.

34. Houle et al., *Armed Services and Adult Education*, 131–33; *What the Soldier Thinks* 4 (1944): 14–15; John MacCormac, "Our Troops Learn Why They Fight," *New York Times Magazine*, 28 June 1942, 10, 23; "Army Orientation: To Make Men Think about Why They Fight Is Now an Official Army Task," *Fortune* 29 (March 1944), 151–55, 166, 168, 171–72, 174, 176, 178; Frank Keppel, "Study of Information and Education Activities World War II," 6 April 1946, 37–38, folder 1, Osborn Papers APA; Louis E. Keefer, "Little Hunks of Home: The School for Army Morale and Washington and Lee University, 1942–1946," *Virginia Cavalcade* 43 (summer 1993), 24–35.

35. Houle et al., *Armed Services and Adult Education*, 46–59.

36. "Army Orientation," 172; *Guide to the Use of Information Materials* quote in Houle et al., *Armed Services and Adult Education*, 134; MacCormac, "Our Troops Learn Why They Fight," 10.

37. *Guide to the Use of Information Materials* quote in Houle et al., *Armed Services and Adult Education*, 135; MacCormac, "Our Troops Learn Why They Fight," 10; Norvin Nathan, "Army Does Educational Work: Men Are Provided with Instruction in Many Extracurricular Courses," *New York Times*, 6 Nov. 1942, 22.

38. Benjamin Fine, "School By Mail Popular in Army," *New York Times*, 28 Nov. 1943, E7; *Catalog of the Armed Forces Institute: What Would You Like to Learn?* (Washington, DC: GPO, 1944); "Soldiers Learn by Mail," *New York Times Magazine*, 8 Nov. 1942, 34.

39. Glenn L. McConagha, "A Service School Looks at Its Program," *Journal of Higher Education* 19 (Feb. 1948): 91.

40. Houle et al., *Armed Services and Adult Education*, 104–5; U.S. Army, *History of the Army Education Branch: 1 July 1944–31 December 1944*, no. 1 (Washington, DC: GPO, 1944–1945), 8–10.

41. Cpl. Laurence H. Slater to USAFI Registrar, 17 April 1943, exhibit O, "Minutes of the Meeting of the Advisory Committee for the United States Armed Forces Institute," 26–27 June 1943, box 49, entry 16, Records of Joint Army/Navy Boards and Committees, RG 225, NARA; T. F. Smith to USAFI Registrar, 15 April 1942, exhibit P, ibid.; McConagha, "Service School Looks at Its Program," 90. For USAFI enrollment data, see Houle et al., *Armed Services and Adult Education*, 96–97. On soldiers' USAFI academic credit options, see Amy D. Rose, "Preparing for Veterans: Higher Education and the Efforts to Accredit the Learning of World War II Servicemen and Women," *Adult Education Quarterly* 42 (fall 1990): 30–45.

42. Frederick C. Painton and Holman Harvey, "School Was Never Like This," *American Legion Magazine* 37 (Dec. 1944), 37; Houle et al., *Armed Services and Adult Education*, 86; Lt. Col. William R. Young to Col. Francis T. Spaulding, 14 April 1944, box 346, entry 285, Records of the Army Staff, RG 319, NARA. See Kenneth H. Bradt, *Why Service Personnel Fail to Complete USAFI Courses* (Washington, DC: Dept. of Defense, Office of Armed Forces Information and Education, Research Division, 1954).

43. Fine, "School By Mail Popular in Army," E7; Painton and Harvey, "School Was Never like This," 22, 34, 37; Pvt. James McElroy to USAFI Registrar, 20 April 1943, exhibit L, "Minutes of the Meeting of the Advisory Committee for the United States Armed Forces Institute," 26-27 June 1943, box 49, entry 16, Records of Joint Army/Navy Boards and Committees, NARA.

44. "A Preliminary Study of Postwar Education for American Soldiers," 14 Sept. 1943, 1–5, box 346, entry 285, Records of the Army Staff, NARA; Adjutant General to

Commanding Generals, European Theater of Operations and Mediterranean Theater of Operations, "Medical Processing of Liberated American Prisoners of War in Europe," memo (by order of the secretary of war), 6 April 1945, box 315, ibid.

45. Houle et al., *Armed Services and Adult Education*, 121–29; U.S. Signal Corps, "U.S. Army to Open Big British School," *New York Times*, 26 July 1945, 5; Gladwin Hill, "Greatest Education Project in History," *New York Times Magazine*, 29 July 1945, 10–11; War Department, *G.I. Roundtable Series: Shall I Go Back to School?* (Washington, DC: American Council on Education, 1945), 5; Kathleen McLaughlin, "1,500,000 Troops Resume 'School,'" *New York Times*, 2 Aug. 1945, 13.

46. John Dale Russell, "The Army University Centers in the European Theater," *Educational Record* 27 (Jan. 1946): 5–23, esp. 11–18; "Truman Hails Opening," *New York Times*, 2 Aug. 1945, 13. Estimated enrollment figures for the four Army University Centers are available in U.S. Army, *History of the Army Education Program: 1 July 1945–31 December 1945*, no. 3 (Washington, DC: U.S. GPO, 1945–1947), 36–42. On the experiences of European soldiers, see Clarence R. Carpenter, "Evaluations of Biarritz American University," *Journal of Higher Education* 18 (Feb. 1947): 63–70. On American veterans' experiences, see Bill Richardson, "On a GI Campus in England," *New York Times Magazine*, 21 Oct. 1945, 21–23.

47. Walter Crosby Eells, "How Mussolini Provided for a GI University," *Educational Record* 27 (April 1946): 188, 185–86.

48. Ibid., 182–83, 185.

49. Ibid., 185–88. Students at the other Army University Centers likewise enjoyed their experiences; see, for example, J. G. Umstattd, *Instructional Procedures at the College Level: An Analysis of Teaching at Biarritz American University* (Austin: University of Texas Press, 1947), 15–16.

50. Soldier discharge data in Herman, *Romance of American Psychology*, 89; and Shephard, *A War of Nerves*, 330. Polling data in Elaine Tyler May, *Homeward Bound: American Families in the Cold War Era* (New York: Basic Books, 1988), 67; and "Fortune Survey," *Fortune* 31 (Jan. 1945), 260, 263–64, 267. "What Combat Soldiers Think the Biggest Problems Are that Will Be Facing Them after the War," 20 June 1945, 1–3, Attitude Reports of Overseas Personnel, box 1014, entry 94, Records of the Office of the Secretary of Defense, NARA.

51. "What Combat Soldiers Think the Biggest Problems Are that Will Be Facing Them after the War," 1–3.

52. Willard Waller, *The Veteran Comes Back* (New York: Dryden Press, 1944), 100–101; Alanson H. Edgerton, *Readjustment or Revolution?* (New York: McGraw-Hill, 1946), 8; May, *Homeward Bound*, 76.

53. Ervin L. Child, ed., *Psychology for the Returning Serviceman* (Washington, DC: Infantry Journal, 1945), 176–77; Carl Rogers, *Counseling with Returned Servicemen* (New York: McGraw-Hill, 1946), 2.

54. James B. Conant, "Wanted: American Radicals," *Atlantic Monthly* (May 1943), 43–44.

55. "Letter from FDR to Stimson, Dec. 1944," box 219, Records of the Army Chief of Staff, RG 165, NARA.

56. On the demise of the NRPB, see Brinkley, *End of Reform*, 258–64. On the contested history of veterans' employment preferences, see John D. Skrentny, *The Ironies of Affirmative Action: Politics, Culture, and Justice in America* (Chicago: University of Chicago Press, 1996), 37–50. For the complete Osborn Report, see Papers of the Armed

Forces Committee on Postwar Educational Opportunities, 30 July 1943, Official File 5182, FDR Library (Hyde Park, NY). See also, Olson, *G.I. Bill, the Veterans, and the Colleges*, 15–16; and Ross, *Preparing for Ulysses*, 93–98.

57. Scholars disagree as to the origins of the G.I. Bill's education provision. For my argument that it primarily emerged out of the U.S. Army and the White House, see Christopher P. Loss, "'The Most Wonderful Thing Has Happened to Me in the Army': Psychology, Citizenship, and American Higher Education in World War II," *Journal of American History* 92 (Dec. 2005): 864–91. For a similar take that privileges the White House's role, see Suzanne Mettler, "The Creation of the G.I. Bill of Rights of 1944: Melding Social and Participatory Citizenship Ideals," *Journal of Policy History* 17.4 (2005): 345–74. For an interpretation that locates the education provision to the American Legion, see Skocpol, "The G.I. Bill and U.S. Social Policy, Past and Future," 95–115.

58. U.S. Congress, Senate, Committee on Education and Labor, *Hearings on S. 1295 and S. 1509*, 78th Cong., 1st sess., 13 Dec. 1943, 49.

59. Message to Congress on the State of the Union, 11 Jan. 1944, in *Public Papers of Franklin Delano Roosevelt*, vol. 13, 194–45 (New York: Macmillan, 1950), 40–41.

60. On previous veterans' legislation, see Theda Skocpol, *Protecting Soldiers and Mothers: The Political Origins of Social Policy in the United States* (Cambridge, MA: Belknap Press of Harvard University Press, 1992); and Ross, *Preparing for Ulysses*, 6–33. On veterans' utilization of G.I. Bill benefits, see Olson, *G.I. Bill, the Veterans, and the Colleges*, 76; and Ross, *Preparing for Ulysses*, 124.

61. U.S. Congress, Senate, Committee on Education and Labor, *Hearings on S. 1295 and S. 1509*, 78th Cong., 1st sess., 13 Dec. 1943, 40; Thomas D. Snyder, ed., *120 Years of American Education: A Statistical Portrait* (Washington, DC: NCES, 1993), 76–77; Alice M. Rivlin, *The Role of the Federal Government in Financing Higher Education* (Washington, DC: Brookings Institution, 1961), 64–70, esp. 67; and Helen Lefkowitz Horowitz, *Campus Life: Undergraduate Culture from the End of the Eighteenth Century to the Present* (Chicago: University of Chicago Press, 1987), 185.

62. Robert M. Hutchins, "Threat to American Education," *Collier's* 114 (30 Dec. 1944), 20–21.

63. Olson, *G.I. Bill, the Veterans, and the Colleges*, 47–56; and student quote in Horowitz, *Campus Life*, 185. On veterans' academic performance, see, for instance, Benjamin Fine, "Veterans in College Are Found to be Making a Better Record than the Nonveterans," *New York Times*, Sunday, 15 Dec. 1946, E9; and Norman Frederiksen and W.B. Schrader, *Adjustment to College: A Study of 10,000 Veteran and Nonveteran Students in Sixteen American Colleges* (Princeton: Educational Testing Service, 1951). Frederiksen and Schrader's study revealed that veterans' academic performance was slightly better than nonveterans, but not dramatically so.

64. See Tom Brokaw, *The Greatest Generation* (New York: Random House, 1998); and Mettler, *Soldiers to Citizens*, in which her subtitle credits the G.I. Bill with "the making of the Greatest Generation."

65. On the white-male heterosexual favoritism of the G.I. Bill, see, for example, Katznelson, "Public Policy and the Middle-Class Racial Divide after the Second World War," in *Social Contracts Under Stress*, ed. Zunz, Schoppa, and Hiwatari, 170–72; Cohen, *Consumers' Republic*, 137–39; and Canaday, "Building a Straight State," 935–57. For the *Ebony* study and quote, see Onkst, "'First a Negro . . . Incidentally a Veteran,'" 522–23.

66. Black students' share of the nation's total college enrollment jumped from 1.08% to 3.6% between 1940 and 1950; see Bennett, *When Dreams Came True*, 260. On black G.I.s, see Olson, *G.I. Bill, the Veterans, and the Colleges*, 74; and Suzanne Mettler, "'The Only Good Thing Was the G.I. Bill': Effects of the Education and Training Provisions on African-American Veterans' Political Participation," *Studies in American Political Development* 19 (spring 2005): 31–52. Mettler concluded that the G.I. Bill was "relatively inclusive in terms of its reach among African-American veterans" ("Only Good Thing," 49).

67. On home front sacrifices, see Allan Winkler, *Home Front U.S.A.: America during World War II* (Arlington Heights, IL: H. Davidson, 1986). On the same, with an emphasis on the fiscal sacrifices made by civilians during the war, see James T. Sparrow, "'Buying our Boys Back': The Mass Foundations of Fiscal Citizenship in World War II," *Journal of Policy History* 20.2 (2008): 263–86, quote on 281.

68. The G.I. Bill was altered and reauthorized during both the Korean War and the Vietnam War before being replaced in 1976 with the Post Vietnam Era Veterans Assistance Program. Following years of difficult recruiting in the late 1970s, however, Congress enacted the All Volunteer Force Educational Assistance Program—better known as the Montgomery G.I. Bill of 1984. In 2008 Congress enacted the Post 9/11 G.I. Bill. For the changes in veterans' benefits from World War II to the Korean War and Vietnam, see Olson, *G.I. Bill, the Veterans, and the Colleges*, 104–8; and Mark Boulton, "A Price on Freedom: The Problems and Promise of the Vietnam Era G.I. Bills" (Ph.D. diss., University of Tennessee, 2005). On the institutionalization of in-service army education programming after World War II, see Owen G. Birtwistle, Jordine Skoff Von Wantoch, and S. A. Witmer, "Extramural Education and Training of Military Personnel," in *The Changing World of Correspondence Study: International Readings*, ed. Ossian Mackenzie and Edward L. Christensen (University Park: Penn State University Press, 1971), 60–74.

69. Charles E. Wilson et al., *To Secure These Rights: The Report of the President's Committee on Civil Rights* (New York: GPO, 1947), x.

70. Ibid., 21.

71. Ibid., 62–67.

72. George F. Zook et al., *Higher Education for American Democracy: A Report of the President's Commission on Higher Education*, 6 vols. (New York: Harper and Brothers, 1948), I, 1–46; V, 59–63.

73. Estimates as to the actual numbers of severely mental disturbed veterans ranged widely. This figure was derived using Veterans Administration pensioner data, which meant that it only captured those veterans enrolled in the program. See Shephard, *A War of Nerves*, 330.

74. Quote in Herman, *Romance of American Psychology*, 118–19. On the psychiatric profession's postwar optimism, see Gerald N. Grob, *The Mad among Us: A History of the Care of America's Mentally Ill* (New York: Free Press, 1994), 191–92.

75. On the NMHA and the NIMH, see Moskowitz, *In Therapy We Trust*, 153–56; quote on 153; Gerald N. Grob, *From Asylum to Community: Mental Health Policy in Modern America* (Princeton: Princeton University Press, 1991), 23–43; and Grob, *The Mad among Us*, 210–11.

76. Aaron L. Friedberg, *In the Shadow of the Garrison State: America's Anti-statism and Its Cold War Grand Strategy* (Princeton: Princeton University Press, 2000), 182. On the cold war draft and deferment policies of the Selective Service Administration, see ibid., 149–98; and Flynn, *Draft*, 88–165.

CHAPTER 5

EDUCATING GLOBAL CITIZENS IN THE COLD WAR

1. Arthur M. Schlesinger, Jr., *The Vital Center: The Politics of Freedom* (1949; New York: Houghton Mifflin, 1988), 1–10.

2. Harold D. Lasswell, "The Garrison State," *American Journal of Sociology* 46 (Jan. 1941): 455–68; Benjamin L. Alpers, *Dictators, Democracy, and American Public Culture* (Chapel Hill: University of North Carolina Press, 2003), 250–302.

3. Sidney Hook, "The Job of the Teacher in Days of Crisis," *New York Times*, 14 Dec.1952, SM9.

4. On higher education's postwar prestige, see Howard Brick, *Age of Contradiction: American Thought and Culture in the 1960s* (New York: Twayne, 1998).

5. Gilbert Bailey, "Picture of a Postwar Campus," *New York Times*, 21 Dec. 1947, MS36.

6. Helen Lefkowitz Horowitz, *Campus Life: Undergraduate Cultures from the End of the Eighteenth Century to the Present* (1987; Chicago: University of Chicago Press, 1988), 132–43.

7. Bailey, "Picture of a Postwar Campus," MS36.

8. Jonathan R. Cole, *The Great American University: Its Rise to Preeminence, Its Indispensable National Role, Why It Must Be Protected* (New York: Perseus, 2009), 77–85.

9. Thomas D. Snyder, ed., *120 Years of American Education: A Statistical Portrait* (Washington, DC: NCES, 1993), 78.

10. UNESCO, *The Bulletin of the Commission for International Educational Reconstruction* 1 (April–May 1947), 2, 3, 5; UNESCO, *The Bulletin of the Commission for International Educational Reconstruction* 2 (29 Feb. 1948), 3–4.

11. Harold E. Snyder, "The Reconstruction of Higher Education in the War-Devastated Countries," *Association of American Colleges Bulletin* 33 (March 1947): 157–58, 166.

12. UNESCO Constitution, Ratified 16 Nov. 1945, available at http://www.icomos .org/unesco/unesco_constitution.html (accessed 26 May 2010).

13. Paul S. Boyer, *By the Bombs Early Light: American Thought and Culture at the Dawn of the Atomic Age* (New York: Pantheon, 1985), 37–38.

14. Benjamin Fine, "Support of UNESCO Is Urged by Benton," *New York Times*, 4 April 1946, 7; "House Votes for UNESCO," *New York Times*, 24 May 1946, 11. Budget data in Waldo Gifford Leland, *UNESCO and the Defenses of Peace* (Stanford: Stanford University Press, 1947), 12–14, 29–32.

15. Walter H.C. Laves and Charles A. Thomson, *UNESCO: Purposes, Progress, Prospects* (1957; New York: Kraus, 1968), 333–36.

16. On the status of the Fulbright Act and the Educational Exchange Act as the centerpiece of the state's postwar educational foreign policy, see State Department, *United States Information Agency: 1953–1983* (Washington, DC: GPO, 1983), 1.

17. Haynes Johnson and Bernard M. Gwertzman, *Fulbright: The Dissenter* (New York: Doubleday, 1969), 12–39.

18. Ibid., 27. Fulbright's tenure as president was short. He was forced out of office in the spring of 1941 by the governor-appointed board of trustees; see ibid., 47–50.

19. Ibid., 69; J. William Fulbright, "The Peace We Want—A Continuing Peace," *New York Times Magazine*, 22 July 1945, 75.

20. U.S. House, Committee on Foreign Affairs, *A Special Report on American Studies Abroad: Progress and Difficulties in Selected Countries (pursuant to PL 87-256)*, H.doc. 138, 88th Cong., 1st sess., 11 July 1963, 3, 33–34.

21. On the IIE's parastatal role, see Margaret P. O'Mara, "The Uses of the Foreign Student" (unpublished ms. in author's possession, 2010), 6–7.

22. Frank Ninkovich, *The Diplomacy of Ideas: U.S. Foreign Policy and Cultural Relations, 1938–1950* (New York: Cambridge University Press, 1981), 140; Paul S. Bodenman, "Educational Cooperation With Foreign Countries," *Higher Education* 9 (1 March 1953): 146–47. For participation levels, see Walter Johnson and Francis J. Colligan, *The Fulbright Program: A History* (Chicago: University of Chicago Press, 1965), 345.

23. Benjamin Fine, "Student-Exchange Program under Fulbright Law Will Give Government Aid to Scholars," *New York Times*, 12 Oct. 1947, E5, Benjamin Fine, "Global Campus," *New York Times Magazine*, 5 Oct. 1947, 24, 26.

24. Michael David-Fox, *Revolution of the Mind: Higher Learning among the Bolsheviks, 1918–1929* (Ithaca: Cornell University Press, 1997), esp. 24–82; John Connelly, *Captive University: The Sovietization of East German, Czech, and Polish Higher Education, 1945–1956* (Chapel Hill: University of North Carolina Press, 2000); Christopher P. Loss, "Party School: Education, Political Ideology, and the Cold War," *Journal of Policy History* 16.1 (2004): 99–116.

25. Allan M. Winkler, *The Politics of Propaganda: The Office of War Information, 1942–1945* (New Haven: Yale University Press, 1978); John MacCormac, "Russia Intensifies Campaign For Sovietizing of Satellites," *New York Times*, 24 Oct. 1949, 1.

26. U.S. Congress, Senate, Committee on Foreign Relations, *Overseas Information Programs of the United States*, 83rd Cong., 1st sess., 15 June 1953, 111–20, 129–30, 139.

27. Nicholas J. Cull, *The Cold War and the United States Information Agency: American Propaganda and Public Diplomacy, 1945–1989* (New York: Cambridge University Press, 2008).

28. Kenneth Osgood, *Total Cold War: Eisenhower's Secret Propaganda Battle at Home and Abroad* (Lawrence: University Press of Kansas, 2006), 15–46.

29. C. P. Trussell, "U.S. Truth Barrage Urged For Europe," *New York Times*, 31 Jan. 1948, 7.

30. "Europe's Collapse Called Complete," *New York Times*, 1 Nov. 1947, 7.

31. U.S. Congress, Senate, Joint Committee on Foreign Relations, *The United States Information Service in Europe*, 80th Cong., 2nd sess., 30 Jan. 1948, 1–6.

32. "Congressmen Pay Call upon Franco," *New York Times*, 9 Oct. 1947, 4.

33. Scott N. Heidepriem, *A Fair Chance for a Free People: Biography of Karl E. Mundt, United States Senator* (Madison, SD: Leader Print Co., 1988), 38–54.

34. Ibid., 43–48.

35. Ibid., 10–17.

36. Sydney Gruson, "U.S. Survey Group Ends Polish Study," *New York Times*, 23 Sept. 1947, 12.

37. On the legislative history of the Smith-Mundt Act, see Heidepriem, *A Fair Chance for a Free People*, 75–79; Ninkovich, *Diplomacy of Ideas*, 128–34; and Johnson and Colligan, *Fulbright Program*, 28–31. For the final legislation, see *Information and Educational Exchange Act of 1958*, P.L. 402, 80th Cong., 2nd sess., 27 Jan. 1948, 62 sta. 6.

38. U.S. Congress, House, Committee on Foreign Affairs, *Hearings on the International Technical Cooperation Act of 1949 (Point IV Program)*, 81st Cong., 1st sess., 27 Sept. 1949, 5.

39. On modernization efforts and its consequences, see, for example, David C. Engerman, Michael E. Latham, Mark H. Haefele, and Nils Gilman, ed., *Staging Growth: Modernization, Development, and the Global Cold War* (Amherst: University of Massachusetts Press, 2003); and Michael E. Latham, *Modernization as Ideology: American Social Science and "Nation Building" in the Kennedy Era* (Chapel Hill: University of North Carolina Press, 2000).

40. Lester Markel, "Opinion—A Neglected Instrument," in *Public Opinion and Foreign Policy*, ed. Lester Markel (New York: Council of Foreign Relations, 1949), 45.

41. On the spread of opinion polling, see Jean M. Converse, *Survey Research in the United States: Roots and Emergence* (Berkeley: University of California Press, 1987), 239–66; and Sarah E. Igo, *The Averaged American: Surveys, Citizens, and the Making of a Mass Public* (Cambridge, MA: Harvard University Press, 2007), 103–49.

42. Donald Fleming, "Attitude: The History of a Concept," in *Perspectives in American History*, ed. Donald Fleming and Bernard Bailyn (Cambridge, MA: Charles Warren Center for Studies in American History, Harvard University, 1967), 287–365.

43. Paul Kecskemeti, "Totalitarian Communications as a Means of Control," *Public Opinion Quarterly* 14 (summer 1950): 224–34.

44. Alex Inkeles, *Public Opinion in Soviet Russia: A Study in Mass Persuasion* (1950; Cambridge, MA: Harvard University Press, 1958), 6. On the development of this view of Soviet society, see David C. Engerman, *Know Your Enemy: The Rise and Fall of America's Soviet Experts* (New York: Oxford University Press, 2009), 182–87.

45. James Madison, "The Federalist No. 10: The Utility of the Union as a Safeguard Against Domestic Faction and Insurrection," 1787, available at http://www.constitution.org/fed/federa10.htm (accessed 15 March 2009).

46. Arthur F. Bentley, *The Process of Government: A Study of Social Pressures* (Chicago: University of Chicago Press, 1908), 447. On Bentley's background and professional life, see Dorothy Ross, *The Origins of American Social Science* (New York: Cambridge University Press, 1991), 308–12, 330–38; and Frank R. Baumgartner and Beth L. Leech, *Basic Interests: The Importance of Groups in Politics and in Political Science* (Princeton: Princeton University Press, 1998), 44–63.

47. David B. Truman, *The Governmental Process: Political Interests and Public Opinion* (1951; Berkeley: University of California Press, 1993).

48. E. E. Schattschneider, *The Semisovereign People: A Realist's View of Democracy in America* (New York: Holt, Rinehart and Winston, 1960); Theodore Lowi, *The End of Liberalism: Ideology, Policy, and the Crisis of Public Authority* (New York: W. W. Norton, 1969).

49. Edgar Lane, "Interest Groups and Bureaucracy," *Annals of the American Academy of Political and Social Science* 292 (March 1954): 109.

50. Gabriel A. Almond, "Public Opinion and National Security Policy," *Public Opinion Quarterly* 20 (summer 1956): 371–78.

51. Martin Kriesberg, "Dark Areas of Ignorance," in *Public Opinion and Foreign Policy*, ed. Markel, 49–64.

52. Ralph O. Nafziger, Warren C. Engstrom, and Malcolm S. Maclean, Jr., "The Mass Media and an Informed Public," *Public Opinion Quarterly* 15 (spring 1951): 105–8.

53. Angus Campbell et al., *The American Voter* (New York: Wiley, 1960), 475–81; V. O. Key Jr., *Public Opinion and American Democracy* (New York: Knopf, 1961), 315–43.

54. Lester Markel, "The Great Need—An Informed Opinion," *New York Times*, 9 April 1950, SM3.

55. Morris Rosenberg, "Some Determinants of Political Apathy," *Public Opinion Quarterly* 18 (winter 1954–55): 349–66, esp. 362.

56. Gabriel A. Almond, *The American People and Foreign Policy* (1950; Westport, CT: Greenwood Press, 1977), 53.

57. *Public Papers of the Presidents: Harry S. Truman* (1952–53), 579; Citizenship Committee of the National Education Association, *Seventh National Conference on Citizenship* (Washington, DC: National Education Association, 1952).

58. Ron Robin, *The Making of the Cold War Enemy: Culture and Politics in the Military-Intellectual Complex* (Princeton: Princeton University Press, 2001), 167–71; Catherine Lutz, "Epistemology of the Bunker: The Brainwashed and Other New Subjects of Permanent War," in *Inventing the Psychological: Toward a History of Emotional Life in America*, ed. Joel Pfister and Nancy Schnog (New Haven: Yale University Press, 1997), 245–67.

59. Malvina Lindsay, "When Men Return from Prison Camps," *Washington Post*, 12 Aug. 1953, 10.

60. Joost A.M. Meerloo, "Pavlov's Dog and Communist Brainwashing," *New York Times Magazine*, 9 May 1954, 3, 30–33; Joost A.M. Meerloo, *The Rape of the Mind: The Psychology of Thought Control, Menticide, and Brainwashing* (New York: Grosset and Dunlap, 1956).

61. "Why Did Many GI Captives Cave In?" *U.S. News and World Report*, 24 Feb. 1956, 56, 61; Edith Evans Asbury, "Airmen Unmoved By Reds' Teaching," *New York Times*, 30 Aug. 1957, 8.

62. Virginia Pasley, *21 Stayed: The Story of the American GI's Who Chose Communist China —Who They Were and Why They Stayed* (New York: Farrar, Straus and Cudahy, 1955), 245–48.

63. Gunnar Myrdal, *An American Dilemma: The Negro Problem and Modern Democracy*, 2 vols. (New York: Harper and Row, 1944).

64. "Ten Christmas Lists of Ten 'Best,'" *New York Times*, 3 Dec. 1944, BR4.

65. Myrdal, *An American Dilemma*, I, 40.

66. Ibid., I, 49.

67. Ibid., II, 882; Walter A. Jackson, *Gunnar Myrdal and America's Conscience: Social Engineering and Racial Liberalism, 1938–1987* (Chapel Hill: University of North Carolina Press, 1990).

68. On the "American Creed," see Myrdal, *An American Dilemma*, I, ch. 1, "American Ideals and the American Conscience," 3–25.

69. Ibid., II, 907.

70. Gordon W. Allport, *The Nature of Prejudice* (Cambridge, MA: Addison-Wesley, 1954).

71. Gordon W. Allport, *The Resolution of Intergroup Tensions: A Critical Appraisal of Methods* (New York: National Conference of Christians and Jews, 1952), 6–7.

72. Max Beloff, "The Real Purpose of the University," *New York Times Magazine*, 26 Sept. 1948, 15.

73. Paul H. Buck et al., *General Education in a Free Society: Report of the Harvard Committee* (Cambridge, MA: Harvard University Press, 1945); George F. Zook et al., *Higher Education for American Democracy: A Report of the President's Commission on Higher Education*, 6 vols. (New York: Harper and Bros., 1948).

74. Benjamin Fine, "Many New Courses in International Affairs Are Offered to Meet Student Demand," *New York Times*, 22 July 1945, E7.

75. F. K. Schaefer, "Area Study and General Education," *School Review* 53 (Feb. 1945): 90–97.

76. David L. Szanton, "The Origin, Nature, and Challenges of Area Studies in the United States," in *The Politics of Knowledge: Area Studies and the Disciplines*, ed. David L. Szanton (Berkeley: University of California Press, 2004), 1–33; Robert A. McCaughey, *International Studies and Academic Enterprise: A Chapter in the Enclosure of American Learning* (New York: Columbia University Press, 1984); Christopher Simpson, ed., *Universities and Empire: Money and Politics in the Social Sciences during the Cold War* (New York: New Press, 1998).

77. Philip E. Mosely, "The Russian Institute of Columbia University," *Proceedings of the American Philosophical Society* 99 (Jan. 1955): 36–38.

78. Gilbert Allardyce, "The Rise and Fall of the Western Civilization Course," *American Historical Review* 87 (June 1982): 695–725; Peter Novick, *That Noble Dream: The "Objectivity Question" and the American Historical Profession* (New York: Cambridge University Press, 1988), 311–14; Louis Menand, *The Marketplace of Ideas: Reform and Resistance in the American University* (New York: W. W. Norton, 2010), 32–34.

79. Richard N. Swift, *World Affairs and the College Curriculum* (Washington, DC: American Council on Education, 1959), 169.

80. Benjamin Fine, "Courses in International Affairs Emphasized In Teachers Colleges of Nation," *New York Times*, 25 May 1947, E9.

81. "St. John's Soviet Course," *New York Times*, 17 June 1951, E7.

82. Fine, "Courses in International Affairs Emphasized in Teachers Colleges of Nation," E9.

83. I. L. Kandel, *The Impact of the War upon American Education* (Chapel Hill: University of North Carolina Press, 1948), 232–34; Ludwig Kahn, "Foreign Languages in the College Curriculum," *Journal of Higher Education* 18 (Feb. 1947): 77–80.

84. Erwin Knoll, "Now They Learn Languages by Practicing on Recorders," *Washington Post and Times Herald*, 13 Oct. 1958, B1.

85. Jacob Greenberg, "The Civilization and Cultural Emphasis in Modern Language Teaching at High School and College Level," *Journal of Educational Sociology* 31 (Jan. 1958): 156.

86. Swift, *World Affairs and the College Curriculum*, 62–63; James I. Brown, "Freshman English and General Education," *Journal of Higher Education* 21 (Jan. 1950): 17–20, 54; Frederick Rudolph, *Curriculum: A History of the American Undergraduate Course of Study since 1636* (San Francisco: Jossey-Bass, 1977), 264–65.

87. Francis H. Horn, "Art and General Education," *Art Education* 7 (Dec. 1954): 7; David Firman, "Geography in General Education," *Journal of Higher Education* 23 (March 1952): 137–38; G. Norman Eddy, "Religion in a General-Education Program," *Journal of Higher Education* 27 (Jan. 1956): 25–34, 56.

88. Allardyce, "The Rise and Fall of the Western Civilization Course."

89. *USNSA Handbook* (Washington, DC: USNSA,1966), 9–10; Eugene G. Schwartz, ed., *American Students Organize: Founding the National Student Association after World War II* (Washington, DC: American Council on Education/Praeger, 2006), viii–ix.

90. "National Organization of College Students Planned at Conclave," *Evening Star*, 29 Aug. 1947, President's Personal File 3394, box 570, Truman Library (Independence, MO).

91. Howard E. Wilson, *American College Life as Education in World Outlook* (Washington, DC: American Council on Education, 1956), 174–76; Martin M. McLaughlin, "National Student Association," *Journal of Higher Education* 22 (May 1951): 261.

92. Karen J. Winkler, "The Central Intelligence Agency Has Long-developed Clandestine Relationships with the American Academic Community," *Chronicle of Higher Education*, 3 May 1976, 1, 7; Doug Rossinow, *Visions of Progress: The Left-Liberal Tradition in America* (Philadelphia: University of Pennsylvania Press, 2008), 202.

93. USNSA "Fact Sheet," n.d., 3, President Personal File 3394, box 570, Truman Library.

94. "Race Issue Solved by Student Group," *New York Times*, 6 Sept. 1947, 10.

95. "McCarthyism Scored as Campus Menace," *New York Times*, 21 Aug. 1951, 21; "To Mark Academic Freedom," *New York Times*, 25 Feb. 1953, 23.

96. Eliot Friedson, ed., *Student Government, Student Leaders, and the American College* (Philadelphia: U.SNSA, 1955).

97. Harry H. Lunn, "A Student Point of View," in ibid., 80–88; Harry H. Lunn, *The Student's Role in College Policy-Making* (Washington, DC: American Council on Education, 1957), 17–19.

98. Wilson, *American College Life as Education in World Outlook*, 117–18.

99. Ibid., 117.

100. Ibid., 119–20.

101. The survey was sent to 655 universities; see, ibid., 120–22.

102. Ellen W. Schrecker, *No Ivory Tower: McCarthyism and the Universities* (New York: Oxford University Press, 1986); Lionel S. Lewis, *Cold War on Campus: A Study of the Politics of Organizational Control* (New Brunswick, NJ: Transaction Books, 1988).

103. Ellen Schrecker, *Many Are the Crimes: McCarthyism in America* (Boston: Little, Brown, 1998), 3.

104. Paul A. Kramer, "Is the World Our Campus? International Students and U.S. Global Power in the Long Twentieth Century," *Diplomatic History* 33 (Nov. 2009): 776.

105. Institute of International Education, *Open Doors 1960: Report on International Exchange* (New York: Institute of International Education, 1960), 6.

106. Diana Galloway, "News and Notes from the Field of Travel," *New York Times*, 21 May 1950, X15; "Students Charter Norwegian Craft," *New York Times*, 9 June 1950, 49; "Student Special Arrives," *New York Times*, 21 June 1950, 55; "New Faces in Port," *New York Times*, 25 June 1950, 96; Erskine B. Childers, "Letters to The Times," *New York Times*, 30 June 1950, 20; Wilson, *American College Life as Education in World Outlook*, 150.

107. Walter H.C. Laves, "Statement Regarding Appropriations for the International Educational Exchange Activities of the Department of State for the Fiscal Year 1958," 9 May 1957, 1–2, folder 18, U.S. Congressional Testimony, box 13/96, American Council on Education Papers, Hoover Institution (Stanford, CA).

108. Ibid., 4.

109. Ibid., 5.

110. John T. Gullahorn and Jeanne E. Gullahorn, "American Objectives in Study Abroad," *Journal of Higher Education* 29 (Oct. 1958): 369–70.

111. Ibid., 370–74.

112. Ibid.

113. Bernard D. Pechter, "Me—Before and After Europe," *Student Government Bulletin* (April 1955): 8–11, publications folder, box 63, Hoover Institution.

114. Mary Anne Sigmund, "Holiday in Europe," *Student Government Bulletin* (Jan. 1955): 19–24, ibid.

115. For the Institute of International Education study, see Gullahorn and Gullahorn, "America Objectives in Study Abroad," 369.

116. Norman Kiell, "Attitudes of Foreign Students," *Journal of Higher Education* 22 (April 1951): 188–94, 225. On foreign students' overall satisfaction with their American educational experience, see Edward Charnwood Cieslak, *The Foreign Student in American Colleges: A Survey and Evaluation of Administrative Problems and Practices* (Detroit: Wayne State University Press, 1955), 144–52.

117. Kiell, "Attitudes of Foreign Students," 188–94.

118. J. Irving E. Scott and Helen Ruth Scott, "Foreign Students in Negro Colleges and Universities in the United States of America 1951–1952," *Journal of Negro Education* 22 (autumn 1953): 489.

119. Jason C. Parker, "Made-in-America Revolutions? The 'Black University' and the American Role in the Decolonization of the Black Atlantic," *Journal of American History* 96 (Dec. 2009): 727–50; Claybourne Carson, *In Struggle: SNCC and the Black Awakening of the 1960s* (1981; Cambridge, MA: Harvard University Press, 1995), 16–17.

120. Scott and Scott, "Foreign Students in Negro Colleges and Universities in the United States of America," quote on 491. On the negative international perception of race relations in the United States, and its influence on civil rights, see Mary L. Dudziak, *Cold War Civil Rights: Race and the Image of American Democracy* (Princeton: Princeton University Press, 2000).

121. J. R. Morton, "University Extension in the United States," *Adult Education* 4 (Sept. 1954): 207–14; Leonard Buder, "Growing Demand for Adult Courses," *New York Times*, 20 March 1949, E11.

122. Bernard J. James and Charles A. Wedemeyer, "Completion of University Correspondence Courses by Adults: The Effects of Goal-Clarity and Other Factors," *Journal of Higher Education* 30 (Feb. 1959): 87–93.

123. Snyder, ed., *120 Years of American Education*, 80.

124. On Hoffman and his team, see McCaughey, *International Studies and Academic Enterprise*, 140–50.

125. H. Rowan Gaither et al., *Report of the Study for the Ford Foundation on Policy and Program* (Detroit: Ford Foundation, 1949), 44, 46, 39; and for the psychosocial aspects of the study, see "Program Area Five: Individual Behavior and Human Relations," 90–97.

126. C. Scott Fletcher, Biographical Information, 22 June 1982, 1–12, quote on 11, box 1, Papers of C. Scott Fletcher, National Public Broadcasting Archives, hereafter NPBA (University of Maryland Library, College Park, MD); Laurie Ouellette, *View-*

ers Like You? How Public TV Failed the People (New York: Columbia University Press, 2002), 44.

127. Funding data in John W. Macy, Jr., *To Irrigate a Wasteland: The Struggle to Shape a Public Television System in the United States* (Berkeley: University of California Press, 1974), 18.

128. C. Scott Fletcher, "The Next Ten Years," Presented at A Conference on Workers' Education, University Park, PA, 20–23 March 1955, 2–3, folder 2, box 4, Papers of C. Scott Fletcher, NPBA.

129. C. Scott Fletcher, "Continuing Education for National Survival," *Annals of the American Academy of Political and Social Science: American Civilization and its Leadership Needs, 1960–2000* 324 (Sept. 1959): 111.

130. Fletcher, "The Next Ten Years," 118.

131. C. Scott Fletcher et al., *A Ten Year Report of the Fund for Adult Education: 1951–1961* (New York: Ford Foundation: FAE, 1961).

132. Ibid.; Benjamin Fine, "Film Discussion Groups Are Carrying Out A Novel Experiment in Adult Education," *New York Times*, 30 March 1952, E11.

133. Fletcher, *Ten Year Report*; Benjamin Fine, "Progress Report on Ford-Sponsored Plan for Liberal Training of Adults in Test Cities," *New York Times*, 18 July 1954, E9.

134. On the FAE's understanding of this point, see *Ford Foundation Activities in Noncommercial Broadcasting, 1951–1976* (New York: Ford Foundation, 1976), 4.

135. George H. Gibson, *Public Broadcasting: The Role of the Federal Government, 1912–76* (New York: Praeger, 1977), 45–59; Glenda R. Balas, *Recovering a Public Vision for Public Television* (New York: Rowman and Littlefield, 2003), 39–92.

136. Susan L. Brinson, *Personal and Public Interests: Freida B. Hennock and the Federal Communications Commission* (Westport, CT: Praeger, 2002), 43–59; Murray Illson, "Series of Televised Home-Study Classes will be Sponsored by University of Michigan," *New York Times*, 20 Aug. 1950, 125.

137. John A. Behnke, "Television Takes Education to the People," *Science* 118 (9 Oct. 1953), 3.

138. Mildred Murphy, "TV Class Opens and a Book Sells," *New York Times*, 24 Sept. 1957, 37.

139. Jack Gould, "T.V.: College in Pajamas," *New York Times*, 24 Sept. 1957, 71.

140. John T. Shanley, "Newton's Law at Dawn," *New York Times*, 2 Nov. 1958, X15.

141. John J. Scanlon, "The Expanding Role of Television in American Education," *Journal of Educational Sociology* 32 (May 1959): 417.

142. Brinson, *Personal and Public Interests*, 40–41, 118–19; John Crosby, "Are We Letting Television Go To—?" *McCall's* (Oct. 1950), 49.

143. Dororthy Brandon, "Miss Hennock Hails Video as Educator," *Washington Post*, 19 May 1950, B11.

144. Brinson, *Personal and Public Interests*, 131–32; Ralph Steetle, "The Changing Status of Educational Television," *Journal of Educational Sociology* 32 (May 1959): 427–33.

145. "Sworn Statement of Miami University," FCC Hearing, 25 July 1951, 1, Educational TV—Sworn Statements, file 1-100, box 14, Freida B. Hennock Papers, Truman Library; J.D. Blackford quote included therein, ibid., 4; "Sworn Statement of Southern Illinois University," FCC Hearing, Sept. 1, 1951, 4, Educational TV—Sworn Statements, file 1-100, box 14, ibid. On the testimony, see also Gibson, *Public Broadcasting*, 74–75.

146. William A. Harper, "The Educational Television and Radio Center," *Quarterly of Film, Radio, and Television* 11 (winter 1956): 197–203, quotes on 198–99.

147. By 1966, 38 of 118 ETV stations were run by colleges or universities. James R. Killian, Jr. et al, *Public Television: A Program for Action* (New York: Bantam Books, 1967), 105–12.

148. Robert L. Hilliard, "The Organization and Control of Educational Television," *Peabody Journal of Education* 40 (Nov. 1962): 170–81.

149. Allan S. Williams, "Television in Education: Possibilities and Obstacles," *School Review* 64 (April1956): 187–90; Charles Side Steinberg, "Educational Television: An Interim Appraisal," *Journal of Educational Sociology* 29 (Oct. 1959): 49–61.

150. "Thanks to TV: Big College Class May Be Going Out," *Houston Post*, 8 June 1953, 9, Publications File, box 23, Freida Hennock Papers, Truman Library; "KUHT Dedication To Inaugurate New Era in Education," *Houston Post*, 9 June 1953, n.p., ibid.

151. Ralph Steetle, "TV Programming — Education's New Frontier," Presented to the Western Radio and TV Conference, San Francisco, CA, 19 Feb. 1954, 6, Speech/Articles, ED TV 1955–56, file 2, box 3, Papers of Ralph W. Steetle, NPBA.

152. On students' dissatisfaction, see Earl G. Herminghaus, "Large-Group Instruction by Television: An Experiment," *School Review* 65 (summer 1957): 119–33; "College TV Class is Found Lacking," *New York Times*, 26 June 1959, 27.

153. Harvey Zorbaugh, "Television—Technological Revolution in Education," *Journal of Educational Sociology* 31 (May 1958): 343.

154. Ratings information on ETV is elusive. The only valid early study was by Wilbur Schramm et al., *The People Look at Educational Television* (Stanford: Stanford University Press, 1963). It revealed a small core audience of middle- and upper-middle-class viewers in the nine ETV markets examined. "Regular viewers," estimated at 10–25 percent of the possible viewing public, watched ETV programming between 1 and 2 hours per week, according to the Schramm study (46–58). On the lack of sound ratings information for ETV, which was due to the lack of funding, see Alan G. Stavitsky, "Counting the House in Public Television: A History of Ratings Use, 1953–1980," *Journal of Broadcasting* and *Electronic Media* 42 (fall 1998): 520–34.

155. P.L. 90129 (81 Stat. 365).

156. Fletcher was not on the commission but helped create it. See Killian et al, *Public Television*.

157. *Public Papers of the Presidents: Lyndon B. Johnson*, 2 vols. (1967), II, entry 474, 995–98, Remarks upon Signing the Public Broadcasting Act of 1967 (Washington, DC: GPO, 1968).

158. Ouellette, *Viewers Like You*?; C. Scott Fletcher, Biographical Information, 22 June 1982, 7, box 1, Papers of C. Scott Fletcher, NPBA.

159. National Defense Education Act of 1958 (NDEA), Pub. L. No. 85–864, 72 Stat. 1580.

160. Gareth Davies, *See Government Grow: Education Politics from Johnson to Reagan* (Lawrence: University Press of Kansas, 2007), 15.

161. For special attention to Elliot and Hill and the NDEA, see Wayne J. Urban, *More Than Science and Sputnik: The National Defense Education Act of 1958* (Tuscaloosa: University of Alabama Press, 2010), 10–72. For the standard political history of the NDEA, see Barbara Barksdale Clowse, *Brainpower for the Cold War: The Sputnik Crisis and National Defense Education Act of 1958* (Westport, CT: Greenwood

Press, 1981). On the relationship between the NDEA and ESEA, see Davies, *See Government Grow.*

162. Clowse, *Brainpower for the Cold War*, 122.

163. National Defense Education Act of 1958 (NDEA), Pub. L. No. 85–864, 72 Stat. 1580.

164. Clowse, *Brainpower for the Cold War*, 79.

165. Davies, *See Government Grow*, 13–17; Arthur S. Flemming, "The Philosophy and Objectives of the National Defense Education Act," *Annals of the American Academy of Political and Social Science* 327 (Jan. 1960): 132–38; Janet C. Kerr, "From Truman to Johnson: Ad Hoc Policy Formulation in Higher Education," *Review of Higher Education* 8 (fall 1984): 15–54.

166. James L. Sundquist, *Politics and Policy: The Eisenhower, Kennedy, and Johnson Years* (Washington, DC: Brookings Institution, 1968), 173–80.

167. Urban, *More Than Science and Sputnik*, 184–89.

168. Ibid., 173.

169. Adam C. Powell, *Adam by Adam: The Autobiography of Adam Clayton Powell Jr.* (1971; New York: Kensington, 1994), 199–205; Julian E. Zelizer, *On Capitol Hill: The Struggle to Reform Congress and its Consequences* (New York: Cambridge University Press, 2004), 77–83.

170. Urban, *More Than Science and Sputnik*, 200; Harold Howe, "Welcoming Remarks (10 Sept. 1968)," Office Files of the Commissioner of Education, 1939-1980, entry A1 122, box 344, Records of the Office of Education, RG 12, NARA (College Park, MD).

171. Ibid., 178.

172. U.S. House, Committee on Education and Labor, *Hearings on H.R. 6774, H.R. 4253, H.R. 7378 and Related Bills to Extend and Improve the National Defense Education Act*, 87th Cong., 1st sess., 1 June 1961, 20–23.

173. Urban, *More Than Science and Sputnik*, 183.

174. Committee on Education and Labor, *Hearings on H.R. 6774*, 22–23.

175. Campbell et al., *American Voter*, 542–44.

Chapter 6
Higher Education Confronts the Rights Revolution

1. John Aubrey Douglass, *The California Idea and American Higher Education, 1850 to the 1960 Master Plan* (Stanford: Stanford University Press, 2000); Nicholas Lemann, *The Big Test: The Secret History of the American Meritocracy* (1999; New York: Farrar, Straus and Giroux, 2000), 125–39.

2. Clark Kerr, *The Uses of the University* (Cambridge: Harvard University Press, 1963), vi.

3. Paddy Riley, "Clark Kerr: From the Industrial to the Knowledge Economy," in *American Capitalism: Social Thought and Political Economy in the American Twentieth Century*, ed. Nelson Lichtenstein (Philadelphia: University of Pennsylvania Press, 2006), 71–87.

4. Ibid., v, 41–45.

5. Mario Savio, "Sproul Hall Steps," 2 Dec. 1964, available at http://www.lib.berkeley.edu/MRC/saviotranscript.html (accessed 13 May 2010).

6. "Port Huron Statement," in James Miller, *Democracy Is in the Streets: From Port Huron to the Siege of Chicago* (New York: Simon and Schuster, 1987), 333–35.

7. "Lyndon B. Johnson, 1908–1973: 'Education President,'" *Chronicle of Higher Education*, 29 Jan. 1973, 3.

8. On K-12 policy, see, for example, Diane Ravitch, *The Troubled Crusade: American Education, 1945–1980* (New York: Basic Books, 1983); Davis Graham, *The Uncertain Triumph: Federal Education Policy in the Kennedy and Johnson Years* (Chapel Hill: University of North Carolina Press, 1984); Patrick J. McGuinn, *No Child Left Behind and the Transformation of Federal Education Policy, 1965–2005* (Lawrence: University Press of Kansas, 2006); and Gareth Davies, *See Government Grow: Education Politics from Johnson to Reagan* (Lawrence: University Press of Kansas, 2007).

9. Graham, *Uncertain Triumph*, xix; "Federal Aid to Colleges Doubles in Four Years; Distribution is Wider, New Statistics Show," *Chronicle of Higher Education*, 27 Sept. 1967, 3.

10. Graham, *Uncertain Triumph*, 3–24; Maurice Isserman and Michael Kazin, *America Divided: The Civil War of the 1960s* (New York: Oxford University Press, 2004), 61–62.

11. *Public Papers of the President: LBJ* (1965), 1102–5.

12. Memo from Richard R. Brown to Aubrey Williams, 2 Feb. 1937, 6, "Reports Received from Field Representatives and Regional Directors, 1935–1938," box 10, NYA, LBJ Library (Austin, TX).

13. Sidney M. Milkis, "Lyndon Johnson, the Great Society, and the Modern Presidency," in *The Great Society and the High Tide of Liberalism*, ed. Sidney M. Milkis and Jerome M. Mileur (Amherst: University of Massachusetts Press, 2005), 3–4.

14. Gareth Davies, *From Opportunity to Entitlement: The Transformation and Decline of Great Society Liberalism* (Lawrence: University Press of Kansas, 1996), 2–3, 37–39.

15. Henry Aaron, *Politics and Professors: The Great Society in Perspective* (Washington, DC: Brookings Institution, 1978), 65–72; Alice O'Connor, *Poverty Knowledge: Social Science, Social Policy, and the Poor in Twentieth-Century U.S. History* (Princeton: Princeton University Press, 2001), 152–58.

16. *Public Papers of the Presidents: LBJ* (1963–64), 112–18.

17. O'Connor, *Poverty Knowledge*, 117–18.

18. Michael Harrington, *The Other America* (New York: Macmillan, 1962), 14–18.

19. O'Connor, *Poverty Knowledge*, 117–18.

20. *Public Papers of the Presidents: LBJ* (1965), 1102–5.

21. Hugh Davis Graham, *Civil Rights and the Presidency: Race and Gender in American Politics, 1960–1972* (1990; New York: Oxford University Press, 1992), 67–86; U.S. Commission on Civil Rights, *Civil Rights under Federal Programs: An Analysis of Title VI* (Washington, DC: GPO, Jan. 1965).

22. Peter Wallenstein, "Black Southerners and Nonblack Universities: The Process of Desegregating Southern Higher Education, 1935–1965," in *Higher Education and the Civil Rights Movement*, ed. Peter Wallenstein (Gainesville: University Press of Florida, 2008), 17–59; Melissa Kean, *Desegregating Private Higher Education in the South: Duke, Emory, Rice, Tulane, and Vanderbilt* (Baton Rouge: Louisiana State University Press, 2008). On Title VI's impact on K-12, see Gary Orfield, *The Reconstruction of Southern Education: The Schools and the 1964 Civil Rights Act* (New York: Wiley-Interscience, 1969).

23. Davies, *From Opportunity to Entitlement*, 30–53; James L. Sundquist, *Politics and Policy: The Eisenhower, Kennedy, and Johnson Years* (Washington, DC: Brookings Institution, 1968), 142–45.

24. James T. Patterson, *Grand Expectations: The United States, 1945–1974* (New York: Oxford University Press, 1996), 564.

25. *Public Papers of the Presidents: LBJ* (1965), 25–33.

26. Julian E. Zelizer, *On Capitol Hill: The Struggle to Reform Congress and its Consequences* (New York: Cambridge University Press, 2004), 77–83; William A. Sievert, "Rep. Edith Green Announces She'll Retire; 'Education Always My First Love,'" *Chronicle of Higher Education*, 25 Feb. 1974, 6; Stephen Crawford Brock, "A Comparative Study of Federal Aid to Higher Education: The Higher Education Act of 1965 and Project Upward Bound" (Ph.D. Diss., Cornell University, 1968), 21–50.

27. At the moment of its enactment, HEA absorbed the student loan provision of the NDEA, the federal work study provision of the OEO, and the Facilities Act of 1963. Following the 1968 amendments, HEA took over the remainder of OEO's compensatory education programs, and by the time of the 1972 Education Amendments, included an affirmative action title (Title IX) all its own.

28. Higher Education Act of 1965, Pub. L. 89-329, 79 Stat. 1219. Two other titles dealt with administrative and definitional, not programmatic, issues.

29. Black enrollment figures in Earl J. McGrath, *The Predominantly Negro Colleges and Universities in Transition* (New York: Teachers College, Columbia University, 1965), 5–6, 172–77. On the state of black higher education, see Fred M. Hechinger, "U.S. Urged to Spur Negro Colleges," *New York Times*, 28 March 1965, 56; and "Negro Colleges Seen Requiring Immediate Aid," *Washington Post*, 28 March 1965, A2.

30. "History of the Office of Education—Higher Education," vol. 1, pt. IV, 181–82, box 3, Administrative History, DHEW, LBJ Library.

31. Benjamin C. Willis et al., *Education for a Changing World of Work: Report of the Panel of Consultants on Vocational Education* (Washington, DC: DHEW, 1963), 19–25; Garth L. Magnum, *MDTA: Foundation of Federal Manpower Policy* (Baltimore: Johns Hopkins University Press, 1968), 19–41.

32. Mark H. Haefele, "Walt Rostow's Stages of Economic Growth: Ideas and Action," in *Staging Growth: Modernization, Development, and the Global Cold War*, ed. David C. Engerman, Michael E. Latham, Mark H. Haefele, and Nils Gilman (Amherst: University of Massachusetts Press, 2003), 80–103.

33. Howard J. Burnett, ed., *Interinstitutional Cooperation in Higher Education: Conference Proceedings* (Corning, NY: College Center of the Finger Lakes, 1969), 91–92; Willa B. Player, "Achieving Academic Strength through Interinstitutional Cooperation: United States Office of Education View of Title III," in *Interinstitutional Cooperation in Higher Education*, ed. Lawrence C. Howard (Washington, DC: DHEW, 1967), 8.

34. Hugh M. Gloster, "Cooperative Programs and the Predominantly Negro College: A Dean's View," in *Interinstitutional Cooperation in Higher Education*, ed. Burnett, 69, 70, 72.

35. McGrath, *Predominantly Negro Colleges and Universities in Transition*, 101–6; Cecil L. Patterson, "Interinstitutional Cooperation: A Professor's Worm's Eye View," in *Interinstitutional Cooperation in Higher Education*, ed. Burnett, 76–77.

36. Harold L. Hodgkinson and Walter Schenkel, *A Study of Title III of the Higher Education Act: The Developing Institutions Program* (Berkeley: University of California, Center for Research and Development in Higher Education, 1974), 259.

37. "White Universities Accused of Luring Southern Negroes," *New York Times*, 2 April 1965, 23; Richard M. Cohen, "Black Colleges Face Brain Drain," *Washington Post*, 23 March 1969, 117.

38. Ben A. Franklin, "Negro Colleges Recruit Whites," *New York Times*, 16 Jan. 1966, 1.

39. Hugh M. Gloster, "The Black College—Its Struggle for Survival and Success," *Journal of Negro History* 63 (April 1978): 104; John Nordheimers, "Negro Colleges Challenged by Soaring Budgets, Rising Enrollments and Competition," *New York Times*, 22 Dec. 1969, 19.

40. Graham, *Uncertain Triumph*, 82–83.

41. Ibid; Brock, "A Comparative Study of Federal Aid to Higher Education," 9–50.

42. Fred M. Hechinger, "Challenge for Colleges," *New York Times*, 9 Nov. 1965, 29.

43. "President's Talk in Texas on Higher Education Act," *New York Times*, 9 Nov. 1965, 28.

44. Howard A. Glickstein, "Federal Education Programs and Minority Groups," *Journal of Negro Education* 38 (summer 1969): 312–14.

45. Maurine Hoffman, "Slum Youth Education Plan Announced," *Washington Post*, 17 June 1965, D23; Gerald Grant, "Upward Bound Set," *Washington Post*, 13 Jan. 1966, G6; Richard L. Plaut, "Plans for Assisting Negro Students to Enter and to Remain in College," *Journal of Negro Education* 35 (autumn 1966): 398–99.

46. Catherine Gavin Loss, "Public Schools, Private Lives: American Education and Psychological Authority, 1945–1975" (Ph.D. diss., University of Virginia, 2005).

47. Jane Brooks, "New Horizons Opened by Upward Bound, Students Say," *Macon News*, 15 Sept. 1967, Upward Bound File, box 347, Office Files of the Commissioner of Education, 1939–80, RG 12, NARA (College Park, MD).

48. Ibid.

49. Arezell Brown, "I Knew It Was Coming," *Seventeen*, Jan. 1968, in ibid.

50. For criticisms, see "Be A Dropout and See the World," *Wall Street Journal*, 1 Nov. 1968, 16, and various responses to it in ibid. See also Gerald Grant, "Education Problems Are Barely Dented," *Washington Post*, 17 Jan. 1967, A1.

51. Lili Marshall, "Officials Well Pleased With Results of Upward Bound Program at Murray," *Paducah Sun-Democrat*, 28 Aug. 1966, Upward Bound File, box 347, Office Files of the Commissioner of Education, 1939–80, RG 12, NARA.

52. Letter from Jerome H. Holland to Thomas Hawkins, 30 Sept. 1966, Upward Bound File, Jerome H. Holland Papers, Hampton University Archives (Hampton, VA). Other presidents of predominantly black colleges felt the same way; see Gerald Grant, "Negro Colleges Grow as Draw in Talent Hunt," *Washington Post*, 15 Dec. 1966, E1.

53. Glickstein, "Federal Educational Programs and Minority Groups," 313.

54. Institute for Higher Educational Opportunity, *The College and Cultural Diversity: The Black Student on Campus* (Atlanta: Southern Regional Education Board, 1971), 7–13, 20–21.

55. HEW Fact Sheet, 1972, BEOG file (tab G), box 31, Office of the Asst. Secretary of Education, Program Files, 1972-75, RG 12, NARA; "Number of Black Students Has Tripled in a Decade," *Chronicle of Higher Education*, 19 June 1978, 8. A majority of the scholarship aid went to black students; see John A. Centra, "Black Students at Predominantly White Colleges: A Research Description," *Sociology of Education* 43 (summer 1970): 328–29.

56. William Borders, "Ivy League Shifts Admission Goals," *New York Times*, 17 April 1967, 1.

57. Ibid; Jerome Karabel, *The Chosen: The Hidden History of Admission and Exclusion at Harvard, Yale, and Princeton* (New York: Houghton Mifflin, 2005).

58. William W. Scranton et al., *The Report of the President's Commission on Campus Unrest* (Washington, DC: GPO, 1970), 42.

59. On the proliferation of competing meanings of alienation, see Doug Rossinow, *The Politics of Authenticity: Liberalism, Christianity, and the New Left in America* (New York: Columbia University Press, 1998), 2–4; and Melvin Seeman, "On the Meaning of Alienation," *American Sociological Review* 24 (Dec. 1959): 783–91.

60. David Riesman, *The Lonely Crowd: A Study of the Changing American Character* (1950; New Haven: Yale University Press, 1989), 242.

61. C. Wright Mills, *White Collar: The American Middle Classes* (1951; New York: Oxford University Press, 2002), xii. On the modern university as one of those impersonal institutions, see ch. 7, "Brains, Inc.," 142–60.

62. Riesman's and Mills's work was also structural-functionalist, if in a different way. Instead of organizational types, which was Parsons's specialty, they focused on individual types, i.e., inner-directed versus outer-directed versus autonomous, in Riesman's case; white-collar versus blue-collar, in Mills's case.

63. Talcott Parson, *The Social System* (Glencoe, IL: Free Press, 1951); Talcott Parsons, *The American University* (Cambridge, MA: Harvard University Press, 1973).

64. Almost half the undergraduate protesters had GPA's higher than 3.0, while two-thirds of the graduate student protesters had GPA's above 3.5. Among the entire undergraduate and graduate student population, by comparison, only 21% and 55%, respectively, had similar or higher GPA's. Charles Muscatine et al., *Education at Berkeley: Report of the Select Committee on Education* (Berkeley: University of California Press, 1966), 24.

65. Seymour Martin Lipset, *Rebellion in the University* (1971; Chicago: University of Chicago Press, 1976), 80–123, esp. 108–9.

66. Thomas D. Snyder, ed., *120 Years of American Education: A Statistical Portrait* (Washington, DC: NCES, 1993), 76–77.

67. Muscatine, *Education at Berkeley*, 218.

68. Mario Savio, "The Uncertain Future of the Multiversity: A Partisan Scrutiny of Berkeley's Muscatine Report," *Harper's* (Oct. 1966), 90.

69. Fred Turner, *From Counterculture to Cyberculture: Stewart Brand, the Whole Earth Network, and the Rise of Digital Utopianism* (Chicago: University of Chicago Press, 2006), 1–2.

70. Lipset and Wolin, *Berkeley Student Revolt*, 214.

71. Ibid., 222.

72. William J. Rorabaugh, *Berkeley at War: The 1960s* (New York: Oxford University Press, 1989), 55.

73. Muscatine, *Education at Berkeley*, 34.

74. Kenneth Keniston, *The Uncommitted: Alienated Youth in American Society* (1965; New York: Harcourt, Brace and World, 1967), 6.

75. Ibid., 7.

76. Ibid., 10–11.

77. Ibid., 183, 199. For Keniston's discussion of the major themes of alienation, see ch. 7, 163–208.

78. Ibid., 404.

79. Ibid., 400.

80. Ibid.

81. Ibid., 442.

82. Ibid., 442–43.

83. Rorabaugh, *Berkeley at War*, 44–45; Mark Gerzon, *The Whole World Is Watching: A Young Man Looks at Youth's Dissent* (New York: Viking Press, 1969), 125–26. For a full account of the alleged therapeutic benefits of political action at the University of Texas-Austin, see Rossinow, *Politics of Authenticity*.

84. King's "I Have a Dream Speech," 28 Aug. 1963, available at http://www.usconstitution.net/dream.html (accessed 29 Sept. 2009).

85. Whitney Young, *To Be Equal* (1964; New York: McGraw-Hill, 1966), 19.

86. Nathan Huggins, *Afro-American Studies: A Report to the Ford Foundation* (New York: Ford Foundation, 1985), 17–18; Daryl Michael Scott, *Contempt and Pity: Social Policy and the Image of the Damaged Black Psyche, 1880–1986* (Chapel Hill: University of North Carolina Press, 1997). According to Scott, "Between 1930 and 1965, few experts who studied blacks questioned the goal of assimilation" (161).

87. George Napper, *Blacker Than Thou: The Struggle for Campus Unity* (Grand Rapids, MI: Eerdmans, 1973), 29.

88. Donald Alexander Downs, *Cornell '69: Liberalism and the Crisis of the American University* (Ithaca: Cornell University Press, 1999), 50.

89. Ibid., 4.

90. Ibid., 50–58.

91. Ibid., 57–58.

92. Ibid., 55.

93. Ibid., 56.

94. Kazin and Isserman, *America Divided*, 183–84; Peniel E. Joseph, *Waiting 'Til the Midnight Hour: A Narrative History of Black Power in America* (New York: Henry Holt, 2006).

95. Stokley Carmichael, "Toward Black Liberation," *Massachusetts Review* 7 (autumn 1966): 639–51; Stokley Carmichael, "What We Want," *New York Review of Books* 7 (22 Sept. 1966), 5–7; Stokely Carmichael and Charles V. Hamilton, *Black Power: The Politics of Liberation in America* (New York: Random House, 1967).

96. Ibid., 34.

97. Ibid., 6.

98. Ibid., 53.

99. Ibid., 44, 173. See also Robert C. Smith, "Black Power and the Transformation from Protest to Politics," *Political Science Quarterly* 96 (autumn 1981): 431–43.

100. Carmichael and Hamilton, *Black Power*, 47.

101. Ibid., 54.

102. On the organization of black student groups at predominantly white universities, see, for example, Richard P. McCormick, *The Black Student Protest Movement at Rutgers* (New Brunswick: Rutgers University Press, 1990); Joy Ann Williamson, *Black Power on Campus: The University of Illinois, 1965–75* (Urbana: University of Illinois Press, 2003); and, for an analysis that focuses on San Francisco State University, Fabio Rojas, *From Black Power to Black Studies: How a Radical Social Movement Became an Academic Discipline* (Baltimore: Johns Hopkins University Press, 2007). For the cases of Harvard, Princeton, and Yale, see Karabel, *Chosen*.

103. Downs, *Cornell '69*, 62.

104. Ibid., 63.

105. Ibid., 51.

106. Ibid., 69.

107. Ibid.

108. Malcolm X, "Black Man's History," in *The End of White World Supremacy: Four Speeches by Malcolm X*, ed. Imam Benjamin Karim (Philadelphia: Temple University Press, 1971), 25–26.

109. Carmichael, "Toward Black Liberation," 639.

110. On the Yale Symposium, see J. Anthony Lukas, "Courses on 'Black Experience' Backed," *New York Times*, 13 May 1968, 1, 47. The symposium was later published as Armstead L. Robinson, Craig C. Foster, and Donald H. Ogilvie, ed., *Black Studies in the University: A Symposium* (New Haven: Yale University Press, 1969).

111. James Sargent Jr., "Faculty Approve Black Major, Seminars in Colleges," *Yale Daily News*, 13 Dec. 1968, 1, 3; "House Proud," *Yale Alumni Magazine* 35 (Jan./Feb. 2005) available at http://www.yalealumnimagazine.com/issues/2005_01/afroam.html (accessed 17 Aug. 2010).

112. "On Being Black at Yale," in *University Crisis Reader: Confrontation and Counterattack*, 2 vols., ed. Immanuel Wallerstein and Paul Starr (New York: Vintage Books, 1971), II, 379, 385.

113. "How Black Studies Happened," *Yale Alumni Magazine* (Oct. 1968): 22.

114. Ibid., 380.

115. Ibid., 384.

116. Donald H. Ogilvie, "A Student's Reflections," in *Black Studies in the University*, ed. Robinson et al., 81.

117. "On Being Black at Yale," in *University Crisis Reader*, ed. Wallerstein and Starr, II, 385.

118. On Robinson, see Barbara J. Fields, "Armstead Robinson, Historian and Discipline Builder," in Armstead L. Robinson, *Bitter Fruits of Bondage: The Demise of Slavery and the Collapse of the Confederacy, 1861–1865* (Charlottesville: University of Virginia Press, 2005), xii–xvi; and Zak M. Salih, "Scholars Remember Armstead Robinson's Intellectual Legacy," available at http://www.law.virginia.edu/html/news/2006_spr/robinson.htm (accessed 3 Oct. 2010).

119. Elliot Moorman, "The Benefits of Anger," in *University Crisis Reader*, ed. Wallerstein and Starr, II, 337.

120. Committee on Race Relations, "The Rationale for Afro-American Studies," in ibid., 339.

121. Lawrence J. Friedman, *Identity's Architect: A Biography of Erik Erikson* (New York: Scribner, 1999).

122. Ibid., 160–62. For Erikson's primary work on identity, see *Childhood and Society* (1950; New York: W. W. Norton, 1985) and *Identity, Youth, and Crisis* (New York: 1968). In *Childhood and Society*, Erickson wrote: "I think that the psychoanalytic method is essentially a historical method. Even where it focuses on medical data, it interprets them as a function of past experience" (17). Later, he elaborated: "One methodological precondition, then, for grasping identity would be a psychoanalysis . . . the other would be a social psychology . . . together they would obviously institute a new field which would have to create its own historical sophistication" (*Identity*, 24).

123. By the late 1960s, the term *identity* was everywhere. As Erikson mused in the prologue to *Identity*: "'Identity' and 'identity crisis' have in popular scientific usage be-

come terms which alternately circumscribe something so large and so seemingly self-evident that to demand a definition would almost seem petty, while at other times they designate something made so narrow for purposes of measurement that the over-all meaning is lost, and it could just as well be called something else" (15).

124. Joseph L. White, *The Psychology of Blacks: An Afro-American Perspective* (Englewood Cliffs, NJ: Prentice-Hall, 1984), 17–21.

125. Joseph L. White, "Toward A Black Psychology," *Ebony* (Sept. 1970), 44–45, 48–50, 52.

126. Wade E. Pickren, "Between the Cup of Principle and the Lip of Practice: Ethnic Minorities and American Psychology, 1966–1980," *History of Psychology* 7.1 (2004): 45. On the history of the black psychology movement, see Robert V. Guthrie, ed., *Even the Rat Was White: A Historical View of Psychology* (New York: Harper and Row, 1976).

127. W.E.B. Du Bois, *The Souls of Black Folk* (1903; New York: Kraus Reprints, 1968), 3.

128. Ibid., 4. See also David Levering Lewis, *W.E.B. Du Bois: Biography of a Race* (New York: Henry Holt, 1993), 279–83.

129. Steven V. Roberts, "Black Studies Aim to Change Things," *New York Times*, 15 May 1969, 93.

130. On the formation of black studies programs, see, for example, Huggins, *Afro-American Studies*; Rojas, *Black Power to Black Studies*; Downs, *Cornell '69*; McCormick, *Black Student Protest Movement at Rutgers*; Williamson, *Black Power on Campus*; Peniel E. Joseph, "Dashikis and Democracy: Black Studies, Student Activism, and the Black Power Movement," *Journal of African American History* 88 (spring 2003): 182–203; Wayne C. Glasker, *Black Students in the Ivory Tower: African American Student Activism at the University of Pennsylvania, 1967–1990* (Amherst: University of Massachusetts Press, 2002); and Jeffrey Ogbar, *Black Power: Radical Politics and African-American Identity* (Baltimore: Johns Hopkins University Press, 2004).

131. Noliwe M. Rooks, *White Money/Black Power: The Surprising History of African American Studies and the Crisis of Race in Higher Education* (Boston: Beacon Press, 2006), 21.

132. Peter Novick, *That Noble Dream: The "Objectivity Question" and the American Historical Profession* (New York: Cambridge University Press, 1988), 477.

133. On this relationship, see Thomas Bender, "Politics, Intellect, and the American University, 1945–1995," in *American Academic Culture in Transformation*, ed. Thomas Bender and Carl E. Schorske (Princeton: Princeton University Press, 1997), 33.

134. Huggins, *Afro-American Studies*, 31–33.

135. Howard Brick, *Age of Contradiction: American Thought and Culture in the 1960s* (New York: Twayne, 1998), 28.

136. Arthur Sandeen, "The New Experimental College: A Challenge to Student Personnel Work," *Journal of College Student Personnel* 9 (Nov. 1968): 391–99.

137. Steven V. Roberts, "Students Demand College Reforms," *New York Times*, 20 Aug. 1967, 38.

138. James W. Brann, "San Francisco Students Run Own 'College,'" *Chronicle of Higher Education*, 21 Dec. 1966, 1.

139. Israel Shenker, "Students Take Over, But It's All Academic," *New York Times*, 7 March 1969, 39; Malcolm G. Scully, "Experimental Programs Aim to Give Students Control of Their Education," *Chronicle of Higher Education*, 7 June 1971, 1.

140. Gregory U. Rigsby, "Afro-American Studies at Howard University: One Year Later," *Journal of Negro Education* 39 (summer 1970): 209–10.

141. Roberts, "Black Studies Aim to Change Things," 49.

142. Rooks, *White Money/Black Power*, 93–122; Ford Foundation, *Widening the Mainstream of American Culture: A Ford Foundation Report on Ethnic Studies* (New York: Ford Foundation, 1978), 1–10, 34–36; Novick, *That Noble Dream*, 477.

143. Thomas A. Johnson, "Colleges Scored on Black Studies," *New York Times*, 7 Dec. 1969, 68.

144. Rojas, *From Black Power to Black Studies*, 167–69.

145. Thomas J. Bray, "Black Studies Boom," *Wall Street Journal*, 3 Feb. 1969, 1.

146. Thomas A. Johnson, "Educators Find Black Studies Are Changing Higher Education," *New York Times*, 4 June 1972, 71.

147. For the contours of the autonomy debate, see Huggins, *Afro-American Studies*, 41–46; and W. Arthur Lewis, "The Road to the Top Is through Higher Education—Not Black Studies," *New York Times*, 11 May 1969, SM34. Not all black studies innovators fell neatly into this framework, of course. Notably, Harold Cruse, author of *The Crisis of the Negro Intellectual* (New York: Morrow, 1967), and the first director of the African American Studies Program at the University of Michigan, eschewed both separation and integration. He favored instead a discipline-based African American Studies program in which "Negro" intellectuals would play a leading part. On Cruse and his ever-changing intellectual framework, see William Jelani Cobb, ed., *The Essential Harold Cruse: A Reader* (New York: Palgrave Macmillan, 2002).

148. Malcolm G. Scully, "A Militant Debates a Moderate on Afro-American Study," *Chronicle of Higher Education*, 27 Jan. 1969, 6.

149. "Nathan Hare on Black Studies," *Integrated Education: Races and Schools* (Nov.–Dec. 1970): 8–15.

150. James Reston, "Black Moderates vs. Black Militants," *New York Times*, 15 Jan. 1969, 46.

151. Scully, "A Militant Debates a Moderate on Afro-American Study," 6.

152. Martin Kilson, "Black Politics: A New Power," *Dissent* 18 (Aug. 1971), 333–45.

153. Roberts, "Black Studies Aim To Change Things," 93.

154. Ernest Dunbar, "The Black Studies Thing," *New York Times*, 6 April 1969, 70, 75.

155. Peter Kihss, "Clark Scores 'Separatism' at Antioch," *New York Times*, 23 May 1969, 29. For more on Clark, see Scott, *Contempt and Pity*.

156. Novick, *That Noble Dream*, 477; Art Harris, "Black Studies Enrollment Shows Dramatic Decline," *Washington Post*, 5 Nov. 1979, A1; Huggins, *Afro-American Studies*, 55–62.

157. Karen J. Winkler, "The State of Black Studies: Reports of Their Demise Are Proving to Be Exaggerated," *Chronicle of Higher Education*, 8 Dec. 1975, 5.

158. Terry H. Anderson, *The Pursuit of Fairness: A History of Affirmative Action* (New York: Oxford University Press, 2004), 150.

159. Novick, *That Noble Dream*, 469–91, quote on 470.

160. Helen S. Astin and Alan E. Bayer, "Sex Discrimination in Academe," in *Academic Women on the Move*, ed. Alice S. Rossi and Ann Calderwood (New York: Russell Sage Foundation, 1973), 333–58; The Carnegie Commission on Higher Education, *Opportunities for Women in Higher Education* (New York: McGraw-Hill, 1973).

161. Florence Howe, "Women and the Power to Change," in *Women and the Power to Change*, ed. Florence Howe (New York: McGraw-Hill, 1975), 136-38; Ruth Rosen, *The World Split Open: How the Modern Women's Movement Changed America* (New York: Viking, 2000), 70- 81; Graham, *Civil Rights and the Presidency*, 102-16; and Andrew Fishel and Janice Pottker, *National Politics and Sex Discrimination in Education* (Lexington, MA: D.C. Heath and Company), 95-136. For NOW's focus on the ERA, see Katherine Turk, "Out of the Revolution, into the Mainstream: Employment Activism in the NOW Sears Campaign and the Growing Pains of Liberal Feminism," *Journal of American History* 97.2 (Sept. 2010): 399-423. On the radical women's movement, and its differences with the liberal women's movement, see Alice Echols, *Daring to Be Bad: Radical Feminism in America, 1967-1975* (Minneapolis: University of Minnesota Press, 1989).

162. Jo Freeman, "The Tyranny of Structurelessness," *Berkeley Journal of Sociology* 17 (1972–73): 151.

163. Robin Morgan, ed., *Sisterhood Is Powerful: An Anthology of Writings From the Women's Liberation Movement* (New York: Random House, 1970), xxviii.

164. Claudia Dreyfuss, *Woman's Fate: Raps from a Feminist Consciousness Raising Group* (New York: Bantam Books, 1973), 10-11. On the context-specific nature of CR, see Anne Enke, *Finding the Movement: Sexuality, Contested Space, and Feminist Activism* (Durham: Duke University Press, 2007), 2.

165. Florence Howe and Carol Ahlum, "Women's Studies and Social Change," in *Academic Women on the Move*, ed. Rossi and Calderwood, 393–424; Rosen, *World Split Open*, 196–201; Ellen Herman, *The Romance of American Psychology: Political Culture in the Age of Experts* (Berkeley: University of California Press, 1995), 297–300.

166. Jack Belden, *China Shakes the World* (New York: Harper, 1970), 166.

167. Miller, *Democracy Is in the Streets*, 333.

168. Sara Evans, *Personal Politics: The Roots of Women's Liberation in the Civil Rights and New Left* (New York: Vintage Books, 1979).

169. Eva S. Moskowitz, *In Therapy We Trust: America's Obsession with Self-Fulfillment* (Baltimore: Johns Hopkins University Press, 2001), 210.

170. Michael Tomasky, *Left for Dead: The Life, Death, and Possible Resurrection of Progressive Politics in America* (New York: Free Press, 1996), 84.

171. For the two most widely cited CR guidelines, see Kathie Sarachild, "Feminist Consciousness Raising and Organizing," in *Voices from Women's Liberation*, ed. Leslie B. Tanner (New York: New American Library, 1970), 154–57; and *Ms.*, "A Guide to Consciousness-Raising," (July 1972), 18, 22–23.

172. Howe, "Women and the Power to Change," in *Women and the Power to Change*, ed. Howe, 148–49; Florence Howe, *Myths of Coeducation: Selected Essays, 1964–1983* (Bloomington: Indiana University Press, 1984), 1–17. See also Jo Freeman, "The Women's Liberation Movement: Its Origins, Structures, Impact, and Ideas," in *Women: A Feminist Perspective*, ed. Freeman (Palo Alto, CA: Mayfield, 1975), 451.

173. Howe, "Women and the Power to Change," in *Women and the Power to Change*, ed. Howe, 137.

174. "Redstockings Manifesto," in *Voices from Women's Liberation*, ed. Leslie B. Tanner (New York: New American Library, 1970), 109–11.

175. Carol Hanisch, "The Personal is Political," 1969, available at http://scholar .alexanderstreet.com/pages/viewpage.action?pageId=2259 (accessed 17 April 2010). On women's contested historical relationship with psychoanalysis, see, for example, Jean Baker

Miller, ed., *Psychoanalysis and Women: Contributions to New Theory and Therapy* (New York: Brunner/Mazel, 1973); Barbara Ehrenreich, *For Her Own Good: 150 Years of the Experts' Advice to Women* (New York: Anchor Press, 1978); Elizabeth Lunbeck, *The Psychiatric Persuasion: Knowledge, Gender, and Power in Modern America* (Princeton: Princeton University Press, 1994); and Mari Jo Buhle, *Feminism and Its Discontents: A Century of Struggle with Psychoanalysis* (Cambridge, MA: Harvard University Press, 1998)..

176. Betty Friedan, *The Feminine Mystique* (1963; New York: W. W. Norton, 1983), 103–25. On Betty Friedan and the writing of *The Feminine Mystique*, see Daniel Horowitz, *Betty Friedan and the Making of the Feminist Mystique* (Amherst: University of Massachusetts Press, 1998). Horowitz argued that Friedan sought to dismantle orthodox Freudianism while still "underscoring the benefits of therapy and self-discovery that she herself had experienced beginning in her Berkeley [college] years" (219). Her book thus condemned and embraced therapy as a technique for the discovery of identity.

177. Friedan, *Feminine Mystique*, 77.

178. Shulamith Firestone, *The Dialectic of Sex: The Case for Feminist Revolution* (New York: Morrow, 1970), ch. 3, "Freudianism: The Misguided Feminism," 46–80, quotes on 72, 78–79.

179. Ibid., 11.

180. Herman, *Romance of American Psychology*, 276–303.

181. Gerald N. Grob, *From Asylum to Community: Mental Health Policy in Modern America* (Princeton: Princeton University Press, 1991), 239–72; James W. Stockdill, "National Mental Health Policy and the Community Mental Health Centers, 1963–1981," in *Psychology and the National Institute of Mental Health*, ed. Wade E. Pickren and Stanley F. Schneider (Washington, DC: American Psychological Association, 2005), 261–94.

182. Grob, *Asylum to Community*, 279–92. Michel Foucault's *History of Madness* appeared in translated form in the mid-1960s. Szasz's *The Myth of Mental Illness: Foundations of a Theory of Personal Conduct* (New York: Harper and Row, 1961) was reprinted five times over the course of the 1960s.

183. Leonore Tiefer, "A Brief History of the Association for Women in Psychology: 1969–1991," *Psychology of Women Quarterly* 15 (1991): 635–49.

184. Martha T. Mednick and Laura L. Urbanski, "The Origins and Activities of APA's Division of the Psychology of Women," ibid., 651–63.

185. Jerome Agel, ed., *The Radical Therapist: Therapy Means Change Not Adjustment* (New York: Ballantine Books, 1971). Grob describes the same phenomenon as a psychiatric counterculture; see Grob, *Asylum to Community*, 273–301.

186. Agel, "Introduction," in *Radical Therapist*, ed. Agel, xi.

187. Marilyn Zweig, "Is Women's Liberation a Therapy Group?" in Agel, *Radical Therapist*, 164.

188. Pamela Allen, "Free Space," in *Radical Feminism*, ed. Anne Koedt (New York: Quadrangle Books, 1973), 278.

189. John D. Skrentny, *The Minority Rights Revolution* (Cambridge, MA: Belknap Press of Harvard University Press, 2002), 130–41.

190. Bernice Sandler, "A Little Help from Our Government: WEAL and Contract Compliance," in *Academic Women on the Move*, ed. Rossi and Calderwood, 451. On Sandler, see Betsy Wade, "Women on the Campus Find a Weapon," *New York Times*, 10 Jan. 1972, E22.

191. Pepper Schwartz and Janet Lever, "Women in the Male World of Higher Education," in *Academic Women on the Move*, ed. Rossi and Calderwood, 57–77.

192. Barbara Sicherman, "The Invisible Woman," in *Women in Higher Education*, ed. W. Todd Furniss and Patricia Albjerb Graham (Washington, DC: American Council on Education, 1974), 161.

193. Friedan, *Feminine Mystique*, 368, 370.

194. "New College Trend," *New York Times*, 7 Jan. 1971, 37.

195. Linda Greenhouse, "A Graduate Program Sets Out to Find History's Women," *New York Times*, 20 March 1973, 34.

196. Joan I. Roberts, "Women's Right to Choose, or Men's Right to Dominate," in *Women in Higher Education*, ed. Furniss and Graham, 53.

197. Roby, "Institutional Barriers to Women Students in Higher Education," in *Academic Women on the Move*, ed. Rossi and Calderwood, 53–54.

198. Adrienne Rich, "Toward a Woman-Centered University," in *Women and the Power to Change*, ed. Howe, 17, 20. On Rich and the "fracturing" of women's studies, see Daniel T. Rodgers, *Age of Fracture* (Cambridge, MA: Belknap Press of Harvard University Press, 2011), 148-49.

199. Howe and Ahlum, "Women's Studies and Social Change," in *Academic Women on the Move*, ed. Rossi and Calderwood, 415.

200. Rich, "Toward a Woman-Centered University," 31–33.

201. The volumes were published by Know, Inc., in Pittsburgh, PA.

202. On Lerner, see Gerda Lerner, *Fireweed: A Political Autobiography* (Philadelphia: Temple University Press, 2002); Gerda Lerner, *A Death of One's Own* (Madison: University of Wisconsin Press, 1985); Lerner, "A Life of Learning," ACLS Occasional Paper Series 60 (2005): 1–21; and Daniel Horowitz, "Feminism, Women's History, and American Social Thought," in *American Capitalism*, ed. Lichtenstein, 191–209, esp. 193–95.

203. Gerda Lerner, *The Grimke Sisters of South Carolina: Rebels Against Slavery* (Boston: Houghton Mifflin, 1967). Lerner's exploration of the relationship between slavery and women's oppression in *Grimke Sisters* continued in her later work. See, for example, her two-volume magnum opus, *The Creation of Patriarchy*, 2 vols. (New York: Oxford University Press, 1986), I; and *The Creation of Feminist Consciousness*, 2 vols. (New York: Oxford University Press, 1993), II. On Lerner's contributions to the field of women's history, see Daniel Horowitz, "Feminism, Women's History, and American Social Thought," in *American Capitalism*, ed. Lichtenstein, 205–9.

204. Lerner, "A Life of Learning," 10–11.

205. She worried about the "straightjacket" of Marxist thought during her graduate school years but did not formally renounce it until several decades later, following the writing and publication of *The Creation of Patriarchy*, which Lerner claimed "shattered the last remnants of my adherence to Marxist thought" (Lerner, "Lifetime of Learning," 19).

206. Lerner, "Lifetime of Learning," 1.

207. Lerner, *Fireweed*, 7, 368.

208. Gerda Lerner, "On the Teaching and Organization of Feminist Studies," in *Female Studies*, 10 vols., ed. Rae Lee Siporin (Pittsburgh: Know Inc., 1972), V, 35–36.

209. In *Creation of Feminist Consciousness*, Lerner wrote: "In the course of the establishment of patriarchy and constantly reinforced as the result of it, the major idea systems which explain and order Western civilization incorporated a set of unstated assumptions about gender, which powerfully affected the development of history and

of human thought" (3). Lerner regarded education and history as the source of and solution to women's oppression; see ch. 2, "The Educational Disadvantaging of Women," and ch. 11, "The Search for Women's History," in *Consciousness*. For the definitive early statement on gender as a historical construct, see Joan W. Scott, "Gender: A Useful Category of Historical Analysis," *American Historical Review* 91 (Dec. 1986): 1053–75; and Joan W. Scott, *Gender and the Politics of History* (New York: Columbia University Press, 1999). For her part, Scott grew weary of gender as a category of analysis, openly worrying about its widespread use by historians from across the subfields. By the late 1990s, according to Joanne Meyerowitz, Scott "turned more concertedly to psychoanalysis, to the fantasies that enable identities, including the 'phantasmatic projections that mobilize individual desires into collective identifications'" (1352), in Joanne Meyerowitz, "A History of 'Gender,'" *American Historical Review* 113 (Dec. 2008): 1346–56.

210. Marcia Landy, "Women, Education, and Social Power," in *Female Studies*, ed. Siporin, V, 53–63, quote on 62.

211. Howe, "Women and the Power to Change," in *Women and the Power to Change*, ed. Howe, 157.

212. "Pressure and Popularity Spur Variety in College Women's Studies Courses," *New York Times*, 7 May 1975, 39.

213. "New College Trend," *New York Times*, 7 Jan. 1971, 37, 70

214. Barbara Isenberg, "Boosting 'Liberation': Women's Studies Rise In College Popularity," *Wall Street Journal*, 9 June 1971, 1.

215. Ibid.

216. Jane Sims, "Colleges Expanding Women's Studies," *Washington Post*, 26 July 1971, A3.

217. "New College Trend," *New York Times*, 7 Jan. 1971, 37, 70.

218. Mari Jo Buhle, "Introduction," in *The Politics of Women's Studies: Testimony from 30 Founding Mothers*, ed. Florence Howe (New York: Feminist Press, 2000), xv.

219. Gene I. Maeroff, "The Growing Women's Studies Movement Gets Organized," *New York Times*, 18 Jan. 1977, 41.

220. Arthur Levine and Jeanette S. Cureton, *When Hope and Fear Collide: A Portrait of Today's College Student* (San Francisco: Jossey-Bass, 1998), 58–63.

221. James T. Patterson, *Restless Giant: The United States from Watergate to Bush v. Gore* (New York: Oxford University Press, 2005), 293–95.

222. National Center for Education Statistics, *Digest of Education Statistics: 2007* available at http://nces.ed.gov/programs/digest/d07/ch_3.asphttp://nces.ed.gov /programs/digest/d07/ch_3.asp (accessed 30 April 2009).

223. Michael Kurlaender and Stella M. Flores, "The Racial Transformation of Higher Education," in *Higher Education and the Color Line*, ed. Gary Orfield (Cambridge, MA: Harvard Education Press, 2005), 11–32.

224. Helen Lefkowitz Horowitz, *College Life: Undergraduate Cultures from the End of the Eighteenth Century to the Present* (Chicago: University of Chicago Press, 1987), 273–79.

225. Gregory L. Schneider, *Cadres for Conservatism: Young Americans for Freedom and the Rise of the Contemporary Right* (New York: New York University Press, 1999), 177–82.

226. Skrentny, *Minority Rights Revolution*, 277, 322, 324; Nathan Glazer, *Ethnic Dilemmas, 1964–1982* (Cambridge, MA: Harvard University Press, 1983), 135–36.

227. Gene I. Maeroff, "White Ethnic Groups in Nation Are Encouraging Heritage Programs in a Trend Toward Self-Awareness," *New York Times*, 28 Jan. 1974, 11.

228. Ibid.

229. Cheryl M. Fields, "White Ethnic Studies Are Spreading: They Focus On European Groups' Experiences in America," *Chronicle of Higher Education*, 16 April 1973, 1.

230. Frank Ching, "Expansion of Asian-American Studies on U.S. Campuses Reflects Growth of Ethnic Consciousness," *New York Times*, 16 July 1973, 18.

231. "C.C.N.Y. Will Add to Ethnic Studies," *New York Times*, 4 April 1971, 49.

232. Roy Lucas, "The Right to Higher Education," *Journal of Higher Education* 41 (Jan. 1970): 56.

233. *Dixon v. Alabama State Board of Education*, 294 F. 2nd 150 (1961); William Van Alstyne, "The Demise of the Right-Privilege Distinction in Constitutional Law," *Harvard Law Review* 81.6 (May 1968): 1439–64; on *Dixon*, see 1462–63.

234. Lisa Tenerowicz, "Student Misconduct at Private Colleges and Universities: A Roadmap for 'Fundamental Fairness' in Disciplinary Proceedings," *Boston College Law Review* 42.3 (2001): 653–94.

235. Human capital theorists affirmed this longstanding assumption. See, for example, Gary Beck, *Human Capital: A Theoretical and Empirical Analysis with Special Reference to Education* (New York: National Bureau of Economic Research, Columbia University Press, 1964), 7–68. For a more popularized version of these findings, see, for example, Christopher Jencks, *Inequality: A Reassessment of the Effect of Family and Schooling in America* (New York: Basic Books, 1972).

236. Quote from *Moore v. Student Affairs Committee of Troy State University*, 284 F. Supp. 725, 729 (M.D. Ala. 1968), cited in William Van Alstyne, "The Tentative Emergence of Student Power in the United States," *American Journal of Comparative Law* 17.3 (summer 1969): 408.

237. Alexander Keyssar, *The Right to Vote: The Contested History of Democracy in the United States* (New York: Basic Books, 2000), 277–81.

238. On the passage of the Education Amendments of 1972, see Lawrence E. Gladieux and Thomas R. Wolanin, *Congress and the Colleges: The National Politics of Higher Education* (Lexington, MA: Lexington Books, 1976); and Fishel and Pottker, *National Politics and Sex Discrimination in Education*, 67-94.

239. Skrentny, *Minority Rights Revolution*, 230-62. See also Edith Green, *Fears and Fallacies: Equal Opportunities in the 1970s* (Ann Arbor: Graduate School of Business Administration, University of Michigan, 1975). On the shift of Title IX from sex equity to athletics, see Amanda Ross Edwards, "Why Sport? The Development of Sport as a Policy Issue in Title IX of the Education Amendments of 1972," *Journal of Policy History* 22.3 (2010): 300-36.

240. Derek V. Price, *Borrowing Inequality: Race, Class, and Student Loans* (Boulder, CO: L. Rienner, 2004), 33–34. The guaranteed loan program was terminated in 2010 when the Health Care and Educational Reconciliation Act shifted the U.S. government to a direct-lending loan model to save money on interest and fees.

241. Lawrence E. Gladieux, *College Opportunities and the Poor: Getting National Politics Back on Track* (Washington, DC: College Board, Center for the Study of Opportunity in Higher Education, 1996), 11.

242. Gladieux and Wolanin, *Congress and the Colleges*, 85–86.

243. Beth Macy, "The Door that Claiborne Pell Opened," *Chronicle of Higher Education*, 13 Jan. 2009, B16.

244. On the specifics of the original BEOG program, see HEW Fact Sheet, 1972, BEOG file (tab G), box 31, Office of the Asst. Secretary of Education, Program Files, 1972–75, RG 12, NARA.

245. George Q. Flynn, *The Draft, 1940–1973* (Lawrence: University Press of Kansas, 1993), 253–82.

246. Family Education Rights and Privacy Act, 20 U.S.C. S.1232g (Supp. IV, 1974).

247. Philip W. Semas, "The Student Mood," *Chronicle of Higher Education*, 24 April 1976, 7.

CHAPTER 7

CONCLUSION: THE PRIVATE MARKETPLACE OF IDENTITY IN AN AGE OF DIVERSITY

1. Robert M. Collins, *More: The Politics of Economic Growth in Postwar America* (New York: Oxford University Press, 2000), 152–60; James T. Patterson, *Restless Giant: The United States from Watergate to Bush v. Gore* (New York: Oxford University Press, 2005), 7–8, 58–62.

2. John Hersey, "Anxiety behind the Façade," *Time*, 23 June 1967, available at http://www.time.com/time/magazine/article/0,9171,839553,00.html (accessed 20 May 2009).

3. Earl F. Cheit, *The New Depression in Higher Education: A Study of Financial Conditions at 41 Colleges and Universities* (New York: McGraw-Hill, 1971).

4. Roger L. Geiger, *Research and Relevant Knowledge: American Research Universities since World War II* (New York: Oxford University Press, 1993), 245.

5. Roger L. Geiger, *Knowledge* and *Money: Research Universities and the Paradox of the Marketplace* (Stanford: Stanford University Press, 2004), 32–35; Bruce Schulman, *The Seventies: The Great Shift in American Culture, Society, and Politics* (New York: Free Press, 2001), 134–35.

6. On the discrediting of academic science and of "expertise" more generally in the early 1970s, see Brian Balogh, *Chain Reaction: Expert Debate and Public Participation in American Commercial Nuclear Power, 1945–1975* (New York: Cambridge University Press, 1991), 221–301; and Thomas L. Haskell, ed., *The Authority of Experts: Studies in History and Theory* (Bloomington: Indiana University Press, 1984), quotes on xvi–xviii.

7. Thomas P. Hughes, *Rescuing Prometheus* (New York: Vintage Books, 1998), 13.

8. Daniel S. Greenberg, "Science and Richard Nixon," *New York Times Magazine*, 17 June 1973, 230.

9. Diane Ravitch, *The Troubled Crusade: American Education, 1945–1980* (New York: Basic Books, 1985), 216–17; "Poll Shows Adult Public Favors Hard Line as Campus Protests Continue to Spread," *Chronicle of Higher Education*, 24 March 1969, 4.

10. "Young Radicals Comprise More than Half of FBI's 'Most Wanted List,'" *Chronicle of Higher Education*, 26 Oct. 1970, 3.

11. Steven V. Roberts, "Conservatives Press Campus Unrest Issue," *New York Times*, 11 Oct. 1970, 1.

12. William W. Scranton et al., *The Report of the President's Commission on Campus Unrest* (Washington, DC: GPO, 1970), 20. The same conclusion was reached by independent researchers. See Alan E. Bayer and Alexander W. Astin, "Violence and Disruption on the U.S. Campus, 1968–1969," *Educational Record* 50 (fall 1969): 337–50.

13. Todd Gitlin, *The Sixties: Years of Hope, Days of Rage* (New York: Bantam Books, 1987), 409.

14. Alexander Keyssar, *The Right to Vote: The Contested History of Democracy in the United States* (New York: Basic Books, 2000); "The Voting Mystery," *New York Times*, 4 Dec. 1976, 38. By 2000, turnout for voters aged 18–29 had slipped to 33 percent for general elections and to 20 percent for midterm elections. See William Galston, "Can Civic Knowledge Motivate the Next Generation?" in *United We Serve: National Service and the Future of Citizenship*, ed. E. J. Dionne Jr. (Washington, DC: Brookings Institution Press, 2003), 176.

15. Paul Starr et al., *The Discarded Army: Veterans After Vietnam* (New York: Charterhouse, 1974); Educational Testing Service, *Final Report on Educational Assistance to Veterans: A Comparative Study of Three G.I. Bills* (Washington, DC: GPO, 1973); John Egerton, "The Vietnam-Era G.I. Bill: Boon or Boondoggle?" *Chronicle of Higher Education*, 9 May 1977, 1, 15.

16. Charles E. Neu, ed., *After Vietnam: Legacies of a Lost War* (Baltimore: Johns Hopkins University Press, 2000).

17. Starr, *Discarded Army*, 232.

18. This argument has been advanced most eloquently by Mark Boulton, "A Price on Freedom: The Problems and Promise of the Vietnam Era G.I. Bills" (Ph.D. diss., University of Tennessee, Knoxville, 2005).

19. Between 1919 and 1995, the psychology profession grew from approximately 300 to 250,000 practitioners, according to James H. Capshew, *Psychologists on the March: Science, Practice, and Professional Identity in America, 1929–1969* (New York: Cambridge University Press, 1999), 1. On the political and professional instability caused by the expansion of expert communities after World War II, see Balogh, *Chain Reaction*.

20. My thoughts on the explosion of public participation in politics after the 1960s have been shaped by the work of Brian Balogh. See Balogh, *Chain Reaction*; Balogh, "From Metaphor to Quagmire: The Domestic Legacy of the Vietnam War," in *After Vietnam: Legacies of a Lost War*, ed. Neu, 24–55; and Balogh, "Making Pluralism 'Great': Beyond a Recycled History of the Great Society," in *The Great Society and the High Tide of Liberalism*, ed. Sidney M. Milkis and Jerome M. Mileur (Amherst: University of Massachusetts Press, 2005), 145–82.

21. John Dittmer, *Local People: The Struggle for Civil Rights in Mississippi* (Champaign: University of Illinois Press, 1994).

22. Cheryl Lynn Greenberg, *A Circle of Trust: Remembering SNCC* (New Brunswick: Rutgers University Press, 1998), 33.

23. Paul Potter, "Name the System" (17 April 1965), in *Debating the 1960s: Liberal, Conservative, and Radical Perspectives*, ed. Michael W. Flamm and David Steigerwald (Lanham: Rowman and Littlefield, 2007), 95; Gitlin, *Sixties*, 422.

24. Ibid., 417.

25. Tom Hayden et al., "Port Huron Statement" (1962), available at http://coursesa .matrix.msu.edu/~hst306/documents/huron.html (accessed 19 May 2009).

26. On the rapid spread of student identity groups, see Arthur Levine and Jeanette S. Cureton, *When Hope and Fear Collide: A Portrait of Today's College Student* (San Francisco: Jossey-Bass, 1998), 58–63.

27. On the Progressive Era origins of interest group mobilizing, see Brian Balogh, *A Government Out of Sight: The Mystery of National Authority in Nineteenth-Century America* (New York: Cambridge University Press, 2009), 352–79; and Elisabeth S. Clemens, *The People's Lobby: Organizational Innovation and the Rise of Interest Group Politics in the United States, 1890–1925* (Chicago: University of Chicago Press, 1997).

28. Jack L. Walker, *Mobilizing Interest Groups in America: Patrons, Professions, and Social Movements* (1994; Ann Arbor: University of Michigan Press, 1991), 19–41.

29. Ibid., 35.

30. On the rise of the New Right, see, for example, Lisa McGirr, *Suburban Warriors: The Origins of the New American Right* (Princeton: Princeton University Press, 2001); and Bruce J. Schulman and Julian E. Zelizer, *Rightward Bound: Making America Conservative in the 1970s* (Cambridge, MA: Harvard University Press, 2008).

31. See, for example, Christopher Lasch, *Culture of Narcissism: American Life in an Age of Diminishing Expectations* (New York: Warner Books, 1979); L. A. Kauffman, "The Anti-Politics of Identity," *Socialist Review* 20 (Jan.–March 1990): 67–80; Todd Gitlin, *The Twilight of Common Dreams: Why America Is Wracked by Culture Wars* (New York: Metropolitan Books, 1995); Michael Tomasky, *Left for Dead: The Life, Death, and Possible Resurrection of Progressive Politics in America* (New York: Free Press, 1996); Arthur Schlesinger Jr., *Disuniting of America: Reflections on a Multicultural Society* (New York: W. W. Norton, 1991); David A. Hollinger, *Postethnic America: Beyond Multiculturalism* (New York: Basic Books, 1995); Richard Rorty, *Achieving Our Country: Leftist Thought in Twentieth Century America* (Cambridge, MA: Harvard University Press, 1997); Alan Brinkley, *Liberalism and its Discontents* (Cambridge, MA: Harvard University Press, 1998), 222–36; and Walter Benn Michaels, *The Trouble with Diversity: How We Learned to Love Identity and Ignore Inequality* (New York: Metropolitan Books, 2006).

32. Hugh Heclo, "The Sixties' False Dawn: Awakenings, Movements, and Postmodern Policy-making," in *Integrating the Sixties: The Origins, Structures, and Legitimacy of Public Policy in a Turbulent Decade*, ed. Brian Balogh (University Park: Penn State University Press, 1996), 34–63.

33. On the trust/distrust paradox and the spread of interest groups, see ibid.; Hugh Heclo, "Issue Networks and the Executive Establishment," in *The New American Political System*, ed. Anthony King (1978; Washington, DC: American Enterprise Institute for Public Policy Research, 1980), 87–124; and Hugh Heclo, "Sixties Civics," in *Great Society and the High Tide of Liberalism*, ed. Milkis and Mileur, 53–82, quote on 54.

34. Kauffman, "Anti-Politics of Identity," 67.

35. Gitlin, *Twilight of Common Dreams*, 147. On higher education's contribution to identity politics in the 1990s, see Robert A. Rhoads, *Freedom's Web: Student Activism in an Age of Cultural Diversity* (Baltimore: Johns Hopkins University Press, 1998).

36. On the longstanding power of occupationally based interest groups, see Walker, *Mobilizing Interest Groups in America*, 57–73; and Balogh, *Chain Reaction*. On the persistence and transformation of identity suggested here, I was aided by the work of Tomasky, *Left for Dead*, 74–95.

37. Jodi Kantor and David Gonzalez, "For Sotomayor and Thomas, Paths Fork at Race and Identity," *New York Times*, 7 June 2009, 1, 21; Amy Goldstein and Alec MacGillis, 1 June 2009, "Sotomayor Was a Passionate but Civil Activist," *Washington Post*, available at http://www.washingtonpost.com/wp-dyn/content/article/2009/05/31/AR2009053101935.html (accessed 8 June 2009).

38. Kate Millett, *Sexual Politics* (New York: Doubleday, 1970), 23, cited in Kaufmanf, "Anti-politics of Identity," 72.

39. The importance of higher education in paving the way for identity politics has been suggested by Hugh Heclo. Though he does not write specifically about colleges and universities, higher education's central role is inferred. See Hugh Heclo, "Sixties Civics," in *Great Society and the High Tide of Liberalism*, ed. Milkis and Mileur, 53–82. On the

importance of the 1960s in teaching average Americans about their rights and duties as citizens, Heclo writes: "In a time when 'teach-ins' became a campus fashion, the sixties as a whole constituted the biggest teach-in of all. The period became a school of sorts for teaching Americans how to think about public affairs" (52). See also Rorty, *Achieving Our Country*, 75–107; and Rhoads, *Freedom's Web*.

40. On the history of affirmative action in general, with special reference to the *Bakke* case in particular, see Terry H. Anderson, *The Pursuit of Fairness: A History of Affirmative Action* (New York: Oxford University Press, 2004), 111–60; and John D. Skrentny, *The Ironies of Affirmative Action: Politics, Culture, and Justice in America* (Chicago: University of Chicago Press, 1996), 225–26. On the *Bakke* case, see also J. Harvie Wilkinson, *From Brown to Bakke: The Supreme Court and School Integration, 1954–1978* (New York: Oxford University Press, 1979); and Howard Ball, *The Bakke Case: Race, Education, and Affirmative Action* (Lawrence: University Press of Kansas, 2000). On the battle between "opportunity" and "merit," see Nicholas Lemann, *The Big Test: The Secret History of the American Meritocracy* (1999; New York: Farrar, Straus and Giroux, 2000), especially 235–351.

41. *Regents of the University of California v. Allan Bakke*, 98 U.S. S.Ct. 2733 (1978).

42. Powell quotes in "What the Court Said in Two 5-to-4 Rulings on the Bakke Case," *Chronicle of Higher Education*, 3 July 1978, 3–7. For the diversity amicus brief, see John Mason Harding and Albert J. Rosenthal et al., *Amicus Brief of Columbia University, et al.* (submitted for *Regents of California v. Bakke*, 1977). On all these subjects, see also Anderson, *Pursuit of Fairness*, 150–55.

43. Lemann, *Big Test*, 169–7; Schulman, *Seventies*, 218–52.

44. Joseph Michalak, "Middle Class Gets More Aid from U.S.," *New York Times*, 16 Nov. 1980, EDUC1.

45. Collins, *More*, 166–213.

46. On this shift, see, for example, Geiger, *Research and Relevant Knowledge*, 310–38; Geiger, *Knowledge and Money*; Sheila Slaughter and Larry L. Leslie, *Academic Capitalism: Politics, Policies, and the Entrepreneurial University* (Baltimore: Johns Hopkins University Press, 1997); Christopher Newfield, *Unmaking the Public University: The Forty-Year Assault on the Middle Class* (Cambridge, MA: Harvard University Press, 2008); and Derek Bok, *Universities in the Marketplace: The Commercialization of Higher Education* (Princeton: Princeton University Press, 2003). Significant base budget cuts occurred during the recessions of the early 1980s, the early 1990s, and after the Terror Attacks of 9/11. For an overview of the decentralization process among the 50 state governments, see Michael K. McLendon, "Setting the Governmental Agenda for State Decentralization of Higher Education," *Journal of Higher Education* 74 (Sep. –Oct. 2003): 479–515.

47. Most of the literature has focused on the privatization of public higher education. See, for example, Newfield, *Unmaking the Public University*; and Christopher C. Morphew and Peter D. Eckel, ed., *Privatizing the Public University: Perspectives from across the Academy* (Baltimore: Johns Hopkins University Press, 2009). But in the three areas discussed here—research, student aid, and citizenship training—the privatization phenomenon has occurred across the entire higher education sector. Geiger's *Knowledge and Money* is especially sensitive to this point.

48. Geiger, *Knowledge and Money*, 230.

49. For the best discussion of the middle-class revolt, see Lara K. Couturier, "The Middle-Class Captures the Debates Over College Student Aid, 1965–2010," Paper de-

livered at the Annual Meeting of the History of Education Society, 7 Nov. 2010, Cambridge, MA. Paper is in author's possession.

50. Ibid., 26–27, 32–35; Patricia Somers et al., "The Government as First Creditor on Student Loans: Politics and Policy," *Education Evaluation and Policy Analysis* 22 (winter 2000): 331–39; American Council on Education, *ACE Issue Brief: Student Borrowing in the 1990s* (Washington, DC: American Council on Education, 2001), 1–10; James C. Hearn, "The Paradox of Growth in Federal Aid for College Students, 1965–1990," *Higher Education: Handbook of Theory and Research* 9 (New York: AERA, Div. J, 1994), 94–153. The guaranteed loan program was terminated in 2010 when the Health Care and Educational Reconciliation Act shifted the U.S. government to a direct-lending loan model to save money on interest and fees.

51. On the 1997 Tax Payer Relief Act, see James J. Duderstadt, *The Future of the Public University in America: Beyond the Crossroads* (Baltimore: Johns Hopkins University Press, 2003), 39–40. For a broader discussion on the role of tax expenditures, such as the Lifetime Learning Tax Credit and the Hope Scholarship, and the middle-class welfare state, see Christopher Howard, *The Hidden Welfare State: Tax Expenditures and Social Policy in the United States* (Princeton: Princeton University Press, 2007).

52. By 2003, the Pell Grant covered 38 percent of the average cost of attendance at a public institution; in 1976, it covered 76 percent. See Andrew Delbanco, "The Universities in Trouble," *New York Review of Books* 56 (14 May 2009), available at http://www.nybooks.com/articles/archives/2009/may/14/the-universities-in-trouble/ (accessed 28 Oct. 2010).

53. Lawrence E. Gladieux, "Statement to the Committee on Governmental Affairs," U.S. Senate Hearing on Rising College Costs, 10 Feb. 2000, available at http://www.ed.gov/about/bdscomm/list/acsfa/edlite-testimonyfeb99.html (accessed 30 April 2009). See also Thomas J. Kane, *The Price of Admission: Rethinking How Americans Pay for College* (Washington, DC: Brookings Institution Press, 1999); and Michael S. McPherson, *The Student Aid Game* (Princeton: Princeton University Press, 1998). By 2000, the aid landscape had become even more privatized as growing numbers of state governments introduced merit-aid scholarships to retain top talent in state. As of 2005, fifteen states had organized merit-aid programs. The total dollar amount was small compared to the federal commitment—at around $1.2 billion—but far from insignificant. Georgia was the first to introduce its Hope Scholarship in 1993; Florida and California followed shortly thereafter; by 2011 seventeen states had programs. See Will Doyle, "Adoption of Merit-Based Student Grant Programs: An Event History Analysis," *Educational Evaluation and Policy Analysis* 28 (2006): 259–85.

54. Helen Lefkowitz Horowitz, *Campus Life: Undergraduate Cultures from the End of the Eighteenth Century to the Present* (New York: Knopf, 1987), 261. See also Arthur Levine, *When Dreams and Heroes Died: A Portrait of Today's College Student* (San Francisco: Jossey-Bass, 1980), 59–83. Levine predicted the coming market model, concluding: "In other words, consumerism may well become the rallying cry of students for the next decade and the dominant theme governing college and university admissions" (83).

55. Haskell, *Authority of Experts*, xviii. On the government's refusal to ask citizens to make sacrifices on behalf of the state since the 1970s, see the wonderful collection of essays edited by E. J. Dionne Jr., *United We Serve*. President Jimmy Carter was arguably the last president to ask the American people to make sacrifices, and he did not get reelected.

56. On the rise of federal K-12 policymaking, see Gareth Davies, *See Government Grow: Education Politics from Johnson to Reagan* (Lawrence: University Press of Kansas, 2007); and Hugh Davis Graham, *The Uncertain Triumph: Federal Education Policy in the Kennedy and Johnson Years* (Chapel Hill: University of North Carolina Press, 1984);

57. See, for example, Matthew D. Lassiter, *The Silent Majority: Suburban Politics in the Sunbelt South* (Princeton: Princeton University Press, 2006); and Kevin M. Kruse, *White Flight: Atlanta and the Making of Modern Conservatism* (Princeton: Princeton University Press, 2005).

58. Patrick McGuinn, *No Child Left Behind and the Transformation of Federal Education Policy, 1965–2005* (Lawrence: University Press of Kansas, 2006).

59. David P. Gardner et al., *A Nation at Risk: The Imperative for Educational Reform* (Washington, DC: GPO, 1983), quotes on 5, 27, 7; see also 8–10 and 23–31. See also Patterson, *Restless Giant*, 33–34.

60. McGuinn, *No Child Left Behind*.

61. William B. Johnston and Arnold E. Packer, *Workforce 2000: Work and Workers for the 21st Century* (Indianapolis: Hudson Institute, 1987), xiii.

62. Peggy Schmidt, "Women and Minorities: Is Industry Ready?" *New York Times*, 15 Oct. 1988, A1.

63. Erin Kelly and Frank Dobbin, "How Affirmative Action Became Diversity Management: Employer Response to Antidiscrimination Law, 1961–1996," in *Color Lines: Affirmative Action, Immigration, and Civil Rights Options for America*, ed. John D. Skrentny (Chicago: University of Chicago Press, 2001), 87–117.

64. Anderson, *Pursuit of Fairness*, 220–21.

65. Heather MacDonald, "The Diversity Industry," *New Republic* (5 July 1993), 22–35; Frederick R. Lynch, *The Diversity Machine: The Drive to Change the "White Male Workplace"* (New York: Free Press, 1997).

66. Tom Engelhardt, *The End of Victory Culture: Cold War America and the Disillusioning of a Generation* (1994; Amherst: University of Massachusetts Press, 2007), x.

67. Levine and Cureton, *When Hope and Fear Collide*, 58–63.

68. David Yamane, *Student Movements for Multiculturalism: Challenging the Curricular Color Line in Higher Education* (Baltimore: Johns Hopkins University Press, 2001), 7.

69. Arthur Levine and Jeanette Cureton, "The Quiet Revolution: Eleven Facts about Multiculturalism and the Curriculum," *Change* (Jan./Feb. 1992), 25–29.

70. Rhoads, *Freedom's Web*; Yamane, *Student Movements for Multiculturalism*.

71. On Duderstadt's education and rise through the professorial and administrative ranks, see James J. Duderstadt, *The View from the Helm: Leading the American University during an Era of Change* (Ann Arbor: University of Michigan Press, 2007), 44–70.

72. James J. Duderstadt et al., "The Michigan Mandate: A Strategic Linking of Academic Excellence and Social Diversity," Draft 6.0 (University of Michigan, March 1990), 1.

73. Ibid., 2–3.

74. Ibid., 2.

75. Ibid., 11.

76. Ibid., 13.

77. James J. Duderstadt, *The Future of the Public University in America: Beyond the Crossroads* (Baltimore: Johns Hopkins University Press, 2003), 44–52.

78. Ibid., 49–50.

79. Ibid., 52.

80. On Proposition 209, see Brian Pusser, *Burning Down the House: Politics, Governance, and Affirmative Action at the University of California* (Albany: State University of New York Press, 2004).

81. For the history of the CIR and its attack on the University of Michigan, see Barbara A. Perry, *The Michigan Affirmative Action Cases* (Lawrence: University Press of Kansas, 2007), esp. 43–86.

82. The two cases were *Gratz v. Bollinger*, 539 U.S. 244 (2003), the undergraduate admissions case, and *Grutter v. Bollinger*, 539 U.S. 306 (2003), the law school admissions case.

83. For the educational benefits of diversity, see Patricia Gurin et al., "The Educational Value of Diversity," in *Defending Diversity: Affirmative Action at the University of Michigan*, ed. Patricia Gurin, Jeffrey S. Lehman, and Earl Lewis (Ann Arbor: University of Michigan Press, 2004), 97-188. Recently, "diversity" has become the focus of a number of new journals, most prominently the *Journal of Diversity in Higher Education*, published by the American Psychological Association for the first time in 2008.

84. Anderson, *Pursuit of Fairness*, 271.

85. *Student Debt and the Class of 2009*, A Report by The Project on Student Debt, Oct. 2010, available at http://projectonstudentdebt.org/files/pub/classof2009.pdf (ccessed 1 Nov. 2010).

86. Nationwide, the average six-year graduation rate at nonprofit four-year institutions is 60 percent, and much lower still, in some cases virtually nonexistent, the lower down the prestige chain you look. Frederick M. Hess, Mark Schneider, Kevin Carey, and Andrew P. Kelly, *Diplomas and Dropouts: Which Colleges Actually Graduate Their Students (and Which Don't)*, A Project of the American Enterprise Institute, June 2009, available at http://www.aei.org/docLib/Diplomas%20and%20Dropouts%20final.pdf (accessed 25 Oct. 2010).

Politics and Society in Twentieth-Century America

❖

Civil Defense Begins at Home: Militarization Meets Everyday Life in the Fifties
by Laura McEnaney

The Politics of Whiteness: Race, Workers, and Culture in the Modern South
by Michelle Brattain

Cold War Civil Rights: Race and the Image of American Democracy
by Mary L. Dudziak

Divided We Stand: American Workers and the Struggle for Black Equality
by Bruce Nelson

*Poverty Knowledge: Social Science, Social Policy, and the
Poor in Twentieth-Century U.S. History*
by Alice O'Connor

State of the Union: A Century of American Labor
by Nelson Lichtenstein

Suburban Warriors: The Origins of the New American Right
by Lisa McGirr

American Babylon: Race and the Struggle for Postwar Oakland
by Robert O. Self

Changing the World: American Progressives in War and Revolution
by Alan Dawley

Dead on Arrival: The Politics of Health Care in Twentieth-Century America
by Colin Gordon

*For All These Rights: Business, Labor, and the
Shaping of America's Public-Private Welfare State*
by Jennifer Klein

Impossible Subjects: Illegal Aliens and the Making of Modern America
by Mae M. Ngai

The Other Women's Movement: Workplace Justice and Social Rights in Modern America
by Dorothy Sue Cobble

*The Radical Middle Class: Populist Democracy and the
Question of Capitalism in Progressive Era Portland, Oregon*
by Robert D. Johnston

Cities of Knowledge: Cold War Science and the Search for the Next Silicon Valley
by Margaret Pugh O'Mara

Labor Rights Are Civil Rights:
Mexican American Workers in Twentieth-Century America
by Zaragosa Vargas

More Equal Than Others: America from Nixon to the New Century
by Godfrey Hodgson

Pocketbook Politics: Economic Citizenship in Twentieth-Century America
by Meg Jacobs

Taken Hostage: The Iran Hostage Crisis and America's First Encounter with Radical Islam
by David Farber

Defending America: Military Culture and the Cold War Court-Martial
by Elizabeth Lutes Hillman

Morning in America: How Ronald Reagan Invented the 1980s
by Gil Troy

Phyllis Schlafly and Grassroots Conservatism: A Woman's Crusade
by Donald T. Critchlow

The Silent Majority: Suburban Politics in the Sunbelt South
by Matthew D. Lassiter

White Flight: Atlanta and the Making of Modern Conservatism
by Kevin M. Kruse

Troubling the Waters: Black-Jewish Relations in the American Century
by Cheryl Lynn Greenberg

In Search of Another Country: Mississippi and the Conservative Counterrevolution
by Joseph Crespino

The Shifting Grounds of Race: Black and Japanese Americans in the
Making of Multiethnic Los Angeles
by Scott Kurashige

School Lunch Politics: The Surprising History of America's Favorite Welfare Program
by Susan Levine

Trucking Country: The Road to America's Wal-Mart Economy
by Shane Hamilton

Americans at the Gate: The United States and Refugees during the Cold War
by Carl J. Bon Tempo

The Straight State: Sexuality and Citizenship in Twentieth-Century America
by Margot Canaday

Little Rock: Race and Resistance at Central High School
by Karen Anderson